GOOD VIBRATIONS

Though used as a healing practice for centuries, only recently have we begun to unravel the science behind music's profound impact on the mind and body. In this book, neuroscientist Stefan Koelsch explores the groundbreaking research behind music's influence on human well-being – emotional, physical, and psychological. Beginning with an account of the human brain's innate capacity for music, Koelsch explains music's potential to evoke emotions and change our moods, soothe anxiety, and alleviate pain. Featuring case studies, he documents the potential of music therapy for a wide range of conditions such as depression, stroke, and Alzheimer's. Filled with fascinating science and concrete tips and strategies, this book encourages anyone to harness the power of music for personal growth, healing, and joy.

Stefan Koelsch is an internationally leading neuroscientist and music psychologist. He earned degrees in violin, psychology, and sociology before receiving his doctorate from the Max Planck Institute. He has held positions at Harvard University and is currently a professor at the University of Bergen, Norway.

CAMBRIDGE FUNDAMENTALS OF NEUROSCIENCE IN PSYCHOLOGY

Developed in response to a growing need to make neuroscience accessible to students and other non-specialist readers, the *Cambridge Fundamentals of Neuroscience in Psychology* series provides brief introductions to key areas of neuroscience research across major domains of psychology. Written by experts in cognitive, social, affective, developmental, clinical, and applied neuroscience, these books will serve as ideal primers for students and other readers seeking an entry point to the challenging world of neuroscience.

Books in the Series

The Neuroscience of Expertise by Merim Bilalić
The Neuroscience of Intelligence by Richard J. Haier
Cognitive Neuroscience of Memory by Scott D. Slotnick
The Neuroscience of Adolescence by Adriana Galván
The Neuroscience of Suicidal Behavior by Kees van Heeringen
The Neuroscience of Creativity by Anna Abraham
Cognitive and Social Neuroscience of Aging by Angela Gutchess
The Neuroscience of Sleep and Dreams by Patrick McNamara
The Neuroscience of Addiction by Francesca Mapua Filbey
Introduction to Human Neuroimaging, by Hans Op de Beeck and Chie Nakatani
The Neuroscience of Sleep and Dreams, 2e, by Patrick McNamara
The Neuroscience of Intelligence, 2e, by Richard J. Haier
The Cognitive Neuroscience of Bilingualism, by John W. Schwieter and Julia Festman
Fundamentals of Developmental Cognitive Neuroscience, by Heather Bortfeld and Silvia A. Bunge
Neuroscience of Attention, by Joseph B. Hopfinger
Good Vibrations: Unlocking the Healing Power of Music, by Stefan Koelsch

GOOD VIBRATIONS

Unlocking the Healing Power of Music

Stefan Koelsch

University of Bergen

Consulting Editor: Scott D. Slotnick, Boston College

Shaftesbury Road, Cambridge CB2 8EA, United Kingdom

One Liberty Plaza, 20th Floor, New York, NY 10006, USA

477 Williamstown Road, Port Melbourne, VIC 3207, Australia

314–321, 3rd Floor, Plot 3, Splendor Forum, Jasola District Centre, New Delhi – 110025, India

103 Penang Road, #05–06/07, Visioncrest Commercial, Singapore 238467

Cambridge University Press is part of Cambridge University Press & Assessment, a department of the University of Cambridge.

We share the University's mission to contribute to society through the pursuit of education, learning and research at the highest international levels of excellence.

www.cambridge.org
Information on this title: www.cambridge.org/9781009366779

DOI: 10.1017/9781009366755

© Stefan Koelsch 2025

This publication is in copyright. Subject to statutory exception and to the provisions of relevant collective licensing agreements, no reproduction of any part may take place without the written permission of Cambridge University Press & Assessment.

When citing this work, please include a reference to the DOI 10.1017/9781009366755

First published 2025

Originally published as *Good Vibrations: Die heilenda Kraft der Musick* by Stefan Kolsch, Ullstein Buchverlage GmbH, Berlin 2019. English translation by Stefan Kolsch, Cambridge University Press & Assessment 2025

Printed in the United Kingdom by CPI Group Ltd, Croydon CR0 4YY

A catalogue record for this publication is available from the British Library

A Cataloging-in-Publication data record for this book is available from the Library of Congress

ISBN 978-1-009-36677-9 Hardback

Cambridge University Press & Assessment has no responsibility for the persistence or accuracy of URLs for external or third-party internet websites referred to in this publication and does not guarantee that any content on such websites is, or will remain, accurate or appropriate.

....

Every effort has been made in preparing this book to provide accurate and up-to-date information that is in accord with accepted standards and practice at the time of publication. Although case histories are drawn from actual cases, every effort has been made to disguise the identities of the individuals involved. Nevertheless, the authors, editors, and publishers can make no warranties that the information contained herein is totally free from error, not least because clinical standards are constantly changing through research and regulation. The authors, editors, and publishers therefore disclaim all liability for direct or consequential damages resulting from the use of material contained in this book. Readers are strongly advised to pay careful attention to information provided by the manufacturer of any drugs or equipment that they plan to use.

Contents

Preface . . . . *page* vii

Introduction: Effects of Music on Health 1

PART ONE: A WORLD WITHOUT MUSIC WOULD BE A WORLD WITHOUT HUMANS

1 Why Humans Would Not Have Survived Evolution without Music . 9

2 Our Innate Sense of Music: Even Non-musicians Are Musical . . . 22

3 Music and Language in the Brain 28

4 Our Engagement Shapes Our Brain 39

PART TWO: MUSIC AND EMOTIONS: A LIFE WITH MUSIC IS A LONGER LIFE

5 How Does Music Evoke Emotions? 55

6 Dance of the Hormones to the Beat of the Music 113

7 Music versus Obstructing Our Natural Healing Powers 123

PART THREE: WHAT HAPPENS IN THE BRAIN WHEN MUSIC EVOKES EMOTIONS?

8 Emotions in the Brain: How Music Truly Affects Us 145

9 What Is an Emotion? 195

10 Morning Dance 203

CONTENTS

PART FOUR: HOW MUSIC HELPS WITH ILLNESS

11 Stroke 207

12 Alzheimer's Dementia: Pioneering Neural Therapy 229

13 Parkinson's Disease: Shall We Dance? 242

14 Autism 255

15 Chronic Pain 266

16 Addiction: Music over Chocolate 272

17 Non-organic Sleep Disorders 281

18 Depression 287

19 How This Book Led Me to a Music Recipe for Patients with Schizophrenia Spectrum Disorder 300

PART FIVE: IN CONCLUSION: AT A GLANCE

20 Music Meditation 307

21 Engaging in Physical Activity with Music 309

22 Negative Side Effects of Music 311

23 Emergency Help for Negative Emotions and Moods 313

24 Concluding Remarks 319

Index 321

Preface

What distinguishes humans from animals? Douglas Adams humorously responded to this question with 'The wheel, New York, the wars.' Some scientists point to 'language', 'mathematics', or 'chess'. And I say, 'music'.

Music calls upon a distinctively human capability that might appear simple yet sets us apart from all other species: the ability to synchronize rhythmically in a group. We can hold a beat, clap in unison, and alter our tempo together. We can also dance, sing, or play instruments in harmony, celebrating a shared musical experience.

The act of creating music together generates positive emotions, which in turn unleash potent healing forces within us. This has provided humans with a crucial evolutionary advantage: to live longer. Music fosters social cohesion, bolsters our endurance, and strengthens our perseverance. Over 100 years ago, Ernest Shackleton, a renowned Antarctic explorer, and his crew were forced to trudge through Antarctica's icy winds after pack ice crushed their ship, *Endurance*. With them, they carried the bare essentials for survival: food, cooking utensils, clothing, tents, and – the banjo! Shackleton later revealed that the hardship and pain of his men were so great that some of them wanted to give up and die. Falling asleep seemed the preferable alternative to further suffering. During these times of despair, music uplifted his crew's spirits, instilling courage and motivation. Despite the harrowing circumstances, all twenty-eight men survived and reached Elephant Island. Shackleton attributed their survival, in a significant part, to music, describing it as 'vital mental medicine'.

For Shackleton's men, music 'invigorated the soul', as Johann Sebastian Bach stated. When music fulfils this role, it exhibits regenerative and healing effects. This book will delve into these effects in detail, explaining how music's therapeutic influence enhances our well-being and health. It will elucidate the changes that occur in our brain and body when music stimulates regeneration and healing.

Music can produce miraculous effects on a range of illnesses: Parkinson's patients find they can dance; Alzheimer's patients start to remember; individuals who have lost their ability to speak after a stroke can still sing, and this singing aids in language recovery; paralyzed stroke patients regain movement; patients in a 'vegetative state' begin to respond to music when all other stimuli have been ineffective. What might sound as if borrowed from biblical miracles has been investigated and confirmed by recent, revolutionary scientific studies.

In writing this book, I have drawn upon hundreds of studies, which I aim to summarize and present in an accessible manner. I have conducted a few of these myself during my time at the Max Planck Institute for Cognitive Neuroscience, at Harvard Medical School, at the Free University of Berlin, and at the University of Bergen. Many of these studies underscore the inherent musicality of human beings, a trait evident already in young children and even infants. Consequently, everyone, regardless of age or musical education, can benefit from the healing effects of music. I will illustrate how individuals of all ages and backgrounds can utilize music for health, as well as for coping with the stresses and challenges of everyday life.

As a professor of biological and medical psychology, I will present numerous findings from brain research. However, because I have a degree in music, I will answer questions that might intrigue both musically trained individuals and those who simply love music. For instance, I will explore how music evokes emotions and will look into the similarities and differences between music and language. Since I also have a background in sociology, I will occasionally examine topics related to societal contexts. For instance, music alone cannot be a panacea for individuals living within a societal context that fosters illness.

I occasionally give concerts, sometimes in conjunction with lectures, on the healing effects of music. Unfortunately, I cannot answer everyone's questions on these occasions. What always moves me, however, is the feedback I receive. A doctor shared with me that without music, he would not have made it through his exams; a man from the former German Democratic Republic told me he would not have survived its regime without the solace music provided; a Parkinson's patient shared how music aided her in managing her illness. Their deep curiosity about the scientific underpinnings of such experiences and the insights we can glean from them has driven me to write this book. I aim to share my fascination with this field of research and communicate the knowledge scientists have amassed about it. How can we use music to stay healthy or regain health? How does music evoke healing and regenerative effects? What happens in our brain and the rest of our body when music plays this role? These are the questions that I will address in this book.

Music can be a valuable and incredibly efficient supplement to conventional medicine, and sometimes, it can even serve as an effective alternative. Despite its potent healing effects, which can often be triggered by the simplest of means, the therapeutic power of music is frequently overlooked. In *Good Vibrations*, I aim to highlight the essential aspects of maintaining health through an interdisciplinary approach and explain how we can bolster our self-healing powers with music.

Introduction

Effects of Music on Health

MICHAEL, A YOUNG ADULT, LIVED IN BERLIN under the care of his aunt. For years, he underwent neurological treatment, plagued by recurrent severe epileptic seizures. In addition, he had long-standing mutism: he could speak and understand others but had said nothing for years. Despite intensive medical treatments by doctors and a psychotherapist, neither the severe epileptic seizures nor his mutism could be controlled. As conventional medicine appeared to exhaust its remedies, the lead neurologist had a moment of insight: what about music therapy? Noting Michael's affinity for music, the neurologist discovered that Michael had frequently sung with his grandfather during his childhood. So he was referred to Julia Kraft, a music therapist and exceptional violinist with whom I have maintained a close friendship since our music studies.

In their initial introductory session, Michael arrived wearing protective headgear. He was completely closed off and had his legs drawn up in a crouched posture. Eye contact and verbal communication were not possible. Laying out a diverse range of instruments, Julia aspired to spark Michael's curiosity and nurture a budding interest. However, he did not initiate any contact or engage with the instruments. Julia went to the soundbed (like a wooden daybed with strings underneath) and plucked the strings. After a few minutes, Michael got up and began to walk around the room, adjusting his pace to the music's rhythm. He appeared to enjoy this 'improvisation', inspired by the music to vary his speed.

After this successful introductory session, Julia was able to build upon it in the subsequent session, during which they 'played' together – Julia

INTRODUCTION

on the soundbed and Michael through his steps. Thus, the two came into direct contact through the music and communicated without using words (recall, Michael had not spoken for years). When the session ended, Michael walked out the door with his aunt, turned towards Julia, and asked clearly 'And dance?' Julia was so delighted that she immediately picked up her violin and played a lively dance, to which Michael and his aunt danced exuberantly and snapped their fingers.

Michael progressed in the following weeks and months, step by step, sometimes faster and other times slowly. The music built trust between them. Julia spoke, commented, and consistently motivated him to join in, to which he increasingly responded with 'yes' or 'no'. Gathering courage, Michael approached the soundbed for their first collaborative session, engaging with the strings alongside Julia. Their interactions, ranging from soft caresses to forceful plucks, co-created moments of profound musical emotion. Michael often revisited their recorded sessions, and in subsequent meetings, he engaged more actively with Julia, as they made music together. This newfound expression through music led him to paint, initially in monochrome and then in vibrant colours, mirroring the depth of their sessions. Julia also discovered that, although Michael hardly spoke, he could sing and enjoyed it. They sang songs such as 'Old King Cole' and others that he knew from childhood, which enhanced his vocal communication. Gradually, he began speaking more frequently and clearly, significantly improving his daily interactions.

As their therapeutic journey neared its end, Michael's communicative skills blossomed, marking a significant turning point. The transition from mutism to verbal communication, coupled with the near disappearance of his epileptic seizures, underscored the profound impact of music therapy. Emboldened by his progress, Michael took up violin lessons, aspiring to play like Julia, and charted a new path for his life with renewed purpose and an apprenticeship. This transformative journey, from mutism to expression through music, exemplifies the profound, holistic impact music therapy can have. It not only illustrates individual growth and healing but also underscores the vast potential within the field of music therapy to effect change. This narrative invites a broader consideration of how music therapy can be further integrated into healthcare practices, advocating for a deeper exploration of its capabilities and applications.

INTRODUCTION

While Michael also underwent speech therapy and took epilepsy medication alongside music therapy, it was music that catalysed the decisive breakthrough. The melodies and rhythms roused a latent part of him, revitalizing his spirit and unlocking his potential. The effectiveness of music in this case was so evident that the consulting physician harboured no doubts about music therapy being an irreplaceable form of treatment.

Michael's story is a testament to the therapeutic effects of music, a compelling case that underscores the need for rigorous scientific research and informed policymaking to unlock the full potential of music therapy for a wider population. Fortunately, the health insurance company approved Michael's music therapy – a form of support that individuals in Germany, and indeed most countries, often cannot rely on. In many jurisdictions, the inability of doctors to prescribe music therapy directly is predominantly due to political reasons, creating a significant gap in healthcare policy. It is imperative for policymakers in these countries to amend legislation to ensure greater access to music therapy for patients in need, a change that should be grounded in the robust scientific evidence that I aim to present in this book.

The past few decades have seen a remarkable increase in research highlighting the therapeutic effects of music, providing compelling evidence of its efficacy. While the field had only garnered a few hundred papers by the year 2000, the subsequent years have witnessed the publication of several thousand more. This surge not only reflects the growing efforts to establish a scientific base for music's benefits but also underscores the urgent need for healthcare systems to adapt and integrate music therapy into their treatment offerings. Yet, a broad spectrum of disorders and diseases exists for which the efficacy of music interventions still needs to be scientifically proven. In medical-pharmacological research, typical studies implement a minimal therapy protocol to ensure precise control of therapy parameters. For instance, participants might take a new medication a specified number of times, with a control group receiving a placebo. However, substantiating the impact of music or music therapy introduces inherent complexities. Questions arise regarding whether the effects are derived purely from the music itself, or if the group experience, the bond with the therapist, a diversion from negative thoughts and emotions, or a combination of these factors play a significant role. Tailoring ideal methods for each individual, whether through singing, playing instruments, speaking, or drumming, poses additional challenges within the confines of a strict clinical study protocol.

Regarding the efficacy of music therapy, reliance on reasonable judgment becomes necessary at times, especially given the inherent challenges in obtaining evidence from placebo-controlled studies for several disorders and diseases. For some conditions, acquiring such evidence may never be feasible. Given that music therapy often extends over longer periods, ethical considerations may preclude the use of placebo controls in studies, particularly when withholding potential treatment could adversely affect patient well-being. Moreover, the rarity of certain conditions, such as Michael's disorder, limits the feasibility of conducting large-scale, randomized controlled trials. Despite these obstacles, the findings presented in this book are underpinned by high-quality empirical research. Focusing on some of the most significant illnesses, this book aims to showcase music's healing potential, offering insights applicable across a broad spectrum of health issues.

Writing a book that enthusiastically listed all kinds of reports on the positive effects of music or music therapy would have been straightforward. However, I have observed that many studies disseminated their findings without the requisite scepticism, leading to biased interpretations by individuals deeply invested in a particular therapy. Thus, despite my enthusiasm for the subject, I aimed at painting an unbiased and scientifically sound picture. To achieve this, I have meticulously reviewed thousands of pages of scientific articles, selecting from a vast collection of papers that cumulatively span tens of thousands of pages. Wherever possible, I placed significant emphasis on systematic reviews and meta-analyses, which compile and evaluate all available studies on a topic, providing a more reliable foundation of information than any single study could offer.

The scientific findings I will share with you draw from a tapestry of disciplines, reflecting the multifaceted nature of music's healing effects. Psychology, medicine, musicology, biology, and music therapy contribute to our understanding of the neurological underpinnings of music perception and processing, the profound emotional responses elicited by music, its cognitive influence, and the targeted therapeutic impacts on specific ailments.

My musical journey through these disciplines is deeply personal. Holding a degree in violin, classical music has not only profoundly influenced my professional path but also many of the examples chosen in this book. However, my appreciation for music transcends genres and cultures. From the intricate rhythms of jazz and the masterful productions of pop to the raw energy of rock, and extending beyond Western music to embrace all cultures across the globe, music in its diverse forms possesses a universal capacity to touch our emotions and facilitate healing. Thus, the principles discussed in this book are broadly applicable, embracing music's diverse impact across genres, cultures, and individual preferences. This diversity underscores the therapeutic versatility of music – a critical point for policymakers, practitioners, and patients alike in advocating for and applying music's therapeutic effects. While delving into the intricacies of emotions and brain functions, I occasionally extend beyond direct ties to music. These explorations are designed for readers with backgrounds in neuroscience, psychology, or sociology and aim to provide a holistic perspective on music's impact on health and well-being. This book, however, is crafted for non-linear exploration – you do not have to read it page by page; feel free to jump directly to sections that most intrigue you or seem most relevant to your interests. Whether you are drawn to a specific topic, a particular disease, or a unique aspect of music therapy, each section offers valuable insights. I hope this book not only informs but also inspires your personal journey through the therapeutic effects of music, contributing to both your overall wellness and personal growth.

PART ONE

A WORLD WITHOUT MUSIC WOULD BE A WORLD WITHOUT HUMANS

CHAPTER 1

Why Humans Would Not Have Survived Evolution without Music

MUSIC IS DEEPLY ROOTED IN OUR SPECIES. While the oldest known musical instruments date back approximately 40,000 to 50,000 years, I shall argue in this chapter that the origins of music are likely to extend much further, probably coinciding with the emergence of *Homo sapiens*, if not predating it. So far, the oldest fossilized remains of *Homo sapiens* date back approximately 300,000 years; however, it is likely that the first humans existed well before this timeframe.[1] Whether the preceding human species made music remains an open question, but it is not improbable. About 1.5 million years ago, the early members of the genus *Homo* discovered the art of cooking. This breakthrough allowed them to get more calories in less time, laying the foundation for the enormous growth of a metabolically expensive organ that accounts for roughly 20 per cent of the resting metabolic rate in modern humans: the brain.[2] Brain evolution brought several new abilities, among them two music-specific skills: holding a pulse in a group and singing tones together.

Together with the birth of music in human evolution, the beneficial effects of music on health and social bonding emerged. Skills essential for communication and cooperation, along with novel forms of social organizations, developed rapidly. As humans started to live in larger

---

[1] Hublin, J. J., Ben-Ncer, A., Bailey, S. E., Freidline, S. E., Neubauer, S., Skinner, M. M., Bergmann, I., Le Cabec, A., Benazzi, S., Harvati, K., and Gunz, P. (2017). New fossils from Jebel Irhoud, Morocco and the pan-African origin of *Homo sapiens*. *Nature*, 546(7657), 289.

[2] Attwell, D., and Laughlin, S. B. (2001). An energy budget for signalling in the grey matter of the brain. *Journal of Cerebral Blood Flow & Metabolism*, 21(10), 1133–1145.

communities, this led to the emergence of more complex social structures. Whether music is a prerequisite or a concomitant of this development remains unknown. However, given its significant effects on social cohesion and health, I posit that humans would not have survived evolution without music.

Music represents a unique category within the realm of sound. More precisely, music is a succession of sounds in which we feel a pulse (usually a beat) and where sounds – if they have pitches – correspond to a scale. Around the globe, there are many scales: in addition to major and minor scales, one finds Gregorian modes, jazz scales, Indian ragas, the Indonesian pelog and slendro, as well as pentatonic and octatonic scales. Among the various scales, the pentatonic scale stands out for its simplicity. It comprises only five notes, and preschool children can easily sing it (as in the song 'Old MacDonald Had a Farm').

When humans produce sounds according to both a scale and a pulse, we recognize these sounds as *music*. With a few exceptions, the musical traditions of the *Homo sapiens* are based on these two characteristics: pulse and scale. They build the core of a universal grammar of music with two basic principles (technically called 'rules'). These two core rules of a universal musical grammar are as follows: 'the time intervals between sounds should be structured such that they fit recognizably into a pulse', and 'the pitches of sounds should be recognizable elements of a scale'. Strikingly, this simple universal grammar has led to the immense variety and diversity of musical systems, styles, and compositions.

However, not all music adheres to the principles of beat and scale. Drum music can get by without scales, and meditation music often has no recognizable beat, as with some pieces of modern art music (for example, Ligeti's 'Atmosphères', which many know from Stanley Kubrick's film *2001: A Space Odyssey*).

The immediate function of beat and scale lies in facilitating *collective* music making. We can best perform movements *together* simultaneously if they follow a beat. If we want to lift a heavy box together 'on three', it makes no sense if I first say 'one' slowly, then wait, and then abruptly and quickly say 'two, three'. You count on *the beat*: 'one – two – three!' To clap, dance, stomp, or shout together, we need a beat. To sing together, a group must agree on which notes to sing, achieved using a scale: a scale provides a set of pitches everyone can follow. Without a scale, there would be no coherent and harmonious blend of musical notes; without a tactus, the resulting sound would be chaotic and disorganized.

The human ability to harmonize pitches and synchronize beats is not coincidental; it has been a vital factor in our evolutionary success. This unique musical ability provided humans with a significant evolutionary advantage – to live longer. This advantage includes the following:

- *Better cooperation and stronger social cohesion.* When people make music together, they engage in cooperative activities that foster a sense of unity and shared purpose. This collaborative spirit extends beyond the realm of music, leading to heightened cooperation and prosocial behaviours in various facets of life. For example, after engaging in joint music making, individuals are more inclined to help each other, enhancing the likelihood of achieving collective goals while minimizing the potential for conflicts. Humans were successful in evolution because they were more potent in groups than individually, and music's role in facilitating a sense of unity through coordinated movement often leads to selfish tendencies evolving into a commitment to the group. When singing or clapping with one voice, individuals transform from 'I' to 'we'. In the subsequent chapters, we will delve deeper into the profound impact of engaging in cooperation on both health and social relationships.
- *More positive emotions and promotion of health.* Music can evoke positive emotions and help regulate negative emotions. Due to this capacity, it can contribute to healing and enhance overall well-being. Whereas prolonged emotional stress has unhealthy consequences, facilitation of relaxation and joy with music has restorative effects. With music, we can relieve pain, and music may support us to persevere during difficult times. Music can invigorate the soul and thereby motivate individuals to persist, even potentially saving lives in extreme cases. (Shackleton's men in Antarctica persevered with music in the face of intense pain and hardships – see the Preface.) As we progress through this book, we will encounter many instances where music's ability to evoke positive emotions has therapeutic effects.

- *Conflict mitigation.* The decrease in physical confrontations within or between groups leads to a corresponding reduction in injuries and fatalities. Various hunter-gatherer cultures have customs where, instead of through duels using weapons, disputes are settled with the use of singing.[3] Such 'song duels' restore peaceful social relations and thus prevent violent confrontations, acts of revenge, or even murder. Because nomadic cultures around the globe practise such conflict-reducing musical customs, they seem to be inherent in human nature, probably dating back to the time the *Homo sapiens* came into existence. In the upcoming sections, we will come to understand how music's social functions contribute to conflict resolution and foster peace.

MUSIC AND LANGUAGE HAVE INTERTWINED EVOLUTIONARY ROOTS

Similarly to music, speech is also structured sound produced by humans. When we speak, we use melody to distinguish between questions and answers, rhythm to help conversation partners follow each other better, and timbre to convey the speaker's mood. However, only *one* person can speak at a time; otherwise, speech sounds unpleasant and challenging to understand. In contrast, with music, several people can produce sounds simultaneously, and it still sounds good and is understandable. This capacity of music to facilitate collective expression surpasses that of language. Therefore, music is the language of the group, while language is the music of the individual.

The evolutionary advantage of language is that a single person can communicate their thoughts, intentions, desires, feelings, and so on. Language is, therefore, a special case of music: language comprises sounds, whereby the beat and the scale are considerably less clear than in music, and the sounds form words with specific meanings. Uli Reich, the linguist, once remarked to me that language is 'music distorted by semantics'. The decisive difference between language and music is that

---

[3] Lehmann, C., Welker, L., and Schiefenhövel, U. W. (2008). The singing controversy in human ethological perspective. *Musicae Scientiae*, 12(1), 115–145.

to fulfil its function, language *does not need* pulse or scale, and music *does not need* sounds with specific meanings.

We can note that the *meaning* of words often relates to their *sounds*, even if it may seem random when we learn a new language. For instance, different languages use different words to express the same concept or property, such as 'tiny' in English, '*winzig*' in German, '*bitte liten*' in Norwegian, '*infima*' in French, and '*piccolissimo*' in Italian. However, a closer listen reveals a striking commonality: these words all contain two or more [i] sounds (English: 'eee'). A scientific study compared a basic vocabulary of 100 words among 4,000 languages, about two-thirds of the known languages.[4] In many words, the investigation discovered systematic clusters of specific sounds, such as the sound 'i' in words for 'tiny', 'r' in words for 'round', or 'n' in words for 'nose'. Because the study's authors observed such similarities across different language families, they assumed these similarities arose independently and did not originate from a common original language. Therefore, the sounds of words are not as arbitrary as was long believed. As we appreciate this connection between the sounds of words and their meaning, we can see how music and language have deep and intertwined evolutionary roots.

THE EMOTIONAL IMPACT OF THE VOICE

The close interconnection between music and language becomes even clearer when considering that musical features encode the emotional content of a voice. Why do we recognize that a voice sounds happy, sad, angry, surprised, or afraid? The music psychologists Patrik Juslin and Petri Laukka analysed data from about forty studies investigating which acoustic features of the human voice characterize certain emotions.[5] For this purpose, actors and actresses recorded words or sentences to express joy, sadness, anger, fear, or tenderness. Some studies also used recordings of real-life emotional voices, such as screams of fear in aircraft accidents. The voice recordings

---

[4] Blasi, D. E., Wichmann, S., Hammarström, H., Stadler, P. F., and Christiansen, M. H. (2016). Sound–meaning association biases evidenced across thousands of languages. *Proceedings of the National Academy of Sciences*, 113(39), 10818–10823.

[5] Juslin, P. N., and Laukka, P. (2003). Communication of emotions in vocal expression and music performance: Different channels, same code?*Psychological Bulletin*, 129(5), 770.

spanned different languages and cultures. Juslin and Laukka confirmed that specific acoustic features in the voice encode each emotion, enabling us to recognize these emotions in speech even without understanding the language. A cheerful voice, for instance, exhibits a faster-speaking tempo than a sad one, with a higher volume and greater variability in pitches, making the speech melody fluctuate and sound active. In contrast, a sad voice sounds darker, less bright, less melodious, with pitches tending to descend. By these acoustic characteristics, a Yanomami man from the Amazon rainforest, who has never had contact with Western culture, would recognize whether I feel happy, anxious, or sad. These acoustic features, encoding emotions in speech, are universal, transcending cultural barriers and highlighting a fundamental aspect of human communication.

The highlight of this study: Patrik and Petri also analysed a dozen studies investigating the acoustic characteristics through which musicians express emotions in music. For this purpose, musicians had played melodies to express joy, sadness, anger, fear, or tenderness. Besides classical music, these studies also used folk music, Indian ragas, jazz, rock, children's songs, and free improvisations played by musicians from different countries and cultures. Results showed that the acoustic features of emotional speech are predominantly the same ones that characterize the expression of emotions in various types of music. The beginning of the *Lacrimosa* ('weeping') from Mozart's Requiem, which sounds so sad, is also slow and quiet (piano), and the melody often descends (the so-called *pianto* motif). The fourth movement from Mozart's serenade 'Eine kleine Nachtmusik' sounds cheerful because it is relatively fast, has a high pitch variability (even just the first four notes played by the first violin span an octave), the melody often goes up, and the frequency register is relatively high.

Digital analysis allows for the precise measurement of these acoustic features from audio files. We took advantage of this for an experiment and selected happy- or scary-sounding music based on computer-calculated acoustic features.[6] We had taken the audio files of the scary

---

[6] Koelsch, S., Skouras, S., Fritz, T., Herrera, P., Bonhage, C., Küssner, M. B., and Jacobs, A. M. (2013). The roles of superficial amygdala and auditory cortex in music-evoked fear and joy. *NeuroImage*, 81, 49–60.

music from soundtracks of thriller TV series and horror movies. The computer analysis showed that this type of music had many noisy, hissing, and percussive sounds, that is, sounds where the determination of the pitch was difficult – which caused uncertainty in the listener. In addition, assigning tones and chords to a key was often tricky, increasing this uncertainty. Finally, many chords were dissonant, which made them more uncomfortable to listen to (think of Bernard Herrmann's music for Hitchcock's *Psycho*, especially the shower scene).[7]

Western music often imitates emotional speech. Consistent with the findings that *emotional speech* is universally recognized, my research group has found that the expression of emotions through the *imitation of emotional speech* in Western music is also universally recognized, regardless of the listener's cultural background. To explore this, Thomas Fritz, then a PhD student in my group, conducted an expedition to a remote region in northern Cameroon. There, he sought out participants from the Mafa people. These participants had never heard Western music before. He played them short piano pieces that sounded like joy, sadness, or fear. After each piece, the participants saw three photos: a happy face, a sad face, and a fearful face. They had the task of pointing to the face that best matched the music. The Mafa recognized all three emotions well above chance level, showing that the expression of happiness, sadness, and fear in Western music is universally recognized, that is, independent of cultural experience.[8]

The Mafa recognized the emotions less successfully than Western listeners, but it is important to note that the concept of expressing emotions with music was entirely new for them. The music of the Mafa people always has a happy meaning, and thus they only know

---

[7] The music used in our experiment can be downloaded and listened to at stefan-koelsch .de/stimulus_repository/joy_fear_neutral_music.zip. When I heard Beat Furrer's piano concerto for the first time a few years ago, it enthralled me how it imitated precisely all these acoustic 'thriller parameters'. Enthusiastically, I listened to the concerto repeatedly because it reminded me of suspenseful car-chasing scenes from older American crime films. When I spoke to Beat Furrer about my observations, he replied, 'Interesting – I didn't mean to express that at all!' Anyway, I'm still a big fan of his concert.

[8] Fritz, T., Jentschke, S., Gosselin, N., Sammler, D., Peretz, I., Turner, R., Friederici, A. D., and Koelsch, S. (2009). Universal recognition of three basic emotions in music. *Current Biology*, 19(7), 573–576.

happy-sounding music. In addition, Western music sounds utterly different to the Mafa than it does to Western listeners. One Mafa man particularly enjoyed the music of Elvis Presley because he thought it sounded just like croaking frogs!

The results of this study reveal that even people unfamiliar with Western music recognize emotions expressed in it as long as the music sounds similar to an emotional voice. Such recognition occurs because recognizing *vocal* expressions of emotion is, to a considerable extent, biologically and genetically inherent to us.[9] The universal recognition of vocal expression of emotions also means that we can formulate universal definitions of how music *sounds* positive (for example, happy) or negative (for example, scary). Whether we *feel* it in that specific way is another question entirely. Sometimes, frightening music (i.e. negative-sounding) makes a thriller film particularly enjoyable for us, or positive-sounding country music gets on the nerves of a heavy metal enthusiast. Of course, music can sound happy to somebody even if it does not imitate or portray any emotions. For the Mafa, their music always has a 'happy' sound, but for listeners from Western cultures, it may sound very much like honking cars.

Thus, the sound of speech conveys the speaker's emotional state, and the sounds of many words are related to their meaning. Since these *musical* aspects of language occur independently of culture, we can conclude that they are part of the essential biological endowment of humans. Babies can already recognize emotional signals that belong to this natural endowment. They are emotionally touched by music and by the sound of language. Therefore, it is important that one's voice sounds warm and calm when interacting with babies and that it conveys security and protection. Singing lullabies to babies helps them calm down, decreasing their heart rate and making their movements and breathing slower and more regular. Such calming effects are particularly important

---

[9] Zimmermann, E., Leliveld, L. M. C., and Schehka, S. (2013). Toward the evolutionary roots of affective prosody in human acoustic communication: A comparative approach to mammalian voices. In Altenmüller, E., Schmidt, S., and Zimmermann, E. (eds). *Evolution of Emotional Communication: From Sounds in Nonhuman Mammals to Speech and Music in Man* (pp. 116–132). Oxford, Oxford University Press.

for preterm infants because agitation is dangerous for them. Moreover, music can help to relieve pain already in these infants.[10]

Interestingly, the acoustic and musical characteristics of lullabies are largely universal, sounding similar across diverse cultures around the globe. The melodies typically descend, are relatively simple in structure, and are repetitive (think of the English 'Twinkle Twinkle Little Star', the Japanese '*Yurikago No Uta*', and the South African '*Thula Baba*').[11] Therefore, today's lullabies probably sound similar to those sung hundreds of thousands of years ago.

Unfortunately, some parents think of themselves as unmusical and do not sing songs to their babies. However, they forget that an infant does not yet have any opportunities for comparison, and thus no parent can embarrass him- or herself in front of their baby by singing. Moreover, the purpose of singing lullabies is not to pave the way for a baby's future career in opera but to support social, emotional, and cognitive development in a playful and engaging manner. That is why singing is important, even if a parent thinks that s/he is unmusical: it promotes social bonding between parent and child, communication, and the learning of speech sounds. It also engages multisensory experiences, that is, experiences of several senses at the same time (hearing, seeing, feeling, sensing the own body moving when being cradled). Even singing these songs *before* birth is helpful because the baby will recognize them after birth, calming them. It can also be beneficial to occasionally place a music box on the pregnant woman's belly because the baby will recognize this song after birth, providing a sense of security for the infant.

SINGING, TALKING, AND DANCING WITH BABIES

Armed with the understanding of music's profound impact on early development, you may be eager to bring its benefits into your

---

[10] Ilari, B. (2002). Music and babies: A review of research with implications for music educators. *Update: Applications of Research in Music Education*, 21(2), 17–26.

[11] Trehub, S. E., Unyk, A. M., and Trainor, L. J. (1993). Adults identify infant-directed music across cultures. *Infant Behaviour and Development*, 16(2), 193–211.

parenting routine. Below are some practical tips to make the most of music in bonding with, comforting, and engaging with your child.

- *The importance of tone in voice.* Infants are immediately influenced by the emotional tone of a voice. If a voice sounds angry, annoyed, or depressed, it inevitably triggers negative emotions, stress, and restlessness in the baby. Therefore, it's essential for one's own voice to sound warm and calm, conveying peacefulness, security, and safety. Singing lullabies and playing songs to an infant come naturally in this manner. Look into the baby's face with a welcoming expression and gently sway them to the rhythm of the music. Singing is particularly helpful during moments when you feel overwhelmed, anxious, or even depressed, as it is difficult to sound angry or upset while singing a gentle lullaby. Additionally, it results in slower and deeper breaths, which will help one become calmer and more relaxed. Thus, singing is *especially* effective when one least feels like it.
- *An alternative to singing – dancing.* If you cannot sing at the moment or it is not working, play some dance music (not too loud) and gently dance with your baby. For example, softly sway with your infant to the beat of the music.
- *Physical comfort through touch.* If the baby still is not calm, make skin contact and slowly stroke up and down one of the baby's arms (this activates nerve fibres that reduce pain).
- *Communication during care activities.* When changing nappies and clothes, calmly and warmly explain to the baby what *you* are doing (you would want the same courtesy if someone was doing things to you without asking). Avoid commenting on everything the *baby* does, as even babies find that annoying.
- *Structured routines and music.* Babies appreciate music, not only for its pleasant sound but also for its clear structure. This makes the world more predictable. Therefore, establishing a daily routine with a consistent rhythm that includes recurring times for sleeping, eating, playing, and singing can help the baby. This structure allows the infant to anticipate what's coming next and even develop a biological daily rhythm. (Of course, this rhythm should never be

> enforced but should correspond to the baby's needs and continuously adapt to their development.)
> - *Professional help for special cases.* In cases of premature birth or postpartum depression, it is highly recommended to seek help from a music therapist. For music therapists: such help should include tips on singing with the baby.

THE HUMAN PREFERENCE FOR RHYTHM OVER CHAOS

Humans also have a biologically deep-rooted predisposition for rhythm. People generally prefer to hear rhythmic information over unstructured temporal information. On top of that, they involuntarily *produce* a rhythm or beat from random sound events. Andrea Ravignani, a mathematician and biologist, asked participants to imitate chaotic-sounding drum sequences generated quasi-randomly by a computer.[12] Then, he played the recordings of the imitated sequences to another group of participants, the 'next generation'. These participants were also asked to imitate the drum sequences in their recordings. This procedure was repeated several times, with each person unconsciously adding more rhythm to the drum sequences than was in the recordings they heard. Eventually, a beat emerged from what was originally a random drum sequence. Thus, the initially chaotic drum sequences gradually evolved into more rhythmic and musical sequences over multiple generations of participants.

Fascinatingly, the rhythmic sequences generated by the participants in Andrea's experiment exhibited musical properties corresponding to several statistical universals observed in music worldwide. Specifically, participants endowed the isochronous pulse with a 'metre', for example, grouping the underlying pulse either in twos (as in a march) or in threes (as in a waltz). Moreover, the resulting rhythmic sequences exhibited a structured pattern in which the bars contained a limited number of note

---

[12] Ravignani, A., Delgado, T., and Kirby, S. (2017). Musical evolution in the lab exhibits rhythmic universals. *Nature Human Behaviour*, 1(1), 0007.

durations, typically no more than five, such as quarters, eighths, and dotted eighths. (Eighth notes have half the duration of a quarter note, and a dotted eighth note is three-quarters of a quarter note.) Finally, participants used these principles to create rhythmic figures, beats, and riffs. This structuring also made the drum sequences easier to learn, as they unconsciously aligned with human memory and cognitive abilities. The innate cognitive and biological properties of the human brain and body predispose musical rhythm to exhibit universal properties.

Many animals also communicate via sounds. Unlike natural sounds and sound textures (such as rain, the crackling of a fire, water splashing, or wind rustling), the sounds produced by animals are structured by living organisms and, therefore, often remind us of music: the songs of birds, whales, or gibbons, the synchronous chirping of cicadas, the drumming on tree roots and body parts by apes. However, as of the present stage of knowledge, there is no animal species where several individuals sing or drum in unison. *Homo sapiens*, by contrast, are the only vertebrate species in which several individuals can produce and keep a beat in a group, sometimes faster, sometimes slower, sometimes accelerating or decelerating. Although some studies reported that animals can synchronize their movements to a beat, their methods and conclusions have been contested by the scientific community, or the reported behaviours cannot be observed in the wild. Yes, whales do sing, but not in a choir. Gorillas pound on their chests together, but not in synchrony, let alone as a combo.

What no other species can achieve, humans are capable of just a few months after birth. The psychologist Marcel Zentner and the musicologist Tuomas Eerola played music to babies between five and ten months old. The pieces were lively classical music, such as the finale from Saint-Saëns' 'The Carnival of the Animals'.[13] As they listened, the babies started kicking so that the pulse of their movements matched the pulse of the music. This fascinating finding shows the innate tendency of humans to engage in music. In addition, the babies smiled when they synchronized their movements to the music – participating in music

---

[13] Zentner, M., and Eerola, T. (2010). Rhythmic engagement with music in infancy. *Proceedings of the National Academy of Sciences*, 107(13), 5768–5773.

naturally gives us humans pleasure. The babies in this study were from Finland and Switzerland. A subsequent investigation obtained nearly identical results with babies from Brazil, except that the Brazilian infants moved significantly more to the same music.[14] They were probably already warming up for Carnival! These studies show that music stimulates a social function in us: moving together. The social effects of this function are prosocial behaviour and cooperation. When fourteen-month-old babies are bounced to music with a matching pulse, they tend to be more helpful afterwards than when bounced to a pulse that does not match the music (they are more likely to help the experimenter retrieve an 'accidentally' dropped pencil).[15] The anthropologists Sebastian Kirschner and Michael Tomasello observed a similar effect: after four-year-old children played music together, they cooperated more with each other and helped each other more.[16] Through this lens, the evolutionarily adaptive functions of music become apparent even in young children, who display increased prosocial behaviour after participating in musical activities.

Human musicality has its roots in the evolutionary development of auditory, vocal, and motor systems in mammals, a journey spanning tens of millions of years. Yet, it is only in humans that we find music characterized by pulse and scale, performed or sung collectively. Therefore, I propose that the simplest mental function distinguishing humans from animals is the ability to synchronize movements in a group to a pulse. This admittedly bold proposal means that music was the decisive evolutionary step of the *Homo sapiens* – possibly even of the genus *Homo*. Precisely this step brought several advantages to humans from which every individual can still benefit today, including positive social, emotional, and health effects. I will deal with these effects in more detail in the following chapters.

---

[14] Ilari, B. (2015). Rhythmic engagement with music in early childhood: A replication and extension. *Journal of Research in Music Education*, 62(4), 332–343.
[15] Cirelli, L. K., Einarson, K. M., and Trainor, L. J. (2014). Interpersonal synchrony increases prosocial behaviour in infants. *Developmental Science*, 17(6), 1003–1011.
[16] Kirschner, S., and Tomasello, M. (2010). Joint music making promotes prosocial behaviour in 4-year-old children. *Evolution and Human Behavior*, 31(5), 354–364.

CHAPTER 2

Our Innate Sense of Music

Even Non-musicians Are Musical

As the first notes of a concert emerge, an intricate cascade of neuronal activity unfolds within the brain, akin to a 'neuronal Big Bang'. This phenomenon triggers a myriad of remarkable effects. The human brain comprises approximately 86 billion nerve cells, of which the cortex alone accommodates around 16 billion.[1] Each cortical cell establishes approximately a thousand connections with other nerve cells, forming trillions of connections within a single brain. (That is many times more than the few hundred billion stars of the Milky Way.) Within moments, musical sounds activate millions of neurons connected by billions of synapses. These dynamic processes engage various brain networks responsible for perception, attention, memory, intelligence, sensorimotor functions, emotion, and communication. As the brain integrates these intricate activities, music brings forth a symphony of cognitive and sensory experiences.

The neuronal Big Bang begins with the activity of nerve cells in the brain stem leading to the perception of direction, volume, pitch, and timbre. Then, we recognize harmonies, differentiate instruments, and group tones and chords into sequences. These processes unfold within the auditory system, involving the brain stem, thalamus, and auditory cortex. Concurrently, diverse memories engage, beginning with *sensory memory* (often termed 'ultra-short-term memory'). This brief memory stage stores and integrates sounds, allowing us to perceive music's pulse, metre, and tone groupings. The sensory memory is a sensory buffer,

---

[1] Herculano-Houzel, S. (2009). The human brain in numbers: A linearly scaled-up primate brain. *Frontiers in Human Neuroscience*, 3, 31.

enabling us to perceive the direction of a melody and recognize whether it is ascending or descending. To remember the beginning of a melody and relate it to its end, we rely on our *working memory*, also known as 'short-term memory'. If we are familiar with the music, our *long-term memory* of the piece is activated. If we have a personal memory of that piece, our *autobiographical memory* comes into play. We also process the music according to our knowledge of musical rules. Even non-musicians have such knowledge, although they are usually unaware of it. Moreover, we experience emotional reactions when listening to music; our heartbeat and breathing change, or we might get goosebumps.

In addition to these functions, the musicians on the stage need sensorimotor functions to play the instruments. They also read the notes and pay attention to each other to coordinate their movements and play together accurately. Finally, the musicians and the audience focus their attention on the music. These processes engage a multitude of brain structures – music can influence neural activity across the entire brain. This insight holds significant relevance for understanding the therapeutic effects of music, a topic we shall explore later in this book.

I became interested in how the brain accomplishes these functions as a psychology student in the mid-1990s. Back then, little was known about how the brain processes music. Therefore, as a starting point, I decided to investigate what happens in the brain when we *listen to* music. Specifically, I started to examine what happens when we hear chord sequences that are 'right' or 'wrong' according to musical rules. This method was analogous to studying brain activity during language processing with 'right' or 'wrong' sentences. During that time, Thomas Gunter and Angela Friederici conducted such language experiments at the Max Planck Institute for Human Cognitive and Brain Sciences in Leipzig, Germany. They compared, for example, brain activity in response to correct and incorrect words in sentences such as 'He sees a cold beer' (singular) and 'He sees a cold beers' (plural).

As a student, I visited Angela Friederici and was fortunate to get an intern offer. During that internship, I planned and conducted my first studies. To explore how the brain processes chord progressions, I incorporated errors in musical grammar into harmonic sequences. More specifically, I composed numerous chord sequences and presented them using a computer connected to a synthesizer piano. Half of the sequences were regular cadences (such as tonic – tonic parallel – subdominant – dominant – tonic); in the other half, one of the chords was replaced by a chord not belonging to the tonal key, that is, by a chord with out-of-key tones. Especially when these out-of-key chords appeared at the end of the sequences, each participant in my studies could immediately discern that they sounded incorrect. (Note that musical tone sequences are not inherently 'wrong' or 'right' but rather more or less conventional, making them more or less expected or unexpected. For example, the unusual harmonic turns in the music of Bach, Mozart, or Beethoven are not necessarily wrong but are often ingeniously surprising. However, for the sake of clarity, I use the terms 'right' and 'wrong' here.)

A Glimpse into the Laboratory: Measuring Brain Electrical Responses to Chords

To investigate the processing of chords in the brain, we first used elect roencephalography (EEG) measurements. An EEG cap is placed on a test subject's head, which already contains numerous electrodes (usually thirty-two or sixty-four). The EEG cap looks like a bathing cap with long cables dangling from it (like a high-tech Medusa look). These electrodes are employed to record the brain's electrical signals. If the cap is mounted correctly, all the electrodes are located in the proper position on the head. The participant is then escorted to an electrically shielded EEG chamber, which includes a comfortable chair, a screen, a touch box, and a speaker. They are informed that they will hear chord progressions and must press a key immediately when another instrument plays a chord. While this timbre-detection task is straightforward and not directly linked to our primary investigation into musical grammar, it serves to maintain the participants' engagement.

During EEG recording, the brain waveforms displayed on the screen do not directly represent the brain's processing of music, as EEG waves are susceptible to noise from head and neck muscle movements. Additionally, the EEG waves capture spontaneous brain activity that is unrelated to the experiment. After all, the brain has tasks other than participating in the study. Compared to this noise in the EEG data, the brain activity that has to do with musical processing is like the buzzing of a bee next to a busy main road. But, as experimenters, we can eliminate such noise by presenting the chord sequences dozens of times and to several (fifteen to twenty-five) participants, enabling us to compute an average brain response. We can then be sure that the brain signal we identify is not simply due to chance. This specific type of brain response is commonly referred to as the 'event-related potential' or 'evoked potential'. The term potential is another word for voltage, created by the electrical activity of the brain. In my research, I focused on the brain potentials triggered by 'incorrect' chords, unveiling that they exhibited distinct differences from those elicited by harmonically correct chords. Fortunately, the experiment yielded enlightening results – I discovered a method for delving into the intricacies of how the brain processes musical grammar.

With such experiments, I discovered that the brain's electrical responses to 'right' and 'wrong' chords differed already about 150 milliseconds after the onset of the chords, that is, after 150 thousandths of a second – that's less than the blink of an eye.[2] The electrical brain potential to wrong *chords* also strongly resembled the typical brain electrical response to syntactically wrong *words*: it had a similar time course and distribution over the head. These findings were among the first indicating that the brain processes music and language in overlapping networks. The only difference was that the brain's electrical responses to unusual chords were more prominent over the *right* hemisphere, while electrical responses to syntactic errors in language experiments were typically more prominent over the *left* hemisphere.

I initially conducted these experiments with musicians and subsequently with individuals who neither played instruments nor sang in choirs. The results were clear: the brains of the non-musicians also reacted to the wrong chords, and their brain activity was very similar to that of the musicians, except for being slightly smaller. This suggests that

---

[2] Koelsch, S., Gunter, T., Friederici, A. D., and Schröger, E. (2000). Brain indices of music processing: 'Nonmusicians' are musical. *Journal of Cognitive Neuroscience*, 12(3), 520–541.

both musicians and non-musicians engage the same neural processes when encountering unusual chords.

Interestingly, I observed brain responses to discordant chords even in participants who claimed, with complete conviction, to be 'completely unmusical'. We can explain this seeming contradiction by the concept of *implicit knowledge*, which refers to knowledge we have although we are not consciously aware of it. Implicit knowledge can be surprisingly precise, which is why many of our participants were surprised by the strength of their brain's response to the wrong chords, even when they had not consciously noticed anything specific while listening to them. I remember how a friend, whom I had shown his brain waveforms after the experiment, asked me, 'So I'm not unmusical after all? Does this mean that I could learn to play an instrument? I've always wanted to learn the saxophone.' I answered his questions with a resounding 'yes'. Sometime later, I saw him playing the baritone saxophone in the university's big band, and it was a truly memorable moment for both of us. Seeing the joy on his face while playing was an unforgettable experience for me.

Thus, we have shown that even individuals who believe they are unmusical possess a sense of music. It is possible to have musical ability without being consciously aware of it. Many assume they are unmusical because they have not received formal music education, cannot read music, do not play an instrument, or have never learned to sing. However, being musically untrained does not mean that someone is unmusical. Every human being has the natural biological capacity for musicality, meaning we are all naturally musical beings. Fortunately, this also means that everyone can benefit from the healing effects of music.

Many groups from different countries have subsequently replicated the results of these studies. Further studies have found that the brain processes 'wrong' chords even when a participant is reading a book and not paying attention to the music. Moreover, it was not just the controlled music stimuli from our experiments that elicited these responses; even compositions by Bach, Beethoven, and Schubert had the same effect.[3]

---

[3] Koelsch, S., Kilches, S., Steinbeis, N., and Schelinski, S. (2008). Effects of unexpected chords and performer's expression on brain responses and electrodermal activity. *PLoS ONE*, 3(7), e2631.

TODDLERS ALREADY RECOGNIZE UNUSUAL CHORDS

We have also conducted several EEG experiments with children. Before that, the conventional academic view was that children could only really begin to understand music from primary school age. However, this prevailing view did not align with my observations – I could see that my children liked music, sang and clapped along, and almost fell off their chairs laughing when I played them the wrong chords from the chord sequences from my experiments.

In a series of experiments with preschool children, we discovered neural responses to unusual chords in youngsters as young as two and a half.[4] Incidentally, a typical comment from parents was, 'Well, I don't hear any difference between these chord sequences – thus, my child won't hear any difference either.' Far from it: children usually perceive much more (and much more accurately) than their parents think or even perceive themselves. Our data revealed that the brains of toddlers responded to the wrong chords. Thus, our results indicated that even toddlers, as young as two and a half, acquire a sophisticated understanding of musical grammar. They acquire musical knowledge based on music that they hear in their everyday life, for example, in kindergarten or on the radio. Toddlers do this naturally without anyone explaining anything to them (none of the children had received music lessons).

However, the brain reactions of these two-and-a-half-year-olds were still relatively small. This leads me to suspect that children begin to recognize and store the syntactic regularities of music and apply them when listening to unfamiliar music around the age of two to two and a half. Intriguingly, that is precisely the age at which they also start to react to incorrect grammar in language. Thus, humans have an innate sense for recognizing and learning the structures and regularities of music and language, which becomes apparent during the third year of life.

---

[4] Jentschke, S., Friederici, A. D., and Koelsch, S. (2014). Neural correlates of music-syntactic processing in two-year-old children. *Developmental Cognitive Neuroscience*, 9, 200–208.

CHAPTER 3

Music and Language in the Brain

WHILE WORKING AS A POSTDOCTORAL FELLOW AT Harvard Medical School, my children and I spent many happy hours exploring sunny Boston playgrounds. They seamlessly switched between English and German, speaking both languages like native speakers. This piqued the interest of another parent, who, curious about their bilingualism, asked me how they had learned German. In spite of my best efforts to suppress my German accent beneath American English, merely uttering my first word gave my origins away, prompting an immediate 'Ah – you are German!' from the other parent.

This encounter highlights the remarkable musicality involved in how we perceive and produce speech sounds. The ability of children to achieve accent-free speech, often even in a specific regional dialect, demonstrates our profound auditory perception and vocal production skills. Language-specific sounds natural to native speakers can pose significant challenges to foreigners. For instance, the nuanced distinction of German umlauts (ä, ö, ü) baffles non-natives, and the Estonian /õ/ straddles somewhere between 'o' and 'ö'. Mandarin vowels carry intricate pitch contours, whereas Japanese speech nuances lie in length differences. These examples from languages around the globe underscore the complexity of human speech and our brain's remarkable musical aptitude in processing language.

Interestingly, the neuronal operations for processing music and language in the brain significantly overlap, reflecting their closely intertwined evolutionary roots. The earliest stages of processing speech and musical sounds in the brain are identical because, from a purely acoustic point of view, speech and music share the same acoustic features. Both are characterized by their frequency spectrum and the way their intensity increases and decreases. This explains why instruments can mimic speech sounds and why acclaimed vocalists such as Bobby McFerrin or celebrated beatboxers such as Tom Thum can produce sounds that resemble musical instruments. A violin tone can sound like an 'eee', a bassoon tone like an 'ooo', a hi-hat tone like a 'tsss', or a castanet like a 'khhh'.

Each *vowel* is a musical tone. The acoustic differences between individual vowels, when spoken at the same pitch, lie merely in the intensity of the overtones – referred to as 'formants' in phonetics. The ability to discern these minute differences is, in essence, a musical feat. Germans can easily distinguish vowels such as 'u', 'ü', 'ö', and 'o', but those who do not speak a language with umlauts can often barely pronounce them or hear any differences between 'o' and 'ö' or between 'u' and 'ü'. Conversely, the Norwegian 'y' sounds between the German 'e' and 'ü'. I have lived in Norway for several years, but even as a musician, I find it challenging to differentiate between the Norwegian 'ü' and 'y'. Intriguingly, research suggests that musicians usually possess an advantage in detecting such subtle acoustic differences.[1] However, the fact that every Norwegian non-musician can readily speak and understand 'y' and that German non-musicians have no problems with umlauts shows how *musically* we humans perceive speech sounds, even without formal musical training. Those who consider themselves unmusical are therefore underestimating the highly admirable musical capabilities of their sense of hearing.

Incidentally, as babies, we can accurately perceive the differences between all these speech sounds. It is only when we reach about nine months of age that we become so accustomed to our mother tongue that our ability to perceive differences in the sounds of other languages diminishes.[2] We 'tune in' to our mother tongue, a process that

---

[1] Kempe, V., Bublitz, D., and Brooks, P. J. (2015). Musical ability and non-native speech-sound processing are linked through sensitivity to pitch and spectral information. *British Journal of Psychology*, 106(2), 349–366.

[2] Kuhl, P. K., Stevens, E., Hayashi, A., Deguchi, T., Kiritani, S., and Iverson, P. (2006). Infants show a facilitation effect for native language phonetic perception between 6 and 12 months. *Developmental Science*, 9(2), F13–F21.

conditions us to focus on the unique phonetic properties of our native language, thus diminishing our ability to recognize speech sounds of foreign languages.

As for vowels, the acoustic features of consonants are the same as those that characterize musical sounds. However, in contrast to vowels, the acoustic characteristics of *consonants* are often a mixture of the frequency spectrum, changes in intensity, and duration. For example, we can use these features to distinguish percussion instruments (such as the hi-hat 'tsss' from a cymbal 'tshhh') or a plucked guitar tone ('deeeng') from a bowed violin tone ('neee').

Both speech and musical sounds are simply air pressure waves with identical physical properties. Consequently, during the initial stages of processing, the brain's auditory system does not differentiate between the two. Even beyond individual sounds, speech has several things in common with music. When several speech sounds are strung together to form words and sentences, they are spoken with a melody that, for example, distinguishes a question from an answer. In tone languages, the melody of a word determines its meaning. We also often speak with a *rhythm* that helps listeners follow the speaker. You can recognize this by purposefully reading this sentence repeatedly with different rhythms. Moreover, accents can convey additional meaning. For example, the emphasis can shift the meaning from 'PETER plays the violin' to 'Peter plays the VIOLIN'. Through the *emotional* prosody of speech – the emotive tonality of speech – we can often gauge the speaker's emotions.

Melody, rhythm, accents, and expressive tone are all characteristics of speech *and* music. No wonder the brain processes music and speech with overlapping mechanisms in overlapping structures.

CHILDREN'S PERCEPTION OF LANGUAGE AS MUSIC

The musical aspects of a language are essential for young children to learn a language. For babies and toddlers, the music of the speech is much more important than its meaning. At first, it is not crucial for them *what* someone says to them or *what* they say (or babble) themselves but *how* something is said. A baby does not yet understand what 'milk' or 'drink' means; it must first learn that language sounds have particular meanings.

Newborns demonstrate remarkable abilities in speech recognition. During the last months of pregnancy, the foetus hears the mother's speech and singing, as well as the music that the mother hears. Although the frequency information is heavily filtered, the foetus already learns the sound of its mother's language, that is, its musical features. An infant can recognize the mother's voice immediately after birth and differentiate it from another woman's voice.[3] They can even distinguish the sound of their mother's language from a foreign language. For example, newborns of mothers who are native English speakers can recognize whether *other* women are speaking Spanish or English.[4]

Newborns recognize voices and languages by the musical aspects of speech, the timbre, the speech melody, and the speech rhythm. This recognition is only possible because we humans are born with spectacular musical abilities. It is through these musical abilities that we learn a language as infants. We, adults, are used to listening to the *meaning* of language, thus often overhearing how much music there is in every spoken sentence. Only when we hear a foreign language, where we cannot understand the meaning, do we hear the music in the speech again – like an infant.

THE MUSIC-LANGUAGE NETWORK IN THE BRAIN

Even at the higher processing stages, such as processing sentence structure and meaning, the brain engages overlapping neural resources for language and music. As a young PhD student, I discovered that the brain's electrical response to 'wrong' chords is generated in a specific part of the frontal lobe. In the brain's left hemisphere, this part is called *Broca's area* (Figure 3.1).[5] Broca's area was one of the first brain areas known to have a specific function. In the 1860s, the French neurologist Paul Broca reported the case of a patient whom he called 'Monsieur

---

[3] DeCasper, A. J., and Fifer, W. P. (1980). Of human bonding: Newborns prefer their mothers' voices. *Science*, 208(4448), 1174–1176.

[4] Moon, C., Cooper, R. P., and Fifer, W. P. (1993). Two-day-olds prefer their native language. *Infant Behaviour and Development*, 16(4), 495–500.

[5] Maess, B., Koelsch, S., Gunter, T. C., and Friederici, A. D. (2001). Musical syntax is processed in Broca's area: An MEG study. *Nature Neuroscience*, 4(5), 540.

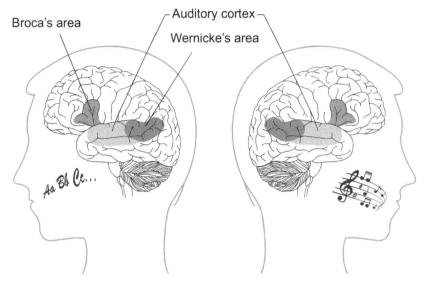

Figure 3.1 The network for language and music in the brain. Left: The classical language network in the brain's left hemisphere with the two language centres, the areas of Broca and Wernicke. Different regions of the auditory cortex also contribute to language processing. Right: The same areas in the brain's right hemisphere serve the processing of music. However, the 'language network' of the left hemisphere also processes music, and the 'music network' of the right hemisphere also processes language. Thus, instead of two separate networks, a single 'music-language network' in the brain processes speech and music. Source: Olga Koelsch

Tan'. This patient could suddenly only slur one syllable ('Tan') but could still understand speech relatively well. After the patient's death, Broca examined his brain and found that a stroke had damaged part of the left frontal lobe. This area is nowadays called Broca's area, and the language disorder after a stroke, in which patients can no longer speak but can still understand language, is called *Broca's aphasia*. Broca's area is a core structure of the language network, and it was long thought that this area was a language-specific brain structure. Nevertheless, my experiments have shown that this particular brain region plays a role in processing musical structures as well.

In addition to conducting studies measuring electrical brain signals, I also conducted an experiment using functional MRI (fMRI). This method is powerful in measuring *where* nerve cells are active in the brain. I still vividly remember the day I showed the results from this fMRI experiment to Yves von Cramon, the head of the Department of

Neurology at the Max Planck Institute. I had prepared the results on a computer screen for the professor. When he entered the room, he looked at the screen and immediately said, 'Ah, a language experiment!' The data he saw on the computer screen seemed so similar to those from language experiments that he thought I had conducted a language experiment. When I informed him of his error, he was so stunned that he could hardly stop scrutinizing the results. He was so fascinated that he spent significantly more time on our meeting than scheduled. For a PhD student like myself, this was a remarkable acknowledgment of the significance of my work.

The fMRI data confirmed that 'wrong' chords evoke neuronal activity in Broca's area. Additionally, they revealed that such chords also evoke activity in a brain region called *Wernicke's area* (Figure 3.1). In the nineteenth century, shortly after Paul Broca had announced his groundbreaking findings, the German neurologist Carl Wernicke reported on patients who had lost their *comprehension* of speech but retained the ability to speak, albeit nonsensically. This condition is now referred to as *Wernicke's aphasia*. After these patients' deaths, Wernicke found that the posterior part of the upper gyrus of the temporal lobe and adjacent regions in the temporal and parietal lobes were damaged. Therefore, this region ('Wernicke's area') is another core structure of the language network. This very network, including Broca's and Wernicke's areas, was clearly visible on the computer screen, which stunned my professor. As in my previous music experiments using EEG, the brain activity was somewhat stronger in the *right* hemisphere, paralleling language experiments where the same brain network is typically more active in the *left* hemisphere.[6] My findings brought to light that the music network in the brain overlaps with the language network: a 'music-language network' in the brain processes both music and language. In this sense, composers actually 'speak' to us with their music.

One year later, when I was a postdoctoral fellow in Gottfried Schlaug's research group at Harvard Medical School in Boston, we conducted a

---

[6] Koelsch, S., Gunter, T. C., von Cramon, D. Y., Zysset, S., Lohmann, G., and Friederici, A. D. (2002). Bach speaks: A cortical language-network serves the processing of music. *NeuroImage*, 17(2), 956–966.

similar fMRI experiment with adults and ten-year-old children.[7] We found activations nearly identical to those in my previous study. Both groups activated the music-language network when hearing chord sequences with 'wrong' chords (again, more strongly in the right hemisphere). That is, both adults and children process music and language in overlapping brain structures in both the left and right hemispheres of the brain.

The Italian neurologist Daniela Perani and I discovered that newborns already respond to music with activity in their music-language network.[8] In this study, classical music was played to newborns. However, sometimes we manipulated the music such that the tonal key shifted abruptly to a different tonal key or the music was permanently dissonant. Thus, whereas the tonal centre of the music was easy to find in the 'original music', it was harder to identify in the manipulated pieces. (The 'tonal centre' in C major, for example, is 'C'.) Brain scans were performed while the newborns listened to the music (most babies were asleep). The manipulated music elicited increased activity in Broca's area. The newborns' brains were likely searching for the tonal centre in the music, using a brain structure critical for learning and processing language. Thus, the human brain naturally processes and recognizes musical structure, including searching for a tonal centre of melodies and harmonies. Already at birth, our brains are endowed with a deep interest in music.

The observation that language is often processed more strongly in the left hemisphere and music in the right hemisphere is related to the fact that the left auditory cortex has a higher temporal resolution and the right one a higher frequency resolution. Speech is *faster* than music, and music has more *pitch* information than speech. In the word 'music', six speech sounds (also called 'phonemes') follow each other within half a second: [m-y-uː-z-ɪ-k]. In a sentence, we can easily speak or perceive ten to twenty sounds per second – considerably more than we typically hear

---

[7] Koelsch, S., Fritz, T., Schulze, K., Alsop, D., and Schlaug, G. (2005). Adults and children processing music: An fMRI study. *NeuroImage*, 25(4), 1068–1076.

[8] Perani, D., Saccuman, M. C., Scifo, P., Spada, D., Andreolli, G., Rovelli, R., Baldoli, C., and Koelsch, S. (2010). Functional specializations for music processing in the human newborn brain. *Proceedings of the National Academy of Sciences*, 107(10), 4758–4763.

in a melody. By contrast, melodies commonly have numerous pitches and easily span an octave (such as the song 'Happy Birthday to You'). Our speech melody rarely spans more than a fifth. Thus, speech is 'super-fast music', and music is 'super-melodic speech'. Hence, it helps children to learn language through songs or nursery rhymes – the speech is slower, and the syllables always occur on the pulse or its subdivisions (quarters, eighths, and so on), making it easier for the brain to recognize and process the syllables.

USING MUSIC TO ENHANCE LANGUAGE SKILLS

Due to the overlap of language and music in the brain, musical skills also strengthen language development. Language is often better developed in children who actively engage in music. Music lessons at preschool age promote speech perception, and kindergarten children who can easily tap to a simple beat can also better distinguish between similar syllables (such as 'ba', 'da', and 'ga'). In addition, their short-term memory for syllables is better developed.[9] These skills are crucial for learning to read at school age.

At school age, musical engagement further supports language development. After I had returned from Harvard Medical School to the Max Planck Institute in Leipzig, my research group carried out an experiment with children of the famous St Thomas Choir of Leipzig, as well as children from a music high school and children without any particular musical engagement. We discovered that language processing in eleven-year-old children with musical training is more developed than in peers without musical training – when listening to spoken sentences with grammatical errors, the brains of children with musical training reacted more sensitively to such errors.[10] (They also responded more sensitively to 'wrong' chords in harmonic sequences, as one would expect.)

---

[9] Carr, K. W., White-Schwoch, T., Tierney, A. T., Strait, D. L., and Kraus, N. (2014). Beat synchronization predicts neural speech encoding and reading readiness in preschoolers. *Proceedings of the National Academy of Sciences*, 111(40), 14559–14564.

[10] Jentschke, S., and Koelsch, S. (2009). Musical training modulates the development of syntax processing in children. *NeuroImage*, 47(2), 735–744.

When the natural musical abilities do not develop properly in a child, language often does not develop properly either. Children with delayed language development usually also have difficulties perceiving sounds and music. They recognize pitches less accurately and sing less precisely than children with typical language development.[11] They also often have problems clapping along to a pulse, moving to a beat, or speaking to a beat.

If a child does not understand what is being said, logically, they cannot learn well. Therefore, children with language development problems often have difficulties in developing acoustic perception and sensorimotor skills. These are precisely the areas that can be practised playfully with music. Often, these children also show learning disorders in school (for example, reading or spelling problems). Interestingly, music lessons with clapping, dancing, and singing games that promote a sense of rhythm can help with language development disorders and dyslexia. Usha Goswami, a psychologist at the University of Cambridge, investigated the effects of a rhythmic musical intervention in children with dyslexia.[12] The intervention included hand-clapping games and nursery rhymes, clapping or walking to a song, and clapping rhythms. Meanwhile, children in a control group played an already-tested computer game for language development: the children had to identify rhyming words or match spoken words to their written counterparts on the screen. After a standard two-month intervention period, both groups could read significantly better than before. Intriguingly, the music-based intervention proved equally effective as the language training in enhancing reading skills, thereby emphasizing the neural interconnectedness of music and language.

Similar results were reported in another study in which researchers assigned preschool children with dyslexia to a music or painting group. The music group played rhythm, clapping, and dance games (based on methods by Kodály and Orff). After seven months of intervention, the

---

[11] Clément, S., Planchou, C., Béland, R., Motte, J., and Samson, S. (2015). Singing abilities in children with Specific Language Impairment (SLI). *Frontiers in Psychology*, 6, 420.

[12] Bhide, A., Power, A., and Goswami, U. (2013). A rhythmic musical intervention for poor readers: A comparison of efficacy with a letter-based intervention. *Mind, Brain, and Education*, 7(2), 113–123.

children with rhythm training could read significantly better and recognize syllables better than those who participated in the painting training.[13] Such results show that *rhythm* training can help children with *language* development disorders as well as reading and spelling difficulties.

Music making has a positive impact on language development by aiding the playful cultivation of children's essential mental faculties: perception, attention, memory, action planning, sensorimotor functions, emotions, and communicative skills. Therefore, it stands to reason that children who engage with music have developmental advantages over children who never experience it. For example, Canadian music psychologist Glenn Schellenberg reported that children who received music lessons had slightly higher intelligence and behaved more helpfully and considerately than control children who did not actively engage in music.[14] Music is part of our human nature. Therefore, musicality is part of the natural endowment of children – just as the ability to learn a language is. Therefore, musical experiences such as singing and dancing are necessary for a child's natural development.

Engaging in Music with Toddlers and Preschoolers

Here are some practical ways to integrate music into the daily lives of toddlers and preschoolers, aiding both their musical and linguistic development.

- *Nursery rhymes and sensory integration.* Singing and playing nursery rhymes is an excellent way to engage children with music. You can also clap and drum while singing or even talking. This helps develop a sense of rhythm, and recognition of syllables and words. Some

---

[13] Flaugnacco, E., Lopez, L., Terribili, C., Montico, M., Zoia, S., and Schön, D. (2015). Music training increases phonological awareness and reading skills in developmental dyslexia: A randomized control trial. *PLoS ONE*, 10(9), e0138715.

[14] Schellenberg, E. G. (2006). Long-term positive associations between music lessons and IQ. *Journal of Educational Psychology*, 98(2), 457; Schellenberg, E. G., Corrigall, K. A., Dys, S. P., and Malti, T. (2015). Group music training and children's prosocial skills. *PLoS ONE*, 10(10), e0141449.

nursery rhymes and songs involve touching (e.g. 'Head, Shoulders, Knees, and Toes'). This assists the brain in processing auditory and sensory information simultaneously.
- *Musical movement in child carriers.* When carrying a child in a child carrier, you can speak, sing, whistle, or play syllable games in sync with the pace of your walking. This is fun and helps the child develop a sense of rhythm and produce speech sounds following a pulse.
- *Exploration of musical instruments.* Provide your child with access to musical instruments. Children are naturally curious about them. Offer the child an opportunity to learn an instrument, or to sing or dance, if they are interested.
- *Multilingual music benefits.* Songs and rhymes are particularly beneficial for children growing up in immigrant or multilingual families, as the syllables are slower and more clearly separated. If both parents are immigrants, a children's singing group and, later on, a children's choir can support language acquisition.
- *Integration of music in speech therapy.* A recommendation for speech therapists is to incorporate musical elements into sessions with children. Train their sense of rhythm, especially for those with language development disorders or dyslexia. Begin with simple exercises aimed at fostering the connection between sensorimotor and auditory processes. For instance, sitting together and clapping a beat with both hands on the table can be an effective way to achieve this. In the next step, speak the child's name syllable by syllable, following a pulse (for example: clap-clap-'An-na'). Also, utilize simple children's songs and nursery rhymes.

CHAPTER 4

Our Engagement Shapes Our Brain

WHEN WE ACQUIRE A SKILL, our brain undergoes transformation; both its structure and function change. Similarly, when we alter our thinking and emotions in ways that promote our health and well-being, new pathways form in the brain. Below, I have compiled two 'hit lists' of pivotal studies exploring the interplay between music, learning, and the brain. The first list examines how engaging with music affects brain *function*, and the second focuses on the impact of musical engagement on brain *anatomy*. In particular, I focus on the most frequently cited scientific papers in these research areas. (The number of citations by other scientists is a key indicator of a research paper's scientific impact.)

Firstly, let us examine the top three studies investigating the effects of music training on brain *function*.

First place: a 1998 study led by Christo Pantev revealed that pianists exhibit greater brain electrical responses to piano tones compared to non-musicians. These responses were traced back to the auditory cortex (refer to Figure 3.1 for an illustration of the auditory cortex).[1] Christo observed that the reactions were most pronounced in musicians who began their piano training at the age of five years. To put it simply, pianists who began their training at a younger age showed stronger brain responses. This result suggests that the observed differences between musicians and non-musicians are not innate but due to

---

[1] Pantev, C., Oostenveld, R., Engelien, A., Ross, B., Roberts, L. E., and Hoke, M. (1998). Increased auditory cortical representation in musicians. *Nature*, 392(6678), 811.

learning effects. This indicates that auditory brain functions vary according to an individual's musical experience. The auditory cortex becomes more responsive to piano tones when learning the piano. Similarly, the auditory cortex of violin players reacts more strongly to violin tones, and the auditory cortex of trumpet players responds more strongly to trumpet tones.

Second place: in 2007, Patrick Wong et al. reported that musicians are better at perceiving minute melodic pitch variations of vowels than non-musicians.[2] Patrick played three very similar-sounding words in Mandarin to the participants several thousand times. All three words sounded like 'me', but Mandarin is a tonal language, meaning the pitch pattern used when pronouncing a vowel can change a word's meaning entirely. For example, the syllable 'ma' can have different meanings based on its tone: with a high-level tone, 'mā' means 'mother'; with a rising tone, 'má' means 'hemp'; with a falling-then-rising tone, 'mǎ' means 'horse'; and with a falling tone, 'mà' means 'scold'. These subtle pitch variations are challenging for non-native speakers to detect and replicate accurately. The research team discovered that the brain electrical responses of musicians reflected these subtle differences more accurately than those of non-musicians.

Similarly, the researchers measured brain electrical responses to similar-sounding syllables – 'ga' and 'ba' – between individuals who had musical training and those who did not. The consonants 'g' and 'b' of these two syllables differ, among other things, in that the sound 'g' is several dozen milliseconds shorter than the sound 'b', and thus the sound 'a' begins earlier with 'ga' than with 'ba'. In adults, brain electrical responses of musicians reflect these subtle temporal differences more accurately than non-musicians. Interestingly, even preschool children who have learned an instrument for one to two years show these differences compared to children who have not.[3] Again,

---

[2] Wong, P. C., Skoe, E., Russo, N. M., Dees, T., and Kraus, N. (2007). Musical experience shapes human brainstem encoding of linguistic pitch patterns. *Nature Neuroscience*, 10(4), 420.

[3] Kraus, N., and Strait, D. L. (2015). Emergence of biological markers of musicianship with school-based music instruction. *Annals of the New York Academy of Sciences*, 1337(1), 163–169.

there is evidence that these effects are due to learning, not innate differences: primary school children at risk for dyslexia received two years of instrumental lessons. Afterwards, their brains were able to distinguish between 'ga' and 'ba' more clearly than before (children in a control group without music lessons did not show these differences).

Third place: in 2008, Sylvain Moreno randomly assigned eight-year-old children with no specific music experience either to a music group or a painting group. The children then received six months of training in either music or painting.[4] Afterwards, the brains of the children in the music group (but not the painting group) reacted more sensitively to minute pitch changes in melodies and spoken sentences. In addition, the children in the music group were better at reading words in a reading-aloud test. These results impressively demonstrate that just six months of regular musical engagement can lead to changes in children's brains associated with better recognition of subtle differences in speech melody and even increased reading skills.

Having discussed the *functional* changes, let us now transition to how these correlate with *structural*, that is, anatomical, changes in the brain. The following provides the 'hit list' of the most cited studies on the effects of learning a musical instrument on brain structure.

First place: in 2003, Christian Gaser and Gottfried Schlaug compared the anatomy of the brains of professional musicians, amateur musicians, and non-musicians. They discovered differences in the grey matter of the auditory and motor cortex.[5] This finding shows that the brains of individuals who learn a specific skill are anatomically different to those who have not. Incidentally, Christian and Gottfried conducted this study when I worked with them in the same research group at Harvard Medical School in Boston. Back then, I brought my violin to Boston to pick up playing again (after a long while of being unable to

---

[4] Moreno, S., Marques, C., Santos, A., Santos, M., Castro, S. L., and Besson, M. (2008). Musical training influences linguistic abilities in 8-year-old children: More evidence for brain plasticity. *Cerebral Cortex*, 19(3), 712–723.

[5] Gaser, C., and Schlaug, G. (2003). Brain structures differ between musicians and non-musicians. *Journal of Neuroscience*, 23(27), 9240–9245.

find the time for it). Gottfried and I took this as an opportunity to investigate whether the structure of my brain would change when I started regularly practising again. We then took multiple brain scans of me over several months and discovered that, with violin practice, some regions of my motor cortex increased in size again.

Christian's research group also explored the effects of juggling training. In one study, after three months of training, an increase in the brain's grey matter was found in regions that have functions for storing and processing visuospatial information.[6] After another three months of not juggling, these changes decreased again. The research group also found similar anatomical changes in sixty-year-olds. Consequently, even in advanced years, the brain remains malleable through the process of learning.[7] In another fascinating study, the researchers observed changes in grey matter after only seven days of training (after which many participants could juggle continuously for one minute).[8]

The alterations in grey matter, as described in these studies, are primarily attributed to the formation of new neural connections. Nerve cells start to sprout new connections to other nerve cells and form new synapses and dendritic spines. (A nerve cell in the brain can pass signals to another nerve cell through a synapse, while a dendritic spine allows a nerve cell to receive input from another nerve cell.) These processes of forming new nerve connections can occur in just a few hours – the brain thus changes amazingly quickly due to what we do. Additionally, the increased activity of the nerve cells and their establishment of connections is accompanied by the formation of additional blood vessels that supply cells with oxygen and nutrients. All these effects contribute to the changes in grey matter in the brain reported in the studies.[9]

---

[6] Draganski, B., Gaser, C., Busch, V., Schuierer, G., Bogdahn, U., and May, A. (2004). Neuroplasticity: Changes in grey matter induced by training. *Nature*, 427(6972), 311.
[7] Boyke, J., Driemeyer, J., Gaser, C., Büchel, C., and May, A. (2008). Training-induced brain structure changes in the elderly. *Journal of Neuroscience*, 28(28), 7031–7035.
[8] Driemeyer, J., Boyke, J., Gaser, C., Büchel, C., and May, A. (2008). Changes in gray matter induced by learning – revisited. *PLoS ONE*, 3(7), e2669.
[9] Jacobs, B., Schall, M., Prather, M., Kapler, E., Driscoll, L., Baca, S., Jacobs, J., Ford, K., Wainwright, M., and Treml, M. (2001). Regional dendritic and spine variation in human cerebral cortex: A quantitative golgi study. *Cerebral Cortex*, 11(6), 558–571.

Learning creates new pathways and new networks in the brain. The more complex a skill is, the more complex networks we need in the brain. When we learn a new skill, change something in our lives, or think or feel in new ways, new connections form within hours, and just a few days of learning are enough to measure such changes with brain imaging. Subsequently, we must keep practising regularly and frequently to keep the neuronal connections fresh – otherwise, they vanish again.

Second place: in 2005, Sara Bengtsson examined the effects of learning on the brain anatomy of eight concert pianists.[10] The research group used a specific MRI method to measure the anatomy of nerve fibres (nerve fibres are the 'wires' connecting nerve cells). The pianists estimated the number of hours they had practised as children, as teenagers, and as adults. The number of practice hours varied among individuals: between 1,000 and 2,000 hours in childhood, between 2,000 and 4,000 hours in adolescence, and between 15,000 and 30,000 hours in adulthood. Additionally, Bengtsson measured the brains of eight non-musicians for comparison.

The measurements showed differences between pianists and non-musicians in a region of the sensorimotor cortex that is important for the execution of finger movements. The more the pianists had practised in childhood, the more pronounced these differences. In addition, the 'corpus callosum' (a thick nerve tract connecting the two brain hemispheres) was thicker in pianists who had practised exceptionally frequently in childhood and adolescence. Specifically, the corpus callosum was larger in places where the nerve fibres were involved in hearing, controlling finger movements, and controlling sequences of movements of fingers and hands.

The noted variances in the corpus callosum arose partly from an increased thickness of the fatty tissue that surrounds and insulates nerve fibres, thereby accelerating information transmission between hemispheres. In addition, the differences originated from the growth

---

[10] Bengtsson, S. L., Nagy, Z., Skare, S., Forsman, L., Forssberg, H., and Ullén, F. (2005). Extensive piano practicing has regionally specific effects on white matter development. *Nature Neuroscience*, 8(9), 1148.

of additional nerve fibres, allowing for a finer resolution of information about the sound of tones and for movement control.

Third place: as early as 1995, Gottfried Schlaug and colleagues reported that the front part of the corpus callosum is thicker in professional musicians than in non-musicians.[11] This difference was most pronounced in individuals who started learning an instrument at seven or younger. Together with the findings of the Bengtsson study, these results support the notion that extensive practising leads to changes in nerve fibres in the brain.

In another study, six-year-old children received thirty-minute piano lessons weekly for fifteen months.[12] Afterwards, the right motor cortex and the right auditory cortex were larger. Likewise, a part of the corpus callosum through which sensory fibres of the fingers cross was thicker. Similar findings were observed in six-year-olds who received instrumental lessons as part of the 'El Sistema' initiative. Sponsored by the Los Angeles Philharmonic Orchestra, children received free instruments and high-quality instrumental lessons. All children came from disadvantaged social backgrounds, and the initiative aims to promote children's social and educational development. That study, too, found anatomical effects of music training in the music group in the area of the auditory cortex and the corpus callosum after two years of music lessons.

'IT'S A LONG WAY TO THE TOP'

The studies above indicate that practice is essential in developing unique skills. Here is a biological illustration of how much time one needs to practise to play an instrument with perfection. Let us assume conservatively that only one-tenth of a concert violinist's brain, that is, about 8.6 billion neurons, is involved in playing the instrument. Let us also estimate conservatively that each of these neurons only forms 100 new

---

[11] Schlaug, G., Jäncke, L., Huang, Y., Staiger, J. F., and Steinmetz, H. (1995). Increased corpus callosum size in musicians. *Neuropsychologia*, 33(8), 1047–1055.

[12] Hyde, K. L., Lerch, J., Norton, A., Forgeard, M., Winner, E., Evans, A. C., and Schlaug, G. (2009). Musical training shapes structural brain development. *Journal of Neuroscience*, 29 (10), 3019–3025.

synapses during training up to concert level, resulting in 860 billion synapses. How many hours must one practise to acquire this number of synapses? If we roughly estimate that, in each practice hour, 400,000 neurons grow new synapses and that each of these neurons forms 100 synapses per hour of practice, then that would result in forty million new synapses (!) per practice hour.[13] Thus, it requires 21,500 hours of learning to reach the number of synapses a concert musician has (860 billion synapses divided by forty million synapses per hour). Suppose one practises three hours every day. In that case, it will take almost twenty years, which is pretty much in line with Bengtsson's observations that concert professionals usually have accumulated more than 10,000 hours of practice by the age of twenty and another 10,000 by the mid-twenties. Thus, even if each hour of learning results in forty million new synapses, it still takes over 20,000 hours for 860 billion connections to form in the brain. Of course, this applies to many other skills besides music. Unfortunately, it also means that millions of synapses are not generated every day we do not practice. Therefore, if you aim to master a new skill, consistent daily practice is crucial. Practising in moderate amounts *every day* is more effective than engaging in erratic bursts of intense training followed by periods of inactivity.

COULD EXCEPTIONAL SKILLS ORIGINATE FROM EPIGENETIC CHANGES?

Whether the special musical abilities of a professional musician are innate or due to extensive training has a long history of hot debates. I propose that our unique skills and talents arise from the interplay between genetics and environment, mediated by *epigenetic* changes: the environment, our experiences, and how we deal with them influence our epigenetics, that is, the *activation pattern* of our genes. Thus, I do not believe that any exceptional talent of an individual is 'innate', that is, due to any extraordinary genes of that individual. Before I lose half of my

---

[13] Kleim, J. A., Hogg, T. M., VandenBerg, P. M., Cooper, N. R., Bruneau, R., and Remple, M. (2004). Cortical synaptogenesis and motor map reorganization occur during late, but not early, phase of motor skill learning. *Journal of Neuroscience*, 24(3), 628–633.

readership now, let me emphasize that I will not argue here about which view ('innate' or 'experience') is right or wrong. Instead, I will say that the mindset that special abilities are due to *experience* and not innate is more beneficial for our *health* and thus puts us in a better position to benefit from the *Good Vibrations* of music. I invite you to follow me through the following train of thought to make this argument.

Music can exert therapeutic benefits most effectively when it strikes a chord with our positive emotions – our inner *Good Vibrations*. Conversely, negative emotions such as anger, depression, and worries hinder our natural healing powers. These negative emotions are associated with the onset and the course of a wide range of diseases, such as cardiovascular diseases, cancer, autoimmune diseases, and neurodegenerative diseases.[14] (The name of the scientific field that has established these links is *psychoneuroimmunology*.)

One of the most common ways we dampen our inner *Good Vibrations* is by judging ourselves or others. Instead, fostering an attitude of unconditional positive regard for all humans – equal in worth, dignity, and rights – can uplift our emotional state. When we judge a person, we tie that person's value to their achievements, intelligence, or character. As soon as we link these value-defining characteristics (intelligence, character, musicality, etc.) with an individual's genes, we also imply that many of our flaws are innate. We then feel *shame* for these flaws (and other negative emotions) and jump through hoops to prove we are worthy. However, as an alternative, we can believe that our genes do not determine our worth, strengths, or flaws. This belief helps us accept ourselves unconditionally and thus let go of shame and self-doubt.

Therefore, I believe that musicality is a natural ability of every human being and that the seemingly unbelievable skills of professional musicians are not innate but the result of tens of thousands of hours of practice, in addition to top-notch instruction.[15] The studies above

---

[14] Kiecolt-Glaser, J. K., McGuire, L., Robles, T. F., and Glaser, R. (2002). Emotions, morbidity, and mortality: New perspectives from psychoneuroimmunology. *Annual Review of Psychology*, 53(1), 83–107.

[15] Ericsson, K. A., Krampe, R. T., and Tesch-Römer, C. (1993). The role of deliberate practice in the acquisition of expert performance. *Psychological Review*, 100(3), 363.

corroborate this belief, showing that intensive practice leads to anatomical changes in auditory and sensorimotor brain regions.

Some ask, 'But what else other than unique genes can explain that only very few individuals become the best of the best?' These people overlook that becoming a unique, world-famous concert musician resulted from countless coincidences that led to that person practising that instrument extensively and effectively from an early age and under excellent guidance. Some factors contributing to a person's exceptional skills may even originate before birth – perhaps the foetus repeatedly heard specific sounds from outside the womb, purely by chance. After birth, the child might have musical experiences that make him/her extraordinarily interested in a musical instrument. Maybe the infant needs to express him- or herself emotionally through music due to certain psychological circumstances. Perhaps the child has parents who encourage him/her to practise regularly, and he/she happens to get an outstanding teacher. In other words, yes, some people have an exceptional talent for playing an instrument, but the presence of such talent is far from proof that this is innate.

The sheer volume of practice and the intricate blend of countless experiences that go into someone becoming a 'genius' are beyond our cognitive grasp. It is then easy to fall for simpler explanations, such as that a person is endowed with unique gifts from God or particular genes. A scientifically more likely explanation is that these experiences influence the activity and expression of genes, which can manifest in epigenetic variations.[16] Thus, special skills originate from the *shaping* of the (epi)genome by experience rather than from a particular innate genome.

THE POSITIVE IMPACT OF UNCONDITIONAL SELF-ACCEPTANCE

Let us briefly return to inhibiting our 'good inner vibrations' (associated with our positive emotions) by judging the value of human beings,

---

[16] Aristizabal, M. J., Anreiter, I., Halldorsdottir, T., Odgers, C. L., McDade, T. W., Goldenberg, A., Mostafavi, S., Kobor, M. S., Binder, E. B., Sokolowski, M. B., and O'Donnell, K. J. (2020). Biological embedding of experience: A primer on epigenetics. *Proceedings of the National Academy of Sciences*, 117(38), 23261–23269.

including ourselves. This judgment puts us under pressure to prove our dignity or worth through our achievements, intelligence, character, and so on. In other words, we often think we can only accept ourselves fully if certain *conditions* are met, such as a certain material wealth, a certain physical attractiveness, a relationship, a family, and so on. However, the psychological burden associated with this attitude is poison for any beneficial effects of music on our health.

One of the most critical findings of clinical psychology in recent decades is that, for the sake of our mental health, we need to practise accepting ourselves *unconditionally*. This means without conditions such as 'I am only lovable *if* I do or achieve this or that' or 'I can only love myself *if* I have improved this or that about myself'. I believe perfection *exists*, and we experience it every day because every human being is perfect as a biological organism, even if their thoughts or actions may be foolish and cause harm. I emphasize this because we can find inner peace and serenity only with an attitude of unconditional respect and dignity towards all human beings. When we have this attitude, music can best stimulate the *Good Vibrations* within us that promote our health.

When we respect others unconditionally, regardless of how likeable we find them, it becomes easier to accept ourselves unconditionally. We can practise meeting other people on an equal footing without judging or evaluating them ('what is wrong with you?'), that is, without assessing how (un)pleasant, (un)attractive, (un)intelligent they seem to us. After all, we do not want to be judged by others either. When we approach others with sympathy, it is natural that they will find us likeable as well. If self-judgment is a struggle for you, try examining the details of any part of your body with a magnifying glass, and allow yourself to be fascinated. With some positive-sounding music, relaxing and finding self-accepting thoughts will be easier.

Likewise, the purpose of our learning must be *growth and development* rather than trying to 'improve' our brains so that we become 'happier', 'richer', or 'better human beings'. We are all worthy as human beings and, therefore, do not need to improve anything about *ourselves*. We can change our behaviour, sharpen our thinking, learn new skills, and strengthen our discipline, which is fulfilling and fun. However, these do not make us more valuable as human beings. Otherwise, according to our standards, those who do not do this would be inferior.

This perspective shifts our understanding of music education: the goal is not to 'upgrade' our childrens' brains but to support their natural progression simply for the sake of growth and development – of their intelligence, knowledge, and skills.

PROMOTING OUR INNER *GOOD VIBRATIONS* ALSO SHAPES THE BRAIN

Just as music or juggling affect neuronal plasticity, all other activities do this too. Our brains change when we change our lives – quickly and with thousands of new connections after the first few hours. In other words, our brains support us powerfully when we learn new skills and even when we change our thinking or behaviour. All we need to do is keep learning and practising. This insight is essential because our way of thinking, feeling, and behaving determines our health. If we create a positive mood daily, regulate our negative emotions and moods, treat ourselves and others humanely, eat healthily and exercise regularly, our brain changes. What seemed difficult at first then becomes increasingly easier. Regrettably, this does not happen miraculously overnight. Nevertheless, the first neuroplastic effects occur after only a few hours, making things a little easier the next time.

I have described above that the brain forms new neural connections when practising a musical instrument. Likewise, when our thoughts and actions cultivate inner peace and serenity, new neural pathways form in the brain. Neuroscientists have unveiled the changes in the brain associated with such emotional skills and their training. Olga Klimecki explored how compassion training affects the brain.[17] She conducted an experiment in which one group received compassion training while another received memory training. *Compassion* involves the motivation to help a suffering person in a spirit of friendship and caring,

---

[17] Klimecki, O. M., Leiberg, S., Lamm, C., and Singer, T. (2013). Functional neural plasticity and associated changes in positive affect after compassion training. *Cerebral Cortex*, 23(7), 1552–1561.

with warm-heartedness and kindness. During the compassion training, participants practised experiencing loving, caring, and gentle feelings, first towards themselves, then towards close people, then towards neutral people, and then towards people in general. This 'Mettā' meditation technique comes from the Buddhist tradition and dates back about 2,500 years. Before and after the training, the experimenters showed the participants video clips of people in distress and asked them to rate their positive and negative feelings after each clip. *Before* the training, participants in both groups empathized with the suffering they saw and were more likely to react with negative emotions – they felt stressed by the suffering of the people in the clips. Brain scans indicated that empathy for people's suffering correlated with activity in the 'anterior insula'. This brain structure is active when we feel pain and even when we *observe* other people experiencing pain. Thus, when we feel empathy, we can suffer with other people (which can lead to emotional burnout in some professions).

In contrast, *after the* compassion training, the participants still experienced negative (sorrowful) feelings while watching the video clips of distressed people. However, they also experienced positive feelings, which arose from a sense of closeness and kindness towards those individuals. Consequently, greater activity in brain structures such as the 'orbitofrontal cortex' was observed, which is implicated in emotion regulation and the control of emotional behaviour. The compassion training thus led to other feelings and neuronal reactions in the brain. Even if witnessing the suffering of others becomes a burden, it does not have to remain that way – emotion regulation exercises can alleviate emotional stress.

We can utilize music as a tool to evoke inner *Good Vibrations*, and transmute negative moods into positive ones. Thus, by altering our emotional state, we can induce corresponding changes in our brain. Such mood alterations are meaningful because negative moods are detrimental to our health. When we consistently engage in these practices, new neural pathways develop in the brain, making it easier to experience fewer unhealthy and more beneficial emotions and moods. In the box below, I demonstrate how we can utilize music to influence our emotions and elevate our moods to benefit our health and well-being.

> **TRANSFORMING NEGATIVE THOUGHTS INTO POSITIVE ONES USING MUSIC**
>
> For optimal health and well-being, concentrating on the positive facets of life and transmuting negative thoughts into positive ones is indispensable. We can harness the power of music to cultivate positivity.
>
> - *Affirm daily*: as a daily exercise, play music that exudes positivity and encouragement. While the music is playing, tell yourself a dozen positive things you are happy about. These can relate to your personal qualities and strengths, your life, your current situation, or positive aspects of your health (even if you currently have health problems!). They could include positive aspects of your job, friendships, relationships, or things that feel pleasant in your body right now. Use complete sentences. For example, start with phrases such as 'I am happy that …', 'I am so lucky that …', 'I am glad that …', 'It is so nice that …', or 'It's very pleasant that …'. Repeat these or similar sentences until the music ends.
> - *Write down or express aloud*: many people find it helpful to write these sentences down or say them aloud rather than merely thinking them silently.
> - *Share the positivity*: whenever it might fit during the day, you can share one or two of these sentences charmingly with someone close to you.
> - *Cultivate resilience*: regular practice of this exercise will cultivate new neural pathways, enhancing your ability to recognize the positive aspects of your life. It will also enable you to notice and stop negative thoughts and emotions more quickly. The psychological term for this enhanced ability is *resilience*, which aids us in coping with traumatizing events or life crises without enduring health impairments.

In this chapter, we have navigated the complex interplay between music, learning, and the brain. We've seen that early musical training can have profound impacts, affecting both brain function and anatomy. The adage 'practice makes perfect' is more than a cliché – it is a scientific truth, demonstrated by extensive research into the brain's remarkable adaptability and plasticity at any age.

So whether you are a musician, an avid listener, or simply someone fascinated by the power of music, remember: the *Good Vibrations* of music can shape not only your mood but also the very structure of your brain. And with that transformative power, you have the capability to shape your life.

As we conclude this chapter, we pave the way for a deeper exploration of the emotional and therapeutic power of music in Part II. We will explore the fascinating ways in which music influences not just our brains but also our emotions and overall well-being. We'll delve into the science of emotion as triggered by music, the intricate dance of hormones orchestrated by musical notes, and the remarkable healing effects music can offer. From hormonal dances to the cultivation of emotional resilience, prepare yourself for an enlightening journey into the profound impact of music on our health and well-being. So, let us advance and tune into the rich emotional symphony that music can compose in our lives.

PART TWO

MUSIC AND EMOTIONS

A Life with Music Is a Longer Life

CHAPTER 5

How Does Music Evoke Emotions?

I N 1930, THE MOTHER SUPERIOR OF THE School Sisters of Notre Dame initiated a unique project: she asked each incoming nun to compose a page detailing her life story before taking her vows. Over the ensuing years, hundreds of nuns, averaging twenty-two years of age, honoured this request by penning their autobiographies. Seven decades on, Deborah Danner analysed 180 of these autobiographical accounts. She tallied the number of positive and negative experiences described and how many positive and negative emotion words each nun had used. Danner investigated whether the nuns who had documented a large number of positive experiences lived longer than those who had described only a few positive experiences. Potential differences could not be attributed to external living conditions, as those conditions were similar for all nuns. Their lifestyles were also virtually the same, as the nuns ate together, had similar daily routines, and neither alcohol nor cigarettes were particularly popular among them. According to Danner, nuns who had described many positive experiences in their early twenties lived longer than those who had described few positive experiences. Care to venture a guess as to how much longer they lived? The answer: on average, ten years.[1]

This astonishing discovery implies that sustaining an optimistic attitude and regularly experiencing positive emotions contribute to a longer lifespan. Thus, when we elevate our mood with the aid of music, we invest

---

[1] Danner, D. D., Snowdon, D. A., and Friesen, W. V. (2001). Positive emotions in early life and longevity: Findings from the nun study. *Journal of Personality and Social Psychology*, 80 (5), 804.

in a longer, healthier life. Conversely, each episode of anger, sadness, or worry, as well as every hateful comment on Facebook or other social media platforms, likely has detrimental effects on one's lifespan.

The healing effects of music are mainly due to the emotions it can elicit. Positive emotions can stimulate our body's healing powers and thus result in positive health benefits. It is worth noting that only our body can heal itself. While doctors and medicines can certainly *facilitate* this innate healing process, we should credit our bodies for the actual *healing*.

Negative emotions, on the other hand, impede regeneration and healing processes – a topic we will explore in greater detail in the next chapter. Hence, regulating our emotions and moods through music takes us straight to music's most important therapeutic effects. Yet, what are the hidden mechanisms that enable music to stir our emotions? How do these emotions originate? While many readers might have ideas for answers, only a few will have a comprehensive knowledge of how music evokes emotions. Such understanding helps us harness music's *Good Vibrations* to support healing. In the following, I will describe seven key mechanisms through which music can evoke emotions. Knowledge of these mechanisms will also facilitate a better comprehension of our feelings and moods in general.

FEWER NEGATIVE EVALUATIONS LEAD TO A MORE POSITIVE LIFE

As a young music student, I had a chance encounter with Christian Tetzlaff while on my way to a concert with the Bremen Philharmonic Orchestra. I was surprised to see him, the violin soloist for the evening, wandering around just minutes before the performance. I offered to show him the entrance to the concert hall, which he gratefully accepted. During our brief walk, he shared he had mistakenly boarded the train to Hannover instead of Bremen. He then resorted to taking a taxi, costing him over an hour of his time. Just the thought of enduring such a stressful ordeal still raises my blood pressure. After hastily changing his clothes, Tetzlaff took the stage and played Beethoven's Violin Concerto, starting with the challenging octaves, with remarkable precision despite all the preceding stress. His composure and confidence were impressive, and his performance – when combined with the knowledge of the chaos that preceded it – made this concert an unforgettable experience. Being aware of the stressful circumstances leading up to Tetzlaff's performance changed how I *evaluated* it. Consequently, this altered the emotions that the music evoked in me. Had I been unaware of these preceding events, my emotional engagement with the music would have undoubtedly been different.

This anecdote illustrates that our evaluations give rise to emotions. Since the brain serves as the agent responsible for these evaluations, it is important to understand that it is the *brain* – rather than external events or objects – that triggers our emotional responses. We learn from an early age that certain events are *followed by* certain feelings. As a result, we may mistakenly come to believe that these events *cause* these feelings. However, the pleasure we feel upon hearing beautiful violin tones originates not from the violin or the ear but from within our brain. If we are about to fall asleep and our neighbour decides to play loud violin music, we become annoyed by those very same tones. This discrepancy arises because our brain *evaluates* the same sound differently in different situations. These evaluations determine whether sounds give us pleasure or displeasure.

As a result, our enjoyment of violin tones does not follow a simple cause-and-effect mechanism – where playing certain notes automatically leads to positive feelings. Instead, a multitude of evaluations comes into play. Of course, this principle applies beyond music-evoked emotions to all emotions. Even in cases of pain or hunger, it is our *brain* that generates the corresponding feelings, not our bodily organs.

CONSCIOUS AND UNCONSCIOUS EVALUATIONS

Our evaluations can be *conscious*, as illustrated when my background knowledge of a concert with Christian Tetzlaff led to particularly positive emotions. However, our brain's emotional systems also conduct their own *unconscious* evaluations. In 2007 Joshua Bell, disguised with a baseball cap, played exquisite compositions for solo violin on his 'Gibson ex Huberman' Stradivarius in an underground station. He performed for forty-five minutes, and among a thousand passersby, only seven paused to listen for more than a minute. Hardly anyone found the music captivating enough to halt, and only twenty-seven people threw money into his violin case, amounting to $32. At a typical concert, Bell earns $1,000 per minute.

How can we explain such a discrepancy? People prefer a piece of music to align with their goals, meaning that music should be appropriate for both the situation and the time. This was not the case for Bach's Chaconne, played in an underground station during the morning rush hour. Even music of the highest calibre can evoke negative emotions if our brains deem it incongruous with the setting or in conflict with our aims.

Most individuals who walked past Bell's rendition of the Bach Chaconne unconsciously decided that the music was not worth pausing to listen to. Had they been *aware* that this was a free, world-class musical performance, their conscious evaluations would have dramatically altered their unconscious assessments. As a result, the music would have elicited quite different emotions.

This example reveals a simple yet fundamental truth: we can always *consciously* re-evaluate our unconscious evaluations. Thus, we are never powerless to transform our negative emotions and moods. Rather than unconsciously dwelling on what we do not have, we can consciously focus on what we do have. Instead of focusing on the aspects of a person that might annoy us, we can consciously focus on those aspects that we appreciate. Rather than focusing on the one tone that we played wrong, we can enjoy all the other tones we played right.

Before delving deeper into the conscious regulation of emotions, it is worth noting that our unconscious evaluations are often irrational. For example, they are often determined by arbitrary conventions. In his book *Das Publikum macht die Musik* ('The Audience Makes the Music'), Sven Müller notes that until the mid-nineteenth century, concert audiences primarily valued the composition and its perceived effects rather than the quality of the performance.[2] At the premiere of Beethoven's 9th Symphony in 1824 at the Vienna Academy, mainly amateurs played with almost no rehearsal. Despite this, the audience and the press were

---

[2] Müller, S. O. (2014). *Das Publikum macht die Musik: Musikleben in Berlin, London und Wien im 19. Jahrhundert.* Göttingen, Vandenhoeck & Ruprecht.

ecstatic about the music. Today, many Beethoven lovers would be annoyed or even leave the hall in indignation at a similar performance. For audiences in the early nineteenth century, technical perfection took a back seat. As long as the composition was recognizable to them, they were satisfied.

This example highlights how often arbitrary social norms can shape our unconscious evaluations of musical performances. When the norms change, so do our evaluations. Those who embrace the listening ethos of nineteenth-century audiences – giving precedence to the composition over the performance – may find themselves less susceptible to irritation. Similarly, giving precedence to the commitment and dedication of musicians can outweigh mistakes and imprecision. Many people practise this listening mode when attending performances by youth orchestras. Equipped with these insights, let us explore further ways to appreciate the positives in a musical performance, even when certain elements are less than perfect.

> **LOOKING ON THE BRIGHT SIDE OF A MUSICAL PERFORMANCE**
>
> Sometimes, certain elements of a performance can be bothersome, such as a conductor who seems to view the music as an accompaniment to their conducting, a soloist who performs poorly, an imprecise or uncommitted orchestra, a poorly mixed band, or a boring piece. Rather than letting these issues get on one's nerves, one might shift attention to less bothersome aspects of the performance. For example, when listening to classical music, one could focus on the tension in the music or the compositional ideas. Alternatively, one might enjoy how the music's vibrations stimulate the mechanoreceptors in the skin and body. Or, one could savour the richness of the three-dimensional sound, a quality yet to be replicated by headphones or stereo systems.

CONTROLLING NEGATIVE EMOTIONS

In preceding discussions, we explored the role of both conscious and unconscious evaluations in shaping our emotional reactions to music.

While these principles are illuminating in a musical context, their applicability extends to the broader sphere of 'real life' as well. Let us now proceed to look into how we can transform negative feelings into positive ones in everyday life.

Currently, the dominant theories in the field of emotion psychology are the 'appraisal theories'. These theories posit that if a factor helps us achieve our goals, we evaluate it as 'good', and such positive evaluation then leads to a positive emotion. We evaluate factors as positive when they satisfy our needs, align with our desires, strengthen our power, and fit our world view. In contrast, our brain evaluates factors preventing us from achieving a goal as 'bad', triggering a negative emotion. Evaluations can be either conscious or unconscious; the majority of our brain's evaluations are of the latter kind, occurring automatically in mere fractions of a second. Each evaluation serves as an impulse, thereby initiating an emotional response.

Critically, when faced with a negative evaluation, we have two options for managing the resultant impulses. One option is to allow the emotional impulse to take its automatic, unconscious course – this is the easy and intuitive route. Alternatively, we can consciously guide our emotions, employing reason, patience, and, ideally, humour. However, the latter approach often seems less attractive because it demands more cognitive effort. Consequently, even though regulating emotions consciously is generally beneficial in the long term, the immediate allure of taking the easy route often wins out.

When we yield to a negative emotional impulse, we risk becoming entrapped in a self-perpetuating cycle that escalates our negative emotions. For instance, think of an event that typically angers us, let us say a train delay. We become angry and immediately look for someone to blame – ideally someone else, in this case 'the stupid railway company'. This compounds our initial anger about the event with new anger directed towards the individual or group we blame, thereby intensifying our negative emotional state. Masters in the art of anger may now start contemplating revenge, or simply become infuriated by their anger. The possibilities for escalating one's own negative emotions seem virtually limitless. In this manner, we become ensnared in continually recycling our negative emotions, whether they be anger, grief, worry, or hatred.

HOW DOES MUSIC EVOKE EMOTIONS?

Besides generating negative emotions, our brains create what I term *emotional attractor effects*. Each instance of negative emotion tends to magnetize additional negative thoughts and evaluations. It also draws our attention to what is bothering us, narrows our perception, and prevents us from seeing the bigger picture. As a consequence, negative emotions can obscure our rational judgment and narrow our perspective – negative emotions can literally make us blind. For instance, when we are furious with someone, it becomes difficult to recall even one of their positive traits. Our brains can automatically perpetuate negative emotion spirals and attractor effects, thereby generating persistent negative moods.

Once caught in this spiral, we often focus on ending what we think is causing our negative emotions, instead of consciously working to end the emotions themselves. We also expect everyone else to take our negative emotions as seriously and significantly as we do. When one is angry, it is a perilously small step to consider it justifiable to eliminate the person triggering the anger, rather than eliminating the anger itself. Although regulating one's emotions may seem more demanding, it leads to healthier and more fulfilling outcomes.

For a fulfilling life, it is crucial to understand that our negative evaluations – rather than the actual events – are the root cause of our negative emotions. Thus, the true origin of our emotions lies not in external events, objects, or individuals but in our own thoughts and evaluations. In everyday life, it is our negative emotions that make us unhappy and ill, rather than the things that do not 'go our way'. The emotional structures in our brains reflexively evaluate certain events as negative, triggering negative emotions. Yet, it is within our power to consciously prevent these negative impulses from evolving into full-blown emotions and enduring moods. By taking the following proactive steps, we can control our negative emotions before they control us.

INTERRUPTING NEGATIVE EMOTIONAL SPIRALS IN FOUR STEPS

To evade negative emotional spirals, we can rely on one of the best-established findings in clinical psychology: the most effective remedy for negative emotions and the stress they bring is deliberate constructive thought. This process involves consciously addressing problems, deliberately invoking relaxation, and actively identifying positive aspects within challenging situations. The best strategies depend on the situation and the individual, considering whether we can change a situation or what resources we have available.

To illustrate this principle, let us revisit the topic of managing anger. When an obstacle is put in one's way, it is normal to feel an anger impulse. However, it is essential to recognize this emotional impulse promptly, and react appropriately: with patience, reason, serenity, and, in the worst-case scenario, even humour. Here are four straightforward steps to manage anger:

First step. The initial and crucial step involves consciously recognizing the negative emotion – for example, by saying to oneself, 'Oh, I realize I am angry right now. This is normal, but now it is time to calm down again.' This way, we add conscious mental activity to the unconscious anger reaction.

Second step. In the next step, the focus is on maintaining composure through three key techniques: deep breathing, relaxation, and 'letting it flow'. At this moment, patience is a sign of inner strength, and anger or rage shows inner weakness. Remember that merely feeling anger does not mean something *is* genuinely infuriating. It is our own view of things that makes them infuriating to us. Consider with a cool head whether or how you can solve the problem (you might need to implement a temporary solution quickly and work on a more permanent one later). Remember, it is healthier to eliminate *your* anger, rather than the person who triggered it. Referring back to the train delay example, no matter how angry someone becomes, their anger and frustration will not change the delay or prevent future delays. If one wishes to make a difference, one can later write a concise complaint with a rational mind. Now, it is more important to take a few deep breaths, relax, and let it flow. ('Letting it flow' refers to the practice of maintaining a relaxed bodily posture to ensure unobstructed blood flow, paired with a mental state that is free from emotional or cognitive blockages.)

Third step. Identify a positive aspect of the situation. Every situation could have been worse, and although it was not our plan, the new situation may also save us some annoyance. The train is delayed, but now the dreaded meeting will be shorter. Finding a humorous aspect of the situation is particularly helpful. For instance, when I am angry, it always makes me laugh when looking at myself in the mirror. By doing so, we consciously take the steering wheel for our thoughts and evaluations into our own hands, thus taking control of our emotions rather than letting them control us.

Fourth step. The final, and often most challenging, step is to let go of the situation and cease dwelling on it. Shift your focus to an activity that aligns with your values and furthers your personal goals. Devote your full attention to this pursuit, instead of wasting it on lingering anger. Now is the time to engage in 'mental decluttering', consciously clearing the mind of lingering negative thoughts or emotions. What has happened is in the past; now you might change something to prevent similar situations from happening in the future. For instance, when you are angry, avoid ruminating on the source of your annoyance, holding grudges, or entertaining thoughts of revenge or retaliation. Otherwise, we end up allowing the person who has caused us distress to occupy valuable mental space, without any benefit to us – essentially, letting them live 'rent-free' in our minds. On the contrary, wish that person happiness and well-being, like you would for any other person, because this is *healthier for you*!

These four steps are applicable to a wide range of negative emotions and moods, including worry, sadness, guilt, shame, anxiety, and hatred. By following these steps, we can maintain an unshakeable peace of mind in all situations in life. Effectively managing negative emotions and moods not only promotes our health but also fortifies our resilience.[3]

---

[3] In emotion psychology, *emotion* refers to relatively brief episodes, typically with a distinct trigger. In contrast, *moods* are longer-term affective phenomena, such as depression, listlessness, or feelings of discouragement. However, the affective mechanisms underlying emotions and moods are similar, which means that negative emotion spirals, rumination, and emotional attractor effects are characteristic of both emotions and moods. Consequently, the methods for dealing with negative moods resemble those for regulating negative emotions. In other words, the four steps mentioned earlier can also be applied to negative moods.

One reason why we can regulate emotional spirals this way is because the interplay between negative and positive affect in the brain resembles a seesaw. When burdened by painful feelings or moods, the release of neurotransmitters associated with pleasure can be triggered by positive thoughts or uplifting laughter. This effectively tips the emotional balance towards a more positive state. Next, we will examine how we can utilize music to trigger the release of these pleasure-associated neurotransmitters, thereby mitigating negative emotions and moods.

TRANSFORMING NEGATIVE EMOTIONS AND MOODS WITH MUSIC

One of music's most important therapeutic effects is its utility to help us break free from negative *emotional spirals* and *thought loops*. In response to uplifting music, our brains naturally respond by steering our thoughts towards optimism and realism. In a study, my colleagues and I observed that individuals who listened to happy-sounding music exhibited greater optimism about their odds in a lottery game. This optimism reduced the 'risk aversion' bias, which is the tendency to avoid risky choices even if they lead, on average, to higher long-term gains.[4]

Upbeat music can also make us perceive the world in a brighter light. Music psychologist Joydeep Bhattacharya and Job Lindsen conducted a study that showed how positive- or negative-sounding music can influence how we judge the brightness or darkness of colours.[5] The researchers presented participants with a grey square on a screen and then played music that sounded happy, peaceful, sad, or scary. After each piece of music, the participants saw the grey square again and judged whether this second square presented after the music was brighter or darker than the first square shown before the music. Unbeknown to the participants, however, all the squares were equally bright. Joydeep discovered that happy-sounding music led participants to rate grey squares as brighter, whereas the same squares appeared darker after listening to sad or scary music.

---

[4] Schulreich, S., Heussen, Y. G., Gerhardt, H., Mohr, P. N., Binkofski, F. C., Koelsch, S., and Heekeren, H. R. (2014). Music-evoked incidental happiness modulates probability weighting during risky lottery choices. *Frontiers in Psychology*, 4, 981.

[5] Bhattacharya, J., and Lindsen, J. P. (2016). Music for a brighter world: Brightness judgment bias by musical emotion. *PLoS ONE*, 11(2), e0148959.

How Does Music Evoke Emotions?

Thanks to its influence on our minds, regulating emotions becomes easier with the aid of music. Simply immersing ourselves in positive-sounding tunes can break the toxic cycle of negative emotions, filling us with fresh, uplifting thoughts and elevating our mood. It facilitates the identification of at least one positive aspect or helps to summon a bit of humour, even amid personal hardship or seemingly insurmountable challenges. By transcending negative emotions in this manner, we can outsmart unhappiness.

Remember, the experience of positive emotions is not a luxury; it is a fundamental human need. Let this need be the motivation to simply play uplifting music as the very first and easy step to positively influence our mood. We can use any music that aids in promoting sensual and mental opening, thus removing cognitive and emotional blockages. (Here are five examples for different tastes: Bach suites, Elvis rock, Mojo Club Edition dance music, Rudy Van Gelder Edition jazz, or Yuval Ron meditation music.) Depending on the situation, it can also help to dance, make music ourselves, sing a song, scat, or whistle. The music will assist us in taking the next step, however small, towards resolving our problem. This might involve doing what we genuinely want, ideally in a way that focuses our thoughts on what we find meaningful, what truly serves our goals, and what can bring us success.

Each time we successfully neutralize a negative emotion or mood, this act stands as one of the most significant personal achievements one can attain in life. The strategic use of music serves as a powerful catalyst in this transformation.

USING MUSIC TO OVERCOME NEGATIVE EMOTIONS AND MOODS

Music can help us break free from negative emotion spirals and attractor effects. For maximum effectiveness, the selection of music should align with the emotional state one aims to *achieve*, rather than merely reflecting one's *current* mood. For example, happy-sounding music can help us feel more cheerful; courageous-sounding music can motivate us; and relaxing-sounding music can help us calm down. Consider the three tips below when improving your mood with music.

- *Transitioning to positive-sounding music*: while some individuals find solace in listening to sad-sounding music as a way to vent their emotions, some individuals prefer to listen to music that resonates with their *current* mood, seeking comfort rather than a way out of their negative emotional state. For individuals with depression or a tendency to depression, who cannot simply listen to positive-sounding music when they suffer from a negative mood, it is okay to use sad-sounding music as a starting point. However, it is important to transition, piece by piece, to more positive-sounding music (e.g. cheerful, peaceful, or motivating). To accomplish this, it is helpful to compile a playlist for such situations on a day where one is not in a trough, starting with music that sounds like the negative mood one typically experiences, and then changing gradually to more positive-sounding music (also see the tips in Chapter 18).
- *Active musical engagement*: to mitigate negative moods, it is essential not only to listen to the music but to actively participate in it. You can tap to the beat, move your body to the rhythm, or sing along, even silently. This usually helps to refocus your mind on positive or constructive thoughts, such as what makes you happy or steps that bring you closer to your goals. If you find yourself ruminating, challenge yourself by asking, 'Do I perhaps have something better to think about?' Then, consciously shift your focus to more positive or meaningful matters. Reflect on how you've handled negative emotions in the past: how quickly did you recognize your negative state? Could you acknowledge it sooner next time? Might you change your response to such triggers in the future? While listening to music, try to imagine confronting the same trigger with complete calm and composure, or visualize your negative emotions dissipating like a cloud in the wind. These mental exercises can significantly enhance your patience and help maintain calmness in future situations.
- *Scheduled positive music breaks*: listening to uplifting and motivating music multiple times throughout the day can help maintain a positive mood, allowing for greater calm and composure when things do not go one's way. This way, we can use music to

> strengthen our mental well-being. Allocating specific times of the day for this practice can be beneficial. For instance, setting aside three to five minutes in the morning, at lunchtime, and in the evening can make a difference. You can start in the morning with 'morning dancing' (see Chapter 10). A positive attitude can help us smile and thus tackle challenges more effectively.

NEGATIVE EMOTIONS AND MOODS ARE DETRIMENTAL TO OUR HEALTH

Frequent negative emotions and moods not only affect our quality of life but are also harmful to our health. Meta-analyses reveal that depression and depressive moods can weaken the immune system and subsequently elevate the risk of conditions such as coronary heart disease.[6] Similarly, worries, anxiety, hostility, and anger can also weaken the immune system.[7] Therefore, contrary to popular belief, getting angry is not a healthy emotional response.

The scientific discipline known as *psychoneuroimmunology* explores the connections between negative moods, chronic psychological stress, and their effects on immunological processes and diseases. Research in this field uncovered that negative moods can make us sick and lead to shorter lives.[8] Specifically, negative moods and chronic psychological stress impair the immune system, affecting healing processes such as defence against infections, inflammatory reactions, and wound healing. When we do not regulate our negative moods, we increase the risk of diseases such as cardiovascular diseases, cancer, or chronic diseases of the immune system, as well as ageing processes such as osteoporosis.

---

[6] Howren, M. B., Lamkin, D. M., and Suls, J. (2009). Associations of depression with C-reactive protein, IL-1, and IL-6: A meta-analysis. *Psychosomatic Medicine*, 71(2), 171–186.

[7] Chida, Y., and Steptoe, A. (2009). The association of anger and hostility with future coronary heart disease: A meta-analytic review of prospective evidence. *Journal of the American College of Cardiology*, 53(11), 936–946.

[8] Kiecolt-Glaser et al., Emotions, morbidity, and mortality; Glaser, R., and Kiecolt-Glaser, J. K. (2005). Stress-induced immune dysfunction: Implications for health. *Nature Reviews Immunology*, 5(3), 243–251.

Ironically, while it is our human right to be happy, we often undermine this right with our negative evaluations and the ensuing negative emotions and moods. Therefore, it is essential to develop strategies that regulate our negative evaluations and promote positive moods, as this will improve our overall health and well-being. Beyond merely improving our health, cultivating positive emotions such as joy, optimism, and contentment is integral to maintaining youthful vitality and enhancing our overall well-being.

'TAKE IT EASY' WITH MUSIC

Music can be a powerful tool to alleviate stress and emotional tension. The next time you encounter a frustrating situation, try the following approach to neutralize the *emotional attractor effects*.

- *Select your mood music*: play some music that expresses a positive mood – be it calm, joy, fortitude, or optimism.
- *Reflect, reassess, and proceed positively*: take a few deep breaths, starting with a long exhale, and relax. Find at least one positive aspect in the situation (there is always one) and think about what you can learn from it, what you can change, or what you still have left in your life despite a loss. Then, try not to dwell on it and continue with your day. Start with small steps to make the process easier, and never give up. Each successful attempt at this exercise contributes to lowering your risk of heart attacks and other chronic diseases.
- *Use proven pieces*: stick to music pieces that have worked well for you in the past. Your brain will associate these tunes with successful emotion regulation, thereby making this technique easier each time you practise it.
- *Practice makes perfect*: remember, repetition breeds mastery. Take any opportunity you find to exercise this technique, as practising it with minor stressors prepares us to better manage major challenges in the future.
- *Seek professional help*: if you frequently struggle with mood issues, consider seeking help from a doctor, clinical psychologist, or music therapist. Taking this step towards better emotional health is both courageous and free of stigma.

PREDICTIVE EVALUATIONS AND THEIR IMPACT ON OUR EMOTIONS

Up to this point, our focus has been on evaluations made in reaction to events. Intriguingly, it is also possible to appraise an event *before* it even occurs. These are what I refer to as *predictive evaluations*: assessments where we anticipate the outcome of an event, and – quite astonishingly – these prophecies often come true. A predictive evaluation can engender a specific emotion, preparing us to react to an upcoming event.

Let us explore this topic, taking our predictive evaluations of the sound of a Stradivari violin as an example. A few years ago, Frank-Michael Erben, the concertmaster of the Leipzig Gewandhaus Orchestra, Zhi-Jiong Wang, and I had the unique opportunity to play six exquisite violins. These ranged from venerated Old Italian masterpieces to modern marvels crafted by the German high-tech company NewStrad. Some of the old instruments cost several million euros, while the NewStrad violins sold for just a few tens of thousands. We played them without knowing which violin was old or new. Several professional musicians and sound designers sat in the audience to rate the sound of the violins. Surprisingly, the new high-tech instruments achieved the best results, not the old master violins. Dr Blutner, the managing director of NewStrad, told me:

> This is not the first time. We have also conducted similar tests with a curtain so that the audience could not see the violins or with violinists playing blindfolded and wearing thin gloves so they could not recognize an instrument by its appearance or feel. We always got the same results. Even when we compared new violins with a Stradivarius, the blinded audience rated the new violins as better.

A research team comprising acousticians, musicologists, and violin makers conducted several scientific investigations to test these observations and found very similar results. In blinded tests, professional violinists preferred new violins to Stradivari and Guarneri violins. The authors concluded that the 'secret of the Stradivarius' is a myth and that musicians would be better served by determining what qualities they prefer in instruments and which instruments measurably best match those qualities, regardless of whether they are old or new.[9] That is why I play a NewStrad violin myself.

The mere belief that every Stradivarius produces an 'unassailably good' sound generates a positive predictive evaluation, which causes these instruments to sound *subjectively superior* in the ears of the beholder. It is like wine: if one believes in the top quality of an expensive wine, it actually tastes better. This phenomenon was demonstrated in a study where participants were told they were sipping either a very expensive or a very cheap wine. In reality, all participants were given the same wine. Not only did the test participants report that the wine they believed to be expensive tasted significantly better, but brain scans also showed heightened activity in their 'orbitofrontal cortex', a brain region involved in unconscious evaluation and reward processes.[10] This underscores that our emotional responses are influenced not just by direct sensory input but also by our brain's predictive evaluations.

These findings are compelling as they show that our emotions can be rooted in *erroneous* evaluations. Inaccurate predictive evaluations can lead to misguided emotional outcomes if we do not consciously revise them. Unfortunately, we often remain unaware of these flawed evaluations, leading us to take our erroneous unconscious expectations, prejudices, or opinions more seriously than we should. Anticipating a dreadful outcome may unintentionally lead to a self-fulfilling prophecy, making the situation as terrible as we feared.

USING MUSIC TO PROMOTE HUMANITY

As we have explored the intricate dynamics of how our evaluations shape our emotional experiences, there remains one final, crucial aspect that merits our attention. While we can use our understanding of evaluations to foster personal well-being, it is equally vital to consider how our judgments can impact our collective humanity. Let us now turn to the

---

[9] Fritz, C., Curtin, J., Poitevineau, J., Borsarello, H., Wollman, I., Tao, F. C., and Ghasarossian, T. (2014). Soloist evaluations of six Old Italian and six new violins. *Proceedings of the National Academy of Sciences*, 111(20), 7224–7229.

[10] Plassmann, H., O'Doherty, J., Shiv, B., and Rangel, A. (2008). Marketing actions can modulate neural representations of experienced pleasantness. *Proceedings of the National Academy of Sciences*, 105(3), 1050–1054.

profound role that music can play in promoting a more compassionate and equitable society.

As a sociologist, I contend that one of the most perilous evaluations we engender subconsciously is to judge others, particularly when we assign greater or lesser value to some people's worth as human beings. This form of evaluation is typically activated when we seek to attribute the causes of our negative emotions to someone else, resorting to derogatory language instead of constructively addressing the matter at hand. Consider instances where one might ask, 'What is wrong with you?', instead of using the more honest statement, 'I would rather you did it my way.' The act of judging others not only manifests as arrogance but also has adverse effects on our well-being.

Judging others or ourselves is not only emotionally harmful, it is ethically questionable as well. The United Nations Charter of Human Rights asserts that every individual deserves life and liberty without discrimination based on 'race, colour, sex, language, religion, political or other opinions, national or social origin, property, birth or other status',[11] and we might well include factors such as health, education, income, and age. Engaging in musical activities that uplift us, while simultaneously harbouring a judgmental mindset, starkly contradicts the healing effects of music. If we wish to fully benefit from music's therapeutic potential, we must avoid undermining both our own well-being and that of others through judgment.

By honing our perception, adopting a constructive mindset, and rigorously seeking factual information, we can attain a greater level of clarity and understanding. In contrast, traits such as arrogance and vanity make us susceptible to negative emotions, as well as the sway of fake news, populism, and manipulation. Although music has the potential to be weaponized for promoting aggression and hostility, its true power lies in its ability to foster peace and unity – most notably when we engage in communal activities such as making music or dancing together.

When we sing or dance together, what matters most is our shared humanity, which renders our differences insignificant. That is one of the profound powers of music. However, it is up to us to utilize music for the

---

[11] www.un.org/en/about-us/universal-declaration-of-human-rights

promotion of kindness, understanding, and compassion, and to reject its use as a tool for sowing hatred and division. We must harness music to encourage a sense of equality and unity. Through kindling the radiant spark of joy with music, we can cultivate a pervasive spirit of community, enriching the well-being of both ourselves and those around us.

EMOTIONAL RESONANCE

Dame Evelyn Glennie is a testament to the remarkable adaptability of the human senses. Despite becoming profoundly deaf as a child, she has become an internationally renowned concert percussionist. This achievement is possible because sounds evoke physical resonance in multiple receptor systems: in the cochlea, the vestibular organ, vibrational receptors in the body (also known as Vater-Pacini corpuscles), and even pressure receptors in the skin. Dame Glennie has refined her perception of these alternative sensory inputs to such an extent that she interacts and performs with a proficiency indistinguishable from those with typical hearing.

You might find it surprising that all of us 'hear' in this multifaceted manner, even if we are not consciously aware of it. In addition to hearing with our cochlea, we also perceive sounds through the vestibular apparatus and other receptors sensitive to vibrations. Many such vibratory receptors are located in various parts of our body, including the skin, some abdominal organs, and sexual organs. (These receptors are particularly sensitive to loud sounds with low frequencies.) The stimulation of these receptors by music is pleasant; it can make music go directly into our stomach.

'To really listen, it is important to use our body as a resonating chamber. It allows us to register rhythms, textures, dynamics, and even pitches,' Evelyn explained to me. 'We need to open our body, and focus our attention on the sound. Similar to taste in food, we need to give sounds time to be processed and perceived in space.' When playing, Evelyn feels low sounds mainly in her feet and high sounds in her face, neck, and chest. 'All sounds develop from the feet. Especially when we play, we can observe and experience sounds like living organisms. Ten instruments that look the same can all sound different. My position to them, my posture, my distance to them – all these influence my perception of sound.' The thickness of clothing and shoes also affects these perceptions.

> **FEELING THE VIBRATIONS OF SOUNDS**
>
> During a concert, try paying attention to the physical vibrations of the sounds (it may help to close your eyes to concentrate better on the sound and the vibrations they cause in your body). Notice how pleasant these vibrations or resonances are and how they contribute to the overall sound experience.

EMOTIONAL CONTAGION

Beyond resonating with our inner ear and vibratory receptors, sounds can also emotionally resonate with us, affecting different levels of brain processing. When I was a young music student rehearsing Viotti's Violin Concerto in A minor with the Bremen Youth Symphony Orchestra, a young girl sat in the front row. At the first notes I played, she immediately cried. Later, she told me that the sad-sounding music had instantly touched her emotions. As concert-goers, many adults find themselves emotionally affected by music, sometimes to the point of tears. Most restrain their emotions in line with cultural norms to avoid embarrassment. Yet, there were times when such conventions were very different. Until well into the nineteenth century, it was normal for listeners to sob and howl fervently to heart-wrenching performances.[12]

This kind of emotional resonance, often called *emotional contagion*, arises mainly without the involvement of the neocortex in phylogenetically older brain structures and without 'higher cognition'. For example, emotional contagion also does not require a distinction between 'I' and 'you', that is, the distinction between oneself and others. Unlike empathy, emotional contagion occurs without conscious intention and usually outside our conscious perception.

---

[12] Müller, *Das Publikum macht die Musik.*

We observe emotional contagion in babies who laugh or cry merely because other babies are doing the same. Similarly, adults can catch 'contagious laughter', even without hearing or understanding the joke. When we hear happy-sounding music, we are more likely to smile and feel happier than after sad-sounding music.[13]

Thus, emotional contagion typically involves the mirroring of an observed emotional expression. When we see a smiling person, we often involuntarily smile ourselves. When people communicate, they often synchronize their facial expressions and movements with each other's facial expressions, voices, and postures. Merely mimicking an emotional expression can often make us feel the same way. Although still a topic of debate in the psychological literature, it is generally easier to feel sad if you maintain a sad expression for several minutes. Conversely, holding a happy expression can actually make you feel happier. Why not experiment with this first thing in the morning upon waking?

Thus, perceiving an emotional expression triggers an involuntary mirroring process where the observed emotion is reflected in our own expressions. In addition to motoric mirroring, emotional contagion influences vegetative activity and hormone release, such as blood pressure, breathing, and heartbeat. Emotional contagion is one reason we usually feel better in the presence of people who radiate positive emotions or in the presence of positive-sounding music.

> **USING THE EMOTIONAL RESONANCE OF MUSIC**
>
> One can get into a positive mood or strengthen one's positive mood simply through the automatic emotional contagion of music. For example, try using music that sounds happy, calm, peaceful, or clear to you and let these *Good Vibrations* resonate within you (ideally avoiding negative thoughts). Try to incorporate this into your daily routine. Determine the time intervals for this according to the

---

[13] Lundqvist, L. O., Carlsson, F., Hilmersson, P., and Juslin, P. N. (2009). Emotional responses to music: Experience, expression, and physiology. *Psychology of Music*, 37(1), 61–90.

> duration for which these effects resonate within you. For example, it can be helpful to use music every morning immediately after getting up and several times during the day (if necessary, only briefly to refresh the positive mood).

THE RELATIONSHIP BETWEEN EMPATHY AND COMPASSION

So far, I have discussed emotional resonance, which occurs unconsciously and without intent. Emotional resonance can also manifest through a different route – *empathy*. In 1992, Eric Clapton and Will Jennings released the song 'Tears in Heaven', widely regarded as one of the saddest songs in pop history. The song was written a few months after Clapton's four-year-old son Conor died in an accident. Why does this song make many people so extremely sad? Compared to songs such as 'Yesterday' by The Beatles, neither the melody nor the harmonies sound particularly sad (the song is in major!). If anything, the music sounds peaceful. Of course, even without background knowledge, we can already tell from the lyrics that it is a sad song. But it is only when we learn that the song is about Clapton's late son – and when we ponder how we might feel under similar circumstances – that we find it difficult to hold back our tears. We then hear the unspeakably painful loss, note for note, from Clapton's singing, his voice sometimes close to crying. Incidentally, Clapton attributed his emotional healing to his work in music. He said, 'I used music almost unconsciously for myself as a "healing agent," and lo-and-behold, it worked. I got a whole lot of happiness and a whole lot of healing through music.'[14]

Empathy involves a more complex neurological layer than emotional contagion, including the neocortex. Empathy requires the intellectual ability to take another person's perspective, enabling us to understand why another person might be crying. If we then become sad ourselves, we

---

[14] ABC News, 7 September 2006. 'Exclusive: Mother of "Tears in Heaven" Inspiration Shares Story.' https://abcnews.go.com/2020/Entertainment/story?id=2404474&page=1

speak of *empathy*. Thus, *empathy* means that the same emotion is experienced by someone who takes part in the emotion of another person.

Empathy can lead to 'empathic stress' and burnout, particularly in professions centred on alleviating the suffering of others. This applies to doctors, therapists, nurses, disaster relief workers, and so on. To prevent such empathic stress, it is helpful to transform feelings of pity into *compassion*.[15] For example, we may feel sympathy, or *empathic concern*, for a person who is worried without being worried ourselves. Compassion means putting one's thoughts in the perspective of solidarity, concern, and care for the other person, as well as the desire to help and thus do something meaningful. We might feel moved or touched by another person crying and feel the motivation to help.

Adopting a compassionate mindset can foster feelings of care, warmth, gentleness, goodwill, and affection. Negative emotions, such as anger, aggression, or hatred, on the other hand, stifle genuine compassion. Thus, compassion is a special case of empathy in which one feels *for* another person, not *with* another person.

Compassion towards others is a fundamental value of many people. It is important to practise compassion regularly to maintain our mental well-being, just like regular physical exercise is crucial for our physical health. Compassion is beneficial both for others *and* ourselves. The more we are committed to our own happiness as well as the happiness of others, the more our well-being grows, and the more inner peace and serenity we experience. Compassion is thus essential for a fulfilled life, alongside love. Individuals whose brains lack the capacity for compassion may still experience fun and pleasure but cannot attain genuine happiness.

Thus, empathy, unlike emotional contagion, involves sharing another person's emotional experience while being aware that the emotion one resonates with is that of another person. Music can motivate us to behave more compassionately, as evidenced by the helpful behaviour of children who make music together and the increased levels of compassion displayed by those who participate in group music lessons.[16]

---

[15] Klimecki, O. M., Leiberg, S., Lamm, C., and Singer, T. (2013). Functional neural plasticity and associated changes in positive affect after compassion training. *Cerebral Cortex*, 23(7), 1552–1561.

[16] Schellenberg, E. G., Corrigall, K. A., Dys, S. P., and Malti, T. (2015). Group music training and children's prosocial skills. *PLoS ONE*, 10(10), e0141449.

Opera or film music can evoke such strong emotional responses because we put ourselves in the emotional situation of a character, which usually leads to much stronger emotions than the music alone. However, if one is oblivious to the plot, it is impossible to empathize with a character, and even the most beautiful opera can quickly become tedious. Soon after my move to Norway, I had the chance to attend a performance of Weber's 'Oberon'. The challenge was that I understood neither the English singing nor the Norwegian supertitles. Not knowing what the characters were singing about was so unnerving that I fled at the intermission.

With music, many people can readily enter the same mood simultaneously and together. Therefore, music can create emotional resonance, even in large groups of people. This capacity is not only effective when listening but also when collectively clapping, jumping, singing, and dancing. This 'collective empathy', which I have termed *co-pathy*, promotes helpfulness, cooperation, peacefulness, and social cohesion.[17]

THE INFLUENCE OF MUSIC ON THOUGHTS

A little-known fact is that even our *thoughts* resonate with music. Music that sounds happy can lead to more positive thoughts, while music that sounds sad or induces nervousness can give rise to negative thoughts and rumination.[18] My research group conducted a series of experiments to assess the impact of music on the nature of spontaneous thoughts. Participants were instructed to listen and relax while being exposed to either uplifting compositions, such as the vivace finale from a Haydn string quartet, or melancholic pieces, such as Nick Cave's 'Song for Bob'. Typically, this setting leads to mind wandering. After the music sessions, participants reported on the nature of their thoughts, specifying whether

---

[17] Page, K. M., and Nowak, M. A. (2002). Empathy leads to fairness. *Bulletin of Mathematical Biology*, 64(6), 1101–1116; Rumble, A. C., Van Lange, P. A., and Parks, C. D. (2010). The benefits of empathy: When empathy may sustain cooperation in social dilemmas. *European Journal of Social Psychology*, 40(5), 856–866.

[18] Koelsch, S., Andrews-Hanna, J. R., and Skouras, S. (2022). Tormenting thoughts: The posterior cingulate sulcus of the default mode network regulates valence of thoughts and activity in the brain's pain network during music listening. *Human Brain Mapping*, 43(2), 773–786.

they were positive or negative. We consistently found that the mind-wandering thoughts were more positive when participants listened to happy music compared to sad music, across four similar experiments.[19] Listening to sad or nervous music can, therefore, negatively affect both our mood *and* our thoughts. To promote more positive thoughts, we can take advantage of the cognitive resonance with music by listening to positive-sounding music in the morning, during meditation, or while working. I often use music by Bach, as I am doing right now while writing this chapter, to help me think clearly and stay focused.

ATMOSPHERES

The amalgamation of physical resonance, emotional contagion, empathy, and cognitive resonance culminates in what we call *atmospheres*. These are perceptual experiences shaped by a rich tapestry of sensory information, encompassing auditory cues such as noise and music, visual stimuli such as facial expressions, and even olfactory signals such as emotional chemosignals.

Babies and toddlers are especially sensitive to atmospheres. They intuitively detect their parents' emotional states, often almost immediately, regardless of the parents' efforts to mask their true feelings. Stress and anger are inevitably passed on to a child through emotional contagion, which in turn triggers stress reactions in the child and further exacerbates the parents' stress. Therefore, the best response of parents to stress with a baby is to keep a stoic calm, take a breath, relax, let it flow, and sing. (Remember, singing makes us breathe deeply and slowly, facilitating physical calmness.)

Atmospheres can correspond to all kinds of moods and have various characteristics, such as relaxed, peaceful, happy, hostile, frightening, or depressing, among others. Atmospheres can be beneficial or harmful to us, so it is important to pay attention to the atmospheres we live in, whether at home, at work, with friends, or in our leisure time. Research in consumer behaviour investigates how creating certain atmospheres in cafes, restaurants, or shops can influence sales. Music also plays a pivotal role here; in some cases, the acoustic atmosphere influences purchasing decisions even more than the actual product itself.

[19] Koelsch et al., Tormenting thoughts.

Music therapists often harness the healing effects of atmospheres, paying particular attention to the emotional resonances of music, voice, facial expressions, and gestures. To promote regeneration and healing, we best create calming, supportive, secure, peaceful, loving, playful, or cheerful atmospheres.

We ourselves contribute to the creation of atmospheres through our moods and emotions. These are also communicated to others via our chemosignals – essentially, the scents our bodies emit. This creates atmospheres and triggers emotional resonance in others, whether relaxed and pleasant or oppressive and tense. The more often we participate in healthy atmospheres, the better for us and our fellow human beings.

A groundbreaking study by chemists and computer scientists analysed the air's chemical composition in cinemas. They discovered that the chemical composition of the atmosphere varied between suspenseful and humorous scenes. (The research team measured the proportion of carbon dioxide, isoprene, and acetone.)[20] Thus, people produce atmospheres related to differences in the chemical composition of the air. Hence, when individuals play together, be it at home, in a concert, or in a music therapy session, they create measurable biochemical atmospheres.

The 'magic moments' in a concert – where musicians play with devotion, the music sounds heavenly, and everyone is in a state of flow – are also a form of atmosphere. These paradisian atmospheres emerge from *shared* emotional experiences by the inspired musicians and a spellbound audience.

MUSICAL MEMORIES: DARLING, THEY ARE PLAYING OUR TUNE!

Is the notion that we form lifelong musical preferences during our teenage years merely a myth, or does empirical data substantiate this claim? To explore this query, data scientist Seth Stephens-Davidowitz

---

[20] Williams, J., Stönner, C., Wicker, J., Krauter, N., Derstroff, B., Bourtsoukidis, E., Klüpfel, T., and Kramer, S. (2016). Cinema audiences reproducibly vary the chemical composition of air during films, by broadcasting scene-specific emissions on breath. *Scientific Reports*, 6, 25464.

conducted an intriguing analysis using listener data from the popular music-streaming service Spotify. Specifically, he scrutinized the ages of listeners alongside the frequency with which they listened to each song on the top 100 charts spanning the years 1960 to 2000.[21] The pattern Stephens-Davidowitz revealed was strikingly consistent: each song found its most frequent listeners among individuals who were aged between eleven and sixteen at the time the song was released. In the early 1980s, during my own teenage years, songs from the Neue Deutsche Welle movement dominated the German music scene. Now, as of 2019, they hold their greatest appeal for those in their fifties. Around 2010, dubstep songs reached their peak, and are now primarily listened to by individuals in their early twenties. It is improbable that dubstep would captivate a fifty-year-old to the same extent as '99 Luftballons' – the famous Neue Deutsche Welle song by Nena, which does not particularly delight today's twenty-year-olds.

According to these analyses, women tend to develop their musical tastes somewhat earlier than men do: for women, the most influential age range for later preferences in pop music is between eleven and fourteen years, while for men, it falls between thirteen and sixteen years. Of course, we often acquire favourite songs at diverse stages of life; however, in the realm of pop music, there is a marked statistical tendency for preferences to cluster around songs released during our teenage years.

The data presents a clear picture, but what underlying factors during our teenage years make them so musically influential? The answer lies in biological factors. Adolescents experience their emotions as particularly intense, uncontrolled, and difficult to regulate due to hormonal changes and neural alterations. For example, during adolescence, the brain's pleasure system is markedly stimulated by the neurotransmitter dopamine.[22] As a result, adolescents actively seek out fun and risky experiences, are drawn to immediate gratification, and tend to consider long-term consequences less. Due to these biological changes in

---

[21] *The New York Times*, 10 February 2018. www.nytimes.com/2018/02/10/opinion/sunday/favorite-songs.html

[22] Galvan, A. (2010). Adolescent development of the reward system. *Frontiers in Human Neuroscience*, 4, 6.

adolescence, music heard at this age may be remembered later in life with a particularly strong emotional connection. Furthermore, most individuals undergo unforgettable emotional experiences during adolescence, such as the first kiss, the first romantic relationship, and other experiences linked to the transition from childhood to adulthood.

Music serves as more than mere entertainment during our formative years; it often acts as emotional scaffolding. Listening to music or creating music can provide young people with a unique sense of comfort and a sanctuary to cope with family issues and childhood traumas. The health repercussions of severe emotional or psychological distress often manifest as psychosomatic symptoms during puberty, such as depression, headaches, or various forms of physical pain. Psychological distress may also translate into a variety of behavioural challenges, including substance abuse, academic difficulties, social withdrawal, and antisocial conduct. Many young people find solace in music while navigating such challenges. They may feel understood, articulate their issues through creating music, distract themselves from immediate problems, or simply derive a sense of comfort.

The music that provided support during those difficult times may offer particular consolation later in life. I thus recommend revisiting such musical experiences and utilizing them as a source of comfort. (However, caution is advised if music is associated with negative experiences, such as drug abuse, criminal behaviour, depression, or suicide attempts; this music should be avoided as it can potentially trigger similar behaviours or moods.)

THE EMOTIONAL POTENCY OF MUSICAL MEMORIES

Music psychologists posit that music evokes emotional memories if we have stored it alongside an emotionally significant autobiographical event. Later, listening to this music can trigger the memory and its associated emotion. Music psychologist John Davies has illustrated this phenomenon with the exclamation, 'Darling, they are playing our tune!' And another music psychologist, Sir John Sloboda, has also noted that many people use music as a 'reminder of valued past events'.[23] Most of us

---

[23] Davies, J. B. (1978). *The Psychology of Music.* London, Routledge.

can identify music that evokes a particular mood because we connect it to an emotionally significant life event. For many, Christmas songs are associated with childhood memories of the festive spirit and thus inspire feelings of Christmas cheer. Christmas songs are also associated with gifts – hence, most stores play this music continuously from the start of the holiday shopping season.

In psychological terminology, the concept of autobiographical memory is often referred to as *episodic memory*, while the memory reserved for general knowledge and facts is termed *semantic memory*. For instance, after a stroke, a patient may remember a vacation in France (with details about the journey, experiences in Paris, and seeing the *Mona Lisa* in the Louvre), but they may no longer recall the name of France's capital or who painted the *Mona Lisa*. Conversely, another stroke patient may know that Paris is the capital of France and that Leonardo da Vinci painted the *Mona Lisa*, but they cannot remember their vacation in France.

Music has the capacity to involuntarily evoke autobiographical memories. If the trip to France is associated with a specific piece of music, this piece will automatically trigger memories of the vacation. Along with the memory, it also elicits the mood linked to the experience – in this manner, music can evoke emotions by triggering memories. One might exploit this phenomenon by curating a playlist that evokes positive autobiographical memories, thereby summoning corresponding uplifting moods – much like creating a musical photo album.

MUSIC EVOKES AUTOBIOGRAPHICAL MEMORIES EVEN IN PATIENTS WITH MEMORY DAMAGE

Remarkably, music has the power to awaken dormant memories, even in individuals who suffer from serious impairments to their autobiographical memory. Neurologist Christoph Ploner illustrated this intriguing phenomenon in a case involving a sixty-eight-year-old cellist, who had once played in prestigious German orchestras. For the purposes of this chapter, I will refer to this patient as 'AC'. As a result of severe brain inflammation induced by herpes viruses, AC had nearly lost all capacity for both semantic and autobiographical memory. He could not name a single German river or chancellor and could not recall any autobiographical details from his childhood, adolescence, or adulthood. He no longer had any memories of relatives or friends, except for his brother and his full-time caregiver. He could neither remember the lyrics of well-known folk or children's songs nor name a single famous cellist. The only composer he could recall was Beethoven.

Astonishingly, however, AC could still play the cello from sheet music, and his memory for music remained extraordinarily precise: he responded clearly to familiar pieces of classical music in a test that included both very familiar and very unfamiliar pieces. Furthermore, he was able to remember newly composed, unknown pieces, even hours after the researchers had played them for him. Although AC's memory for faces and objects was destroyed, he retained the ability to remember and learn new music.[24]

Upon hearing about this extraordinary case from Christoph Ploner, I immediately recommended that the patient take up his cello once again. I suggested enlisting a music therapist for this task, and I knew just the right one: Julia Alexa Kraft. We were together in the same violin class during our music studies, and later, during her time playing in the Gewandhaus Orchestra in Leipzig, she was among the very first participants in my experiments at the Max Planck Institute.

What Julia experienced in her work with patient AC is one of the most remarkable things I have ever learned about patients with memory disorders. When she first visited AC, he had regular contact with only a caregiver and lived in relatively humble circumstances, considering his high-profile cellist career. He had not played the cello for years and was adamant about not picking it up again. Nevertheless, Julia unpacked her violin and opened the sheet music for a Beethoven duet. While conversing with AC, she started playing the violin part of the duet. 'Hmm, but now the cello part is missing,' she said – a statement that instantly resonated with the musician in AC. He jumped up, fetched his cello, and they both began playing together. Despite a lengthy break from playing, AC, once one of Germany's finest cellists, performed the Beethoven Duo without any major difficulties. He was dissatisfied with the quality of his playing and wanted to stop after the first movement, but

---

[24] Finke, C., Esfahani, N. E., and Ploner, C. J. (2012). Preservation of musical memory in an amnesic professional cellist. *Current Biology*, 22(15), R591–R592.

MUSIC AND EMOTIONS

the act of playing had triggered something in his memory: AC spontaneously recounted to Julia how he had studied abroad – a memory that contradicted the neurological diagnosis of a severe loss of episodic memory.

From that moment, each subsequent session followed a similar pattern: AC would initially resist the idea of playing, often saying, 'We'll play again next time, not today.' However, in the secure and trusting atmosphere that Julia had cultivated, he would eventually find the courage to play. A neighbour kept knocking on the door, complaining about the noise – unaware that he had just witnessed a medical marvel. Every time AC played, memories began to pour out of him: he recounted his cello studies abroad, auditions, concerts in different countries, and interactions with his colleagues. He could also remember his birthday again and spoke about his family members. Within a few sessions, it was possible to reconstruct his life. AC played recordings of earlier concerts for Julia, while he passionately engaged with the music, swaying along, giving cues, and reminiscing about the past. After playing together, he once said blissfully, 'That sounds so beautiful!', and then, more seriously, 'I know now that I have to play again; it's good for me.'

From a neurological perspective, this remarkable case challenges conventional medical understanding. Importantly, it demonstrates that joy in music and enthusiasm for making music can have profound healing effects, even when medical knowledge has reached its limits. 'Music opens the door to all kinds of experiences,' says Julia.

A Personal Music Vault

Creating a personalized collection of music associated with beautiful experiences can serve as a resource for emotional resilience and well-being.

- *Assemble positive tracks*: begin by identifying musical pieces that are linked solely to positive memories. Then, obtain recordings of these selected pieces and store them in a designated place.
- *Elevate your spirits*: whenever you are experiencing melancholy moments, use this personalized music vault to uplift your mood.

> Moreover, you will have a treasure trove of memories to access through music in your later years.
> - *Turn to music during illness*: if you are grappling with an illness, turn to the music that brought you joy during times of good health. Then, close your eyes and vividly recall yourself at a time when you were in good health. Engaging in this form of musical reminiscence can support your self-healing powers.

THE SYMPHONY OF PREDICTIONS

Have you ever considered that your brain is constantly making predictions while you are awake? As you read this sentence, your brain automatically predicts the next... word. When we flip the light switch in the morning, we expect illumination – and are disoriented if the bulb burns out. If an egg slips from our hand during breakfast, we can reflexively catch it because our brain calculates the egg's trajectory and anticipates where it will fall. When we listen to a piece of music, we automatically predict what might come next.

Anticipation, or prediction, constitutes a fundamental function of not just the human brain but likely of all nervous systems as well. Prediction plays a role in both perception and motor activity, such as when we observe an action and anticipate its outcome, or when we perform an action and expect a specific result. In this way, our senses often alert us to forthcoming events even before they transpire, allowing for rapid responses. Our predictions even influence how we *perceive* sensory information. When we listen to someone speaking in a noisy environment, such as a bar, our brain fills in the gaps, resulting in the perception of continuous speech.[25] Even the most skilled violinist does not play every note perfectly in tune; instead, our brain creates the illusion of pitch perfection by continuously predicting pitches and automatically ignoring minor prediction errors. Our perception is thus always a blend of what our brain has predicted and actual sensory information.

---

[25] Kashino, M. (2006). Phonemic restoration: The brain creates missing speech sounds. *Acoustical Science and Technology*, 27(6), 318–321.

Through the manipulation of our predictions or expectations, composers are capable of stirring a broad spectrum of emotions, from certainty and uncertainty to tension, surprise, and resolution. Making a prediction always involves some degree of uncertainty about the outcome. During the initial notes of an unknown piece, we are uncertain about what comes next and lack specific expectations. However, after a few tones or chords, we can usually predict the next event with some certainty. When we hear a cadence, we can predict the final tonic chord with high certainty (e.g. in the key of C major, the tonic chord is a C major chord). We often perceive uncertainty as curiosity or suspense, and such curiosity motivates us to continue listening.

The excitement of uncertainty increases with the importance of the outcome – an audition in front of a world-class orchestra is more thrilling than performing a serenade for one's family. We perceive the excitement of uncertainty as a pleasant form of tension in scenarios such as awaiting a birthday present or watching a thriller. Conversely, we perceive it as unpleasant stress when awaiting a medical diagnosis or exam results.

Beyond the period of uncertainty, emotions also come into play when that uncertainty is *resolved* – that is, upon discovering the accuracy of our prediction. If our prediction comes true, we may feel a sense of reward, relief, or relaxation, and this feeling is more significant when the previous tension or stress was high. Conversely, when a prediction proves incorrect, we experience surprise. Depending on whether the outcome is better or worse than expected, surprises can be pleasant or unpleasant. What, then, renders musical predictions pleasant? To address this particular query, we shall delve into how music perpetually creates and resolves uncertainty.

THE EPISTEMIC OFFERING OF MUSIC

In music featuring a pulse and a scale, the timing of musical events aligns with the tactus (beat), and the pitches align with the underlying scale. As a result, music consistently presents us with plausible outcomes through its rhythm and tonality, enabling us to anticipate the timing of subsequent notes and their likely pitches. However, the absolute certainty of our predictions remains elusive. Not every tone falls on the beat, and the succeeding pitch or harmony eludes precise prediction. This element of uncertainty can be highly engaging, as it piques our curiosity about the music's progression and motivates us to continue listening.

At this juncture, the magic unfolds: each new tone reveals whether our predictions were correct. Every new tone offers satisfaction of our curiosity. This rewarding and pleasurable experience engages us in a constant dance of prediction and resolution. This dynamic interaction keeps our brains intrigued as music continuously 'informs' us by confirming or defying our expectations. I have termed this property of music the 'epistemic offering', in homage to Johann Sebastian Bach's 'Musical Offering'.[26] Music continuously invites us to expand our knowledge by resolving the uncertainty tied to our predictions, providing us with insights about its underlying structure and allowing us to evaluate the accuracy of our anticipations.

The allure of the epistemic offering entices people to listen to music, read books, watch films, play games, and attend sporting events – we want to know what happens next and how accurate our predictions were. This implies that we must be able to make predictions, and that the information we gain is rewarding. In a piece featuring only one repeating note or chord, we could make flawless predictions but the epistemic offering would be minimal. There would be no surprises, and the piece would quickly become monotonous. It would, therefore, not constitute art. Conversely, a piece with entirely chaotic notes or chords would also be unappealing, as we could not make any predictions, learn anything, or be surprised. At most, we would predict that it will end eventually and eagerly look forward to that. Both music pieces scarcely provide an epistemic offering.

This is why Chinese Peking opera may initially appear disconcerting to many Europeans – they are unfamiliar with the patterns and can only make a limited number of predictions. For analogous reasons, contemporary art music frequently appears perplexing. We desire a fair amount of predictability and a rewarding amount of epistemic offering. This amount varies depending on the intended purpose of the music – whether for dancing, meditation, aesthetic enjoyment, or

---

[26] Koelsch, S., Vuust, P., and Friston, K. (2019). Predictive processes and the peculiar case of music. *Trends in Cognitive Sciences*, 23(1), 63–77.

background ambience. Surprising events contain more information than events of a monotonous sequence, as they inform us that our prediction was incorrect. The unexpected can captivate us by expanding our horizons and presenting learning opportunities.

THE ART OF PLEASANT SURPRISES

But what makes musical surprises pleasant? For a long time, academics believed that it was the right *amount* of surprise – arousing enough but not too much. However, this notion is incorrect. For music to be truly engaging and captivating, it requires a well-balanced blend of certainty and surprise. My friends and colleagues Marcus Pearce and Peter Harrison devised a computer model into which they input hundreds of Billboard songs. The model computed, for each harmony, how certain one could be about how the harmonic progression continued and the degree to which it was surprising.[27]

We then asked study participants to rate how pleasant they found each harmony to be. The data revealed that it is actually the right build-up of predictions that makes musical surprises pleasant. For example, at the beginning of a melody, we might be able to sing a tone that could come next, but we are very uncertain about what will actually follow. In such a situation, we find it pleasant when the music is highly regular and not surprising at all. But once we are quite certain about where the music is going, we like to be surprised. Thus, the key lies in finding the sweet spot between certainty and surprise: first leading us along a predictable path and then, just when we feel we have grasped the musical journey, surprising us. *That* is the formula that makes musical structure pleasant, and when composers find this sweet spot, musical surprises can be so pleasant that some of us even get goosebumps.

Endeavour to listen to an unfamiliar piece, making continuous predictions regarding the melody's next note or the ensuing harmony, while also weighing the level of certainty or uncertainty in your predictions. It helps to attempt to sing along with the melody, even with unfamiliar pieces. Though

---

[27] Cheung, V. K., Harrison, P. M., Meyer, L., Pearce, M. T., Haynes, J. D., and Koelsch, S. (2019). Uncertainty and surprise jointly predict musical pleasure and amygdala, hippocampus, and auditory cortex activity. *Current Biology*, 29(23), 4084–4092.

it may seem challenging at first, this method effectively reveals how composers set up contexts to meet, partially meet, or cleverly subvert our expectations, thereby delivering delightful surprises. The impact is particularly striking when listening to composers with a remarkable intuition for balancing predictability and surprise – such as Mozart, Verdi, or Elton John.

This way, surprises can also acquire a humorous quality. In the second movement of his 'Surprise Symphony', Joseph Haydn establishes a context of quiet tones for eight bars, then of very quiet tones (*pianissimo*) for another seven bars, and then a sudden, very loud sound (*fortissimo*) erupts with the booming kettledrum stroke. This surprise is amusing for the audience, and Haydn likely enjoyed a private moment of mirth upon witnessing the audience's startled reactions.

HOW DO WE MAKE MUSICAL PREDICTIONS?

The most straightforward prediction we can make in the context of most music is the timing of the next note – typically aligning with the next beat of the measure – and its stress level, whether stressed or unstressed. Moving our body helps in making such predictions. One reason we dance to captivating grooves lies in the music's rhythmic nuances: in dance music we find 'groovy', a note may be conspicuously absent where we expect it – on the beat of the measure – and instead appear just before or after as an *off-beat*. Such off-beats challenge our cognitive model of the rhythm, prompting us to stabilize this mental representation through *movement*. Due to our intrinsic need for a stable model, we feel compelled to restore a deviation from the structure through dance movements. (Of course, other aspects, such as the pleasure of dancing together, also motivate us to dance.)

If the rhythm is perfectly predictable and our rhythmic model remains unchallenged, we experience no 'groove' and feel less urge to move. Likewise, if everything is entirely irregular and no model can be established, we also perceive no groove. It is only the optimal level of predictability that kindles our desire to move, leading us to find such grooves exceptionally enjoyable.[28]

---

[28] Witek, M. A., Clarke, E. F., Wallentin, M., Kringelbach, M. L., and Vuust, P. (2014). Syncopation, body-movement and pleasure in groove music. *PLoS ONE*, 9(4), e94446.

Figure 5.1 Excerpts from Mozart's Symphony No. 31. Top: The beginning of the symphony. The end of the scale (in D major) features the 'correct' note (a D) concluding the sequence. Since we are familiar with scales, we expect the final tone with high certainty. Bottom: The development section begins with the same passage (transposed to A major), but here, the concluding note is 'incorrect' (not an A but a B flat, which does not belong to A major). This note defies our expectation or prediction (made with great certainty) and surprises us. Source: Olga Koelsch

The prediction of melodic tones and harmonies presents a more complex task. A substantial understanding of a particular music genre is required to make accurate predictions. In Western music using major or minor keys, certain tones belong to the key while others do not. For example, in the key of C major, the white keys on a piano, that is, C, D, E, F, G, A, B, belong to C major, while all the black keys do not. Playing all the notes of a key in ascending pitch, starting with the root note, results in a scale. Now, imagine a piece with a scale as melody, that is, 'C–D–E–F–G–A–B ...' – we would then expect 'C' as the next note (similarly, after '1–2–3–4–5–6–7 ...', we expect the '8'). Mozart incorporated this in his 31st Symphony (Figure 5.1): the beginning starts with a complete scale (where anyone familiar with a scale expects the last tone). This sequence repeats a few more times – and then, at the beginning of the development (bar 132), the strongly expected final scale tone does *not* appear. Instead, a tone that does not belong to the scale emerges and surprises us (my favourite expectancy violation in Mozart's music).

The same principle applies to harmonies: customarily, a dominant seventh chord towards the end of a chord progression gives way to a tonic chord. Anyone who has listened to Western music for some time learns these regularities involuntarily – without intention and unconsciously. We acquire *implicit knowledge* about the regularities underlying sequences of notes and chords. Then, we apply this knowledge when listening to music, automatically making predictions about what will happen next.

Certain chord progressions are uncommon and therefore perceived as unexpected, such as a *deceptive cadence* with a submediant (instead of a tonic) following a dominant. Similarly, a chord sounds unexpected when it suddenly contains notes that do not belong to the key of the preceding harmonies. This transpires in the first movement of every classical sonata or symphony, where the key of the initial theme shifts to the key of the subsequent theme – a process termed *modulation* in music theory. In my lectures, when presenting such musical excerpts, even trained musicians frequently find it challenging to identify the precise moment of modulation, as non-musicians often cast helpless glances in my direction. Interestingly, although many people may not consciously notice a modulation of key, their brains do register it. (Even in non-musicians, 'wrong' chords evoke activity in the brain's music-language system, as discussed in Chapter 3.)

HOW THE BODY REACTS TO MUSICAL SURPRISES

In a study on the emotional effects of chord progressions, my research group used musical excerpts analogous to the Mozart example in Figure 5.1. We utilized original excerpts, as written by the composers, featuring moderately unusual chords such as a deceptive cadence. Furthermore, we adapted these excerpts to feature chords that were either completely regular, such as a perfect cadence, or highly irregular, such as chords with several out-of-key tones. The latter chords sounded very unexpected even to non-musicians.[29]

To gauge the physiological reactions of our participants as they engaged with the music, we employed electrodes placed on their palms to measure sweat secretion. Approximately two to three seconds after hearing a moderately unusual chord progression, we recorded a significant increase in sweat secretion, compared to the responses elicited by standard chord sequences. This increase was even more pronounced for the particularly unusual chord progressions. Interestingly, although non-musician participants often struggled to consciously recognize the moderately unusual chord progressions, their palms still perspired more.

---

[29] Koelsch, S., Kilches, S., Steinbeis, N., and Schelinski, S. (2008). Effects of unexpected chords and performer's expression on brain responses and electrodermal activity. *PLoS ONE*, 3(7), e2631.

This effect is in line with prior findings by my research team, thus affirming its reliability.[30] This means that each time you hear unusual chord progressions, such as when the music's key changes or a deceptive cadence occurs, *your* palms react in the same way. This occurs even if you are not consciously aware of the unusual harmonies or key transitions. It is astonishing to observe how sensitively our bodies respond to even the subtlest harmonic nuances.

PARADOXICAL PREDICTIONS: WHEN FAMILIAR PIECES REMAIN SURPRISING

Remarkably, even when one is familiar with a musical piece and capable of making accurate predictions, the brain continues to respond to uncommon tones. In an experiment, we played musical excerpts similar to those from Mozart's Symphony shown in Figure 5.1 repeatedly, for both non-musicians and amateur musicians. After a few repetitions, the listeners became familiar with the excerpts. Nevertheless, when exposed to these uncommon chords, the brain's electrical activity remained strikingly similar to initial responses, demonstrating a remarkable resilience to familiarity. Our predictions are based on implicit knowledge accumulated over thousands of hours, which is why certain parts of our brain involuntarily make predictions for the typical case, even when we *consciously* know that the music will proceed differently.

This establishes a paradox: our brain's predictions may well conflict with our conscious knowledge regarding the unfolding of the music. Consequently, we can still experience musical surprises even when listening to a piece multiple times. For example, even after hearing the unexpected twist in Mozart's 31st Symphony multiple times, I still enjoy the surprise it elicits in my brain.

TENSION ARCS

Musical expectancy violations seldom stand alone; they usually precede a resolution. In the interim between the two, an intermediate phase exists

---

[30] Steinbeis, N., Koelsch, S., and Sloboda, J. A. (2006). The role of harmonic expectancy violations in musical emotions: Evidence from subjective, physiological, and neural responses. *Journal of Cognitive Neuroscience*, 18(8), 1380–1393.

in which we, as experienced listeners, anticipate the resolution. During this phase, our uncertainty about what will happen next is sustained. When the resolution finally arrives, we experience a sense of resolution and relaxation.

Emotions elicited by the architecture of music are collectively referred to as *musical tension*. We typically experience musical tension as a *tension arc*. Such an arc begins with the *development* of a musical structure, which can be perceived as more or less *stable* (for instance, a structure is stable when the tonal centre is always clear). We can also make *predictions* about what will happen next and be more or less confident in their accuracy. When a prediction is incorrect, we feel surprise. A tonal expectancy violation is usually followed by a *transitional phase* where tension is suspended – we become curious about how the violation will be resolved, anticipating the relaxation brought by the upcoming resolution. This *resolution* eliminates the previous uncertainty and tension, which we perceive as pleasurable.

In grander compositions such as symphonies, composers often adroitly interweave multiple tension arcs that correspond to various structural layers – from individual themes to comprehensive movements, culminating in the unified symphonic entity. As a result, the end of a piece, where all open tension arcs are resolved, is often the moment of greatest musical relaxation.

Even if you have never considered musical tension arcs, certain parts of your brain are always monitoring them. Moritz Lehne, Martin Rohrmeier, and I discovered this in a study where we played piano pieces by Mendelssohn ('Venetian Gondellied', Op. 30, No. 6) and Mozart (the beginning of the second movement of the Piano Sonata KV 280) to non-musicians and amateur musicians.[31] Their task was to continuously indicate their perceived tension using a slider interface. The tension curves recorded by the individuals while listening to Mendelssohn's piece are shown in the upper part of Figure 5.2. We found that these curves increased or decreased in several places for all participants. As a result,

---

[31] Lehne, M., Rohrmeier, M., Gollmann, D., and Koelsch, S. (2013). The influence of different structural features on felt musical tension in two piano pieces by Mozart and Mendelssohn. *Music Perception: An Interdisciplinary Journal,* 31(2), 171–185.

MUSIC AND EMOTIONS

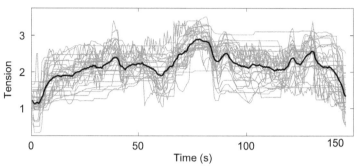

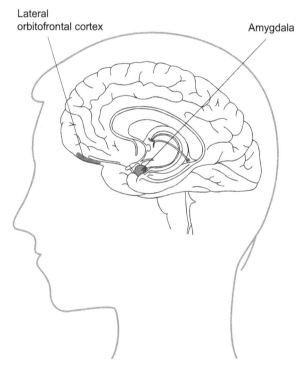

Figure 5.2 Tension curves observed during listening sessions featuring Mendelssohn's 'Venetian Gondellied', Op. 30, No. 6. Each grey curve corresponds to the curve of one participant. The black curve shows the average tension curve. Bottom: Even when not focusing on tension, activity in the lateral orbitofrontal cortex is related to the tension curve. When the tension curve rises, neural activity in this area of the brain also increases. Furthermore, moments when tension rises sharply activate the amygdala in the brain. Note that in this medial view of the brain, only a small part of the lateral orbitofrontal cortex is visible. Source: Olga Koelsch

musical perceptions of tension display remarkable consistency across a wide range of listeners.

BRAIN CORRELATES OF MUSICAL TENSION

My colleagues and I also conducted a parallel experiment involving some of the participants, utilizing functional MRI (fMRI).[32] During the measurements, the participants listened to the pieces again; however, this time they did not provide tension ratings but simply listened to the music. Using the average tension curve from Figure 5.2, we identified regions in the brain whose activity correlated with the tension curve: activity in the 'lateral orbitofrontal cortex' increased or decreased in correspondence with the tension curve (bottom of Figure 5.2). This brain region is implicated in forming expectations and processing their violation, among other roles. Moreover, activity in the amygdala increased when the tension curve rose sharply (bottom of Figure 5.2).

When I saw these results for the first time, I could not have been happier, because the amygdala is a central structure for emotional processes, akin to a conductor of the emotion orchestra in the brain.[33] It registers signals relevant to the individual's well-being, and it initiates, coordinates, or inhibits the activity of emotional structures in the brain. The fact that music can influence the activity of the amygdala and the orbitofrontal cortex demonstrates that music can indeed activate central structures of emotional processing in the brain. Thus, the emotions evoked by music are not mere epiphenomena; they stem from core brain activity responsible for emotional experience.

Furthermore, the activations of the amygdala and the orbitofrontal cortex were measured in both musicians and non-musicians, even though they had not consciously paid attention to the musical tension at all. This means that *your* brain also automatically follows musical tension arcs – every time you listen to music.

---

[32] Lehne, M., Rohrmeier, M., and Koelsch, S. (2013). Tension-related activity in the orbitofrontal cortex and amygdala: An fMRI study with music. *Social Cognitive and Affective Neuroscience*, 9(10), 1515–1523.

[33] Mears, D., and Pollard, H. B. (2016). Network science and the human brain: Using graph theory to understand the brain and one of its hubs, the amygdala, in health and disease. *Journal of Neuroscience Research*, 94(6), 590–605.

On a lighter note, a musicologist once expressed the concern that measuring musical tension with fMRI lacks real-world applicability, as participants lie in a narrow tube with the loud noise of the brain scanner. I acknowledged his point but noted that our experimental setting had some unexpected parallels with classical concert experiences: much like at some real concerts, in our experiments, some participants drifted off to sleep, while others couldn't wait until it was finally over!

> **FOLLOWING TENSION ARCS TO REDUCE NEGATIVE THOUGHTS AND PAIN**
>
> While listening to music, focus on the musical structure of the piece. Try observing how phrases start, develop, and conclude. Or pay attention to how expected or unexpected the musical events sound. This can be particularly effective if you internally sing along with the melody – even if you are unfamiliar with the piece. Follow the tension of the music and feel your emotional reactions to it. If your thoughts wander away from the music, gently redirect them back. This approach can help free your mind from negative thoughts or thought loops, as focusing on the music draws cognitive resources away from ruminating. Similarly, focusing on music can alleviate pain. Embrace the relaxation and inner peace that come with immersing yourself in music. This enjoyable and regenerative experience can have positive effects on your well-being.

TENSION ARCS AS AESTHETIC DEVICES ACROSS ART FORMS

We also appreciate tension arcs in many other art forms, such as drama, novels, short stories, and poems. In Western culture, tension arcs are an essential aesthetic tool. A sequence of chords achieves in miniature what a play unfolds over several hours, but the underlying principle of creating tension and release is the same.

For example, Shakespeare's *Romeo and Juliet* opens with a prologue, comparable to *setting up* a musical structure by establishing a key. Then, Act I introduces the characters and a plot constellation, analogous to establishing a harmonic configuration in music, where relations between chord functions become evident, and the tonal structure of the phrase remains relatively *stable*. In Act II, the plot's content develops and the conflict sharpens, but a simple solution is still possible (Romeo and Juliet could simply marry, the opposing families could make peace, and the play would be over, with a happy ending). Similarly, the harmonic sequence leads towards a clear goal. We *predict with certainty* that this goal is a tonic, which could conclude the sequence. In Act III, the hero's fate takes a critical turn, termed 'peripeteia', as Romeo stabs Tybalt and subsequently gets banished. Similarly, a deceptive cadence represents a *breach of expectation*. Act IV further delays the inevitable end. A positive outcome is unlikely but still possible, increasing the tension further (Juliet drinks the potion to appear dead). This mirrors a *transitional phase* in a harmonic sequence, where the resolution to the tonic is delayed, sustaining tension. Finally, Act V concludes the action (Romeo and Juliet die), akin to the chord sequence reaching its resolution with the final tonic.

The same principle applies to many television series as well. Being an aficionado of both Shakespeare and *Star Trek*, it is noteworthy that almost all episodes of *Star Trek: The Next Generation* adhere to a prologue and five-act structure. If you are more into electro, house, dubstep, or techno, you will find the same principle at work: a 'siren' prepares the 'drop', increasing the tension. Then, there is a brief delay at the tension climax (between the siren and the drop), which serves to sustain the tension at its peak, before the relaxing drop finally follows.

In a survey, music psychologist John Sloboda discovered that new or unexpected harmonies frequently evoked goosebumps.[34] Artists often push tension and release to levels that such chords or tones elicit intense reactions. Even without goosebumps, the confirmation or violation of our expectations, along with the associated excitement and relaxation, brings us pleasure. A unique allure of the arts lies in their ability to let us savour the intellectual and emotional thrills of unpredictability and expectation, all within a context devoid of real-world risks and consequences.

---

[34] Sloboda, J. A. (1991). Music structure and emotional response: Some empirical findings. *Psychology of Music*, 19(2), 110–120.

FANTASY AND IMAGINATION

Try the following experiment: listen to the beginning of a Tango Argentino by Astor Piazzolla (for example, 'Libertango'), close your eyes, and focus only on the musical structure: the beginning and the end of the phrases, rhythm, harmonic sequences, and musical expectations, as delineated in the previous section. Then, while keeping your eyes closed, switch to imagination mode: envision a couple passionately tangoing, the dancers circling each other, touching or almost touching, moving together with relish, stepping back and forth, and gazing at each other passionately. Most people will now experience entirely divergent (and frequently quite potent) emotions, including goosebumps or even tears. Imagining a couple dancing a tango to Mozart's Requiem does not work as well. In such a case, imagining the choir members passionately and emotionally singing together might do the trick.

Visual imagery emanates from our minds and frequently triggers powerful emotions. When music stimulates our imagination, we think imaginatively and inventively, which brings pleasure and provokes positive emotions. Ideas of something particularly positive, such as a beautiful landscape or children playing, elicit particularly positive emotions. Imagery with music is especially powerful, similar to films where the strongest emotions are usually evoked by a combination of images and music.

Of course, an entire genre exists – *programme music* – in which composers craft narratives that listeners can vividly imagine as they listen. Prominent examples include Modest Mussorgsky's 'Pictures at an Exhibition', Camille Saint-Saëns' 'Carnival of the Animals', Paul Dukas' 'The Sorcerer's Apprentice', and Bedřich Smetana's 'Vltava'.

Consider the first 'Mephisto' waltz by Franz Liszt. It tells the story of Mephistopheles and Faust arriving at a village tavern where a wedding party is taking place (one can hear a fiddle represented by violin fifths). Mephistopheles persuades Faust to enter the tavern (one can hear them ascending the steps). They join the celebration, and Mephistopheles grabs a musician's fiddle and plays a wild, intoxicating waltz. Then, he seduces a village beauty with a romantic, passionate melody. Mephistopheles grins diabolically and dances his enchanting waltz with her. The two of them then leap out of the tavern and into the forest, where a nightingale sings, and Mephistopheles and the village beauty give in to their unrestrained desires – Liszt depicts a sexual act in tones. About one minute later, the waltz is over!

In our research, we have discerned that music with a sadder tone often evokes imaginations of melancholic scenes in listeners, while music with a happier tone tends to inspire visions of celebrations and dancing.[35] In another study, we found that listening to music that sounds powerful and heroic frequently evoked images of encouraging moments that motivated participants to think more constructively and become more active.[36]

If you want to boost your motivation, you may experiment for yourself with the compositions employed in our study: 'Heroic March' by Spirit of America Ensemble, 'Legendary' by Epic Soul Factory, and 'Addicted to Success' by Epic Instrumental Background Music/Fearless Motivation Instrumentals. For classical music fans, the last movements of Beethoven's symphonies are suitable. Of course, there is a plethora of other music that fits perfectly; here are just a few examples for different styles or tastes: Elvis, AC/DC, Janis Joplin, Odetta, the film music by Hans Zimmer for *Planet Earth II*, and, of course, 'Eye of the Tiger' by Survivor. Everyone should curate their own collection according to personal preferences and the most potent personal effects. This facilitates the easy use of music for motivational purposes and for activating one's imagination (see the box below).

In the same vein, when we feel emotionally drained and low on energy, we can use highly expressive music to imagine ourselves conveying emotions with equal power and intensity. This identification with the music is akin to connecting with a protagonist in theatre or film. When listening to music, it's also enjoyable to visualize ourselves playing the music, complete with fitting gestures and facial expressions. Everyone has conducted music at home at some point (please tell me everyone has …). This activity is enjoyable because it allows us to

---

[35] Taruffi, L., Pehrs, C., Skouras, S., and Koelsch, S. (2017). Effects of sad and happy music on mind-wandering and the default mode network. *Scientific Reports*, 7(1), 14396.

[36] Koelsch, S., Bashevkin, T., Kristensen, J., Tvedt, J., and Jentschke, S. (2019). Heroic music stimulates empowering thoughts during mind-wandering. *Scientific Reports*, 9(1), 1–10.

imagine creating the music ourselves. The same concept applies to playing air guitar, where we envision ourselves as rock stars. Interestingly, there are even world championships for air guitar playing, which have garnered significant public attention.

In creative pursuits such as composing, improvising, or dancing, imagination takes on an active role; it becomes 'creativity' in action, transforming our ideas into tangible expressions. We invent, experiment, and see if it works. Engaging in creativity is enjoyable and also rewarding when our improvisations prove successful.

Achieving Goals and Influencing Moods with Musical Imagery

Utilize the power of musical imagery to elevate your emotional state and achieve your goals. Below are key techniques to help you achieve this.

- *Accomplish goals with heroic music*: when formulating a plan to accomplish a goal, listening to encouraging or heroic music can be beneficial. Envision yourself taking the first step, then another, and so on. Visualize the moment when you reach your goal, such as raising your arms in the air, laughing, and jumping for joy. Employing such musical imagery not only helps in achieving set goals but also serves as a motivational catalyst for initiating activities that have been previously delayed.
- *Overcome discouragement with courageous tunes*: if one feels discouraged, listless, or anxious, listening to courageous or heroic-sounding music may assist. Imagine tackling a task heroically, perhaps in slow motion, with head held high, chest puffed out with courage, and feet planted firmly.
- *Revitalize energy levels with uplifting melodies*: should one feel listless, playing energetic music and envisioning oneself imbued with a zest for action can be effective.
- *Lift your emotions during low moods*: during a depressed or sad mood, listening to uplifting melodies can aid in vividly imagining oneself in a more cheerful state.

- *Boost motivation to learn or practise:* simply imagining oneself learning or practising an instrument helps to motivate oneself to engage in these activities.
- *Boost workout motivation:* analogously, imagining oneself engaging in physical activity helps to motivate oneself to exercise and not to give up when working out.
- *Alleviate stress with relaxing rhythms:* relaxing music can facilitate imagining yourself in a comfortable place, such as a beautiful spot with sunshine and pleasant temperatures. Also, try envisaging any negative thoughts and emotions drifting away like clouds, dispersed by the wind.

HARNESSING IMAGINATION IN MUSIC THERAPY

One music therapy technique that capitalizes on the positive effects of fantasy and imagination is composing one's own songs, or 'songwriting'. Songwriting offers a playful way to address emotionally challenging topics and express one's feelings, thoughts, desires, and values. The subject matter can encompass a wide array of life experiences, for instance, relationships, break-ups, illnesses, problems, worries, and fears. Songwriting can stimulate creativity, spark insightful realizations, serve as a distractor from psychological stress, and provide valuable material for discussion and self-reflection. This process can be liberating, open up new perspectives, and be enjoyable. When the song is completed, it serves as a snapshot of one's life, which can be revisited later. Naturally, the practice of writing one's own song can also be undertaken independently, without the assistance of a music therapist.

Imagination is also utilized in the music therapy method *Guided Imagery and Music* and its variations. In this method, the client's music-evoked visual imaginations aim to help overcome inner conflicts and traumas with the assistance of the therapist (the 'guide'). During this process, the therapist provides a simple image (a house, an island, a city) and invites the client to explore this image while listening to music, thus initiating a story (such as entering and exploring the house). The client narrates their imaginings, and the therapist serves as a facilitator, guiding them through these 'imaginative journeys'. In doing so, the therapist can help confront and address stressful memories, negative imaginings, and emotions, or focus on positive imaginings and relaxation. The client is like a creative 'composer of the soul', a composer of their own psychological themes and personality developments.

Music therapists apply the positive effects of fantasy and imagination on emotions and health also in other ways. In the context of patients afflicted with pain or cancer, therapists occasionally employ techniques prompting these individuals to recall instances from their past when they felt notably well. The conceptualization of a healthy self, as evoked by these memories, engenders positive emotions and appears to promote the patient's self-healing capabilities. Upon these premises, it becomes plausible that imagining oneself in good health, while engaged in listening to uplifting and soothing music, is beneficial during periods of illness.

> **USING MUSICAL IMAGERY TO SUPPORT RECOVERY**
>
> To promote recovery, play calming and uplifting music, close your eyes, and relax. Vividly imagine a time when you were healthy. Next, envision yourself or specific organs in your body as healthy *now*, even if you are currently ill – this exercise is all about imagination. Maintain your engagement with this mental imagery for the entire duration of the musical piece, akin to a focused-attention meditation. Should your thoughts stray from the intended focus, gently steer them back towards the affirmative visualization of your state of well-being.

UNDERSTANDING AND THE PLEASURE OF 'AHA' EXPERIENCES

Gioachino Rossini once made a comment about Wagner's 'Lohengrin': 'One can't judge Wagner's Lohengrin after a first hearing. I don't intend to hear it a second time.'[37] When we are unfamiliar with musical patterns

---

[37] Sherrin, N. (ed.) (2008). *Oxford Dictionary of Humorous Quotations*. New York, Oxford University Press.

and regularities, predicting what comes next becomes difficult, making the music sound chaotic and irritating. On the other hand, understanding the music leads to pleasure. By listening to a complex piece multiple times, we become better at recognizing the melodies and themes. We learn how they are structured and interrelated.

The more familiar we become with a particular style of music, the more pleasure it provides. Simply by resolving the uncertainties associated with our predictions, music continuously offers us a series of 'aha' experiences (the epistemic offering of music). Moreover, understanding the structure of a sequence, section, or entire piece also leads to 'aha' experiences. Consider a tension arc, for example: after an expectancy breach, the moment of resolution helps us comprehend the coherence of the entire sequence. Much like a riddle that arouses our curiosity, a deceptive cadence piques our interest. Its resolution satisfies this curiosity, offering an opportunity to comprehend the entire sequence.

Our brains are naturally driven to make sense of the world; each 'aha' moment fulfils this innate need and thus provides pleasure. Such experiences expand our horizons and enhance our competence. With every problem we solve, we accomplish a goal. Understanding and learning are fundamental human needs at any age. We experience the satisfaction of this need as enjoyable and fulfilling. Imagine the effectiveness of schools that focus primarily on fostering interest and deriving satisfaction from learning. Pupils would only have to engage with topics that genuinely intrigue them, without being lectured. As I have not yet encountered a child who is disinterested in music, incorporating it as an integral part of every school's curriculum would be only natural.

THE REWARDS OF UNDERSTANDING MUSICAL STRUCTURE

Delving into the architecture of a piece of music can be a fascinating and informative experience. This is the foundation of the fields of music theory known as *musical analysis* and *Formenlehre* (the theory of form). For example, to understand classical symphonies and sonatas, it is helpful to know their underlying structure. Typically, the first movement follows the *sonata form*, which consists of three distinct sections: an exposition, the development, and the recapitulation.

During the exposition, the composer introduces what is known as the 'first theme', usually the initial melody of the piece. This is followed by a transition to another key, leading into the 'second theme'. This second theme is intended to contrast the first theme and is therefore presented in a different key. After the second theme, the exposition concludes. The exposition is usually repeated to help listeners better understand and remember the themes presented. In the *development* section, the composer varies, combines, and develops the themes and motifs introduced in the exposition. This creates numerous 'aha' moments for listeners due to the musical exploration and innovation. Finally, the *recapitulation* returns to the exposition's basic structure, with the first and second themes presented again, but this time united in the same key.

Throughout the history of music, the sonata form has undergone various modifications and expansions, with numerous composers adding their unique style and flair to this foundational structure. For example, Brahms occasionally included four themes in the exposition of his works. It is fascinating to discover the intricate structure of his complex compositions, and an in-depth analysis of just one of them can easily run to over 100 pages. Nevertheless, many concert guides also offer brief analyses of various works, aiding listeners in following the piece's form and comprehending its structure – leading to a more enjoyable emotional experience of the music.

Similarly, an opera only becomes truly enjoyable when we understand the plot and become familiar with the melodies. Otherwise, we glance at our watch after hours, and only twenty minutes have passed. When I listen to an opera for the first time, I find it difficult to fully appreciate it. However, upon the second or third listen, I start to recognize the passages. As I listen to it more, I eagerly anticipate those passages, and eventually, I can hardly wait to attend the opera again and hear them once more. By investing time in deepening one's understanding of an opera, everybody will be rewarded with an abundant release of dopamine in the brain, sometimes accompanied by goosebumps or tears of emotion. For most, it will be easiest to begin with the classics: 'Carmen' by Georges Bizet, 'The Barber of Seville' by Gioachino Rossini, 'La Traviata' by Giuseppe Verdi, 'The Magic Flute' by Mozart, or 'La Bohème' by Giacomo Puccini.

ENHANCING MUSICAL APPRECIATION AND BRAIN HEALTH

'Aha' experiences are good for the brain because the enjoyment and release of dopamine associated with them have an anti-sclerotic effect on the brain, thus keeping it young.

- *Programme music*: an easy start is to grasp the narrative of a piece of *programme music*. Concert guides and recordings for children that explain the programme can be useful (for example, a recording of Prokofiev's 'Peter and the Wolf' or 'The Carnival of the Animals' by Saint-Saëns). One can have fun with the 'aha' experiences associated with the discovery of how the programme is expressed in the music. In addition, one can then enhance the emotional experience by engaging one's visual imagery.
- *Context through a composer's life*: another approach is to learn about a composer's life and explore how specific life events influenced their compositions or are reflected in their music. This added context can deepen one's appreciation and understanding of a piece, revealing new layers of meaning and emotional connection.
- *Advanced analysis*: for those with prior knowledge of music theory, analysing the structure of a cherished piece – be it classical, jazz, or other genres – can yield numerous pleasurable 'aha' experiences. This enjoyment arises from understanding how the composer constructed the piece, developed themes, or organized chords and keys.

THE EXPERIENCE IS THE RESULT: SOCIAL FUNCTIONS OF MUSIC

The 'Singing Hospitals' initiative serves as a pioneering effort, providing opportunities for singing across healthcare facilities in Germany, Switzerland, and Austria. When patients and singing leaders from a 'Singing Hospital' gather, they sing simple melodies without the need for sheet music or lyrics. They choose easy songs such as the African 'Bele Mama' or empowering phrases such as 'I am all I need, yes I can do it the way I am', accompanied by clapping, drumming, and moving to the rhythm of the music.

The atmosphere reminds me of the communal music making in many indigenous cultures around the world, where the focus lies on fostering a sense of community through singing, rather than delivering a polished performance. In this setting, equality prevails, transcending distinctions of age or social status. Here, community and solidarity are experienced through the shared act of making music. The sense of togetherness visibly moves everyone involved; emotional tears, smiles, laughter, and spontaneous hugs can be seen among participants. Illness often exposes our vulnerability, and in these moments, we simply seek relief from our suffering and a path to recovery. Patients have reported feeling renewed strength, energy, liberation, relaxation, and openness during these singing sessions. Elke Wünnenberg, Chair of the initiative, said to me: 'Singing together can aid in coping with illness and contribute to healthcare. We want people in our healthcare system to experience the healing effects of singing.'

Singing together can cultivate positive emotions by fostering a sense of community. Some feel more energetic, hopeful, serene, courageous, and calm after singing together; others experience reduced anxiety and worry. These positive emotions possess healing properties; they alter brain chemistry and promote balance in both the autonomic nervous system and the hormonal system. In turn, these changes positively impact the immune system. We can sleep better at night and experience enhanced regeneration and recovery.

THE SEVEN C'S

Music is a unique tool for fostering community and social cohesion; it enables large groups to perform synchronized movements, thus engendering a sense of unity and togetherness. The need to participate in communal activities is an intrinsic part of human nature, and the emotional effects of such participation often manifest as joy and happiness. Music facilitates engagement in social functions in seven distinct ways, which I have coined as *The Seven C's*.

1. *Contact.* Making music together establishes social interaction, thereby counteracting loneliness and isolation. This is vital because loneliness

and isolation can result in unhappiness, illness, and reduced lifespan.[38] Social contact is a fundamental human need, and the absence of it can be so distressing that it is sometimes used as a form of punishment, such as house arrest for children, solitary confinement in prisons, or even torture. Attending concerts and 'just listening' also provides opportunities for social interaction and becoming part of the concert community. Similar to activities such as playing games in a group, or doing team sports, engaging in musical activity facilitates social contact. Taking each other's hand while dancing together naturally involves physical contact. The importance of human contact for overall health and well-being is often underestimated. However, research showed that children require physical contact and hugs for healthy brain development, and adults also benefit from physical contact for their overall health.[39] Gentle touch, such as slow stroking, alleviates pain by activating C-tactile nerve fibres. Furthermore, individuals with more frequent physical contact tend to have a weaker response to unhealthy stress and challenging life events.

2. *Social cognition.* When we hear someone's voice or see their face, our brain engages automatically in a sort of 'detective work' to determine how the person is feeling, what they are thinking or intending, and the extent of their desires. This process is known as social cognition, which occurs without conscious intent and often without our awareness. In social cognition, we develop a mental model, or a 'theory of mind', to understand what is happening in another person's mind. For example, through the tone of the request, 'Can you please take the rubbish down?', a husband can gauge his wife's mood, the degree of her annoyance, and how urgently she wants it to be done right now.

Listening to music involuntarily activates our social cognition. Nikolaus Steinbeis and I investigated this in a brain-imaging study where we played music by Arnold Schönberg, Alban Berg, and Anton

---

[38] Holt-Lunstad, J., Robles, T. F., and Sbarra, D. A. (2017). Advancing social connection as a public health priority in the United States. *American Psychologist,* 72(6), 517.
[39] Gallace, A., and Spence, C. (2010). The science of interpersonal touch: An overview. *Neuroscience & Biobehavioral Reviews,* 34(2), 246–259.

Webern for participants.[40] However, they were told that only some of the pieces were composed by a composer, while others were generated by a computer. When participants believed they were listening to music created by a composer, their 'theory of mind' network was engaged – the brain network responsible for processing information about what another person might be thinking, wanting, knowing, or believing. Specifically, they felt that the composers (but not the computers) had an intention to convey something through their music. This means that even if you have not noticed it before, when you listen to music, your brain is constantly assessing what the composer likely intended to express with their composition.

3. *Co-pathy.* When we listen to music together or create music in a group, we often experience similar emotions and moods. We resonate emotionally in a similar manner, and feel a shared sense of tension and resolution. Often, music evokes emotions such as peacefulness, joy, or triumph across all participants. As a result of this co-pathy, group members tend to exhibit more prosocial behaviour than before, since shared emotional experiences promote cooperation, helpfulness, and fairness.[41]

Co-pathy – the phenomenon of experiencing emotions together – powerfully amplifies these emotions. Consider the heightened emotions experienced when singing in a choir, dancing in a crowd at a rock concert, or cheering in a football stadium. The reason mass events can be so overwhelming is that many people are experiencing the same emotions simultaneously (including the shared sense of being overwhelmed). In fact, emotions typically become truly overwhelming only when shared with others. This collective emotional experience can be harnessed for either positive outcomes, such as during peace demonstrations, or negative outcomes, as seen in events such as the Nuremberg party rallies or demonstrations that fuel

---

[40] Steinbeis, N., and Koelsch, S. (2008). Understanding the intentions behind man-made products elicits neural activity in areas dedicated to mental state attribution. *Cerebral Cortex*, 19(3), 619–623.

[41] Page and Nowak, Empathy leads to fairness; Rumble, Van Lange, and Parks, The benefits of empathy.

hatred and exclusion. Music is often present at such events because it can readily evoke these powerful 'pack emotions'.
4. *Communication.* Music serves as a versatile medium for communication, whether we create it with others or individually. Even when simply listening to music, we can feel a sense of understanding as we realize that other people may share similar emotions or face similar challenges. Since babies are already capable of understanding some musical elements (see Chapter 3), we can communicate with them through music. In music therapy, patients can employ music to express emotions or convey issues that they find challenging or impossible to articulate in words.
5. *Coordination.* When making music, dancing, or clapping along, humans can naturally and effortlessly synchronize their movements to the beat, coordinating them to move together in time. We can speed up and slow down in a group – a feat unmatched by any other species. Our attention becomes focused on creating music together, fostering shared intentions and a common goal, and we enjoy such shared engagement. We also simply enjoy coordinated movements in groups, whether it be drumming, dancing, or participating in stadium waves. Already, infants enjoy synchronizing their movements to a beat (see Chapter 1).

Such coordination of movements has a multitude of fascinating effects: Robin Dunbar and his team at the University of Oxford suggest that synchronizing movements within a group activates the endogenous opioid system, including the release of endorphins.[42] In addition to reducing pain – one of music's most well-established therapeutic effects – the release of endogenous opioids is perceived as pleasurable and relaxing and helps alleviate anxiety and stress.[43] Importantly, synchronizing movements together to a beat makes people more likely to cooperate with each other afterwards. They then behave more fairly and peacefully towards one another,

---

[42] Tarr, B., Launay, J., and Dunbar, R. I. (2014). Music and social bonding: 'Self–other' merging and neurohormonal mechanisms. *Frontiers in Psychology*, 5, 1096.

[43] Werner, L. M., Skouras, S., Bechtold, L., Pallesen, S., and Koelsch, S. (2023). Sensorimotor synchronization to music reduces pain. *PLoS ONE*, 18(7), e0289302.

exhibit greater trust, and even sacrifice personal advantages for the group's benefit.[44]

Nonetheless, it is essential to note that synchronizing to the beat of music also predisposes individuals to comply more readily with requests from fellow group members, even if such requests are directed at aggression towards individuals from other groups.[45] This demonstrates that while music possesses significant potential for promoting peace, its effective use ultimately depends on our values.

6. *Cooperation.* When we make music together, we engage in cooperation; otherwise, the music would lack harmony. Cooperation with others is a human need and stimulates neuronal activity in the brain's 'fun motor' (the nucleus accumbens).[46] Furthermore, people who have cooperated once are more likely to cooperate with each other again in future encounters. In evolutionary terms, cooperation, alongside mutation and selection, is a fundamental principle of human evolution.[47] Promoting cooperation through music was, therefore, evolutionarily adaptive, meaning it was beneficial for the survival of humankind. When members of a tribe, or even different tribes, played music together, they subsequently behaved more cooperatively and peacefully.

7. *Social cohesion.* Participation in the aforementioned social functions leads to stronger social cohesion – a reinforced social bond. As a result, group members experience heightened unity, deeper connections, increased willingness to offer assistance, and fortified trust among each other. Members can also trust that this prosocial behaviour will continue and that they will be included in future social

---

[44] Wiltermuth, S. S., and Heath, C. (2009). Synchrony and cooperation. *Psychological Science*, 20(1), 1–5; Launay, J., Dean, R. T., and Bailes, F. (2013). Synchronization can influence trust following virtual interaction. *Experimental Psychology*, 60(1), 53–63.

[45] Wiltermuth, S. S. (2012). Synchronous activity boosts compliance with requests to aggress. *Journal of Experimental Social Psychology*, 48(1), 453–456.

[46] Rilling, J. K., Gutman, D. A., Zeh, T. R., Pagnoni, G., Berns, G. S., and Kilts, C. D. (2002). A neural basis for social cooperation. *Neuron*, 35(2), 395–405.

[47] Nowak, M. A. (2006). Five rules for the evolution of cooperation. *Science*, 314(5805), 1560–1563.

activities. For instance, when a parent sings to a child, the child trusts that the parent will continue to provide care and support.

Engaging in these social functions satisfies a fundamental human need, bringing us pleasure, happiness, and a sense of deep fulfilment. This is why participation is so beneficial for our health, while exclusion from such activities can lead to unhappiness and illness. When we partake in these communal activities, certain moments may evoke powerful emotional experiences that one could describe as *spiritual*. 'Spiritual' here refers to a sense of harmony – neither religious nor esoteric, but the experience of being part of a larger, meaningful whole that transcends our understanding (some religions refer to this as 'God'). We find a sense of purpose and fulfilment when we engage as parts of this greater whole in ways that bring happiness to ourselves and others. In such transcendent moments, our mundane concerns appear to shrink into insignificance. We feel *Good Vibrations* resonating within ourselves, in connection with others, and perhaps even with the universe at large. These vibrations can have a healing effect, but only if we treat ourselves and others *humanely* – with respect, peacefulness, friendship, compassion, and warm-heartedness towards *every* human being.

For the sake of our health or recovery, it is essential that we uphold the dignity and human rights of *every* individual. We damage our mental well-being when we place ourselves above or below others in terms of our value as human beings. Making music together on this foundation helps each participant experience and strengthen their sense of dignity and worth. Experiencing this while singing together *is* already an important outcome – the quality of the performance is secondary in this context. That is why participating in music making or dancing can support the health of *all* individuals – including those who may not consider themselves as musical.

> **PARTICIPATING IN MUSICAL ACTIVITIES**
>
> Consider immersing yourself in musical activities alongside others in diverse formats. This can include singing in a choir, dancing, playing chamber music, performing in an orchestra, joining a band, or

finding others to attend concerts with. Dust off your old instrument and start playing again, begin learning a new instrument, or sign up for a dance course. This is particularly important for older individuals who live alone, as it greatly contributes to their health and well-being. (Remember, even the companionship of a pet cannot replace the experience of a choir.)

CHAPTER 6

Dance of the Hormones to the Beat of the Music

THE ACTIVITY OF OUR INTERNAL ORGANS IS incessantly coordinated and regulated by our brain. When we engage in physical activity, our heartbeat and breathing rates increase, intestinal activity decreases, sweat production rises, and blood pressure adjusts accordingly. Conversely, when we lie down and relax, we switch to 'recovery mode', allowing for regeneration. Under normal circumstances, the body maintains an optimal balance within its internal environment. In situations of physical or psychological stress (such as extreme cold, heat, or danger), our organ capacities are pushed to their limits to maximize our chances of survival.

Fortunately, we are relieved of the need to consciously govern these processes as they fall under the automatic regulation of two systems: the *autonomic nervous system* and the hormonal system, also known as the *endocrine system*. Both systems work closely together and influence the activity of organs and glands in the body. They also collaborate with the immune system. In the case of inflammation, the brain registers messenger substances from the immune system and triggers autonomic and hormonal responses such as sweating, fever, fatigue, a need for rest, and difficulties with attention and concentration.

Each emotion manifests effects upon the body, signifying that any emotional experience is accompanied by vegetative and even hormonal changes. Consequently, emotions also impact the immune system; these effects might be minimal in the case of mild, short-lived emotions but become significant when negative emotions frequently recur or when experiencing prolonged negative moods.

This implies that when music evokes emotions, it instigates changes within the vegetative, hormonal, and immune systems – in addition to alterations in brain neurotransmitter systems. These alterations form the biological basis of music's healing effects. Positive emotions support regeneration and healing, while persistent stress negatively affects immune functions and leads to illness. Naturally, this pertains to both healthy individuals and patients grappling with psychological or physical challenges. Every occasion of laughter or rejoicing ignites a biochemical fireworks display, benefiting our health. Music has the ability to evoke positive emotions, positively influence our moods, help us relax, and cope with stress – thus bolstering our healing powers.

AUTONOMIC NERVOUS SYSTEM

The autonomic nervous system, also known as the *vegetative nervous system*, regulates processes in our bodies. We cannot directly control these processes at will – for example, we cannot stop or speed up our heartbeat. However, we can voluntarily calm ourselves down ('take a deep breath, relax, let it flow'), which can slow down our heart rate.

The autonomic nervous system consists of two branches that maintain nerve connections to all of our organs: the *sympathetic* and *parasympathetic nervous systems* (see Figure 6.1). The sympathetic nervous system orchestrates the rapid activation of organs, acting as a nervous accelerator pedal. Stimulation of sympathetic nerves leads to an increase in heart rate and beat volume, perspiration, and a decrease in bowel movements. Conversely, the parasympathetic nervous system organizes deactivation, relaxation, and regeneration, acting as a nervous brake. Excitation of parasympathetic nerves leads to a decrease in heart rate, an increase in intestinal movements, and relaxation of the urethral sphincter.

In response to stress, the sympathetic nervous system organizes activation, releasing energy for actions such as fleeing or fighting. Conversely, the parasympathetic nervous system handles deactivation, with extreme fear even leading to freezing. During intense stress, the brain cannot simply lift its foot off the accelerator or brake pedal. Instead, in extreme situations, the opposing branch of the autonomic nervous system must counteract: if the sympathetic accelerator pedal is pushed to the limit, as in the case of intense worry, overagitation, or panic, the parasympathetic nervous system must simultaneously apply

DANCE OF THE HORMONES TO THE BEAT OF THE MUSIC

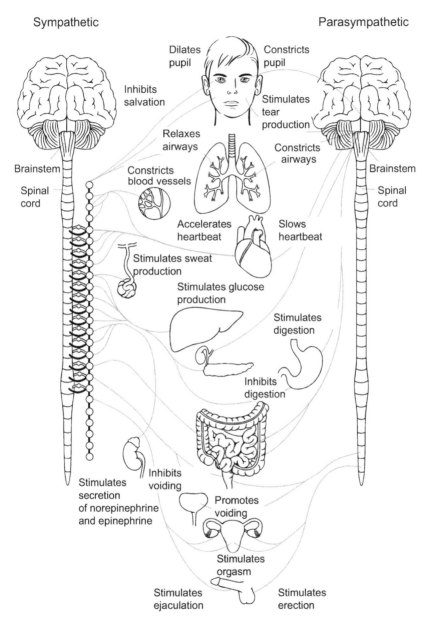

Figure 6.1 The autonomic nervous system, consisting of the sympathetic branch (the 'accelerator pedal') and the parasympathetic branch (the 'brake pedal'). Music can influence the activity of the autonomic nervous system and, consequently, the activity of various body organs. Source: Olga Koelsch

the brake to restrain sympathetic effects, preventing the metaphorical fuses from blowing and keeping the heartbeat in check. On the other hand, if the parasympathetic brake pedal is fully engaged, such as during mortal fear, the sympathetic nervous system must simultaneously step on the accelerator pedal to ensure the heart continues to beat and the individual does not suffocate. Clearly, such states are not conducive to good health.

Incidentally, both the heart and the intestines possess their own independent nervous systems, comprised of numerous clusters of nerve cells, also known as 'ganglia'. In the intestines, these ganglia regulate peristalsis – the contraction of individual sections of the intestine to move its contents along. In the heart, such ganglia organize the contraction of heart muscles to pump blood through the ventricles. The *enteric nervous system* in the gut is occasionally considered a third component of the autonomic nervous system, alongside its sympathetic and parasympathetic counterparts. However, if we were to adopt this view, we would also need to recognize the 'cardiac nervous system' as another part of the autonomic nervous system. Furthermore, calling the enteric nervous system the 'little brain in the gut' can be misleading, as it might suggest that it generates intuitions, performs cognitive processes, or even possesses consciousness. If we were to refer to a 'brain in the gut', we would then also have to acknowledge a 'brain in the heart' – and wouldn't that be painfully unromantic?

The intestinal and cardiac nervous systems interact with the autonomic and hormonal systems, which in turn interact with the immune system. As a result, psychological stress or negative emotions, which invariably involve the autonomic and hormonal systems, can cause dysregulation of activity within the gut or the heart, and, consequently, diseases of these organs. Fortunately, because of these interactions, it is also possible to positively influence intestinal and cardiac diseases through psychological processes – particularly by promoting positive emotions and moods.

Given that every emotion involves some level of activity within the autonomic nervous system, this system's functioning can be influenced by emotions elicited by music. In a 2015 review paper, Lutz Jäncke and I analysed available studies on the impact of music on the autonomic nervous system. Despite the limited number of high-quality investigations on this subject, we determined that heart rate and breathing rate increase with stimulating music, while they decrease with slow and calming music.[1] Furthermore, calming music can help reduce blood pressure. Such effects are fundamental to the therapeutic benefits of music.

> **A GLIMPSE INTO THE LABORATORY: EXPLORING THE EFFECTS OF MUSIC ON HEART RATE, RESPIRATORY RATE, AND PERSPIRATION**
>
> In a series of experiments, my research group studied the impact of music on autonomic activity.[2] To do this, we measured the heart rate using electrodes, similar to a normal electrocardiogram. From the heart recordings, we also computed the breathing rate. Additionally, we attached electrodes to the palms of participants to measure their level of sweat production, which varies with emotional arousal.
>
> In one experiment, participants listened to cheerful, pleasant-sounding music from various eras and styles, including classical pieces by Vivaldi and Bach, 'Take Five' by Dave Brubeck, or a stomp by Louis Armstrong. As comparative stimuli, they also heard simple tone sequences of ascending semitones or distorted, unpleasant music-like noises. All stimuli had the same tempo, which allowed us to examine whether pleasant or unpleasant music resulted in different heart rate responses.
>
> After a period of two and a half seconds, we observed that pleasant music induced slightly more perspiration in the participants than did the unpleasant music. Within a span of six seconds, the heartbeat of the participants increased by approximately two beats per minute.

---

[1] Koelsch, S., and Jäncke, L. (2015). Music and the heart. *European Heart Journal*, 36(44), 3043–3049.

[2] Krabs, R. U., Enk, R., Teich, N., and Koelsch, S. (2015). Autonomic effects of music in health and Crohn's disease: The impact of isochronicity, emotional valence, and tempo. *PLoS ONE*, 10(5), e0126224; Orini, M., Bailón, R., Enk, R., Koelsch, S., Mainardi, L., and Laguna, P. (2010). A method for continuously assessing the autonomic response to music-induced emotions through HRV analysis. *Medical & Biological Engineering & Computing*, 48(5), 423–433.

Furthermore, after ten seconds had passed, we noted an acceleration in the breathing rates of the participants. Thus, music automatically elicits a chain of physiological reactions. Interestingly, the heart rate also rose with simple tone sequences consisting of semitone steps. This finding suggests that as soon as we hear a beat at a tempo noticeably faster than our resting pulse, our heart rate marginally increases (compared to a relaxed resting pulse).

Altering the tempo of the musical stimuli to be either slightly faster or slower did not lead to a significant change in heart rate. This result indicates that the heart rate does not simply follow a music's beat. Thus, fortunately, from a cardiological standpoint, listening to music appears to be harmless.

HORMONES

Autonomic responses can trigger significant changes in target organs within mere milliseconds due to their transmission via rapid nerve pathways. Conversely, hormones, travelling through the bloodstream, take longer to influence their target organs or tissues. The pituitary gland in the brain plays a crucial role in releasing hormones into the bloodstream. The hypothalamus regulates the release of hormones from the pituitary gland. It also coordinates hormone secretion with the autonomic nervous system located in the brainstem.

Some hormones trigger activity within the hypothalamic–pituitary–adrenal (HPA) axis, leading to the release of cortisol from the adrenal cortex. Cortisol, often referred to as a 'stress hormone', is more accurately described as an 'energy-releasing' or 'stress-sensitive' hormone. This is because its release occurs not only during stressful situations but also under non-stressful conditions. One of cortisol's primary roles is to promote the release of glucose, increasing available energy in the bloodstream. For example, cortisol levels naturally rise in the morning, even before we wake up, providing renewed energy to start the day. These levels continue to increase when we experience stress, such as during an uneasy day at work. For individuals who are chronically stressed and need relaxation or sleep, reducing cortisol levels is essential. Cortisol also plays a role in overall health by interacting with various molecules in the bloodstream, including those of the immune system. Therefore, appropriate cortisol levels are crucial for overall health.

A true 'stress hormone' is noradrenaline, also known as norepinephrine. It is released prominently during instances of intense, short-term distress. Among its various effects, noradrenaline constricts blood vessels, leading to an increase in blood pressure. This elevated pressure makes the pumping of blood more strenuous for the heart. As a response, adrenaline is concurrently released, which elevates the heart rate to meet the body's increased demands.

Contrary to the common misconception that cortisol and adrenaline are strictly 'stress hormones', it's crucial to understand that not all stress is detrimental. Certainly, strong negative stressors such as looming threats, persistent conflicts, or witnessing violence can have harmful effects. Such *unhealthy stress*, particularly when chronic, can place a substantial psychological and physical burden on an individual. This distress can lead to harmful hormonal changes and weaken the immune system, with persistently elevated cortisol levels contributing to a decrease in the immune system's activity.

However, there also exists *healthy stress*, which arises from enjoyable, stimulating activities such as sports, dancing, playing music, or even taking a cold shower (best starting from the extremities and progressing towards the torso). Such eustress usually lasts from a few moments to several hours. It involves minimal mental strain and can even be perceived as a positive experience. The stress response under these conditions is quick to initiate and rapidly subsides once the stressor is removed, generally having a fortifying effect on the immune system. Recognizing the difference between *healthy eustress* and *unhealthy stress* is a key aspect of maintaining overall well-being.

Research into the effects of music on the endocrine system has predominantly focused on its influence on cortisol. In a review that my colleague Thomas Stegemann and I conducted a few years ago, we analysed nearly sixty studies examining the impact of music on cortisol levels.[3]

---

[3] Koelsch, S., and Stegemann, T. (2012). The brain and positive biological effects in healthy and clinical populations. In MacDonald, R., Kreutz, G., and Mitchell, L. (eds). *Music, Health, and Wellbeing* (pp. 436–456). Oxford, Oxford University Press.

Our findings showed that relaxing music tends to decrease cortisol levels, while activating, energizing music tends to increase them – often in conjunction with physical activities such as dancing or singing. Notably, both the decrease and the increase in cortisol levels can be beneficial to health. For example, lying down with relaxing music for half an hour, which decreases cortisol, can be as healthful as dancing or playing music for a while, which increases cortisol. Therefore, an increase in cortisol is not inherently detrimental unless it is associated with frequently recurring emotions of distress, such as anxiety, anger, or hostility.

Music's effects extend beyond cortisol, influencing other hormones such as adrenaline and noradrenaline, which modulate stress responses, as well as oxytocin and prolactin, associated with social bonding. However, only a few studies have investigated these and other hormones, making it necessary to await the results of further research before we can draw definitive conclusions.

In addition to studies measuring hormones, we have also used functional MRI (fMRI) to examine music's effects on neural activity in the hypothalamus, the brain's hormonal control centre. In one experiment, participants listened to either joyful-sounding music, such as Irish folk or upbeat rhythm and blues, or frightening music typical of horror films.[4] When the music evoked feelings of joy, the neural communication between the hypothalamus and several other brain structures increased, compared to instances when the music induced feelings of fear. This finding suggests that even a few minutes of listening to music can influence activity in the hypothalamus, potentially reducing the production of hormones associated with distress.

THE IMMUNE SYSTEM

Emotions always affect the immune system. Hence, both positive and negative stress invariably exert an impact on this system. In music-related studies, immunoglobulin A – an antibody produced by white blood cells

---

[4] Koelsch, S., and Skouras, S. (2014). Functional centrality of amygdala, striatum and hypothalamus in a 'small-world' network underlying joy: An fMRI study with music. *Human Brain Mapping*, 35(7), 3485–3498.

known as 'leukocytes' – often serves as a parameter for immune responses. Immunoglobulin A levels can be easily assessed in saliva. In the aforementioned review conducted by Thomas Stegemann and I, we discussed thirteen studies, of which ten reported an increase in immunoglobulin A when participants were engaged in creating or listening to music. However, only a handful of these studies adhered to rigorous methodologies, including the incorporation of control conditions. A notable exception was research led by musicologist Gunter Kreutz, which found elevated immunoglobulin A levels in choir singers as compared to those who merely listened to choir performances. This study and four others also observed a positive increase in participants' mood. Therefore, when musical experiences foster a positive mood or even mitigate distress, they positively influence the immune system, manifesting as increased antibody levels in the blood. This effect appears to be stronger when making music, but is also present when listening to music.

> **A GLIMPSE INTO THE LABORATORY: EFFECTS OF MUSIC ON HORMONAL AND IMMUNE RESPONSES**
>
> In a collaborative study, my research team and Ulrich Sack's immunological research group investigated the effects of music on stress reduction.[5] At the beginning of the experiment, each participant inhaled a gas mixture with a relatively high concentration of carbon dioxide, inducing a noticeable physical stress reaction. One participant exclaimed after inhaling, 'Wow, it feels like someone hit you over the head with a frying pan.' Another, apparently familiar with the drug scene, enthusiastically enquired about the substance and expressed surprise that it hadn't gained popularity yet!
>
> Hormonally, this physical stress reaction manifested as a rapid increase in blood noradrenaline levels, followed by a sharp rise in adrenocorticotropin levels. The latter hormone is secreted from the

---

[5] Koelsch, S., Boehlig, A., Hohenadel, M., Nitsche, I., Bauer, K., & Sack, U. (2016). The impact of acute stress on hormones and cytokines, and how their recovery is affected by music-evoked positive mood. *Scientific Reports*, 6, 23008.

pituitary gland and stimulates cortisol release in the adrenal cortex. Subsequently, cortisol levels also increased, albeit at a slower pace, reaching their maximum concentration in the blood after fifteen minutes.

Shortly after the stress test, half of the participants listened to pleasantly cheerful music for an hour, while the other half listened to a neutral control stimulus comprising sound sequences that were perceived as neither pleasant nor unpleasant. Within minutes, the cortisol levels in the music group surpassed those in the control group, a difference that persisted throughout the duration of the experiment. The difference was especially pronounced in individuals who experienced a boost in positive mood during the experiment, which primarily included participants from the music group (but also a few from the control group). This finding demonstrates that a positive mood promotes a 'healthier' response to short-term stress, as cortisol levels adequately rise to provide the necessary energy for coping with a stressor.

In addition to hormones, we also measured the immune signalling molecule interleukin-6 (a 'cytokine'). Its concentration in the blood significantly increased one hour after the stress test. However, this increase did not (yet) differ between the groups. In my forthcoming research, I aim to determine the timeframe needed for the beneficial effects of music on the immune system to become evident.

CHAPTER 7

Music versus Obstructing Our Natural Healing Powers

PLACEBO EFFECTS

OUR BODIES HARBOUR A POTENT NATURAL ABILITY for self-healing. This self-healing capacity is evident in the *placebo effect*. A placebo is a tablet or other treatment that patients believe to be a genuine medication or procedure, even though it lacks any active ingredients or offers no genuine medical intervention. Placebos can also include sham treatments, such as fake surgeries. The placebo effect, then, is the positive impact on health that occurs without any real medical or pharmacological measures, simply triggered by the belief in healing and prompting the body to heal itself.

Placebo effects are surprisingly large, so much so that any high-quality medical study includes a placebo group for comparison. When I once mentioned to a pharmacist friend that placebo effects, on average, account for approximately 66 per cent of healing success, she passionately disputed, asserting, 'No, it is only 46 per cent!' The existence of placebo effects and their considerable impact are undisputed, even within the field of pharmacy.

The exact magnitude of placebo effects varies depending on factors such as the illness, the individual, and the treatment. Most studies show that placebo effects account for between 40 and 80 per cent of healing success, with an estimated average of 66 per cent. This highlights that the most potent healing power resides within our own bodies. Contrary to popular belief, doctors and medications do not *heal* the body; instead, they assist in *facilitating* the body's inherent healing process.

Studies have shown that various factors influence the effectiveness of placebos: larger pills work better than smaller ones; multiple pills have a greater effect than just one; placebo injections are more effective than placebo pills; and placebos administered by a doctor work better than those dispensed by a machine. For sedation, blue pills are more effective than red ones, while red pills provide more stimulation than blue ones. Interestingly, placebos retain some level of effectiveness even when patients knowingly take them, although to a lesser degree than 'genuine' placebos.[1]

Placebo effects have been convincingly demonstrated for various conditions, including chronic pain, migraines, Parkinson's disease, osteoarthritis, restless legs syndrome, and depression.[2] One of the most striking examples of the placebo effect was reported in a study of osteoarthritis patients who underwent sham knee surgery. Doctors made incisions around the knee, sprayed salt water, and then stitched the incisions back up without performing any actual therapeutic intervention. Remarkably, the results of the placebo surgery were just as good as those of the real knee surgery.[3] While these results cannot be generalized to all types of surgeries, similar findings have emerged from subsequent research, leading the authors of a highly regarded review paper to conclude that about half of the surgeries in the analysed studies were pointless because they were no more effective than placebo surgeries.[4]

Given that placebo effects are often substantial and pharmacological substances sometimes provide little additional benefit (and can even

---

[1] Kam-Hansen, S., Jakubowski, M., Kelley, J. M., Kirsch, I., Hoaglin, D. C., Kaptchuk, T. J., and Burstein, R. (2014). Altered placebo and drug labelling changes the outcome of episodic migraine attacks. *Science Translational Medicine*, 6(218), 218ra5.

[2] Price, D. D., Finniss, D. G., and Benedetti, F. (2008). A comprehensive review of the placebo effect: Recent advances and current thought. *Annual Review of Psychology*, 59, 565–590.

[3] Moseley, J. B., O'Malley, K., Petersen, N. J., Menke, T. J., Brody, B. A., Kuykendall, D. H., Hollingsworth, J. C., Ashton, C. M., and Wray, N. P. (2002). A controlled trial of arthroscopic surgery for osteoarthritis of the knee. *New England Journal of Medicine*, 347(2), 81–88.

[4] Wartolowska, K., Judge, A., Hopewell, S., Collins, G. S., Dean, B. J., Rombach, I., Brindley, D., Savulescu, J., Beard, D. J., and Carr, A. J. (2014). Use of placebo controls in the evaluation of surgery: Systematic review. *BMJ*, 348, g3253.

have harmful side effects, especially with psychotropic drugs), it has been suggested for some conditions, such as depression, that it might be better to administer placebos rather than pharmaceuticals right away.[5]

The placebo effect does not mean we merely imagine illnesses; rather, it demonstrates the remarkable self-healing capacity of our bodies. Various factors can promote healing, such as positive emotions arising from support and care or from faith, hope, and confidence in our recovery. Music can serve as a catalyst for harnessing this intrinsic power by evoking positive emotions such as encouragement, hope, and joy. These regenerative effects are conducive to healing processes, while negative emotions are detrimental to our health.

The brain can *learn* to associate certain experiences, such as taking medicine (even a placebo), with feeling better, enhancing the effectiveness of the placebo over time. For instance, if a child is given chicken soup for a cold or flu and the brain forms a connection between the soup and recovery, the healing effect of the soup strengthens, even if some of the effect is 'only' in the brain. We can employ music in a similar fashion: listening to a particular musical piece every time we recover from an ailment can enhance our propensity for future healing.

It should be noted that the placebo effect can significantly bolster the perceived effectiveness of any therapy, no matter how esoteric (e.g. past life regression, crystal healing, astrology, pilgrimages, or water from the spring of Lourdes). The occurrence of healing *during* a course of therapy does not necessarily imply that the therapy itself was the *cause* of that healing.

NOCEBO EFFECTS

Unfortunately, the placebo effect has a dark counterpart: the *nocebo effect*. When we read the long list of potential negative side effects on a medication's package insert, we might begin experiencing some of those effects before even taking the medication. The nocebo effect also manifests when heightened *expectations* of pain, similar to a self-fulfilling prophecy, directly result in increased worry, anxiety, and pain.

---

[5] Kirsch, I. (2014). Antidepressants and the placebo effect. *Journal of Psychology*, 222(3), 128.

Nocebo effects are comparable in magnitude to placebo effects, meaning that our beliefs can make us sick or even prove fatal. Walter Cannon, a Harvard physiologist and renowned emotion researcher, detailed numerous cases in his 1942 anthropological paper '"Voodoo" death', illustrating how deeply beliefs of being cursed can impact physical health.[6] In one instance, a man from a Congolese tribe discovered that years earlier, he had inadvertently consumed a chicken, which was considered absolutely taboo. Overwhelmed with panic, he began to tremble, and tragically passed away the following day. Fear, anxiety, and the belief in imminent death can quickly debilitate the body to the point of severe illness or death.[7] This phenomenon, colloquially termed 'give-up-itis', is a universal occurrence, noted among diverse cultures as well as in historical and more recent contexts, including prisoners of war and concentration camp inmates.[8]

Indeed, perseverance can be a transformative factor. In the context of patient care, nocebo effects and 'give-up-itis' are highly relevant because negative prognoses from doctors and the associated bad expectations or hopelessness in patients can become self-fulfilling prophecies. Conversely, when a doctor treats a patient with kindness, reassurance, and encouragement, instilling positive expectations and describing the therapy as effective, safe, and beneficial, the success of the treatment is greater – patients recover faster or live longer.[9]

USING MUSIC TO FACILITATE NATURAL HEALING PROCESSES

Placebo and nocebo effects stem from beliefs, expectations, and the emotions or moods they generate. Beliefs trigger processes in the brain

---

[6] Cannon, W. B. (1942). 'Voodoo' death. *American Anthropologist*, 44(2), 169–181.

[7] While Cannon's observations provide crucial insight into the power of belief over physical health, it is important to view such historical research within its time, acknowledging the evolution of ethical standards and cultural sensitivities in anthropological studies.

[8] Leach, J. (2018). 'Give-up-itis' revisited: Neuropathology of extremis. *Medical Hypotheses*, 120, 14–21.

[9] Di Blasi, Z., Harkness, E., Ernst, E., Georgiou, A., and Kleijnen, J. (2001). Influence of context effects on health outcomes: A systematic review. *The Lancet*, 357(9258), 757–762; Stewart, M. A. (1995). Effective physician–patient communication and health outcomes: A review. *CMAJ: Canadian Medical Association Journal*, 152(9), 1423.

that can contribute to our health or illness. This is where music comes into play, as it can influence emotions, moods, and even thoughts. By using music, we can affect various brain activities in a way that supports our body's natural self-healing processes. Even if music does not provide immediate and complete relaxation or the desired happiness during challenging situations or crises, its influences on our brain chemistry and body are nonetheless beneficial. Even the darkest crisis cannot prevent encouraging-sounding music from triggering the release of at least one molecule of a mood-enhancing neurotransmitter. And once one such molecule is released, a thousand more will readily follow.

Such neurotransmitter release has effects on the autonomic nervous system, hormone release, and, in turn, the activity of bodily organs and the immune system. As seen in the placebo effect, our bodies possess a powerful innate inclination – a robust physiological drive – to heal. We can support our body's healing powers by believing in its unwavering will to heal, rather than obstructing these capacities with negative thoughts or emotions and other unhealthy lifestyle habits.

Negative thoughts and related emotions, such as worry, fear, anger, or hostility, can weigh us down and cause distress. As we suffer from these negative feelings, our body's healing powers are compromised. The same is true for negative stress, which may arise, for example, from workplace demands, personal issues, or excessive expectations from others or ourselves. When we are burdened by negative thoughts or stress, other factors often contribute to hindering regeneration, such as lack of exercise, social isolation, sleep deprivation, and substance abuse.

Right nutrition is also important for our health; this was recognized in both Western and Asian medicine thousands of years ago. In addition, we need physical exercise. The World Health Organization recommends 150 to 300 minutes of exercise per week. Positive social contact with other people is also important, because feeling alone and helpless makes us sick. Lastly, we frequently sap our bodies not only through insufficient sleep but also through substance abuse – regrettably, this includes the excessive consumption of sugar, alcohol, and cigarettes. These are all aspects that we can influence ourselves. By taking care to nurture our body's healing abilities, we can enjoy better health, well-being, andlongevity.

This book describes how music can assist us in this endeavour. Through music, we can exert a positive influence on both our emotions and our conscious and subconscious thoughts. This enables us to relax, alleviate stress, and attain inner peace. Furthermore, music can aid in fostering a sense of community with others and serve as a catalyst for motivating ourselves to exercise or to tackle our addictions.

INDIVIDUAL WELL-BEING REQUIRES A HEALTHY SOCIETY

Negative stress diminishes our overall quality of life. Therefore, it is crucial to prioritize stress reduction and the promotion of healthy living conditions, especially in affluent, industrialized nations that have both the means and the responsibility to do so. For instance, it is illogical that while many individuals endure financial worries, others amass excessive wealth, as this contradicts the fundamental human values of fairness and equality. Similarly, the imbalance of experiencing excessive work stress for some while others remain unemployed is nonsensical.

As a sociologist, I propose that any prosperous country should strive to lead the way by making it a right for every citizen to be needed by the community, including the right to well-compensated employment and a high minimum wage. Would it not be commendable for a nation to lead international rankings in terms of minimum wage? Currently (as of 2024), in many of the top fifty richest nations worldwide, a feasible minimum wage would be around 30 euros per hour, as demonstrated by Scandinavian countries. The resulting costs will be offset in the long run by reduced healthcare expenses, as decreased worries and a sense of purpose promote better health and combat depression. In Germany alone, expenditure on this condition exceeds twenty billion euros annually. Eliminating tax loopholes provides another financial means to combat poverty. In 2016, every fifth person in Germany was affected by poverty or social exclusion, while approximately 10 per cent of the wealthiest Germans owned as much as the remaining 90 per cent.

Conversely, when most individuals experience economic well-being, it leads to an enhanced quality of life for all (one of the main reasons I relocated to Norway). Scandinavian countries finance this approach through comparatively high taxes for high earners. This way, the affluent contribute to a fair society. Sharing and solidarity bring happiness; even the most luxurious car cannot evoke the same sense of fulfilment as helping someone in need.

The reason I am devoting significant attention to this message is that music *alone* cannot lead us to long-term, holistic well-being. Our health relies on living in a society that fosters well-being for everyone, rather than causing harm to ourselves or others. The more individuals unconditionally align their inner attitudes with reason and ethics, the closer we come to building a society that fosters holistic well-being. This attitude is championed by organizations such as the International Humanist and Ethical Union or the European Humanist Federation.

A humanistic attitude encompasses recognizing and upholding human rights for all individuals, respecting the inherent worth of every person as a human being, and not privileging one over another based on factors such as race, gender, wealth, age, religion, or world view. Labelling someone as subhuman, a monster, an idiot, or using any derogatory term signifies a departure from a humanist orientation. A humanist perspective also involves respecting the intrinsic dignity of every human being, *irrespective* of how we evaluate their actions or opinions. It further entails practising fairness towards others and extending help to those in need, regardless of personal sympathies. Finally, this orientation calls for respecting the freedom of each human being, including oneself, without compromising the freedom or dignity of others. Embracing and defending these values epitomizes humanity.

To fully experience the therapeutic effects of music's *Good Vibrations*, it is essential to embrace a humanistic approach towards ourselves and others. Otherwise, we impede our biological healing powers by inciting conflict and stress stemming from judgment, blame, or the need to prove our worth. One fundamental principle of effective psychotherapies for maintaining mental health is accepting ourselves and valuing our dignity *unconditionally*. This includes that we are not ashamed of any aspect of ourselves as *human beings*. If we genuinely desire to act in the best interests of our well-being, this acceptance is imperative. We need not jump through any hoops or meet specific criteria (such as a certain income, social status, partnership, family, physical attractiveness, etc.) to fully accept ourselves. Is not each individual a marvel of nature and fully acceptable as a human being, even if their past *behaviour* has been erroneous, flawed, or harmful? The less we doubt our intrinsic, unconditional value as human beings, the more *Good Vibrations* contribute to our health and well-being.

HOW MUSIC HAS HEALING EFFECTS

Listening to music can have positive effects on health and well-being, and these effects are perhaps even stronger when one engages in music making and dancing. Active engagement in music even contributes to keeping our brains youthful. *Brain age* can be estimated by analysing anatomical MRI scans of the brain. A recent study examined the brain age of three groups: professional musicians, amateur musicians, and non-musicians.[10] The participants' average age was mid-twenties. The average brain age of non-musicians aligned closely with their actual age. In contrast, the brain age of professional musicians was over three years younger than their chronological age. This indicates that engaging in music making helps maintain youthfulness in the brain. The results for amateur musicians were particularly noteworthy: their brain age was found to be four and a half years younger than their chronological age. The rejuvenating effects of music were likely most potent in amateur musicians because they often take a more stress-free approach to music making than professional musicians.

A study led by my research group identified a similar but less pronounced trend: the average brain age of amateur musicians was slightly younger than that of non-musicians – about one year.[11] Interestingly, this study also discovered that individuals who engaged in physical activity had a younger brain age than those who did not (the difference in brain age was more than two years). These findings bolster the notion that dancing, by amalgamating musical engagement and physical activity, is especially beneficial for enhancing overall health.

---

[10] Rogenmoser, L., Kernbach, J., Schlaug, G., and Gaser, C. (2018). Keeping brains young with making music. *Brain Structure and Function*, 223(1), 297–305.

[11] Matziorinis, A. M., Gaser, C., and Koelsch, S. (2023). Is musical engagement enough to keep the brain young? *Brain Structure and Function*, 228(2), 577–588.

One factor that helps keep the brain young is the release of the neurotransmitter dopamine. This neurotransmitter is essential for various brain functions, including sensorimotor activity, learning, memory, and emotions. Furthermore, it safeguards the brain from sclerosis, thereby helping to sustain its youthful state.[12] Therefore, to maintain youthfulness, it is important to keep the brain active and stimulate the dopamine system. Music is an ideal way to achieve this (also see Chapter 8).

SEVEN KEY FACTORS UNDERLYING THE THERAPEUTIC EFFECTS OF MUSIC

Beyond its rejuvenating effects, music stimulates healing, particularly when complemented by a balanced lifestyle that includes physical activity, a balanced diet, and avoidance of negative stress and emotions. The following details seven key factors through which music can aid in healing. (I will provide brief examples of these effects here, with more details presented in Part V.) Although these factors are presented separately, several or even all of them ideally come together when making music or dancing – music can have multidimensional healing effects.

1. *Perception.* Music sharpens the senses. Even preschool children who learn to play an instrument or sing can recognize finer differences in pitch and changes in pitch. This ability also enables them to distinguish similar-sounding syllables (such as 'ga' and 'ba') more precisely.[13] This is important because children with language development disorders often struggle not only with speaking correctly but also with *understanding* speech accurately (for example, for some of them, 'ga' and 'ba' sound the same). Early introduction to learning an instrument might prevent language development disorders in many

---

[12] Seidler, R. D., Bernard, J. A., Burutolu, T. B., Fling, B. W., Gordon, M. T., Gwin, J. T., Kwak, Y., and Lipps, D. B. (2010). Motor control and aging: Links to age-related brain structural, functional, and biochemical effects. *Neuroscience & Biobehavioral Reviews*, 34 (5), 721–733.

[13] Kraus, N., and Strait, D. L. (2015). Emergence of biological markers of musicianship with school-based music instruction. *Annals of the New York Academy of Sciences*, 1337(1), 163–169.

of these children. Addressing these disorders as early as possible is crucial, as they increase the risk of learning and reading problems. It should be noted that children with these ailments are not less intelligent; they struggle to follow the lessons because they have difficulties understanding spoken language. Full participation in class and feeling included are vital for a child's carefree and happy development.

Middle-aged people and older adults also hear better if they have learned an instrument, facilitating the separation of speech from background noise in challenging auditory settings such as traffic or pubs.[14] This is important because understanding others significantly contributes to quality of life.

Similar positive effects of making music or dancing also affect other senses: the sense of movement, the sense of balance, and the sense of touch. Musicians train their body perception through practice, enabling them to detect tensions in their muscles more effectively and relax tense muscles more easily. A finer sense for signals from one's own body makes one more resistant to mental illnesses and disorders, as shown for depression, eating disorders, and addictions.[15]

2. *Attention.* Playing music requires a deliberate focus of attention on sensory perceptions and the execution of movements, often over an extended period. Unlike many stimulus–response video games (which primarily involve eye–hand coordination), making music necessitates a flexible focus on multiple senses and their interplay. For example, when I play the violin, I must shift attention between hearing, the perception of arm and finger movements, and vision for reading the

---

[14] Parbery-Clark, A., Strait, D. L., Anderson, S., Hittner, E., and Kraus, N. (2011). Musical experience and the aging auditory system: Implications for cognitive abilities and hearing speech in noise. *PLoS ONE*, 6(5), e18082; Zendel, B. R., and Alain, C. (2012). Musicians experience less age-related decline in central auditory processing. *Psychology and Aging*, 27(2), 410.

[15] Khalsa, S. S., Adolphs, R., Cameron, O. G., Critchley, H. D., Davenport, P. W., Feinstein, J. S., Feusner, J. D., Garfinkel, S. N., Lane, R. D., Mehling, W. E., and Meuret, A. E. (2017). Interoception and mental health: A roadmap. *Biological Psychiatry: Cognitive Neuroscience and Neuroimaging*, 3(6), 501–513.

next notes. Additionally, when making music with others, it is essential to be attentive to their playing or intentions.

Given that our attentional capacities are limited, focusing attention on music can serve to direct it away from negative thoughts and their associated emotions, thereby reducing their impact and promoting inner peace. Music has a natural capacity to capture attention, making it easy to concentrate on it or engage in music making or dancing. This concentration, similar to meditation, has restorative and healing effects.

Focusing on music can also reduce pain, such as during medical procedures or treatments.[16] For individuals with autism, engaging in music making or dancing can improve attention to socio-emotional cues from others. Likewise, practising focus with music can help adolescents with attention and hyperactivity disorders concentrate and better organize their movements.[17] Finally, for some types of tinnitus, voluntarily directing attention to other stimuli (such as music or conversation) can help the tinnitus sound fade into the background or disappear altogether.

3. *Memory*. Making music activates multiple long-term memories simultaneously. For instance, when I play Bach's 'Chaconne' on my violin, I recall the stored tone and harmony sequences of the piece, the techniques for playing these sequences, the stylistic interpretation of the piece, and the general process of playing the violin. Additionally, I remember past experiences of playing this piece and the people who were present during those events. Practising or performing the piece also means that my brain stores new information in its long-term memory.

Apart from long-term memory, engaging in music also requires short-term memory, where information is temporarily stored to solve a task at hand. Exercising both types of memory helps to maintain or improve their fitness. For Alzheimer's patients who struggle with

---

[16] Werner et al., Sensorimotor synchronization to music reduces pain.

[17] Rickson, D. J. (2006). Instructional and improvisational models of music therapy with adolescents who have attention deficit hyperactivity disorder (ADHD): A comparison of the effects on motor impulsivity. *Journal of Music Therapy*, 43(1), 39–62.

memory problems, music can even revive memories that already appeared to be lost.
4. *Intelligence.* The human brain is the most complex, mysterious, and intelligent structure known to us in the universe. Since everyone has a brain, everyone possesses remarkable intelligence. However, effectively *using* it depends on various factors, such as practice and knowledge. Importantly, intelligence should not be confused with knowledge or education: even educated individuals can exhibit poor judgment, while uneducated people can demonstrate clever thinking.

Examples of intelligent cognitive abilities in humans include drawing logical conclusions and planning ahead. These skills require the ability to hold multiple pieces of information in short-term memory simultaneously and combine them in a way that makes sense – for instance, arranging words or sounds in an order that forms a sentence or melody. Thinking in words or sounds is already an intelligent feat, especially when we express and understand thoughts that are embedded in other thoughts. Consider the sentence 'The boy who kissed the girl plays the cello': although the second half of the sentence says, 'the girl plays the cello', we correctly understand that it is the boy who plays the cello and has kissed the girl. This ability to interpret such embedded constructions showcases the sophisticated cognitive abilities exclusive to humans. No other species can produce or recognize constructions with the same level of complexity that humans can.

In music, we can train ourselves to produce, hear, and understand embedded constructions. For example, in Elton John's 'Goodbye Yellow Brick Road', the harmonies following 'This boy's too young to be singing the' are succeeded by 'blu-uh-hues, ahh-ah-ah-ahh' for five bars in a key different from the original key of the piece. Only in the sixth bar does the piece return to the dominant of the original key, followed by a return to the original key. Thus, the song begins in one key, transitions to a sequence of harmonies that do not belong to that key, and then returns to the original key. The 'blu-uh-hues' part is embedded in a larger harmonic structure.

Every first movement of a sonata or a symphony also follows this principle: the movement begins in one key, transitions to the second theme in another key, enters the development (with passages from several keys), and finally returns to the original key. Often, we encounter multiple embeddings in such movements. Following and understanding these intricate constructions challenge our intelligence. Some musicians can even improvise such embeddings.

For advanced thinking skills, such as applying logic or understanding embeddings, we require attention and a well-functioning short-term memory (also referred to as 'working memory'). In both children and adults, musical abilities are related to auditory working memory skills.[18] This may explain why children learning a musical instrument score slightly better, on average, in intelligence tests. Similarly, cognitive training with music helps seniors maintain their mental acuity, especially if they sing, dance, or play an instrument themselves.

In contrast to intelligence or the use of logic, irrational thoughts often cause distress, particularly when they lead to a downward spiral of negative thoughts. Logical and rational thinking is needed to address these issues, such as mental work to identify the exact problem, determine its causes, and develop strategies for improvement in the future. Music can help in disrupting irrational thought loops through intelligent, conscious thinking (for tips, see Chapter 8).

5. *Sensorimotor function.* 'Sensorimotor' refers to the interplay of motor and sensory functions, particularly the perception of one's own movements and the tension of muscles and tendons. Motor and sensory skills are intrinsically connected, as motor skills always require sensory processing.

Engaging in well-coordinated movements while making music or dancing helps maintain the elasticity and fitness of muscles, joints, tendons, and the nerve cords leading to and from the muscles. (Exceptions occur when musicians or dancers overexert their motor skills, or when excessive stress and psychological pressure lead to motor disorders.) For patients with movement disorders such as those

---

[18] Sallat, S., and Jentschke, S. (2015). Music perception influences language acquisition: Melodic and rhythmic-melodic perception in children with specific language impairment. *Behavioural Neurology*, 2015(1), 606470; Franklin, M. S., Sledge Moore, K., Yip, C. Y., Jonides, J., Rattray, K., and Moher, J. (2008). The effects of musical training on verbal memory. *Psychology of Music*, 36(3), 353–365.

caused by strokes, Parkinson's disease, osteoarthritis, or 'motor aphasia' (where individuals can no longer speak), music making or physiotherapy with music can facilitate the recovery of both gross and fine motor skills.

6. *Emotion.* Positive emotions are beneficial to health – they have regenerative effects and support our body's natural healing abilities. Music can evoke numerous positive emotions, calming us down or invigorating us, encouraging us, moving us, making us feel joyful or even happy.[19] Another positive emotion is the feeling of beauty, which can be readily evoked through music. Beautiful sounds, melodies, or harmonies, and the communal experience of music, all contribute to this sense of beauty. My tip: consciously experience a moment of beauty at least once every day – through music or other arts, in nature or the company of others.

Music can also help to regulate negative emotions and moods. The negative impact of such emotions on health is considerable: they adversely affect blood pressure and heart function (thus increasing the risk of cardiovascular disease), impair regenerative and restorative functions, slow wound healing, weaken the immune system, disrupt sleep, and hinder physiological recovery. Thus, one of music's most crucial therapeutic effects stems from lightening the mood.

As I will show in the next part, music has the potential to influence the activity of all brain structures involved in emotions, as well as the autonomic and hormonal systems, which are closely linked with the immune system. Therefore, music can elicit therapeutic effects in mental health conditions associated with emotions, such as depression, anxiety disorders, phobias, post-traumatic stress disorder, and schizophrenia, as well as in chronic diseases of the immune system and other somatic conditions linked to hormonal and immune dysfunctions, including cancer, cardiovascular diseases, and Type 2 diabetes.

---

[19] Koelsch, S., Offermanns, K., and Franzke, P. (2010). Music in the treatment of affective disorders: An exploratory investigation of a new method for music-therapeutic research. *Music Perception: An Interdisciplinary Journal,* 27(4), 307–316.

7. *Social participation.* Making music together often leads to the formation of a community, and participating in music making allows individuals to become part of that community. We communicate with others, coordinate our movements, and cooperate with each other. This creates sympathy and often fosters social bonding and cohesion. Participating in a community fulfils a basic human need – to belong. Fulfilling this need elicits attachment-related emotions, such as trust, joy, and happiness. Thus, peaceful togetherness through music has regenerative and healing effects. We can see the importance and benefits of participating in a community, as social isolation, exclusion, or marginalization increase the risk of disease and mortality – social isolation and loneliness cause emotional stress, often with painful intensity.

Engaging in communal activities, such as music making, can bolster one's self-confidence. This is the reason why music or music therapy proves beneficial when social separation, experiences of loss, traumas, disorders, and illnesses undermine self-confidence. Many patients experience social isolation due to their illness, often associated with broken partnerships and fractured social networks. Therefore, music therapy places great emphasis on human connection, both with the music therapist and with other patients. The therapist supports the patients, and group participants support one another, empathizing, sympathizing, and giving each other hope. Given its potential to facilitate human connection, music therapy is particularly recommended for addressing social problems.

In summary, music stands as a versatile therapeutic instrument, having multidimensional healing effects through numerous factors. Synergizing music with other healthy lifestyle choices significantly magnifies its healing impact. Supported by our research, we assert that music evolves beyond art, actively enhancing human physiology and psychology. As we turn to 'Cultivating Resilience', we see music as a key architect in shaping life's quality.

CULTIVATING RESILIENCE

We can tap into the therapeutic power of music to bolster our *resilience* – a necessary ingredient in any recipe for long-term health and well-being.

When confronted with highly adverse life events, individuals are at an elevated risk of developing mental health conditions such as post-traumatic stress disorder or depression. Resilience is the ability to recover from such highly challenging events in a healthy manner, without succumbing to long-term mental health conditions. The following key strategies show how we can use music to build and nurture resilience.

- *Regulating negative emotions and fostering positive ones.* The more we divert from dwelling on negative thoughts and emotions, the greater the room we create for positive ones. By utilizing music, we can evoke positive emotions, elevate our spirits, and disrupt negative thought loops by redirecting our focus towards positivity. Positive emotions and moods – such as enjoyment, being moved, happiness, and peacefulness – have regenerative effects and thus support healing processes and overall well-being.

    Tip: savour beauty. Making it a daily habit to embrace beauty and pleasure is crucial for your holistic well-being. Do this even if you think you do not deserve it right now. The practice involves consistently participating in activities that not only bring you joy but also enhance your overall well-being. For the readers of this book, the enjoyment of beautiful music would be a natural choice. Yet, other ways to savour beauty can include indulging in at least one healthy meal each day that delights your palate, or taking a moment to appreciate the beauty of nature or a piece of art.
- *Engaging in healthy nutrition, sleep, and exercise.* Beyond emotional regulation, a healthy lifestyle comprises sufficient quality sleep, balanced nutrition, regular physical activity, social interaction, and steering clear of substance abuse.

    For tips on how to leverage music to cultivate these habits, refer to Chapters 16, 17, and 21.
- *'Love thy neighbour.'* Promoting the resilience of *others* also builds our own inner strength. This encompasses compassion and prosocial behaviour. The goal here is to help others and to evoke positive emotions in other people, even if they are initially unsympathetic to us. Music is especially potent in fostering social cohesion, and we can leverage this attribute to encourage peaceful and prosocial human interaction.

Moreover, aiding others not only strengthens our sense of hope but also affirms the presence of kindness in the world, thereby creating a virtuous cycle of support. It can also offer perspective, making us realize that our challenges may be minor in comparison to those faced by others.

Tip for professional helpers: continual exposure to the suffering of others can lead to emotional exhaustion. This holds especially true when helping others is associated with stressful emotional resonance, rather than compassion. To prevent emotional burnout, it is crucial to approach those suffering and in need of help with a spirit of friendship, care, respect, and warm-heartedness, rather than being stressed by feelings of sorrow, sadness, or anger. It is equally vital to remain mindful of the rate at which you might deplete your own resources. Ensure that you allocate sufficient time to care for yourself, thus avoiding the pitfall of self-sacrifice. Music can be a helpful tool for self-care of professional helpers: psychiatrists, psychologists, and neurologists at Berlin's Charité hospital have founded a 'shrink choir', where they support each other in reducing stress and preventing emotional burnout through singing.

- *Building self-confidence.* This involves having faith in one's personal strengths (without arrogance or vanity), a firm belief in one's inherent dignity and unconditional value, as well as the wholehearted acceptance of oneself as worthy of being loved. The symptoms of low self-confidence include thinking negatively about one's personal abilities, pessimism, indecisiveness, excessive worry or anxiety about forthcoming difficulties, envy of others, feelings of demotivation, passivity rather than activity, difficulty in initiating tasks, and physical symptoms such as a slumped posture and tension.

Tips to build self-confidence: to instil trust in your personal strengths, you first need to identify and appreciate them. Achieving this can be facilitated by writing down seven personal strengths on a piece of paper. Playing positive-sounding music in the background can make this task easier, as the 'cognitive resonance' with the music encourages positive thoughts, including those about one's personal strengths. You can use this list in difficult moments as a reminder of your strengths – I keep such a list in my wallet. Musicians struggling with stage fright might compile a list detailing their specific strengths as a musician, and focus on these strengths rather than their worries and anxiety, before stepping on stage. In addition, individuals who tend towards depression can enhance their list with seven joyful life experiences. If any of these happy memories are associated with a particular piece of music, the title of that music should also be included on the list. Ideally, an electronic copy of the music will be readily accessible, for instance, on a smartphone. In moments of negative mood, consulting this list and listening to the corresponding music can act as a poignant reminder that life also has its positive moments, despite any present adversity.

- *Establishing clear values and goals.* It is important to act in line with one's personal values and goals. This requires an understanding of what one deems important in life, which values guide one's actions, and what one's current short- and long-term goals are. To acquire such an understanding, it is beneficial to have a clear awareness of one's values and goals.

  Tips for identifying personal values and goals: play encouraging music in the background while engaged in this task, as the mental alignment – or 'cognitive resonance' – with this music can facilitate setting adequate goals driven by self-confidence, rather than by risk aversion. Subsequently, it is essential to spend your time on activities that align with your values, and that bring you closer to your goals. These are the activities that are truly important to you, and they include, besides professional pursuits, leisure activities, family, and friends. This also means that you must say 'no' occasionally.

- *Cultivating self-efficacy and taking initiative.* When confronted with a problem, it is crucial to take steps to overcome it, rather than simply enduring the problem and hoping that it will resolve itself or be solved by others. By solving problems, we grow and develop. Life inevitably brings changes and problems, but most can be managed. When faced with negative events, we can acknowledge that while we cannot change the past, we do have control over our actions and emotions, which allows us to adapt to new circumstances. For instance, in the event of loss or trauma, we can intentionally carve out a daily emotional time-out to meditate with music. By focusing on the melody or breathing

MUSIC VERSUS OBSTRUCTING NATURAL HEALING POWERS

based on the pulse of the music, we can regenerate in the absence of negative thought loops or memories.

Tip: a brief manual for problem-solving. Start with selecting music that specifically energizes you and enhances your focus. Leave this music playing softly in the background as you proceed through the problem-solving steps outlined here. The first step is to clearly state the problem. Secondly, brainstorm as many solutions as possible, even those that may seem unrealistic – this will stimulate your creative thinking. Choose one solution and give it a try. If it does not yield satisfactory results, do not give up – return to the first step and try again. Focus on altering your own actions, thoughts, and feelings, rather than attempting to change others. Remember that solving even a single problem is worthwhile, regardless of how many other problems appear to persist. Often, only a few problems are responsible for a significant portion of our difficulties. Therefore, by tackling the most critical issues step by step, we can eliminate a major part of our problems. However, abstain from dwelling on unsolvable challenges. As the German saying goes, '*Der Narr tut, was er nicht lassen kann, der Weise lässt, was er nicht tun kann*' (the fool is ensnared by compulsions he cannot resist, while the wise man abstains from what he knows he cannot achieve).

- *Balancing life's various domains.* Life comprises various important domains. These may include work, family, friends, hobbies, and other interests. Each of them deserves a fair allocation of time and energy. However, be cautious not to put all your eggs in one basket by excessively focusing your time and energy on one single facet, such as your job. Should this particular area falter, it may feel as though your entire world has crumbled, increasing the risk of a severe crisis.

Tip for work-centric individuals: if you realize that you are dedicating over forty-five hours a week solely to work, contemplate the potential benefits of redistributing some of those hours to spend quality time with family, engage with your children, or reconnect with friends from whom you have become distant. Often, music can serve to combine several of these domains, for instance when engaging in music making with family and friends. Remember, your social network plays a significant role in your happiness, and you will need this network to lean on when times get tough.

Thus, personal growth and development reinforce resilience. In turn, resilience facilitates growth. This holds true even amid crises, however painful they may be. We learn some of the most significant life lessons through mistakes, failures, and crises. Cologne has a humorous 'Carnival Law', actually known as 'The Kölsch Consitution', and fittingly for this compendium, one article reads, 'In the end, it has always worked out.'[20] The earlier a person learns not to give up in difficult situations, the better equipped they are for serious crises. Therefore, we should foster behavioural patterns that strengthen resilience already in preschool children, for instance, through kindergarten programmes. This includes lessons on kindness, mutual respect, patience, empathy, helping each other, awareness of one's own body, and understanding one's own feelings as well as those of others. What more potent medium for embracing these virtues than through active engagement in music!

---

[20] Beikircher, K. (2016). *Et kütt wie't kütt: das rheinische Grundgesetz.* Köln, Kiepenheuer & Witsch.

PART THREE

WHAT HAPPENS IN THE BRAIN WHEN MUSIC EVOKES EMOTIONS?

CHAPTER 8

Emotions in the Brain

How Music Truly Affects Us

MORE THAN TWO DECADES AGO, I WAS an aspiring doctoral student at the Max Planck Institute in Leipzig. At that time, no brain-imaging studies were available on music-evoked emotions with functional MRI (fMRI) (the primary brain-scanning technique in many brain research studies). I was eager to initiate such a study. However, when I proposed my experiment to my professors, they questioned its relevance, asking, 'Why would music stimulate any significant emotional structures within the brain? It isn't food, sex, or a predatory animal – it's *only* music.'

I argued that for numerous individuals, including myself, music listening could give rise to profound emotional experiences often accompanied by significant physiological reactions – such as goosebumps, teary eyes, and variable heart rates. The prevailing belief of that era – that music, while enjoyable, did not engage key emotional structures in the brain – has been thoroughly revolutionized over the past two decades. My study became one of those that have been instrumental in this paradigm shift, and it is now among the most frequently cited in the field.[1]

In this chapter, I explore the profound impact of music on all emotional systems within the brain. Understanding this concept is crucial for fully appreciating the therapeutic effects of music. Initially, I describe the brain activity associated with emotions, and elucidate how music can modulate this activity. My explanations draw upon the 'quartet theory

---

[1] Koelsch, S., Fritz, T., von Cramon, D. Y., Müller, K., and Friederici, A. D. (2006). Investigating emotion with music: An fMRI study. *Human Brain Mapping*, 27(3), 239–250.

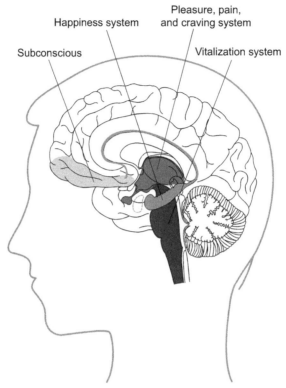

Figure 8.1 The quartet of affect systems. The vitalizing system in the brainstem, the fun, pleasure, and pain system in the diencephalon, the happiness system in the hippocampus formation, and the subconscious in the orbitofrontal cortex. Source: Olga Koelsch

of human emotions', a neurobiological framework that I co-published with my distinguished colleagues at the Free University several years ago.[2] As depicted in Figure 8.1, this model posits four distinct *affect systems* within the brain. In this context, the term *affect* refers to the initial provocation of emotions and moods, while *affect systems* signify the primary biological instigators of these emotions and moods in the brain. Music has the capacity to modulate the activity within each affect system, thereby promoting health and well-being. Thus, it either energizes or

---

[2] Koelsch, S., Jacobs, A. M., Menninghaus, W., Liebal, K., Klann-Delius, G., von Scheve, C., and Gebauer, G. (2015). The quartet theory of human emotions: An integrative and neurofunctional model. *Physics of Life Reviews*, 13, 1–27.

calms us, offers pleasure or alleviates pain, evokes happiness, or inspires optimism amid negative moods.

THE VITALIZATION SYSTEM

Mrs A was in her mid-fifties when she suffered a heart attack. The subsequent cessation of her circulation meant her brain was no longer supplied with oxygen, plunging her into an *unresponsive wakefulness syndrome* (previously known as a vegetative state). Although Mrs A exhibited sleep cycles and kept her eyes open during the day, her gaze was vacant. Doctors diagnosed her as unconscious, immobile of her own volition, and unable to communicate with her surroundings. Her anxiety was palpable; she exhibited excessive salivation and seemed perpetually asleep, even though her eyes were open.

After spending four years in this condition, she was transferred to a hospital in Lower Austria, to a ward where she received dedicated care, including music therapy provided by Astrid Heine, a music therapist at the Krems University of Applied Sciences. In her first music therapy session, Ms Heine sang a song softly while playing her guitar. Mrs A, however, seemed stiff and stressed. Learning from Mrs A's daughter that her mother had once enjoyed singing Austrian folk songs, Ms Heine decided to incorporate these into their sessions. She emphasized the calm, rhythmic elements of these songs and kept conversation to a minimum. This approach appeared to comfort Mrs A, who began breathing more evenly and seemed increasingly relaxed.

Ms Heine conducted three sessions per week with Mrs A, singing songs, speaking gently, and attempting to establish a sensitive and personal connection. After only a few sessions, Mrs A showed astonishing progress. Upon hearing the music, her laboured breathing eased, and her excessive salivation stopped. She began sighing deeply and relaxing noticeably. Video recordings also revealed a profound change: Mrs A was no longer looking past Ms Heine but instead was looking at her.

Mrs A's case serves as a compelling illustration of a phenomenon I have termed the *music reflex*. Music can reflexively invigorate and encourage, or relax and soothe. During this process, it can trigger physical reactions, such as changes in heartbeat and breathing, and it can evoke or synchronize movements. The music reflex is governed by the brainstem (Figure 8.1), the phylogenetically oldest structure of our brain. The brainstem not only regulates vital functions such as heartbeat, blood pressure, respiration, and digestion but also performs several roles that significantly affect our emotional states, particularly in terms of activation and calming. These are intrinsically linked to vitalization (or invigoration) and regeneration (or recovery). Consequently, the brainstem houses a *vitalization system*, effectively acting as a wellness centre in the brain.

The vitalization system modulates activation and calming through the *reticular formation*, a complex network of neurons extending throughout the entire length of the brainstem (Figure 8.2). This network is the core of the vitalization system, and we can refer to it as the brain's courage centre. On one hand, it modulates the activity of higher brain structures through an *ascending system*. On the other hand, it governs the function of organs and various glands outside the nervous system via the *autonomic nervous system*.

Through ascending nerve connections to other parts of the brain, the 'courage centre' regulates the sleep–wake cycle and modulates attention and alertness. A person sleeping can be immediately awakened by sudden loud music. When the courage centre stimulates both the brain and the body, it can engender sensations akin to vitality, manifesting as feelings of being 'fit', 'fresh', 'courageous', or even, at times, 'frightened' and 'panicked'. Conversely, deactivation of this centre can result in sensations such as 'calm' and 'relaxed', or even 'drained', 'tired', and 'sick'.

Music travels from the inner ear into the vitalization system through only one single neuronal connection (Figure 8.2). Acoustic information is transmitted from both the cochlea and the vestibular apparatus, which serves as our balance system. Thus, we 'hear' not only with the cochlea but also with the vestibular organ, as it is sensitive to vibrations and sounds – particularly those of low frequencies, such as bass tones, as well as sudden loud noises, including those produced by percussion instruments.[3] The nerve impulses from the inner ear are conveyed to the courage centre and the autonomic system, activating or deactivating

---

[3] Todd, N. P., Paillard, A. C., Kluk, K., Whittle, E., and Colebatch, J. G. (2014). Vestibular receptors contribute to cortical auditory evoked potentials. *Hearing Research*, 309, 63–74.

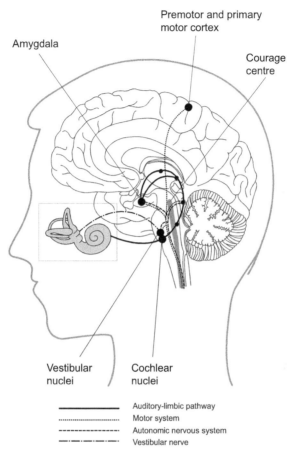

Figure 8.2 The rectangle highlights the inner ear, which comprises the cochlea (auditory cochlea) and the vestibular apparatus (balance organ). The inner ear transmits nerve impulses to the brainstem, specifically the cochlear nucleus and vestibular nucleus. (Note that both left and right ears project into distinct cochlear and vestibular nuclei, which is why the figure uses the plural form.) The cochlear nucleus is the first stop on the 'auditory-limbic pathway' (depicted by a solid line). This pathway serves acoustic perception and initiates emotional processes. Certain stations along this pathway, such as the amygdala, send nerve impulses to the motor system (indicated by a dotted line) and the autonomic nervous system (depicted by a dashed line). The vestibular nucleus also sends impulses to these systems. Moreover, the cochlear nucleus and the vestibular nucleus relay impulses to the 'courage centre' (the reticular formation). These neural pathways enable music to evoke responses in both the viscera and skeletal muscles, and thus to vitalize us, calm us, and aid our regeneration. Source: Olga Koelsch

both the brain and the body. As a result, music can have direct effects on our organs (affecting heartbeat, breathing, etc.) while simultaneously activating and invigorating, or calming and relaxing our minds. Most individuals can identify particular musical genres or pieces that either uplift or soothe them. Personally, the music that most elevates my mood varies; while writing this chapter, it happens to be Bach's cantatas.

Additionally, acoustic information has the capacity to excite skeletal muscles via neural pathways within the brainstem. A powerful musical beat can involuntarily stimulate our skeletal muscles, whereas a sudden loud noise can make us reflexively startle and turn our head – these motor effects are illustrated by the dotted lines in Figure 8.2. This provides further explanation as to why we commonly assert that music 'propels us into motion' or 'infuses rhythm into our limbs'.

> **ENGAGING YOUR 'COURAGE CENTRE' THROUGH MUSIC**
>
> Identify your go-to 'courage songs' – the tracks that invigorate and propel you into action. (For examples, also see Chapter 10.) Keep these courage songs readily available on devices such as your smartphone, laptop, or a CD that's within arm's reach of your stereo.
>
> Play these songs when you find yourself feeling sluggish or dispirited. Increase the volume slightly more than usual, as this will stimulate your vestibular apparatus, thus contributing to your bodily activation. However, avoid excessive volume to prevent potential hearing damage – and to maintain harmony with your neighbours. Implement this strategy especially when you are contending with a lack of motivation or drive, finding it challenging to start a task promptly, or needing a little boost to commence physical exercise. You may also use this method to address tasks that you tend to procrastinate on. Use music not only to uplift your spirit but also to awaken your body by engaging your inner courage centre directly.
>
> If getting up in the morning seems unacceptably arduous, consider using invigorating music regularly to help kick-start your day. Preparing your playlist the night before aids in morning routines and primes your subconscious for an active and productive day.

USING MUSIC FOR PHYSICAL EXERCISE

We can also harness the activating effects of music in sports. Music can be a powerful aid in motivating ourselves to exercise and maintaining perseverance. A review article established that music does even more than simply boost engagement in sports; it also enhances the quality and level of physical activity by elevating physical arousal and positively affecting mood. Interestingly, the authors report that synchronizing movements to the beat of music helps individuals endure longer and train more intensively. Athletes who train with music often exhibit smoother movements, improved balance, and enhanced motor coordination. Synchronizing repetitive movements or movement patterns with music thus significantly enhances endurance, intensity, movement coordination, and movement accuracy.[4]

Music becomes particularly effective against exhaustion when it is produced or influenced by the athletes themselves. Thomas Fritz has developed modified fitness equipment such that exercise movements produce musical sounds, resulting in music that is directly connected to the individual's actions. Individuals utilizing this innovative equipment report decreased levels of fatigue and an elevated pain threshold when compared to those exercising while simply listening to music.[5]

Similarly, singing songs during activities such as marching or working serves as a source of unity and strength, promoting endurance in the face of adversity and hardship. Marching songs have long kept soldiers in step and lifted their spirits, whether on long deployments or in the heat of battle. Shanties, sung by sailors, synchronized the strenuous labour on ships, turning hard work into a collective endeavour.

The brainstem houses movement or rhythm generators, which I refer to as 'puppet neurons'. These puppet neurons take charge of organizing a range of repetitive movements, from walking and running to actions such as sucking and swallowing. When these neurons are activated, the

---

[4] Clark, I. N., Baker, F. A., and Taylor, N. F. (2016). The modulating effects of music listening on health-related exercise and physical activity in adults: A systematic review and narrative synthesis. *Nordic Journal of Music Therapy*, 25(1), 76–104.

[5] Fritz, T. H., Hardikar, S., Demoucron, M., Niessen, M., Demey, M., Giot, O., Li, Y., Haynes, J. D., Villringer, A., and Leman, M. (2013). Musical agency reduces perceived exertion during strenuous physical performance. *Proceedings of the National Academy of Sciences*, 110(44), 17784–17789; Fritz, T. H., Bowling, D. L., Contier, O., Grant, J., Schneider, L., Lederer, A., Höer, F., Busch, E., and Villringer, A. (2018). Musical agency during physical exercise decreases pain. *Frontiers in Psychology*, 8, 2312.

organism performs rhythmic movements in a quasi-puppet-like manner, without the need for continuous movement commands from higher processing centres of the brain. Importantly, these neurons are also connected to the courage centre, allowing them to be set in motion by the beat of music.

This means that music not only aids individuals in finding the courage to exercise and persevere in sports but also has profound effects on various movement patterns. For example, in patients diagnosed with unresponsive wakefulness syndrome, the rhythmic pulse of music is likely to influence breathing and other repetitive motions through the activation of puppet neurons. Likewise, for individuals living with Parkinson's disease, the therapeutic influence of music may aid in restoring their walking abilities upon hearing a rhythmic beat.

Motivate Yourself to Exercise with Music

Every small step is easy, except for the first one. Getting started is often the hardest part, but taking that initial step towards physical activity is crucial for our health. You can make the process easier and more enjoyable by incorporating music into your workout routine.

- *Set the stage for success.* According to the World Health Organization, adults are recommended a minimum of two and a half hours of exercise per week, with the ideal target being five hours. Try incorporating exercise into your regular weekly routine, preferably at consistent times. This allows your body to adapt to a predictable rhythm. Focus on maintaining a consistent duration, while adjusting the intensity of your workouts to match your fitness level.
- *Preparation is key.* Plan in advance when you will start exercising the following day, set aside your sports gear, and select suitable music that is both encouraging and activating. Consider songs such as 'Eye of the Tiger' or choose one of your personal courage songs.
- *Visualize success.* Imagine yourself turning on the music, engaging in your chosen activity, working up a sweat, and persevering throughout your workout. If it helps, imagine yourself with the determination and strength of a tiger.

- *Execute your plan.* On the following day, stick to your plan and start exercising promptly without allowing any delays. Aim to maintain the activity for at least twenty minutes. As for motivation, after this duration, the body starts releasing hormones that aid in reducing body fat. Even if you do not manage to exercise as long as you had planned, acknowledge your exercise time as a success.
- *Synchronize with music.* During your exercise session, sync your movements and breathing with music, either by listening to music or by singing to yourself, even if it's covertly. Remember to exhale longer than you inhale. You may also try imagining that your movements produce the musical beat. Next time, reuse the music that has proven effective in motivating you; this reinforces the neural association between music and exercise.
- *Post-workout wisdom.* Stay hydrated by drinking water or herbal tea instead of sugary beverages, fruit juices, smoothies, or vitamin drinks. Opt for a post-workout meal that is healthy, rich in vitamins, and free from added sugars.

USING MUSIC TO RELAX

In addition to systems within the brainstem that organize stimulation, mechanisms also exist to facilitate relaxation and tranquillity. These mechanisms are especially vital for the regenerative effects of music. A meta-analysis has reported that music can significantly reduce physiological arousal.[6] However, it should be noted that many of the studies included in the analysis combined music with relaxation techniques, making it unclear how much the music specifically contributed to relaxation. Among the relaxation programmes studied, the combination of relaxing music and verbal relaxation instruction proved to be particularly effective. This suggests that music for relaxation can be especially helpful when one focuses on relaxation, similar to a meditation.

---

[6] Pelletier, C. L. (2004). The effect of music on decreasing arousal due to stress: A meta-analysis. *Journal of Music Therapy*, 41(3), 192–214.

Relaxation is crucial for our health because regeneration requires inner peace. Negative emotions and stress hinder the regenerative process. It is important to note that relaxation music does not always have to be slow and deactivating. Its primary purpose is to evoke *Good Vibrations* within our soul and spirit, helping us let go of negative thoughts, brighten our mood, and find inner peace. When music assists us in relaxing and calming down, it has positive effects on the balance of autonomic nervous system activity, hormonal activity, and, ultimately, the immune system. Therefore, music's capacity for calming and relaxation can have a regenerative impact.

Similar to the other three affect systems, the brainstem features antennae that sense both danger and protective signals. These antennae are particularly sensitive to emotional expressions from others, including vocalizations. Music is rich with sounds that resemble such emotional vocalizations. When listening to orchestral music, one can perceive Bach's cheerful exclamations, Beethoven's defiant accents, or Brahms' expressions of bliss and delight. Music can sound like sighing, cheering, crying, or protesting.

The brainstem antennae also register the emotional tone of speech. When someone speaks to us gently and calmly, we feel more comfortable than when they shout at us in anger. When these antennae are activated by music that sounds warm and gentle, it has a calming and relaxing effect. In such a situation, the brainstem initiates regenerative processes and prompts the individual to, for instance, make themselves comfortable. Signals that are classified as threatening or stressful by the brainstem antennae have the opposite effect.

In patients in a vegetative state, intact brainstem functions enable them to respond to threatening stimuli with negative emotions and to positive signals with a sense of calm and relaxation. This phenomenon is similar to that observed in infants, who sense safety and react with fear or panic when they perceive danger, such as feeling abandoned. For them too, a threatening acoustic environment automatically leads to agitation and tension, whereas music can soothe and comfort. Incidentally, the nerve connections from the vestibular apparatus to the brainstem ensure that rocking also induces relaxation. Therefore, for babies, the combination of music and rocking or cradling can have a particularly calming effect.

'MUSITATION': A SIMPLE MUSIC MEDITATION

Put on pleasant, relaxing music, lie down, and close your eyes. The more relaxed and inviting the environment, the better. Wear comfortable clothing or loosen your belt. Turn off your phone, the internet, and so on during this time. First, focus on your breathing. Breathe calmly and evenly. You can exhale either through your nose or your mouth. When exhaling through the mouth, it may help to purse your lips as if to whistle (or even actually whistle while exhaling). However, inhale only through your nose. Breathe out completely (until there is no more air in your stomach), then allow the air to flow into your stomach as you inhale. Imagine your stomach is like a balloon that expands and contracts with each breath – your chest barely moves during natural breathing.

Count the beats of the music while you breathe in and out. Adjust your breaths to match the beat, but feel free to change the length of your breaths as it feels natural. Exhale for longer than you inhale, for example, six beats out and four beats in.

If you feel dizzy or experience a tingly sensation due to the deep breaths, you can pause after exhaling (before you inhale). Do not pause after inhaling; instead, always move directly to exhaling. Proper exhalation will automatically slow and calm your heartbeat, contributing to immediate relaxation.

With each breath, aim to exhale tension and negative emotions and inhale calm, relaxation, and recovery.

Next, mentally scan your extremities, torso, and head, and focus on relaxing each part of your body one by one. Intentionally tense each part slightly (or move, lift, or lower it slightly) to feel how it then relaxes again (this technique is known as 'progressive muscle relaxation'). You can choose the sequence; I recommend starting with your legs or arms (as these are typically easier to relax than your shoulders or neck), moving progressively from upper arms, forearms, palms, fingers, and so on. Do not forget about your eyelids, forehead, and other facial muscles when focusing on the head. Be mindful of your breathing throughout the process.

> It is important to concentrate solely on your relaxation, your breathing, or the music. Do not let your mind wander and do not entertain any negative thoughts. It is normal for thoughts to drift – but as soon as you notice this, gently bring your attention back to your relaxation, your breathing, or the music. If you feel deeply relaxed and wish to prolong the exercise, feel free to imagine positive, relaxing places (such as a sunny spot on a beach) or happy situations or experiences. Try to practise this form of relaxation daily. Over time, this ability to relax can help you identify and alleviate tension more quickly in your everyday life.

THE PLEASURE, PAIN, AND CRAVING SYSTEM

Joke Bradt, a music therapist based at Drexel University in Philadelphia, specializes in treating chronic pain through music therapy. To this end, she has devised a method wherein a group of patients convenes weekly for an hour-long session. Ten patients sit in a circle. Joke takes to the keyboard, guiding everyone to breathe deeply and calmly, synchronizing their breaths with the music. This enables the patients to concentrate on both the musical experience and their bodily sensations. Then the breathing transitions into relaxed humming along with the music. Afterwards, each person gets a percussion instrument. Joke initiates a short melody that is sung repeatedly, and the patients start to chime in with it. Some play rhythms on drums and rattles. The sound of the singing, the improvisations of some group members, and the rhythm remind me of a lively gospel song or the 'circle songs' of Bobby McFerrin. Joke calls over the song into the circle, and some from the circle call back. Despite the simplicity of the musical material, it evokes goosebumps in me.

What particularly strikes me is a woman who had struggled into the session groaning and leaning on a crutch. She suddenly springs to her feet and begins to sing and dance – leaving her crutch behind. Joke tells me later that this patient has been unable to walk unaided for two years due to debilitating back pain. Now she dances so freely that Joke almost becomes worried. After the session, after the room has been empty for a few minutes, the patient re-enters, exclaiming, 'I forgot my stick!'

Music can evoke feelings of pleasure, enjoyment, and delight, a phenomenon facilitated by a network of structures distributed throughout the brain. The epicentre of this pleasure network resides in the *diencephalon* (refer to Figure 8.1). The primary structures of the diencephalon encompass the thalamus, the hypothalamus, and the pituitary gland. Research utilizing electrical brain stimulation to map areas associated with pleasure has demonstrated that the most potent responses come from specific nuclei within the hypothalamus. For example, some readers may be familiar with self-stimulation experiments where rats incessantly press a lever to administer electrical pulses to their brain's pleasure centre, sometimes to the point of exhaustion or even death. The specific nuclei stimulated in these experiments are also involved in releasing endogenous opioids, including endorphins. These findings allow us to identify the hypothalamus as a key *pleasure centre* of the brain.

In contrast, electrical stimulation of specific nuclei in the thalamus can provoke the most intense pain responses. Therefore, we can identify the thalamus as the centre of the brain's pain network. This means that the diencephalon hosts key structures for both the pleasure and the pain systems. (Only a few nuclei within the thalamus are involved in pain, while others participate in various other functions, including pleasure. Similarly, within the hypothalamus, only certain nuclei are involved in pleasure, while others participate in different functions, including pain and analgesia.)

Beyond generating sensations of pleasure and pain, the diencephalon has multifaceted roles in homeostasis, regulating factors such as body temperature, water–electrolyte balance, appetite, and blood pressure. When we start to feel cold, or experience hunger or thirst, these are indicators that something within the body has become imbalanced. The diencephalon then generates signals akin to pain signals ('hunger hurts'), which motivate us to perform activities that restore this internal balance, such as eating or drinking. We perceive these impulses or urges as intense cravings. When we restore this balance, we experience it as satisfaction, pleasure, and delight.

The diencephalon, therefore, acts as the central hub for a *pleasure, pain, and craving system*. It is important to note that this affect system encompasses numerous additional affective functions. For instance, the hypothalamus also generates defensive, offensive, caring, and sexual behaviour, while the thalamus registers signals of danger or reward, imbuing them with an affective tone. Remarkably, this takes place even before the information reaches the neocortex and enters our conscious perception, indicating that most of the brain's emotional evaluations occur outside our conscious awareness.

Intriguingly, this pleasure, pain, and craving system has notably expanded the capacity for learning through trial and error during the course of evolution. This form of learning hinges on the capacity to judge whether an action yields a 'success' or 'failure' – in essence, attributing a 'score' to each behaviour. The pleasure, pain, and craving system plays a crucial role in this process by generating feelings of pleasure and satisfaction for positive outcomes, and feelings of pain or discomfort for negative outcomes. Therefore, the evolution of the diencephalon above the brainstem not only granted species new homeostatic functions but also bestowed them with additional capabilities, such as advanced types of learning.

GOOSEBUMPS AND THE FUN MOTOR

Pleasure and delight originate from a specific brain system, which I will henceforth refer to as the *pleasure system*. Neuroscientists commonly label this the 'reward system' because it has been extensively studied in the context of various rewards, including food, sex, money, and drugs. Intriguingly, this system can also be activated by music.

The capacity of music to activate the pleasure system was first explored through instances of 'goosebumps', one of the most intense expressions of pleasure or delight. This phenomenon, familiar to many when listening to or playing music, is characterized by a pleasant shiver, the emergence of goosebumps, an increased heart rate, and reduced sweat production.[7] Jaak Panksepp used the term 'skin orgasm' to describe this experience.[8] All kinds of music, from classical to jazz, rock,

---

[7] Grewe, O., Kopiez, R., and Altenmüller, E. (2009). The chill parameter: Goose bumps and shivers as promising measures in emotion research. *Music Perception: An Interdisciplinary Journal*, 27(1), 61–74.

[8] Panksepp, J. (1995). The emotional sources of 'chills' induced by music. *Music Perception: An Interdisciplinary Journal*, 13(2), 171–207.

heavy metal, pop, or techno, can trigger these goosebumps. However, the specific songs that elicit such responses vary from person to person. Sensuous individuals may also experience goosebumps from other intense sensory pleasures, such as savouring a particularly delightful wine, inhaling the aroma of delicious food, or during intimate moments. Interestingly, some people, myself included, can also get goosebumps when we encounter or conceive a particularly compelling idea, helping us to identify such ideas.

There is no need to worry if one has never experienced goosebumps while listening to music. One in ten people has never had such experiences, neither when listening to music nor in other situations, and one in three people only rarely experience goosebumps, even if they enjoy music.[9] Some individuals do not experience particularly strong positive emotions from music at all. This phenomenon is known as 'musical anhedonia'.[10] People with specific musical anhedonia experience normal emotional reactions to stimuli such as food, money, sports, sex, and drugs, whereas music hardly elicits any emotions in them, let alone goosebumps.

Experiences of goosebumps are generated by the brain's pleasure system. This was researched by Anne Blood and Robert Zatorre in one of the first neuroscience studies on music and emotion, published in 2001.[11] They asked each participant to bring in a piece of music that reliably elicited goosebumps for them. Brain activity was then measured using positron emission tomography (PET). Among other findings, the data revealed signal changes in the 'nucleus accumbens' – a structure that is part of the brain's pleasure system (refer to the middle panel of Figure 8.3). I often refer to this structure as the 'fun motor' because it motivates, initiates, and reinforces behaviours that can result in rewards. In the study conducted by Blood and Zatorre, the signal measured in this

---

[9] Panksepp, The emotional sources of 'chills' induced by music.
[10] Mas-Herrero, E., Zatorre, R. J., Rodriguez-Fornells, A., and Marco-Pallarés, J. (2014). Dissociation between musical and monetary reward responses in specific musical anhedonia. *Current Biology*, 24(6), 699–704.
[11] Blood, A. J., and Zatorre, R. J. (2001). Intensely pleasurable responses to music correlate with activity in brain regions implicated in reward and emotion. *Proceedings of the National Academy of Sciences*, 98(20), 11818–11823.

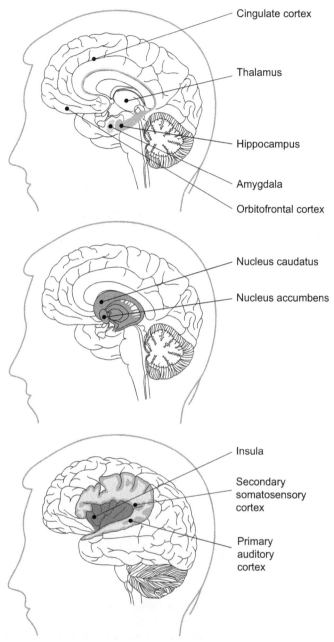

Figure 8.3 Emotional structures in the brain activated by listening to music in various studies. These structures include all components of the pleasure network (also referred to as the 'reward network'), in addition to the anterior hippocampus. The pleasure network overlaps significantly with the pain network: all shown structures, except auditory cortex and

'fun motor' increased in correlation with the intensity of the goosebumps experience.

The activation of the fun motor indicates that music can modulate activity within a significant emotional structure of the brain. The fun motor is sensitive to various 'rewards'. For instance, it gets activated when participants drink water while being extremely thirsty, or consume delicious wine even when not thirsty. It is also triggered when participants receive monetary rewards (e.g. 'You've won ten euros!'), or when a negative consequence is unexpectedly avoided (e.g. 'You don't lose ten euros after all!'). Moreover, the fun motor activates during the consumption of substances such as cocaine or chocolate, as well as during sexual activity (yes, even such experiments are conducted in brain scanners).[12] Therefore, within the fun motor of the brain, they all truly come together: 'Sex, Drugs & Rock 'n' Roll'.

The main fuel for this fun motor is the neurotransmitter dopamine, which is released during instances of pleasure and delight. In another groundbreaking study by Robert Zatorre's research team, they investigated whether music could trigger the release of dopamine into the fun motor.[13] Once again, the participants brought their own pieces of music to the experiment, ones that typically gave them goosebump

---

Figure 8.3 (*cont.*) hippocampus, belong to both networks. Because of this overlap, music can help with pain. Even the nucleus accumbens (the fun motor), which is primarily known for its role in pleasure, is involved in pain, especially in the regulation of analgesic effects. Like the caudate nucleus, the nucleus accumbens is part of the basal ganglia (shown in dark grey in the middle image). The secondary somatosensory cortex is the 'feeling cortex', which is located mainly above the insula (shown in dark grey in the bottom image). The anterior hippocampus (show in the top image) is the centre of the happiness system.
Source: Olga Koelsch

---

[12] Di Chiara, G., Bassareo, V., Fenu, S., De Luca, M. A., Spina, L., Cadoni, C., Acquas, E., Carboni, E., Valentini, V., and Lecca, D. (2004). Dopamine and drug addiction: The nucleus accumbens shell connection. *Neuropharmacology*, 47, 227–241; Holstege, G., Georgiadis, J. R., Paans, A. M., Meiners, L. C., van der Graaf, F. H., and Reinders, A. S. (2003). Brain activation during human male ejaculation. *Journal of Neuroscience*, 23(27), 9185–9193.

[13] Salimpoor, V. N., Benovoy, M., Larcher, K., Dagher, A., and Zatorre, R. J. (2011). Anatomically distinct dopamine release during anticipation and experience of peak emotion to music. *Nature Neuroscience*, 14(2), 257.

experiences. They then underwent a special PET scan that could visualize dopamine availability in the brain. The data showed that the availability of dopamine in the fun motor increased during goosebump experiences.

Several studies have shown that activating the fun motor does not necessarily require the extraordinary sensation of goosebumps. Simply finding music pleasurable is already sufficient. Thus, merely by listening to music we find enjoyable – or engaging in any other pleasurable activity – we can flood certain regions of our brain with dopamine.

Pleasure yields significant therapeutic effects; for instance, the release of dopamine keeps the brain young, counteracting dementia and neurodegeneration.[14] In addition, the release of dopamine during the activation of the fun motor by music suggests that music or music therapy can likely assist patients who have reduced dopamine release. This is pertinent to a range of conditions including depression, post-traumatic stress disorder, substance use disorders, attention deficit hyperactivity disorder, schizophrenia, and Parkinson's disease. Research into the therapeutic use of music in these disorders and diseases, as well as the exploration of the neural basis of such therapeutic effects, remains an important quest for ongoing and future studies.

> **UNLOCKING PLEASURE AND ENJOYMENT WITH MUSIC: SIMPLE STEPS**
>
> Encouraging the release of dopamine in the brain could be as straightforward as listening to enjoyable music, making music, or dancing. These activities help to keep the brain young and counteract dementia and degeneration. One can savour the sound of beautiful music or have fun with cheerful or amusing music by simply listening, tapping along, covertly singing, or even dancing.

---

[14] Seidler, R. D., Bernard, J. A., Burutolu, T. B., Fling, B. W., Gordon, M. T., Gwin, J. T., Kwak, Y., and Lipps, D. B. (2010). Motor control and aging: Links to age-related brain structural, functional, and biochemical effects. *Neuroscience & Biobehavioral Reviews*, 34(5), 721–733.

> If certain pieces of music or videos trigger pleasant goosebumps, consider assembling a 'goosebump vault'. From time to time, select pieces from this vault and savour the thrilling sensation. Sharing the vault with others and asking about their goosebump-triggering music can further enhance the enjoyment of music.

THE PLEASURE NETWORK

Until now, our focus has been primarily on two key regions of the brain: the 'fun motor', also known as the nucleus accumbens, and the 'pleasure centre', or the hypothalamus. These two brain structures communicate through the midbrain, situated in the upper region of the brainstem. The pleasure centre within the hypothalamus transmits signals to the midbrain via a collection of nerves termed the medial forebrain bundle. Subsequently, dopaminergic neurons in the midbrain connect to the fun motor via the mesolimbic pathway. However, besides these structures, the brain's pleasure network also encompasses several other structures located in various parts of the brain.

A few years ago, I discovered that music can activate this entire pleasure network.[15] I made this discovery while computing a meta-analysis on music, emotion, and the brain. This analysis identified brain areas that consistently respond to music across multiple studies. The studies included explored the effects of various musical elements: consonant and dissonant sequences, emotionally cheerful and sad-sounding compositions, tension-inducing and fear-evoking tracks, as well as musical passages that induce goosebump experiences.

Figure 8.3 schematically illustrates the results of this study. We can see here that music can activate the entire reward network. This network includes the following:

- The nucleus accumbens (the fun motor)
- The caudate nucleus (part of the basal ganglia akin to the nucleus accumbens, particularly involved in movements)

---

[15] Koelsch, S. (2014). Brain correlates of music-evoked emotions. *Nature Reviews Neuroscience*, 15(3), 170; Koelsch, S. (2020). A coordinate-based meta-analysis of music-evoked emotions. *NeuroImage*, 223, 117350.

THE BRAIN WHEN MUSIC EVOKES EMOTIONS

- The amygdala (the 'conductor' of the brain's emotional orchestra, with the capacity to initiate, sustain, modulate, and cease emotions)
- The mediodorsal thalamus (part of the diencephalon, i.e. part of the pleasure, pain, and craving system)
- The orbitofrontal cortex (where the subconscious is located)
- The insula (which receives information concerning the body's internal state and, in turn, also regulates it)
- The cingulate cortex, which plays a role in emotions, emotional regulation, and musical memory (it hosts an 'emotion-memory tunnel')
- The secondary somatosensory cortex, which hosts the 'feeling cortex'

Intriguingly, this identical network is stimulated not only by primary rewards, such as food and sex, but also by secondary rewards, including money and power. This clearly indicates that, contrary to the scepticism of my professors at the Max Planck Institute all those years ago, music indeed has the potential to modulate the activity within a fundamental emotion network of the brain.

THE PLEASURE NETWORK OVERLAPS WITH THE PAIN NETWORK

Similar to pleasure, pain does not originate from a solitary pain centre in the brain but from a complex pain network. A noteworthy aspect of this network is its substantial overlap with the pleasure network (refer to Figure 8.3). Both pain and pleasure networks share several identical structures or encompass structures situated close to each other, such as thalamic nuclei for pain or pleasure. Notably, even structures unique to the pain network are susceptible to the influence of music. For instance, the parabrachial nucleus, a component of the pain network in the brainstem, is susceptible to influence from auditory-induced vestibular information.

The significant overlap between the pleasure and pain networks, when combined with music's ability to stimulate the entire pleasure network, contributes to the efficacy of music in pain management. Although George Herbert once said, 'music helps not the toothache',[16] music can indeed alleviate both acute and chronic pain. During medical

---

[16] Sherrin, Oxford Dictionary of Humorous Quotations.

procedures, music can ease severe pain as well as emotional states of anxiety, helplessness, and distress. Several studies show that music during medical procedures lowers both the heart and breathing rates, and results in less release of the stress hormone norepinephrine.[17] Listening to music can not only elevate the pain threshold but also improve overall pain tolerance. Additionally, music can decrease physical restlessness, muscle tension, tremors, and reduce instances of vomiting. It also distracts attention, making it easier to focus on positive thoughts, thus alleviating worries and fears. These effects contribute to a more relaxed interaction between patient and practitioner. Consequently, music is increasingly being incorporated into clinical settings, including during catheter examinations and other procedures involving local anaesthesia, at dental clinics, during childbirth, and during vaccinations.

Remarkably, research has primarily utilized *passive* music listening to investigate the pain-reducing effects of music, finding that such effects are relatively small.[18] However, *active* music listening results in significantly more potent effects. Recent findings from my research group indicate that merely tapping along to the beat while listening to music significantly enhances its pain-reducing effects.[19] One reason for this is that tapping necessitates a stronger focus on the music, leaving fewer resources for attention and thought to be directed towards pain processing. In addition, participants in our experiment reported feeling more pleasant during the trials in which they tapped to the beat, and the subsequent release of pleasure molecules, such as dopamine and endogenous opioids, contributes to pain reduction. Thus, active engagement with music while listening, such as discreetly tapping along to the rhythm, internally singing along, or synchronizing one's breathing with the beat, enhances the pain-reducing effects of music.

The calming effects of music also result in a reduced requirement for anaesthetics among patients. In another study, my research group

---

[17] Spintge, R. (2015). Music medicine interventions in clinical medicine for pain, anxiety and stress. In *Music and Medicine* (pp. 71–83). Vienna, Springer.
[18] Cepeda, M. S., Carr, D. B., Lau, J., and Alvarez, H. (2006). Music for pain relief. *Cochrane Database of Systematic Reviews* (2), 1–45.
[19] Werner, L. M., Skouras, S., Bechtold, L., Pallesen, S., and Koelsch, S. (2023). Sensorimotor synchronization to music reduces pain. *PLoS ONE*, 18(7), e0289302.

measured the consumption of Propofol during knee surgeries under local anaesthesia. We found that when listening to music, a lower dose of Propofol was necessary to achieve a light level of sedation.[20]

For medical practitioners, allowing patients to choose their preferred musical genre can be significantly beneficial. It gives them a sense of control over their environment, rather than leaving them feeling subjected to the choices of their doctor. While it is encouraged for patients to bring their own music, doctors might also consider curating a selection of diverse playlists across various genres – such as rock, pop, classical, jazz, folk, and country. This approach not only empowers patients with the freedom to select their music but also ensures that the music environment is conducive to the well-being and comfort of both patients and healthcare staff. In addition, offering such 'prescribed' playlists can mimic the effect of different 'musical medicines', amplifying placebo effects and thus providing more substantial relief from both pain and psychological stress.

Music has demonstrated particular benefits for children. A meta-analysis demonstrates that they experience diminished levels of pain, fear, and anxiety when exposed to music during medical procedures, including dental visits. Although the reduction in pain was moderate and some studies lacked robustness, the authors considered the findings clinically relevant. This is because reduced fear and anxiety mean less psychological stress for the child, and often a reduced need for pharmaceutical pain relievers.[21]

> **USING MUSIC DURING MEDICAL PROCEDURES**
>
> If you have to undergo a medical procedure, consider bringing music and headphones with you. Of course, ask your doctor in advance, but if the procedure permits, many doctors will gladly approve. Music is

---

[20] Koelsch, S., Fuermetz, J., Sack, U., Bauer, K., Hohenadel, M., Wiegel, M., Kaisers, U. X., and Heinke, W. (2011). Effects of music listening on cortisol levels and Propofol consumption during spinal anesthesia. *Frontiers in Psychology*, 2, 58.

[21] Klassen, J. A., Liang, Y., Tjosvold, L., Klassen, T. P., and Hartling, L. (2008). Music for pain and anxiety in children undergoing medical procedures: A systematic review of randomized controlled trials. *Ambulatory Pediatrics*, 8(2), 117–128.

already widely used in clinical settings today, and it makes for a more conducive environment when the patient is less tense. Choose music that usually evokes positive and hopeful emotions within you. The pieces in your playlist should be calming, but not too slow, so that they can distract effectively. Try to concentrate fully on the music to help divert attention from worries and pain. To enhance the pain-reducing effects, lightly tap along to the beat, sing along internally, or synchronize your breathing with the music (also refer to tips on 'music for chronic pain'). Even if the music only prompts the release of a few pleasure molecules in the brain, each one serves to counteract pain – and every little bit helps!

CRAVING

The hypothalamus, in conjunction with the pituitary gland, controls and regulates both the hormonal system and the autonomic nervous system. It plays a crucial role in maintaining the body's internal equilibrium, a process known as 'homeostasis'. This encompasses the generation of physical needs and the motivation of behaviours to satisfy these needs. For instance, in cases of advanced dehydration, the hypothalamus triggers a sensation of thirst and directs our focus accordingly. Suddenly, all matters related to water or drinking come into sharp focus, and we experience a compulsion to drink. The more acute the thirst (and the accompanying craving), the more inclined we are to undertake even or risky actions to satisfy it. Similarly, the hypothalamus generates feelings of hunger when our blood glucose level drops, drawing our attention towards food sources. Moreover, the hypothalamus also works to keep all brain-regulated chemical processes within the body in balance, including those related to body temperature, electrolyte balance, and oxygen levels.

Hence, the hypothalamus also is a 'craving centre'. It acts as a linchpin in the regulation of addictive behaviours and substance use disorders. Remarkably, the brain structures that constitute the craving network significantly overlap with those of the pain network, explaining why cravings can be agonizing. However, it is worth noting that the craving network also overlaps with the pleasure network. This overlap provides an opportunity: we can counteract painful cravings and addiction using pleasurable stimuli such as music (see Part IV for more details).

Finally, I wish to make two observations. Firstly, the 'fun motor' can be activated not only by the pleasure centre in the diencephalon but also by other areas such as the happiness system or the subconscious. Compassion, the thrill of epiphanies, and the joy of humour can all ignite this fun motor. Similarly, the pleasure system is stimulated by social interactions such as bonding with others, helping them, sharing with them, or cooperating. Consequently, our fun motor engages during activities that cater to social needs, such as the natural inclination for communal interaction. This underlying mechanism sheds light on why communal music making is such a pleasurable experience: we engage in social functions such as communication, movement coordination, and cooperation.

My second observation pertains to the findings from music studies that have been presented thus far. By juxtaposing Figures 8.1, 8.2, and 8.3, we ascertain that music stimulates or alters activity across all four affect systems, in addition to structures such as the fun motor and the amygdala. Each of these systems and structures plays a vital role in the emergence of emotions; if any become damaged, a patient may lose the ability to experience or recognize certain emotions. This presents a critical insight: music possesses the power to influence activity in all brain structures that are pivotal for emotions. Therefore, it can be an instrumental aid in the therapy for a broad range of disorders and diseases, which are often associated, at least in part, with dysfunction in these emotional brain structures.

And to conclude with a special surprise, my meta-analysis on music and emotion revealed something intriguing. Many studies showed measurable changes in activity within the hippocampus (see Figure 8.3). This structure does not form part of the pleasure system, suggesting that the emotional response to music is not solely tied to the sensation of reward. It implies that music can elicit emotions that extend beyond mere pleasure and delight. This intriguing aspect will be the focus of the next section.

THE HAPPINESS SYSTEM: SOUL WITHIN THE BRAIN

Misaki Matsumoto, an extraordinarily gifted pianist, became a cherished friend when our paths intersected during my violin studies, specifically through rehearsals for a joint concert. Unsurprisingly, our time was largely devoted to making music rather than conversing during these rehearsals. Despite our limited verbal interactions and scant understanding of each other's opinions, attitudes, or personal histories, a remarkable human bond emerged over just a few days of rehearsals and the subsequent concert. This bond proved stronger than any other I had formed over a similar timeframe with individuals with whom I had not shared the experience of making music. Those fortunate enough to have made music with others will likely concur: music possesses a unique capacity to facilitate deep human bonds.

The very structure of music invites *communal* experience or participation: music's rhythm is based on a pulse that everyone can clap or dance along to, and melodies consist of the few notes of a scale that everyone can sing along to. This enables anyone to readily become an integral part of the community. When making music together, it is as though we sing with a single voice. The experience of shared emotions, the synchronization of movements, and the cooperation taking place all contribute to strengthening the sense of community. Those who have revelled in the joy of collective music making rarely become adversaries in serious conflicts – at least, not in the experience of initiatives like the West–Eastern Divan Orchestra, where musicians from traditionally opposing sides have found common ground through their shared love of music!

During social encounters and communal activities, we can experience emotions that touch, move, and fulfil us, such as sympathy, joy, and happiness. The capacity of musical engagement to cultivate social bonds and evoke such attachment-related emotions is vividly apparent in the brain. In the preceding section where I introduced a meta-analysis on the neuroscience of music and emotion, I highlighted that along with the entire pleasure network, the anterior part of the hippocampus is also significantly involved (see Figure 8.3 for details).

To illuminate the implications of these activations of the hippocampus, let us delve into some of its functions. Commonly, textbooks depict the hippocampus as a brain structure associated with learning, memory, and spatial orientation – a notion that won the Nobel Prize in 2014. Typically, patients with bilateral lesions of the hippocampus suffer from severe 'anterograde amnesia', rendering them incapable of learning new information. For example, they might read a magazine and, mere minutes after setting it aside, forget its entire content along with the very act of having read it. They also cannot remember individuals they frequently interact with – every encounter with their neurologist seems like the first time. Nonetheless, they fully retain the capacity to remember individuals and locations with which they were familiar before their hippocampal damage. Intriguingly, even those with severe anterograde amnesia display the capacity to learn and retain new musical skills. Musicians with anterograde amnesia, for instance, can acquire and perform new pieces, despite an inability to remember ever having learned or played them – imagine the astonishment when they unexpectedly play a difficult 'new' piece.[22]

ATTACHMENT-RELATED EMOTIONS AND SOCIAL BONDING

In addition to its well-documented roles in memory and spatial orientation, the hippocampus plays a pivotal role in emotional processing. Despite being proposed by scientists decades ago, these roles have regrettably been overshadowed and forgotten within the field of neuroscience – a significant oversight, given that the hippocampus generates a unique class of emotions: *attachment-related emotions*. As a result, the exploration of attachment-related emotions has largely fallen out of focus in neuroscience.

What evidence supports the claim that the anterior hippocampus is responsible for generating attachment-related emotions? The structure of this region undergoes notable changes upon the birth of offspring; during this period, the neural connections within the hippocampus transform, and its volume increases in both mothers and fathers.[23] Furthermore, the anterior hippocampus, precisely the part that emerges

---

[22] Cavaco, S., Feinstein, J. S., van Twillert, H., and Tranel, D. (2012). Musical memory in a patient with severe anterograde amnesia. *Journal of Clinical and Experimental Neuropsychology*, 34(10), 1089–1100.

[23] Galea, L. A., Leuner, B., and Slattery, D. A. (2014). Hippocampal plasticity during the peripartum period: Influence of sex steroids, stress and ageing. *Journal of Neuroendocrinology*, 26(10), 641–648.

in studies on music and emotion, has direct neural connections to regions of the hypothalamus that regulate reproductive, bonding, recognition, and social behaviours.[24] Through these neural pathways, the hippocampus can trigger the hypothalamus to release hormones such as oxytocin and vasopressin. These hormones are instrumental in social bonding and nurturing behaviour: oxytocin alleviates stress during encounters with members of the same species, and vasopressin diminishes fear – these effects facilitate approach and social contact.[25] Additionally, the hippocampus can influence the release of other hormones, such as prolactin and oestrogen. Levels of these hormones experience a surge in both mothers and fathers following the birth of their offspring; in some instances, the hormonal levels in fathers can even surpass those in mothers – besides its role in milk secretion, prolactin is also important for nurturing behaviour and social bonding.[26]

The hippocampus also contains receptors for dozens of hormones and various signalling molecules, many of which play significant roles in bonding behaviour.[27] These include endorphins, which are opioids produced by the brain. While many people are familiar with their pain-relieving and euphoric effects, endorphins also foster the formation of social bonds and encourage behaviours associated with these bonds.[28] Such behaviours include laughter, play, tender touch, and coordinated movements, such as those seen in music making or dancing. The release of these endogenous opioids inclines people towards engaging in music making, with music, in turn, further stimulating the secretion of these naturally produced opioids. The hippocampus can generate opioids and

---

[24] Strange, B. A., Witter, M. P., Lein, E. S., and Moser, E. I. (2014). Functional organization of the hippocampal longitudinal axis. *Nature Reviews Neuroscience*, 15(10), 655.

[25] Heinrichs, M., and Domes, G. (2008). Neuropeptides and social behaviour: Effects of oxytocin and vasopressin in humans. *Progress in Brain Research*, 170, 337–350.

[26] Leuner, B., Glasper, E. R., and Gould, E. (2010). Parenting and plasticity. *Trends in Neurosciences*, 33(10), 465–473.

[27] Lathe, R. (2001). Hormones and the hippocampus. *Journal of Endocrinology*, 169(2), 205–231.

[28] Panksepp, J., Herman, B. H., Vilberg, T., Bishop, P., and DeEskinazi, F. G. (1980). Endogenous opioids and social behavior. *Neuroscience & Biobehavioral Reviews*, 4(4), 473–487.

distribute them to various brain regions, including the pleasure system. Furthermore, the hippocampus can instigate the hypothalamus, a major producer of endogenous opioids, to release endorphins. It is also noteworthy that endorphin receptors can be activated by substances such as morphine, heroin, opium, and other opiates. However, in stark contrast to these substances, music does not lead to addiction.

Hence, I posit that the hippocampus serves as the core structure for a social bonding system within the brain. I will refer to this social bonding system as the *happiness system*. It has notably evolved in species that necessitate parental care for their offspring, chiefly among mammals and birds. From this perspective, altruism appears to hold an evolutionary advantage over egoism. After all, the majority of fish, amphibian, and reptile species do not engage in parental care, and a lizard would not shed tears of emotion upon hearing its child sing a solo!

The happiness system motivates parents to care for their offspring, to provide for and defend them. Moreover, memory systems have evolved to support the care of offspring, enabling parents to recognize their young and find their way back to the nest after foraging for food. Therefore, it is evolutionarily logical that these functions – memory, navigation, scent recognition, and attachment-related emotions – are colocalized within the hippocampus, the core of the happiness system.

In humans, the relative volume of the hippocampus surpasses that of any other species, underlining its crucial role in social bonding – a function that has culminated in humans, in association with their complex social structures. The hippocampus consists of the most evolutionarily ancient and simplest form of cortex – the 'archicortex'. This stands in contrast to the vitalization system, as well as the pleasure, pain, and craving system, which exclusively encompass 'subcortical' structures.

THE HIPPOCAMPUS AS THE NEUROBIOLOGICAL SUBSTRATE OF THE SOUL

Emotions related to attachment frequently manifest in feelings such as sympathy, love, joy, or even happiness. These feelings are marked by their peaceful, gentle, and warm-hearted qualities. Given these qualities, it is fitting to consider the anterior hippocampus – serving as the centre of the happiness system – as what could be termed the *soul*.[29] Apart from the capacity to love, the soul can also generate feelings of being 'moved' or 'touched' – especially in response to music. Even the most hard-boiled individuals I know have confided in me that they have shed tears in response to music – and only to music. One of them, a hard-boiled fighter pilot whose poker face seldomly gave away any inner emotion, shared with me that he wept with emotion while listening to Nathan Milstein perform the Mendelssohn Concerto. As he watched the small man with his violin playing in front of the huge orchestra, tears rolled down his cheeks.

The power of music to touch our souls was succinctly captured by Shakespeare in *Much Ado about Nothing*, when Benedick expressed astonishment that sheep guts, used for instrument strings, could 'hale souls out of men's bodies'. Particularly when we hear children singing or playing music together, many of us shed tears of emotion. Some people find themselves moved to tears by operatic performances, while nearly everyone has experienced such emotionally potent moments in cinema. Heart-wrenching film scenes are almost always accompanied by music, or outright singing scenes, such as those from *Volver* or 'When She Loved Me' from *Toy Story 2* – Hollywood has turned this into a whole industry. Note that all these scenes have a social element: when the students in *Dead Poets Society* shout 'O Captain! My Captain!', it is a moment of human solidarity. So, when we feel moved or touched, it involves emotions related to human bonds – love, sympathy, or solidarity.

We can also recognize the soul's particular sensitivity in its physiology: the hippocampus is the only brain structure where severe emotional stress due to violence and inhumanity leads to the death of nerve cells.

---

[29] In this context, the term 'soul' is used not in a religious or metaphysical sense but rather as a metaphor for the neurobiological substrate within our brains, primarily located in the anterior hippocampus, which harbours our deepest emotions and feelings. This conceptualization aims to capture the rich and complex emotional experiences of humans, including the capacity for love, joy, and the profound effects of music on disorders associated with dysfunctions in the anterior hippocampal formation. It is crucial to clarify that any discussion of conditions affecting the hippocampus – such as changes in hippocampal volume – should not be misconstrued as suggesting a diminished 'soul' or its value. Rather, such discussions emphasize the soul's vulnerability to trauma and its remarkable resilience, underscored by the hippocampus' ability to recover and regenerate, thereby healing emotional wounds over time.

In this sense, the soul can be wounded by emotional traumatization and strong chronic emotional stress. The death of nerve cells in the hippocampus results in a reduced volume of the hippocampus, which can be seen in MRI scans. Meta-analyses have revealed a smaller hippocampal volume in both women who were sexually abused as children and in soldiers suffering from post-traumatic stress disorder.[30] Some of these soldiers were traumatized not just by the violence they witnessed but also by the violence they inflicted upon others. Hence, it is not only the experience but also the perpetration of extreme violence that leads to nerve cell death within what we term the soul.

Moreover, psychiatric disorders such as schizophrenia and borderline personality disorder, commonly associated with childhood trauma, exhibit a correlation with reduced hippocampal volume.[31] Similarly, depression – a state characterized by prolonged, intense unhappiness, coupled with feelings of helplessness, worthlessness, futility, and despair – also leads to a decrease in hippocampal volume.[32]

In addition to these clear anatomical findings, which reveal the unique sensitivity of the soul, numerous studies demonstrated *functional* changes in the hippocampus across an astonishingly large number of diseases and disorders. In individuals with depression, the hippocampus responds more strongly to emotionally negative stimuli than to positive ones.[33] For

---

[30] Smith, M. E. (2005). Bilateral hippocampal volume reduction in adults with post-traumatic stress disorder: A meta-analysis of structural MRI studies. *Hippocampus*, 15(6), 798–807; Kitayama, N., Vaccarino, V., Kutner, M., Weiss, P., and Bremner, J. D. (2005). Magnetic resonance imaging (MRI) measurement of hippocampal volume in posttraumatic stress disorder: A meta-analysis. *Journal of Affective Disorders*, 88(1), 79–86.

[31] Haijma, S. V., Van Haren, N., Cahn, W., Koolschijn, P. C. M., Hulshoff Pol, H. E., and Kahn, R. S. (2012). Brain volumes in schizophrenia: A meta-analysis in over 18 000 subjects. *Schizophrenia Bulletin*, 39(5), 1129–1138; Nunes, P. M., Wenzel, A., Borges, K. T., Porto, C. R., Caminha, R. M., and de Oliveira, I. R. (2009). Volumes of the hippocampus and amygdala in patients with borderline personality disorder: A meta-analysis. *Journal of Personality Disorders*, 23(4), 333–345.

[32] Koolschijn, P. C. M., van Haren, N. E., Lensvelt-Mulders, G. J., Hulshoff Pol, H. E., and Kahn, R. S. (2009). Brain volume abnormalities in major depressive disorder: A meta-analysis of magnetic resonance imaging studies. *Human Brain Mapping*, 30(11), 3719–3735.

[33] Diener, C., Kuehner, C., Brusniak, W., Ubl, B., Wessa, M., and Flor, H. (2012). A meta-analysis of neurofunctional imaging studies of emotion and cognition in major depression. *NeuroImage*, 61(3), 677–685; Groenewold, N. A., Opmeer, E. M., de Jonge, P.,

chronic diseases of the immune system such as ulcerative colitis, reduced hippocampal activity in response to emotional images was observed.[34] In individuals with Crohn's disease, the hippocampus reacts more strongly to stress stimuli. Many of these individuals also show a smaller volume of the anterior hippocampus as the duration of the disease increases.[35] This part of the hippocampus also regulates bodily stress responses, which in turn influence the activity of the immune system.

These are just examples – the list of other diseases and disorders associated with abnormalities in the structure or function of the hippocampus is long and includes Alzheimer's disease, Parkinson's disease, multiple sclerosis, anxiety disorders, obsessive-compulsive disorder, bipolar disorder, attention deficit hyperactivity disorder, as well as autism – and as I am writing this, more and more chronic diseases are being found to present such abnormalities. These findings show that we must consider the soul when we think about the causes and the healing of diseases, and our overall health.

THE INVIGORATING POWER OF MUSIC ON THE SOUL

Intriguingly, music possesses a unique capability to activate the anterior region of the hippocampus – the exact emotional structure in the brain that presents abnormalities across a wide range of previously mentioned diseases and disorders. This insight suggests that the stimulation of the

---

Aleman, A., and Costafreda, S. G. (2013). Emotional valence modulates brain functional abnormalities in depression: Evidence from a meta-analysis of fMRI studies. *Neuroscience & Biobehavioral Reviews*, 37(2), 152–163.

[34] Agostini, A., Filippini, N., Cevolani, D., Agati, R., Leoni, C., Tambasco, R., Calabrese, C., Rizzello, F., Gionchetti, P., Ercolani, M., Campieri, M., and Leonardi, M. (2011). Brain functional changes in patients with ulcerative colitis: A functional magnetic resonance imaging study on emotional processing. *Inflammatory Bowel Diseases*, 17(8), 1769–1777.

[35] Agostini, A., Filippini, N., Benuzzi, F., Bertani, A., Scarcelli, A., Leoni, C., Farinelli, V., Riso, D., Tambasco, R., Calabrese, C., Gionchetti, P., Ercolani, M., Nichelli, P., Campieri, M., and Rizzello, F. (2013). Functional magnetic resonance imaging study reveals differences in the habituation to psychological stress in patients with Crohn's disease versus healthy controls. *Journal of Behavioural Medicine*, 36(5), 477–487; Agostini, A., Benuzzi, F., Filippini, N., Bertani, A., Scarcelli, A., Farinelli, V., Marchetta, C., Calabrese, C., Rizzello, F., Gionchetti, P., Campieri, M., Nichelliand, P., and Ercolani, M. (2013). New insights into the brain involvement in patients with Crohn's disease: A voxel-based morphometry study. *Neurogastroenterology & Motility*, 25(2), 147–182.

happiness system with music may have therapeutic effects, especially when we consider this crowning circumstance: the soul can regenerate. Directly adjacent to the hippocampus lies another component of the happiness system, the 'dentate gyrus'. This structure is capable of generating new nerve cells. Indeed, you have read that correctly: the human brain houses a structure capable of generating stem cells throughout the course of one's life, even into advanced age. These stem cells migrate into the hippocampus and differentiate into different cell types, including nerve cells. Considering that music can effectively activate the happiness system, this offers a highly intriguing healing perspective for individuals with chronic diseases or disorders: music can revitalize the soul and thereby stimulate the formation of nerve cells in the happiness system.

While music therapy is actively utilized to mitigate a range of the previously mentioned diseases and disorders, meta-analyses have so far been confined to depression, autism, and schizophrenia. These analyses suggest that while the results are promising, the quality of many studies leaves room for improvement, emphasizing the need for more robust research.[36] In addition, neuroscientific investigations into the healing effects of music on these conditions are scarce. Yet, the clear association between music, the activation of the soul, chronic diseases, and the capacity for neurogenesis within the happiness system argues for the therapeutic use of music in these conditions.

Due to the extraordinary vulnerability of what we term here the soul, the brain has developed neuronal safeguards to protect it from cellular death. There are mechanisms within the brain that inhibit activity in the hippocampus when the environment becomes dangerous, loud, or

---

[36] Aalbers, S., Fusar-Poli, L., Freeman, R. E., Spreen, M., Ket, J. C. F., Vink, A. C., Maratos, A., Crawford, M., Chen, X. J., and Gold, C. (2017). Music therapy for depression. *Cochrane Database of Systematic Reviews* (11), 1–87; James, R., Sigafoos, J., Green, V. A., Lancioni, G. E., O'Reilly, M. F., Lang, R., Davis, T., Carnett, A., Achmadi, D., Gevarter, C., and Marschik, P. B. (2015). Music therapy for individuals with autism spectrum disorder: A systematic review. *Review Journal of Autism and Developmental Disorders*, 2(1), 39–54; Mössler, K., Chen, X., Heldal, T. O., and Gold, C. (2011). Music therapy for people with schizophrenia and schizophrenia-like disorders. *Cochrane Database of Systematic Reviews* (12), 1–70.

stressful. Consequently, while a dangerous situation may evoke a sense of thrill, it cannot induce genuine happiness. Emotions such as fear, anxiety, and worry suppress neuronal activity in the happiness system, just as anger, hostility, and aggression do. In these circumstances, music can serve as a soothing balm, helping to evoke positive emotions, uplift the mood, and thereby reignite the neuronal activity of the soul.

It merits attention that excessive noise potentially inflicts damage upon the hippocampus. Interestingly, both the hippocampus and the inner ear harbour receptors for stress hormones, such as cortisol. Thus, both are particularly sensitive to stress. Because the hippocampus is involved in regulating stress hormones, both acoustic and emotional stress can trigger tinnitus. Hence, tinnitus may be a hippocampal signal for emotional distress. Conversely, tinnitus resulting from acoustic stress appears to be associated with the loss of nerve cells in the hippocampus, much like purely emotional stress.[37] Consequently, music with a calming tone may prove advantageous for managing types of tinnitus that are stress-induced. This approach serves not just to alleviate stress and soothe the soul but also to enhance our refined perception of the 'soft tones'.

HOW MUSIC PROMOTES HAPPINESS

Why do I refer to the system for attachment-related emotions as the *happiness system*? When you enquire of older individuals about the sources of their happiness, the prevalent answer is 'social bonds' – surprisingly, not 'money' or 'cheesecake'. A study from Harvard University recently corroborated these findings. That study examined several hundred people over nearly eight decades and found that the most crucial factor for personal happiness is good relationships – and a few truly reliable ones rather than many superficial ones.[38] In addition to contributing to our happiness, strong interpersonal connections are crucial for our resilience and overall health.

As humans, we are by nature dependent on each other and need community experiences for our happiness – kind and loving interaction

---

[37] Kraus, K. S., and Canlon, B. (2012). Neuronal connectivity and interactions between the auditory and limbic systems: Effects of noise and tinnitus. *Hearing Research*, 288(1–2), 34–46.

[38] www.adultdevelopmentstudy.org

with others. Even if someone has remarkable abilities, physical attractiveness, success, and wealth, that person becomes happy just like everyone else: by loving, being loved, feeling compassion, and supporting others. Regardless of how strong and independent someone may feel in the successful times of their life, sooner or later there are situations in which they will depend on the help and support of others. *Every* individual inherently desires love and is born with the ability to give and receive it. Because we need our reciprocal loving and our human bonds, we are naturally motivated at our core to risk love and compassion. The happiness system readily facilitates this endeavour by releasing hormones such as oxytocin and vasopressin. These hormones alleviate anxiety and stress, encouraging us to bond with other people.

The intrinsic human desire for communal inclusion, termed 'the need to belong' by social psychologist Roy Baumeister,[39] encompasses the vital imperatives of communication, cooperation, and mutual support. Furthermore, our happiness system naturally motivates us to recognize and respond to *others'* feelings and needs – our soul endows us with the innate ability to love our neighbours. Although it makes us vulnerable to love, feel compassion, and allow ourselves to be loved by others, such vulnerability is not a weakness or something to be ashamed of. Rather, these capabilities glue every human community together, making it stronger than the sum of its members. Friendship, sympathy, love, and compassion can profoundly touch us, and even move us to tears. Hence, our happiness system is to blame when we shed tears at concerts, operas, or cinemas.

Harnessing Music to Foster Happiness

Music is a powerful catalyst for communal connection and happiness. We can use it as a platform to engage in communal activities such as making music with others, joining a choir, or even dancing. Such communal experiences can be particularly beneficial for those grappling with social isolation – which often accompanies severe chronic

---

[39] Baumeister, R. F., and Leary, M. R. (1995). The need to belong: Desire for interpersonal attachments as a fundamental human motivation. *Psychological Bulletin*, 117(3), 497–529.

illnesses or mental disorders. In these cases, music therapy can be a valuable tool.

To ignite the 'happiness system', or the 'soul in the brain', we can utilize music and musical activities to alleviate negative emotions and brighten the mood. This requires that the music feels pleasing and positive, a characteristic that depends on personal taste. Music that gives you goosebumps or moves you emotionally in a positive way is a perfect choice.

Recall that the happiness system flourishes optimally in tranquil settings. Therefore, it can be a good idea to avoid loud noise, over-stimulation, or negative stress for a few days. Instead, establish a serene and safe space where you can enjoy or create music, either solo or with others.

Nurturing the happiness system through music gains particular importance for individuals grappling with chronic ailments, including those affecting the immune system. A special focus should be placed on using music to foster inner peace and relaxation. This aids the hippocampus in its regeneration, bringing both the stress system and the immune system back into harmony.

HEDONIC HAPPINESS, EUDAIMONIA, AND BEYOND

Our exploration of the pleasure, pain, and craving system in the previous section introduced us to the feelings of pleasure. These feelings lead to what is philosophically understood as *hedonic happiness*. Notably, philosophers distinguish between hedonic happiness and *eudaimonic happiness*, a differentiation akin to the neurobiological separation between the *pleasure system* and the *happiness system*. So, why is it crucial to distinguish between these two affect systems and the emotions they generate: pleasure and happiness?

The feelings generated by the pleasure system have a different quality to those of the happiness system. For instance, the pleasure of satisfying homeostatic needs – such as relishing a hearty sandwich when famished – is hardly experienced as 'moving' or 'touching'. We are moved when a social element comes into play – for example, when a hungry girl shares her last piece of bread with her younger brother.

THE BRAIN WHEN MUSIC EVOKES EMOTIONS

For one thing, experiencing pleasure does not necessitate the involvement of the happiness system, meaning we can feel fun without true happiness. Fun can rapidly alleviate pain and lighten our mood. However, fun *alone* is relatively short-lived and not truly fulfilling. The exhilaration of a shopping spree frequently leads to swift disillusionment, particularly when there is no more space in the wardrobe. Consuming fast food provides immediate satisfaction but often leaves us feeling heavy afterwards. Drugs can temporarily diminish feelings of unhappiness or depression, but once their effects fade, one feels as miserable as before. Occasionally, the aftermath of a fun experience can leave one feeling empty or worse.

Fun, in itself, is not detrimental. It stimulates dopamine release and keeps our brains young. Pleasure contributes to our quality of life – 'Those who don't savour, become hard to savour.' However, fun alone often saturates quickly. While it is pleasurable to satisfy physical needs, once inner equilibrium is achieved, previously rewarding stimuli become neutral or even negative, as too much of a chemical compound can harm the body. The first bites of a cheesecake are pleasant, but overindulging leads to nausea.

In contrast, the positive emotions associated with social bonding do not saturate – parents do not get nauseous from caring for their babies. One can enjoy music for extended periods without ill effects, and the joy experienced during communal music making can linger. The pleasant memories can provide emotional warmth for days afterwards. The evolutionary advantage of having two separate affect systems – the 'pleasure system' and the 'happiness system' – becomes evident when we consider a hypothetical species in which parents could become satiated from loving their children, akin to overindulging in cheesecake.

Another evolutionary advantage is that 'eudaimonia' imparts more than pleasure: the happiness system can motivate actions that lack immediate gratification, such as gathering food for offspring or building a nest. Parents often endure hardship and discomfort to care for their children, driven by their happiness system. When we engage in meaningful challenges and personal growth, it is often not pleasurable in the moment, yet it contributes significantly in the long run to our overall sense of fulfilment and happiness.

Finally, the happiness system has evolved to establish direct neural connections with the pleasure centre (hypothalamus and medial forebrain bundle) and the fun motor. These connections ensure that the moments of happiness during social bonding are also pleasurable. In such moments, 'hedonic' and 'eudaimonic' happiness unite, providing experiences of 'true happiness'.

BUYING PLEASURE AND EARNING HAPPINESS

Another fundamental difference in the emotional quality between the pleasure system and the happiness system is that pleasure can be purchased. Chocolate, drugs, food, and sex can be bought. Such purchases can induce intensely pleasurable feelings, but not happiness. Conversely, attachment-related emotions cannot be bought, which is fortunate since it implies these emotions do not need to be purchased and, therefore, are affordable for everyone.

Given everyone's inherent pursuit of happiness, there is a significant economic interest in profiting from this desire. This is why advertising often attempts to sell pleasure as happiness, seeking to persuade us that happiness can be bought. For instance, a renowned ice cream company advertises with the slogan, 'This is what happiness tastes like.' However, as discussed above, activating the pleasure system does not equate to attaining true happiness. Despite the alluring promises, chocolate, cheesecake, ice cream, stylish furniture, or impressive cars cannot bestow happiness. While they can offer immense pleasure, and be perceived as highly rewarding, becoming truly happy requires something more.

The biology of the happiness system also reveals that we can only become happy without hatred, violence, and aggression. Thus, by violating another person's dignity, we obstruct our pursuit of happiness. Posting hate-filled comments may be fun, but it is a sure-fire way to personal unhappiness. Instead, it is crucial to treat oneself and others with kindness, contributing constructively to both one's individual happiness and society as a whole.

Unfortunately, the fact that an action triggers positive feelings does not necessarily denote that it promotes true happiness or that it is ethically right. For instance, exerting power and asserting dominance can elicit feelings of fun, even when it is unethical. Power, akin to money, is a 'secondary reward' that can be used to obtain 'primary rewards' such as food, drink, and sex. Both primary and secondary rewards activate the pleasure system. Emotional systems, however, cannot rationally discern what is beneficial for us and our community in the long run – we must engage our reason and intelligence for that. Before engaging in an activity that promises pleasure, we need to ensure this behaviour is ethical and aligns with human values. Thus, we have to aim not only to pursue hedonic happiness but also to strive for eudaimonic happiness. Only then can we pave the way towards achieving true happiness and health.

THE SUBCONSCIOUS: BLAME AND SHAME IN THE BRAIN

I have named the fourth affect system the *subconscious*. Located in the 'orbitofrontal cortex' above the eyes, this cortex has evolved in mammals that live in larger groups. It evolved after the happiness system but earlier than the neocortex, which implies that the subconscious lacks neocortical functions such as logical, deductive reasoning. However, the subconscious has astonishing capabilities of decoding complex patterns of sensory information, predicting potential rewards and dangers. Consider an experiment where you observe visual patterns containing hidden clues that signal whether the patterns forecast a positive or negative outcome. Although you cannot consciously tell why you should choose one pattern over the other, your orbitofrontal cortex quickly picks up these patterns and generates an intuition about which one is more beneficial. This intuition entails the generation of impulses designed to respond aptly to these patterns.

During our childhood, the subconscious internalizes the cultural rules or norms of our culture, our tribe or clan. When we adhere to these rules, the subconscious evaluates this compliance as positive. Conversely, deviating from these rules results in 'bad vibrations' – feelings of guilt and *moral emotions* such as shame, disgrace and embarrassment and regret. If others break these rules, it instigates indignation, outrage, contempt, or a desire for revenge.

Social rules must be learned, just as the environmental cues indicating rewards or punishments. Consequently, unlike the other three affect systems, the subconscious is not biologically pre-programmed but is shaped and influenced primarily by our experiences. This trait allows humans to adapt to vastly different environments and cultures. However, the subconscious neither possesses language nor can it solve problems. Instead of logical thoughts, it produces intuitions: spontaneous, emotionally imbued thoughts or thought fragments.

The psychologist and Nobel laureate Daniel Kahneman refers to the system that produces these types of thoughts as 'System 1'.[40] In contrast, the neocortical 'System 2' is capable of rational, logical thinking, although it can often be perceived as slow and tedious. Here is a simple arithmetic problem, inspired by Kahneman, to illustrate how these two systems function: an apple and a cherry together cost €1.10, with the apple costing €1 more than the cherry. How much does each fruit cost? Our 'System 1' quickly generates an answer to this question, marking the puzzle as solved, and is typically reluctant to abandon its conclusion. The advantage of the response is its simplicity and convenience ('the apple costs €1, the cherry €0.10'). However, the downside is that it is incorrect. To logically verify and correct our answer, we need to engage our 'System 2', which is often uncomfortable and takes longer than an intuitive response. If the cherry indeed costs €0.10, and the apple is €1 more expensive, then the apple should cost €1.10, bringing the total to €1.20 for both – not €1.10. Therefore, the answer must be incorrect. Kahneman has demonstrated, through numerous experiments, that individuals operating in 'System 1' mode often reach incorrect conclusions, misjudge risks, and are guided by prejudices.

It is vital to comprehend that our brain houses a system generating thoughts devoid of rationality. Such irrational thoughts can easily lead us astray because they are difficult to identify: the subconscious does not doubt its own thoughts, even when these are indeed errors. Consequently, we frequently conflate the mere existence of subconscious thoughts with their accuracy (as with the notion of the apple costing €1) unless we subject them to rigorous, albeit laborious, scrutiny through conscious reasoning. However, the mere *existence* of a thought does not necessarily evince its *truth* or logic; the cherry does not cost €0.10, but €0.05. (Incidentally, *deliberately* producing false thoughts

---

[40] Kahneman, D. (2011). *Thinking, Fast and Slow*. New York, Farrar, Strauss and Giraux.

switches our thinking directly from System 1 to System 2, helping to gain conscious control over one's mind.)

Alongside intuitions and irrational thoughts, the subconscious generates impulses that drive action or inaction, which we perceive as *volition*. We not only 'feel' these subconscious thoughts, but we also 'want' them. When the subconscious generates thoughts, it ascribes to them the highest importance and urgency, demanding immediate attention and absolute priority. Fortunately, in addition to our subconscious will, we have a conscious, free will at our disposal. This conscious will enables us to identify and regulate impulses originating from the affect systems, including those generated in the subconscious. Through our conscious will, we can guide our thoughts, actions, and emotions in the direction that aligns best with our long-term interests. For example, should we find ourselves unconsciously reaching for a biscuit during a meeting, we have the capacity to consciously recognize this impulse and retract our hand. Likewise, upon identifying a subconscious thought – whether it is racially biased or an impulse to assign blame – we can consciously acknowledge and retract it, replacing it with an attitude of kindness.

SOCIAL NORMS AND IRRATIONAL BELIEFS

Why do our brains employ the same system to store social rules and generate irrational thoughts? The answer lies in the nature of social norms themselves. Many social norms, family roles, and cultural customs are not inherently logical. This becomes clear when we consider the vast diversity of cultural norms, some of which are diametrically opposite to each other – 'different strokes for different folks'. Most individuals tend to view their own culture or family as the standard for rational or logical norms. This skewed perception, however, results from our subconscious having internalized these norms and customs. If we wanted them to be logical, we would entrust logicians to devise them.

Consider, for instance, the unwritten rules of attending a classical concert. Nowadays, coming in or going out during the performance is frowned upon – a stark contrast to societal norms 200 years ago when such behaviour was normal.[41] You are expected to occupy the seat

---

[41] Müller, *Das Publikum macht die Musik.*

specified on your ticket, rather than choosing one based on your preference. There is also a dress code – even on sweltering days, turning up in a bikini is a no go. During the concert, engaging in conversation or clapping between movements attracts unwanted attention, again a stark departure from the practices of two centuries ago. Using your phone during the performance is a sure-fire way to attract the ire of those around you. A musician from Zimbabwe once told me that for many people in his community, it would be challenging to comprehend why it is unacceptable to join a classical concert performance with their own drums and flutes. It would be even harder to explain to them why clapping, singing, or dancing along is discouraged, and that the social requirement is to sit uncomfortably motionless and quiet for hours on end.

Patients with damage to the orbitofrontal cortex often exhibit significant alterations in social behaviour, including a notable disregard for social norms and moral principles. This is often because they do not experience guilt or regret after violating these norms as their subconscious no longer generates such feelings. For instance, a person with this condition might make unwanted sexual advances, despite being aware that such actions are inappropriate. They might not perceive any reason to restrain these impulses.

Likewise, these patients frequently display emotions inappropriately, failing to adhere to socially accepted norms. This highlights the role the subconscious plays in controlling emotional expression in line with cultural norms. These norms essentially dictate who is to express which emotion, to whom, under what circumstances, and with what degree of intensity. Note that such norms can differ significantly, or even contradict, between societies. For instance, cultural practices surrounding funerals exhibit wide variations across the globe. In some cultures, funerals involve solemn and reflective rituals, whereas in others, they may be marked by exuberant parades and music, celebrating life and the strength of community bonds. Each practice is deeply rooted in its specific cultural context, and might be perceived as inappropriate or even unacceptable in a different cultural setting.

Though it may not seem applaudable to harbour an 'irrational thought catapult' in the form of the subconscious within our frontal lobe, our social coexistence would be markedly less tolerable without this affect system. If everyone plays by the rules, there are fewer conflicts and living together is easier. However, in the long run, irrational thoughts cannot logically lead to advantageous outcomes, and cultural or family rules often entail irrational thought patterns that lead to unhappiness and sickness.[42] I will provide examples of such irrational thoughts in the following. It is essential to address these because we cannot expect music to make us healthy and happy if we are constantly entertaining thoughts that make us unwell. Subsequently, I will discuss how music can help us to let *bad vibrations* of the subconscious subside, and transform them into *Good Vibrations*.

Commonly Held Irrational Beliefs

- *The belief that humans are innately flawed*, typically labelled as 'wrong', or 'sinful'. This belief sharply contradicts biological reality. From a biological perspective, every human is a marvel of existence, perfectly human even if their actions may cause harm or suffering. If we perpetually harbour shame about ourselves, we cannot truly feel entitled to our existence. Negative emotions and resultant stress from this belief in intrinsic inadequacy can cause illness. Therefore, for the sake of our health, distancing ourselves from this belief is logically imperative.
- *The belief that individuals differ in their intrinsic worth.* With this mindset, it is but a short leap to ranking one individual as superior or inferior to another. The *halo effect*, as described by Kahneman,[43] 'assists' with this: we tend to infer other traits of a person from one trait – for example, we tend to overlook the positive traits of a criminal. However, every person possesses a wealth of positive traits and nobody is a monster. When we evaluate *people* (instead of merely criticizing their *behaviour*, as would be logical), we must constantly prove our own worth too – and can thus never feel truly adequate as a human being.
- *The propensity to incessantly find fault*, fixating on what is missing for our ultimate happiness. However, if we persistently believe that something is lacking for our happiness, attaining it becomes impossible. We may

---

[42] Weiss, J. (1993). *How Psychotherapy Works: Process and Technique.* New York, Guilford Press.
[43] Kahneman, *Thinking, Fast and Slow.*

be overlooking that the present moment is already truly golden – such as maybe right now.
- *The belief that undesirable events inherently make life difficult.* In actuality, it is our irrational attitudes in dealing with such events that pose the real problem. Albert Ellis, a clinical psychologist, characterized irrational beliefs along the lines of 'I/others/the world *must* be a certain way' and 'it's an absolute *catastrophe* if it is not'.[44] However, such notions are self-defeating. They bring about headaches and provoke negative emotions: fear or depression when I am not the way I *must* be; anger or vindictiveness when others are not the way they *must* be; frustration or procrastination when the world is not the way it *must* be.

HOW MUSIC AFFECTS THE SUBCONSCIOUS

Fortunately, music holds the power to sway the subconscious, facilitating the transformation of detrimental negative thoughts into positive ones. This process starts by mitigating the impact of negative emotions and moods on our cognitive functions – such as attention, memory, motivation, and thought processes (remember, I refer to these impacts as 'emotional attractor effects', a concept detailed in Chapter 5). When engulfed in negativity, our conscious thinking can be overwhelmed by the subconscious, which narrows our focus solely on elements that echo the negative mood. This leads us to generate thoughts, initiate actions, and recall memories that are congruent with our negative feelings. For instance, during bouts of depression, the subconscious limits our capacity to recognize positive attributes in ourselves, remember joyful moments, or even muster the energy to get out of bed. Phrases such as 'I can't think of anything else' reflect the powerful influence of emotional attractor effects. Nevertheless, such claims are generally overstated, unless confirmed by a medical diagnosis.

Despite the formidable nature of these attractor effects, which often appear stronger than our conscious will, the subconscious is surprisingly receptive to music. For most individuals, it usually suffices to play music mirroring the positive mood they seek, and then actively engage with it.

[44] Ellis, A., and Blau, S. (eds) (1998). *The Albert Ellis Reader: A Guide to Well-Being Using Rational Emotive Behavior Therapy.* New York, Citadel Press.

Such engagement can be tapping to the beat, singing along, dancing, or breathing in time with the music (for tips on this, again refer to Chapter 5). Those who are drawn to music that sounds sad or melancholic can commence with tunes that resonate with their *current* negative mood and gradually transition to those that evoke the positive mood they aim to *achieve*. Here too, active engagement with the music is crucial (for more guidance, refer to Chapters 18 and 20).

In addition to neutralizing emotional attractor effects, music can also assist in managing negative *thought loops*. When we are not engaged in conscious thought or actively directing our attention, our subconscious swiftly takes the helm, activating the brain's subconscious autopilot mode. Our subconscious then generates thoughts on its own, unsolicited and at will. It throws thoughts into existence, often imbuing them with a sense of truth. Psychologists and neuroscientists refer to these phenomena as *mind wandering*, during which we may daydream, ponder, or brood over thoughts.

In subconscious autopilot mode, we sometimes keep repeating negative thoughts, over and over. Such negative thought loops typically revolve around issues that distress us emotionally; for example, a situation that might turn out negatively and thus worries us, or an event that angered, disappointed, or demotivated us, such as a break-up or dispute. Subconscious thought loops may even revolve around destructive themes, such as aggression or revenge. (Not all types of mind wandering are negative. Consider, for instance, a constructive inspiration occurring during the morning shower. However, such epiphanies are typically the result of intense, intelligent contemplation from the previous day.)

Many individuals let their minds wander approximately half of their waking hours. During this time, they often slip into negative mind wandering and are then unhappier than when they consciously focus on a task or actively control their attention and thoughts.[45] Isn't it startling how much of our precious lifetimes we throw out the window with negative thoughts? If someone else were to squander our time in such a way, we would instantly deem them our worst enemy.

---

[45] Killingsworth, M. A., and Gilbert, D. T. (2010). A wandering mind is an unhappy mind. *Science*, 330(6006), 932.

Disrupting negative thought loops is crucial; enduring unhappiness not only undermines our well-being but also jeopardizes our health. For instance, depression is associated with biochemical processes that promote the growth of cancer tumours. Moreover, depression impairs immune system communication, putting the brain in a state comparable to real inflammation, where concentration becomes challenging and even simple tasks seem daunting.[46] To break off negative thought loops, techniques such as meditation and mindfulness exercises have been developed (see Chapter 20 for further insights). These exercises become especially effective when integrated with music, as music acts like a potent 'attention magnet', reducing the pull of emotional attractor effects and engaging mental resources, leaving little room for negative thought cycles.

Furthermore, music can induce positivity in our mind-wandering thoughts. Mind wandering correlates with the activity of a particular network within the brain, which I refer to as the *autopilot network* (the scientific term is *default mode network*). The subconscious is a part of this network, and music can modulate its activity. The following illuminates how researchers explore this phenomenon.

A Glimpse into the Laboratory: Music's Impact on the Subconscious

In an experiment, participants listened to either cheerful pieces, such as 'À La Folie' by Michael Nyman, or more melancholic compositions, such as 'Death is the Road to Awe' by Clint Mansell.[47] We asked participants to close their eyes and relax while listening to the music. In such a setting, it is common for individuals' minds to wander. Even when consciously trying to focus on the music, thoughts tend to stray. Our study sought to determine whether music could influence these wandering thoughts to be either more positive or negative. To measure participants' brain activity, we utilized fMRI.

---

[46] Reiche, E. M. V., Morimoto, H. K., and Nunes, S. M. V. (2005). Stress and depression-induced immune dysfunction: Implications for the development and progression of cancer. *International Review of Psychiatry*, 17(6), 515–527.

[47] Taruffi, L., Pehrs, C., Skouras, S., and Koelsch, S. (2017). Effects of sad and happy music on mind-wandering and the default mode network. *Scientific Reports*, 7(1), 14396.

We discovered that thoughts veered more towards positivity during cheerful music compared to the melancholic compositions. Likewise, another study by my team discovered that heroic-sounding music prompted more positive and motivating thoughts than sad-sounding music.[48] Brain scans indicated that the orbitofrontal cortex, part of the default mode network, communicated more with other brain structures when listening to sad music. Given that I refer to the orbitofrontal cortex as the subconscious, and to the default mode network as autopilot network, the results reflect that the subconscious aspect of the autopilot network played a more dominant role during the melancholic music, in contrast to the cheerful compositions. This heightened influence could be compared to a concertmaster who, during specific passages, establishes eye contact with other section leaders, thus exerting greater influence over the orchestra's performance.

In a follow-up study, we found that the subconscious influenced the brain's pain network during sad or nervous-sounding music.[49] This unveiled a neural mechanism where subconscious negative thoughts manifest as emotional discomfort or even physical pain.

In summary, our research shows that listening to music that mirrors negative emotional states such as sadness or nervousness makes our wandering thoughts more negative. It also allows our subconscious to wield greater influence over other brain areas, including those that form the brain's pain network.

Counteracting Thought Loops with Music

1. *Awareness.* The initial and most crucial step to counteract negative thought loops is to recognize them. How long did it take for you to become aware of them last time? Could you perhaps identify them sooner next time?

---

[48] Koelsch et al., Heroic music stimulates empowering thoughts during mind-wandering.
[49] Koelsch et al., Tormenting thoughts.

2. *Musical tools.* Once you acknowledge these loops, music can serve as a potent tool to dismantle their cycle. Choose music that emanates positivity – be it joyful, motivating, empowering, or calming.
3. *Active engagement.* Next, direct your focus towards the music and engage actively by tapping to the beat, singing along, or dancing. Breathing in synchrony with the music's rhythm while counting the beats of each inhalation and exhalation is also remarkably effective. Such a level of engagement consumes your working memory resources, thereby effectively stripping the subconscious thought loops of their power. Should you notice these loops reappearing, immediately disrupt them by refocusing on the music.
4. *Immediate impact.* Committing to this for just a few minutes will already have an impact. No matter how modest this impact may seem initially, not even the deepest depression can entirely suppress the release of at least one positive neurotransmitter when we engage with music. And once we trigger the release of one such molecule, thousands more will follow.
5. *Background benefits.* Bear in mind that when positive-sounding music plays in the background, mind-wandering thoughts are more apt to take a positive turn. We can leverage this effect to prevent the inception of negative thought loops. Occasionally, let positive music play in the background, especially during activities that do not require high concentration. If your mind starts wandering, the presence of this music can help steer these thoughts in a positive direction.
6. *Starting the day.* To set a positive tone for the day, consider starting your morning routine with uplifting music, avoiding tunes that evoke feelings of sadness, melancholy, nostalgia, or nervousness.
7. *Daily practice.* Incorporate positive music into your daily routine and use it several times throughout the day to positively influence your thoughts and refresh your mood.

MUSIC'S PEACEMAKING POTENTIAL

There is another positive effect of music on subconscious thoughts: with music, it is easier to steer our attention towards *commonalities.*

As discussed in the previous sections, the subconscious is concerned with influencing thoughts, behaviours, and emotions according to *social norms* – it wants us and others to be 'normal'. Deviations from social norms and cultural practices are subconsciously perceived as threats, provoking fear, concern, or outrage. Because the subconscious is a threat-sensitive system, it allocates more attention to differences than to similarities. And because the subconscious prioritizes our need to belong and be accepted by our group, it compels us to align our views with those prevalent within it, disregarding their logical or factual validity. In this process, the subconscious selectively filters information that corroborates the pre-existing world view of the group – even when such pieces of information are 'fake news'. From a neurobiological viewpoint, we do not live in a 'post-truth' era; we simply have a 'pre-factual' affect system within our brain.

During a *conflict*, the views and opinions of individuals differ. The subconscious focuses on such differences and blows their importance out of proportion. Yet, it is the *commonalities* of the conflicting parties that attenuate conflicts, and we only identify them when we consciously seek them out. Ironically, recognizing similarities should be straightforward, especially considering their abundance. For example, all humans crave social interaction and a sense of belonging. We all desire respect, love, individual freedom, justice, and fairness. Everyone seeks happiness, purpose in their actions, societal recognition, avoidance of suffering, the welfare of children, personal integrity, honour, health, and well-being. Moreover, on a lighter note, everyone has their moments of looking rather peculiar!

These extensive similarities among all people, irrespective of skin colour, religion, gender, or wealth, signify a shared plethora of interests and needs. Instead of *moral emotions* that assign blame and generate outrage, we need *ethical emotions* that are rooted in human values. Instead of subconscious biases that accentuate differences, we need to focus on shared interests and needs to foster compassion and kindness. As these interests and needs are universal, they form the basis of the human rights that every individual inherently deserves.

When we make music together, we inherently share significant commonalities. Everyone focuses their attention on the music, we share a goal, and our movements and even our emotions synchronize. Our participation in collective music making thus becomes a *natural sign* of the desire to experience music together. Some academics refer to this natural sign as an *honest signal*. Because music is a means to demonstrate an abundance of commonalities in large groups, it possesses a substantial capacity for fostering peace, perhaps more than any other medium.

The Role of Music in Conflict

A beautiful example of music's peacemaking potential are the *singing duels* in hunter-gatherer cultures and tribal societies.[50] These typically occur between members of different clans or tribes with the intention to resolve disputes, such as those concerning interpersonal conflicts or territorial claims. The tribes or village communities gather for a large celebration, during which two participants – one from each conflicting party – participate in the singing duel, alternately singing and improvising about the conflict and the opposing party.

These singing duels adhere strictly to established rules. The duels follow a prescribed order, have a fixed duration, and the consequences for winners or losers are well defined. The duels prohibit lies or insults, but wit, irony, and sharp repartee are welcomed. They are intended to be fair and peaceful, working to de-escalate conflicts and re-establish amicable social relationships, and thus prevent violent confrontations, revenge, or even murder. Often, these duels result in the conflicting parties transforming their strife into long-lasting friendships.

The essence of these practices can be seen across various cultures worldwide, where music and performance serve as mediums for conflict resolution and community bonding. Rap battles, for instance, transform verbal aggression into a creative and non-violent form of competition, showcasing lyrical agility and wit. Capoeira sessions in Brazil, with their emphasis on call and response and fluid movements, blend elements of martial arts, dance, and music to foster community and teach respect and discipline. Sean-nós dancing in Ireland, often performed in communal settings, encourages participation and celebrates cultural heritage while showcasing individual expression. These events not only highlight

---

[50] Lehmann et al., The singing controversy in human ethological perspective.

individual talent but also underscore the importance of respect, unity, and peaceful competition across diverse traditions.

Why can singing resolve conflicts more effectively than just speaking? The answer lies in the power of singing to amplify *shared* experiences and, by extension, our perception of commonalities. The pulse of a song prompts participants' minds and bodies to 'swing together in time', stimulating a collective engagement with the rhythm. The melodies heighten this effect: they are typically simple, making it easy for everyone to follow and resonate with. Such mental and physical synchronization among the conflicting parties and the audience fosters a deep sense of *community*. It makes everyone feel they are part of a larger collective, with shared objectives, needs, and values. Through this experience, it becomes clear that the commonalities they share significantly outweigh their differences.

The widespread prevalence of these customs across diverse and independent cultures suggests that singing duels form part of our species' biological behavioural repertoire, akin to language, music, and dance. Unfortunately, our modern civilization has largely overlooked this innate human capacity for conflict resolution through music. Imagine this – a legal system where all court proceedings unfold in *song*.

Certainly, music is not a magic pill that would instantaneously induce love and peace. While music has the *potential* to foster peace, it is not a panacea for conflict. On the contrary, by reinforcing social identities, music can also function as a barrier against other groups or societies. This is evident in the hate music of neo-Nazis, 'white power music', or war songs rallying troops into battle. Numerous subcultures celebrate with their unique music and dance but often leave outsiders unwelcome. The emotional effects of music can be exploited to incite aggression, manipulate others, or even serve as a means of torture. However, with a *humanistic orientation*, the community-building potential of music can unfold, and music can aid in the cultivation of peace, prosocial behaviour, and harmony. When we swing together in time with a peaceful, community-focused attitude, music can serve as a more potent catalyst for peace and unity than any other medium in the world.

CHAPTER 9

What Is an Emotion?

EVERYONE KNOWS WHAT AN EMOTION is – until they are asked to elucidate it. While people intuitively describe their feelings when discussing emotions, from a scientific standpoint, a feeling is just one component of an emotion, specifically the *percept* of an emotion. Another key component is the activity of the affect systems, which we explored earlier. These systems function as the 'wellsprings' that generate our emotions, with each system creating a distinct class of emotions imbued with unique qualities. Other components of an emotion include the physiological changes within the body, our evaluation of the current situation, the motivation driving a particular behaviour, shifts in attention and memory, and the expression of the emotional state.

Consider, for instance, the experience of listening to groovy funk music in a club. This might activate the pleasure system, alter your heartbeat, prompt you to evaluate the music positively within the given context, instigate an urge to move, direct your attention towards the music, and elicit a joyful facial expression. The cumulative *result* is the experience of a pleasurable feeling. However, this feeling does not originate in the pleasure system itself; rather, it stems from the 'feeling cortex' within the brain. Similarly, the changes in heartbeat and expressions of joy are *effects* of activity in the pleasure system, but are not produced by the pleasure system itself.

Therefore, when an affect system becomes active, it instigates effects in other brain systems, and it is the combination of these components that contributes to our emotional experience. Let us look more closely at these components. I have outlined them in detail in the *four-component theory of subjective feelings* that follows.[1]

FOUR BIOLOGICAL COMPONENTS CONTRIBUTE TO OUR FEELINGS

The first element is the *affective component*, which involves the affect systems sending neural impulses directly to the 'feeling cortex'. The role of the affect systems in directly eliciting emotional sensations becomes evident in patients with damage or disruption to an affect system, who show profound anomalies in their feelings. Over a century ago, neurologists Henry Head and Gordon Holmes documented this phenomenon in patients with damage to one side of their thalamus, a crucial structure within the pain system. When these patients were emotionally moved by music, such as during hymns in a church service, the sensations on the side of their body affected by the damage were overwhelmingly intense, almost to the point of being unbearable.[2]

The second ingredient in our emotional experience is the *somatic component*. Every emotion involves autonomic and hormonal effects (some autonomic effects are illustrated in Figure 6.1). Sensations arising from such somatic responses form an integral part of our feelings. These can manifest in feeling cold or warm, tense or relaxed, feeling goosebumps, a pounding heart, a gasp for breath, or the sudden onset of perspiration. Many languages have idiomatic expressions to reflect these sensations: one might feel 'butterflies in the stomach', find a situation so unnerving that 'one's blood freezes in their veins', or become so flustered that 'words stick in one's throat'. Emotions may even affect our vision, hearing, and balance, given that all sensory organs are influenced by autonomic nerves and hormones. This can result in phenomena such as blurred vision, dizziness, or tinnitus.

---

[1] Koelsch, S., Jacobs, A. M., Menninghaus, W., Liebal, K., Klann-Delius, G., von Scheve, C., and Gebauer, G. (2015). The quartet theory of human emotions: An integrative and neurofunctional model. *Physics of Life Reviews*, 13, 1–27.

[2] Head, H., and Holmes, G. (1911). Sensory disturbances from cerebral lesions. *Brain*, 34 (2–3), 102–254.

WHAT IS AN EMOTION?

It is worth noting that disrupted or underdeveloped *interoception* – the perception of internal body states – is implicated in various health conditions, including depression, anxiety, eating disorders, and addictions.[3] It also plays a role in somatoform disorders, where individuals experience pain in an organ despite the absence of any detectable physical cause. Thus, a sensitive perception of one's body is indeed beneficial for our health and well-being. Musical activities such as learning to play an instrument, singing, or dancing are excellent means to cultivate this interoception.

Our internal organs relay sensory information to a specific brain region, the 'insula' (refer to Figure 8.3 for a depiction). Thus, this region registers the internal state of our body – it harbours our primary interoceptive cortex. In addition, the insula receives information from our muscles, tendons, and joints, thus contributing to *proprioception* – our sense of bodily position and movement. Proprioception is critical for self-recognition, determining whether a body part that we see or feel belongs to us. This notion is exemplified in patients with disrupted proprioception, who, in stark disorientation, might perceive an arm extending from their body as alien, failing to identify it as their own.

The insula integrates interoception and proprioception, extending the capacity for self-recognition beyond the physical to the emotional domain. This enables us to distinguish our own feelings from those of others, in addition to defining the borders between self and others. This process is not innate but develops over time. For example, initially, a newborn lacks the capacity to distinguish between their own body and that of their mother; similarly, they are unable to separate their emotions from those of their mother. Upon the infant's learning of this distinction, the insula gains crucial importance for empathy and compassion, owing to its ability to distinguish between one's own feelings and those of others.

The third element contributing to our feelings is the *motor component*. Each emotion inherently involves a motivation to act or, alternatively, an impulse to inhibit action. We perceive this motivation as the urge to act or abstain, to approach or avoid. Take, for instance, the infectious beat of

---

[3] Khalsa, S. S., Adolphs, R., Cameron, O. G., Critchley, H. D., and Davenport, P. W. (2018). Interoception and mental health: a roadmap. *Biological Psychiatry: Cognitive Neuroscience and Neuroimaging*, 3(6), 501–513.

a dance band, which may elicit an urge to draw nearer, partake in clapping, and join the dance. Conversely, we have all encountered music that makes us wish to make a swift exit!

The fourth constituent of our emotional experience is the *cognitive component*. Cognitive evaluations influence our emotions by assessing the potential benefits or hazards of a situation, a topic we explored in Part II. For instance, consider the apprehension many students feel when preparing for an exam. Initially, they may worry about falling short of their performance expectations. However, upon realizing they can devise a study plan and collaborate with peers, their anxiety may lessen. As previously discussed, we also possess the ability to consciously regulate negative emotions through simple measures such as deep breathing, relaxation, and identifying positive elements in our situation.

WHERE IN THE BRAIN DO WE FEEL OUR FEELINGS?

The affect systems, the motor areas of the brain, and the interoceptive cortex of the insula all dispatch nerve signals to a brain region that I have termed the *feeling cortex*. This region, identified anatomically as the 'secondary somatosensory cortex', is indicated in the bottom panel of Figure 8.3. In addition, the feeling cortex receives sensory information from the skin, making it responsive to a variety of tactile stimuli including touch, pressure, and temperature, alongside pain and even a gentle slow caress. Drawing from these diverse sources throughout the brain and body, the feeling cortex synthesizes an *emotion percept*, transforming objects or situations into *emotionally felt* experiences.

Brain areas involved in conscious thought also project to the feeling cortex. This establishes a neural foundation for our ability to consciously regulate our feelings. Intriguingly, the feeling cortex also receives an abundance of neural projections from the auditory cortex. This implies that sounds carrying emotional information, such as affective vocalizations of others or music, can directly influence our feelings. Consequently, from a neuroanatomical perspective, music can modulate our feelings even without necessarily evoking any specific emotion. Recall the last time you used music to calm your nerves. Beyond the soothing impact that the music likely exerted on your vitalization system, it also *directly* influenced your feelings. This effect occurred simply because the auditory cortex was sending calming signals to the feeling cortex. These direct effects can be compared to the immediate impact a calming thought has on our feelings when we are agitated.

Intriguingly, the feeling cortex engages not only during our *own* sensory experiences but also activates when we witness *others* undergoing such experiences. It reacts both to receiving a slow gentle touch and to watching another person experience such a touch. In parallel, it responds to our personal perception of pain as well as when we witness another person getting hurt. For instance, when we watch someone stumble and crash to the ground, our feeling cortex activates almost as if we were falling ourselves. In a similar vein, the insula, which processes information about our *own* bodily sensations, also becomes active when we observe *others* experiencing specific feelings, including pain. (For reference, the insula is depicted in Figure 8.3.) Hence, the neural codes involved in experiencing our *own* emotions significantly overlap with those activated when we empathize with the emotions of others. This overlap provides a neurobiological underpinning for our capacity to share, and understand, the emotions of others.

WHEN MUSIC IS WORTH A THOUSAND WORDS

A feeling is the *percept* of an emotion. While many of us are accustomed to verbalizing our feelings, these feelings do not inherently possess a verbal component. As a result, attempts to articulate our internal emotional states often prove both imprecise and unreliable. This is because the distinct feeling components – affective activity, unconscious evaluations, motor impulses, and interoception – collectively contribute to our emotional experience, merging indistinguishably within the emotion percept. For example, when we feel 'happy', we cannot delineate the individual contributions of these elements. This dilemma deepens when we acknowledge that our emotion percepts cannot be externally observed. If someone says, 'I have a severe toothache', we cannot gain direct access to their experience to confirm the statement or interpret what 'severe' means to them. Consequently, we can never ascertain whether *another* person's verbal description of a feeling precisely aligns with our *own* interpretation.

In contrast, other sensory percepts are externally observable and measurable. If we hear a violin sound, we need to find words for this auditory percept to communicate it, and someone could correct us by saying, 'No, that's not the sound of a violin.' It would be baffling, though, if someone were to tell us, 'No, you aren't experiencing a toothache.'

Thankfully, the feeling cortex possesses the capacity for emotional resonance, enabling us to communicate feelings *without* using words. Hearing emotions such as joy, surprise, sadness, or fear in someone's voice elicits corresponding sensations in our feeling cortex. Additional emotional cues include smell, facial expressions, and gestures. Through these signals, we share and understand another person's feelings. The intensity of someone's toothache can be inferred from their anguished voice, contorted, sweat-beaded face, dramatically dilated pupils, and overall physical tension.

This power of emotional resonance is why music outperforms words in communicating feelings. Music – this *super-expressive voice* – allows us to establish a more accurate correlation between feelings and sounds. In Beethoven's 'Moonlight Sonata', we can hear the emotional distress caused by his struggles with hearing loss and isolation – an experience we broadly label as 'melancholy'. Through Arnold Schönberg's String Trio Op. 45, we can vicariously experience the chest pangs he endured during a heart attack. Gustav Mahler famously asserted that if he could articulate his experiences in words, he would not need to compose music.

Music therapy improvisation capitalizes on this unique expressive capacity of music, facilitating emotional articulation where words prove insufficient. For instance, a patient with depression might 'finally let it all out' through *music* when they find themselves inhibited and unable to *verbalize* their distress. Furthermore, music therapy can assist individuals with autism – who often struggle to associate feelings with words – by enabling them to label their feelings with the titles of music pieces rather than words. This method also aids them in understanding emotion words, thereby enhancing their ability to verbally express their emotions.[4]

---

[4] Allen, R., and Heaton, P. (2010). Autism, music, and the therapeutic potential of music in alexithymia. *Music Perception: An Interdisciplinary Journal*, 27(4), 251–261.

MIXED EMOTIONS

In the preceding sections, we explored how *emotions* consist of various components: the activities within our affect systems, physiological changes, modulations in attention and memory, emotional expressions, motor impulses, and the subjective experience of feelings. We can name these feelings using language, and our conscious cognitive evaluations can exert influence over these emotions. Each of these phenomena represents ingredients of emotions, and it is their combined interplay that constitutes an emotion.

Frequently, multiple affective components coalesce to shape a single emotion. For example, music that incites joy may also concurrently mitigate pain, or an episode of happiness could simultaneously provide a sense of pleasure. I have observed a baby's face displaying pain and a social smile concurrently. Particularly within the arts, these *mixed emotions* offer fascinating nuances. Listening to melancholic music, for instance, can engender *bittersweet emotions*, where melancholy blends with the pleasure derived from the beautiful sound of the music.

EMOTIONS AND CONSCIOUSNESS

Viewed biologically, emotions serve as survival mechanisms, instrumental in preserving the individual and the species. They motivate specific behaviours, maintain an optimal level of arousal, communicate information to those around us, and swiftly direct attention and memory – all without necessitating any contemplation. Emotions aim to help us navigate immediate situations, secure instant advantages, avoid discomfort, and experience positive sensations. Thus, our emotional systems favour immediate rewards, such as 'receiving five euros now', over potentially larger future gains, such as 'receiving eight euros next month'.

However, our emotional systems often fall short in assessing the long-term repercussions of our actions. Fortunately, humans possess a conscious mind that can help evaluate the long-term ramifications of behaviour or regulate negative emotions. It can assist us in discerning whether the behaviours that our emotions so urgently impel us towards are truly aligned with our self-interest. For example, if the craving system evokes a desire for alcohol or cheesecake, we can consciously control our actions, even though it may seem enormously challenging at times. If we find it difficult to motivate ourselves to exercise, we can consciously remind ourselves that physical activity is crucial for our long-term health. If a music student's subconscious tempts him/her to opt for the immediate pleasure of watching Netflix instead of rehearsing a demanding sonata, he/she can consciously motivate him- or herself to practise. He/she might achieve this by reminding him- or herself that an hour of focused practice, devoid of negative thoughts, can serve as a form of meditation conducive to good health. Lastly, our conscious mind can assist us in determining whether our subconscious thoughts and emotional behaviours align with peaceful, humane principles. Such conscious mental activity creates room for the emergence of those positive emotions that offer sustained benefits to us and others.

CHAPTER 10

Morning Dance

ACCORDING TO FRIEDRICH NIETZSCHE, A DAY WITHOUT dancing is a day wasted. For Charlie Chaplin, a day without a smile is a day wasted, and a day devoid of joy or fun hardly qualifies as a truly happy one. Fortunately, we can accomplish all these in one fell swoop, through dancing. Furthermore, dancing carries a plethora of health benefits. It bolsters physical fitness, keeps our brains young through enjoyment, reduces stress, and encourages positive emotions. It also enhances balance, and it can even improve mobility for those with Parkinson's disease.

Therefore, I extend an invitation to each reader: engage in a morning dance. Let us dance in such a way that we all dance together: if you are willing, play one of the songs I have listed below between 6 and 10 a.m. (each day has its song) and dance. Naturally, you are free to use your own favourite tunes. Sway your hips, nod gently with your head, stretch your arms towards the sky. Dance while brewing your coffee, brushing your teeth, or showering, either alone, as a duo, or even in a group. If there is no stereo in the room you are dancing in, you can play the songs on a mobile device, perhaps with a Bluetooth speaker. If a high number of readers participate, we can envision others dancing simultaneously, all experiencing *Good Vibrations*, perhaps even to the same tune.

Most of the songs are dance music 'classics', spanning the last hundred years, covering a broad array of genres. In the list below, songs are arranged according to the day of the week and the week of the month. For instance, Aretha Franklin's 'Think' is the tune of the day for the first Monday of a month; the following day, it is 'Everybody Needs Somebody' by the Blues Brothers. If a song evokes negative associations for you, please feel free to replace it. If you wish to dance for longer than the duration of a song, set it on repeat or play other songs listed for the day.

	Week of the month				
	1	2	3	4	5
Day of the week					
Monday	Aretha Franklin, 'Respect'	Blues Brothers, 'Everybody Needs Somebody'	ZAZ, 'Paris sera toujours Paris'	Daft Punk, 'One More Time'	Elvis, 'A Little Less Conversation' (JXL remix)
Tuesday	Gilberto Gil, 'Bat Macumba'	Clean Bandit ft. Jess Glynne, 'Rather Be'	Elvis, 'King Creole'	Manny Corchado, 'Chicken and Booze'	Christina Aguilera, 'Candyman'
Wednesday	Aretha Franklin, 'Think'	Jimmy Smith, 'Stay Loose'	Chic, 'Le Freak'	Green Hill, 'The Charleston'	Elvis, 'Jailhouse Rock'
Thursday	Ritchie Valens, 'La Bamba'	Earth, Wind & Fire, 'September'	Stevie Wonder, 'Sir Duke'	Jackson Five, 'Blame It on the Boogie'	Ray Charles, 'Shake Your Tailfeather'
Friday	Ella Fitzgerald and Duke Ellington, 'It Don't Mean a Thing'	Chuck Berry, 'Johnny B. Goode'	The Trammps, 'Disco Inferno'	Benny Goodman, 'Sing, Sing, Sing'	Justin Timberlake, 'Can't Stop the Feeling'
Saturday	Blues Brothers, 'Soul Man'	Prince, 'Let's Go Crazy' (live)	Mark Ronson ft. Bruno Mars, 'Uptown Funk'	Pharrell Williams, 'Happy'	Outkast, 'Hey Ya!'
Sunday	Ella Fitzgerald, 'Blue Skies'	Kool and the Gang, 'Celebration'	Avicii, 'Levels'	Shakira, 'Waka Waka'	Milton Nascimento, 'Cravo e Canela'

PART FOUR

HOW MUSIC HELPS WITH ILLNESS

In the chapters that follow, I will illustrate the healing effects of music on a variety of diseases and disorders. This exploration will shed light on the astonishing and, from a medical perspective, often inexplicable effects that music can wield – effects that are, nonetheless, well substantiated by scientific evidence.

If there are certain diseases and disorders for which I have not dedicated a separate chapter, it is generally because the current body of research has yet to entirely convince me. However, this should not be misconstrued as music being incapable of assisting with such conditions. On the contrary, the field of music therapy research is still young and burgeoning. I am confident that, in due course, we shall accumulate scientific evidence that underscores the therapeutic impacts of music on a wide range of chronic diseases and disorders. Therefore, many of the findings and the suggested treatment techniques that I discuss in this book can be adapted and applied to a host of other ailments.

CHAPTER 11

Stroke

GLOBALLY, STROKES ARE AMONG THE MOST PREVALENT diseases and the leading causes of death. In the United States alone, approximately 795,000 individuals experience a stroke annually, making strokes one of the main reasons for loss of life in the country. Typically, a stroke is caused by the occlusion of a blood vessel in the brain, although cerebral haemorrhages can also be a less common cause. This blockage and the resulting circulatory disruption deprive a part of the brain of its vital oxygen supply. Typical indications of a stroke include unilateral paralysis, speech difficulties, loss of consciousness, dizziness, nausea, and visual disturbances such as sudden double or blurred vision, or even a complete loss of vision within a certain field.

Because a stroke usually does not cause pain, the seriousness of the situation is often dismissed and immediate medical intervention is not sought. However, the most critical response to a stroke is to get to a hospital as swiftly as possible. The longer the delay in receiving adequate treatment, the more extensive the potential brain damage. Every minute counts. When calling for emergency medical services, it is vital to clearly express the suspicion of a stroke. Additionally, the precise time when the initial symptoms emerged should be noted, as medical interventions to clear blocked blood vessels are most effective within the first few hours of symptom onset – any delay can be detrimental.

While a stroke may seem to strike suddenly, transient disruptions in the brain's circulation often trigger warning signs days or even months prior. These can include mild dizziness, flickering vision, transient paralysis, or speech difficulties. As these minor episodes usually dissipate within minutes or hours, most individuals tend to downplay their significance. However, the appropriate response to such occurrences is immediate medical consultation.

Surviving a stroke usually leads to moderate to severe disabilities, which may be temporary but often become chronic. Consequently, a stroke represents a severe personal crisis for the individual, eliciting a range of emotional responses such as sadness, a sense of impending disaster, hopelessness, frustration, or even aggression. However, in the weeks and months following a stroke, the brain works tenaciously to rectify and compensate for the damage. This effort leads to substantial changes within the brain: it forms new synapses, generates new blood vessels, and develops new brain tissue, albeit not new nerve cells. Furthermore, the nerve cells neighbouring the damaged area or those in the opposite hemisphere strive to take over the functions of the lost cells.

These neurological changes can be significantly influenced by music. The most compelling evidence for the therapeutic effects of music has been produced for therapies administered following strokes. The brain's adaptive changes necessitate practice – and the more enjoyable the process, the more effectively the brain can reorganize itself. The emotional effects of music have a tangible impact on brain chemistry, creating positive implications for the healing processes within the brain. Moreover, the brain can reorganize more proficiently when engaged 'multimodally', such as when movement exercises are paired with moving to music.

When patients actively participate in their exercises, they can positively steer their healing trajectory. Furthermore, rehabilitation measures that incorporate music often outperform those without such inclusion. Up until recently, it was widely believed that post-stroke assistance was often very limited. However, in many cases, the appropriate rehabilitation measures had simply not yet been discovered. Some of the most promising, effective therapeutic measures have emerged from the domain of neurocognitive music therapy.

DURING THE ACUTE PHASE

Approximately fifteen years ago, a groundbreaking study by Finnish doctoral student Teppo Särkämö captivated the medical community.

He revealed that stroke patients who had listened to music during their hospital stay exhibited superior mental faculties and fewer depressive symptoms in the months following their stroke, compared to a control group of patients who had listened to audiobooks.[1]

In his research, Särkämö classified patients afflicted with middle cerebral artery strokes into one of three groups within a week of hospitalization: a music group, an audiobook group, or a passive control group. Participants in the music group were given a CD player featuring their favourite tunes, while those in the audiobook group received CD players with their selected audiobooks. Conversely, participants in the passive control group received neither music nor audiobooks. Teppo instructed the first two groups to listen to their respective CDs for at least one hour per day over the subsequent two months, whether they were in the hospital or at home. Both of these groups devoted about the same amount of time to their listening exercises during this period – on average one and a half hours per day.

Six months post-stroke, all three groups exhibited cognitive improvement – a testament to the brain's intrinsic ability for recuperation. However, a fascinating distinction emerged: the individuals in the music group exhibited a greater increase in their verbal memory and concentration test scores than those in the other two groups. In the verbal memory test, patients were asked to recall a list of ten words, while the concentration test challenged them to solve mental arithmetic problems. Notably, these improvements in the music group were most pronounced among patients with left-hemispheric strokes – likely because music stimulated the 'musical' right hemisphere more effectively.

Thus, the mere act of daily music listening enhanced the recuperation of particular cognitive functions in stroke patients. Furthermore, those in the music group reported feeling less depressed and less disoriented – in other words, less forgetful, uncertain, and unfocused – in evaluations conducted three and six months post-stroke. Consequently, the emotional state of the patients in the music group was noticeably

---

[1] Särkämö, T., Tervaniemi, M., Laitinen, S., Forsblom, A., Soinila, S., Mikkonen, M., Autti, T., Silvennoinen, H. M., Erkkilä, J., Laine, M., and Peretz, I. (2008). Music listening enhances cognitive recovery and mood after middle cerebral artery stroke. *Brain*, 131(3), 866–876.

more positive at both the three- and six-month intervals than that of the patients in the other two groups.

In addition to the observed effects of music listening on cognitive functions and mood, Teppo also noticed differences in the brain's reorganization.[2] Through MRI data, grey matter in the brain was measured one week and six months post-stroke. The results indicated that the music group experienced a significantly stronger increase in grey matter within the *healthy* hemisphere compared to the audiobook group. The latter, in turn, demonstrated a slightly more pronounced grey matter increase than the passive control group. Thus, it became apparent that music listening markedly bolstered the reorganization of brain functions within the hemisphere unaffected by the stroke.

What, then, accounts for the salutary effects of music listening on cognitive recuperation and cerebral reorganization? Music, it appears, activates an array of brain functions: perception, attention, memory, sensorimotor skills, along with emotion, intelligence, and language – particularly when the music includes lyrics. Therefore, music triggers a plethora of processes within the brain, stimulating numerous regions, including the area surrounding the lesion and its 'partner areas' in the unaffected hemisphere. Such stimulation not only triggers nerve cell activity but also enhances blood flow within the region. This augmentation aids in the compensation of functions from damaged areas, forming new synapses, dendritic spines, capillaries, and new tissue supporting nerve cells. Depending on the brain area, reorganization can even result in the settlement of new nerve cells. These processes particularly flourish in an environment that is gentle, pleasant, and emotionally positive, ideally engaging multiple sensory channels and cognitive functions – simultaneously as music so readily does.

The emotional benefits of music listening also encompass that patients worry less, focus on the music, relax more, and experience greater joy. This regulation of emotion impacts brain chemistry, affecting

---

[2] Särkämö, T., Ripollés, P., Vepsäläinen, H., Autti, T., Silvennoinen, H. M., Salli, E., Laitinen, S., Forsblom, A., Soinila, S., and Rodríguez-Fornells, A. (2014). Structural changes induced by daily music listening in the recovering brain after middle cerebral artery stroke: A voxel-based morphometry study. *Frontiers in Human Neuroscience*, 8, 245.

neurotransmitters such as dopamine, serotonin, and glutamate, as well as messengers of the immune system. Furthermore, emotions in the brain generate hormonal and vegetative effects in the body, including positive effects on blood pressure – which must not become too high post-stroke.

So, following medical emergency care upon hospital admission, music listening can provide substantial aid. It draws attention towards the music, away from worries, and promotes positive effects on brain regeneration. Therefore, family members, doctors, and nursing staff are advised to encourage stroke patients to listen to music (also see the box below). The specific genre of music appears unimportant, as long as it provides enjoyment and pleasure to the patient. The music selection in Teppo's study primarily consisted of popular genres (pop, rock, rhythm and blues), although some patients opted for classical, jazz, folk, or meditation music. Listening to music with vocals is particularly advantageous, as it also engages the brain's language functions.

However, it is crucial to prevent any overwhelming exposure to stimuli when listening to music, as this could create undue stress that would be counterproductive during this vulnerable period of recovery. In the weeks and months following a stroke, the brain is exceptionally receptive, aiding in its reorganization but also rendering it particularly sensitive.

Notably, during the acute phase, several stroke patients – especially those with right-hemispheric strokes – may develop *amusia*.[3] This means that patients frequently struggle to hear or understand music properly. While amusia can sometimes improve, it can also persist over the long term. Nonetheless, Teppo has shared with me that even when patients have difficulty perceiving the melody or the sound of the music, they can often still appreciate other aspects of it, such as rhythm or emotional expression. Moreover, music can often evoke memories in these patients. Therefore, even for patients with amusia, music can still hold significance, and listening to it can still be a beneficial activity.

---

[3] Särkämö, T., Tervaniemi, M., Soinila, S., Autti, T., Silvennoinen, H. M., Laine, M., Hietanen, M., and Pihko, E. (2010). Auditory and cognitive deficits associated with acquired amusia after stroke: A magnetoencephalography and neuropsychological follow-up study. *PLoS ONE*, 5(12), e15157.

RECOMMENDATIONS FOR THE IMMEDIATE AND SUBSEQUENT PHASES AFTER A STROKE

- Initiate music listening as soon as is feasible after receiving emergency medical treatment. However, there's no rush – music continues to offer benefits even days or weeks post-stroke.
- Family members should equip the patient with a device for playing music, perhaps along with headphones if they are sharing a room with other patients. Only play music that the patient enjoys or requests, using what you know they enjoyed before their stroke. If the patient struggles to express themselves, observe their reactions attentively to prevent any music-induced stress. If needed, adjust the volume, experiment with different genres, or switch the music off. When using headphones, always try them out on yourself first to check the volume. Note that safe listening levels for a healthy person might still be too loud for a stroke patient with heightened sensitivity. Consider headphones with volume-limiting features for additional safety.
- Exercise caution to prevent overstimulation or sensory overload, especially in the initial phases. Choose soothing music and introduce it gently. Opt for calming rather than stimulating music, and aim for a quieter rather than louder volume. Yet, it should remain engaging enough to provide a mental distraction. Keep in mind that, due to heightened sensitivity, music will sound much louder and more intense to the patient than usual.
- Include songs with comprehensible lyrics in the playlist, to stimulate both music and language processes in the brain.
- Let the patient listen to music for as long as they wish, ideally for at least one hour per day, over a period of no less than two months.
- When the patient is ready, encourage them to select and listen to their music on their own, or even begin making music again if they enjoyed playing an instrument before their stroke. Empowering patients to take an active role in music selection and creation can significantly enhance their recovery experience, providing both comfort and a sense of agency. The following chapters offer a wealth of recommendations and examples to help patients incorporate music into their recovery journey.

APHASIA: PATIENTS WHO SING EVEN WHEN THEY CAN NO LONGER SPEAK

Mrs N was in her late forties and staying in France when she awoke one morning to discover she had lost her ability to speak. Despite her capability to form sentences in her mind, she lost control over her speech-motor skills – she could no longer produce words. This harrowing ordeal, not unlike a nightmare, became her chilling reality. Fortunately, her husband acted quickly and ensured she was rushed to a hospital, where she was diagnosed with a stroke in the left hemisphere of her brain. Upon her subsequent transfer to a German clinic, she remained speechless – unable to voluntarily produce even a single vocal sound. Additionally, she suffered from hemiplegia, although this condition receded shortly after.

The stroke, coupled with the sudden inability to speak, plunged Mrs N into a deep well of distress and despair. She was frequently overwhelmed by bouts of weeping; although she could *hear* her emotional vocalizations, she remained unable to produce a single speech sound *intentionally*. Ultimately, she decided to pursue music therapy.

At a rehabilitation clinic, she encountered Claudia Dill-Schmölders, an experienced music therapist. Mrs N wept, and Claudia responded compassionately through music. Playing the piano, she improvised a tune for Mrs N, who gradually calmed down and began to synchronize her breathing with the rhythm of the music. Then, just before the final note of the melody, Claudia stopped playing – and to her surprise, Mrs N softly echoed the final tone. As the inaugural music therapy session progressed, Mrs N began to vocalize the melody's tones, one by one. She discovered that, although spoken language eluded her, she was still capable of singing tones. This realization evoked profound relief, along with a sense of potent internal liberation and relaxation. Finally, a glimmer of hope emerged for Mrs N. Within that very first music therapy session, she started to hum simple songs. Then, Claudia suggested she would *sing* the first syllable of the word 'hello', inviting Mrs N to complete the word with a sung tone. She voiced, 'Hel ...' and Mrs N replied, with a fragile yet clear, '... lo'.

In the weeks that followed, Mrs N participated in both speech and music therapy. She attended a singing group specially designed for aphasia patients, which incorporated not just singing but also breathing and rhythmic exercises. Additionally, she joined the 'therapeutic singing group', an initiative open to all patients in the hospital. Her extensive experience with choir singing proved beneficial, providing her with a broad repertoire of songs.

In music therapy, she began by learning to supplement words with singing, then progressed to singing whole words. This feat could only be achieved through *singing*; when she attempted to *speak*, she was unable to form sentences or even parts of words. Her attempts to speak were evident; she tirelessly sought a way to articulate speech sounds. However, barely any speech sounds emerged from her mouth, and those that did were scarcely audible and lacked resonance.

Consequently, Claudia worked with Mrs N on controlling her breathing, concentrating on eliciting speech sounds by way of singing – beginning with simple syllables and gradually advancing to entire words. It was highly effective to incorporate movements with the music or speech melody. They would tap along to the music with one hand or clap with both hands, for example. Additionally, music-therapeutic relaxation exercises on a soundbed assisted Mrs N in loosening her facial muscles.

Before long, she was capable of *singing* brief sentences, though she still found it impossible to replicate them while attempting to *speak*. In a mere span of two weeks, she progressively mastered singing words, parts of phrases, and, ultimately, entire phrases for a growing number of songs. She then embarked on melodious speaking, a fusion of singing and speaking. She had discovered that her voice could find flow through singing, which eased her effort to speak. Gradually, she began to initiate speech independently. After a period of three months, Mrs N had successfully regained her ability to articulate words clearly and bid farewell to the clinic.

Roughly a third of all stroke patients struggle with aphasia, a condition characterized by the loss of the ability to speak or understand language. When the left frontal lobe, particularly Broca's area, suffers damage, it often results in what is known as 'Broca's aphasia' or 'motor aphasia'. Interestingly, these patients retain the capacity to *comprehend* simple sentences spoken to them. They can think in words and sentences, but they face a significant obstacle when it comes to *speaking*; typically, they can only babble one or a few sounds. One of the most compelling phenomena in neurology is that many of these patients preserve the ability to sing and, even more remarkably, to sing *with words*. I have encountered patients who have lost their capacity to utter the phrase 'happy birthday', yet they can melodiously voice 'happy birthday', with the words often articulated with such clarity and precision that it contradicts their speech impairment. This fascinating observation has catalysed the development of various therapeutic techniques that exploit this unique phenomenon.

MELODIC INTONATION THERAPY

One such approach is *melodic intonation therapy* (MIT). In this therapeutic framework, patients with motor aphasia are guided to sing simple sentences, using a rhythm and melody that mimic an exaggerated form of natural speech intonation. They might be directed to sing the phrase 'I-am-hun-gry' with just two pitches, where each syllable is sung for an equal duration. Unstressed syllables are sung on the lower pitch, while stressed ones take on the higher pitch. Concurrently, patients tap the rhythm of the sentence with their left hand, reflecting each syllable's beat. Along with the therapist, they start by singing phrases with simple rhythms on two or three notes, gradually transitioning to sing these independently. Over time, they learn to verbalize the phrases they have been singing and later expand this capability to singing or speaking entirely new sentences.

The act of singing inherently decelerates the pace of speech, making the production of words more manageable and less stressful. The rhythm proves vital in temporally structuring speech, and music's emotional uplift, brought about by the melody and the act of singing, motivates the patients. The early stages of therapy also place significant emphasis on using *speech formulas* – commonplace phrases such as 'How are you?', 'Good morning', 'Excuse me', 'I'm sorry'. These have been voiced countless times in one's life; therefore, we do not have to mentally construct or comprehend word by word each time. Speech formulas are uniquely represented in the brain, spanning *both* hemispheres. Hence, if the right hemisphere remains functional in aphasia patients, its resources can aid in the verbalization of these formulas, facilitating the relearning of the articulation of new sentences.

Several studies have attested to the efficacy of MIT, not only during the subacute phase – a few weeks to a few months post-stroke – but also in patients with chronic aphasia, in whom language capabilities have not naturally improved or resurfaced with speech therapy.[4] In the subacute phase, initiating the therapy sooner tends to yield greater benefits, especially for those with more severe motor aphasia.

Owing to its straightforward and well-defined methodology, MIT serves as an excellent resource for both neuroscience and medical research. Neurologists are particularly interested in the underlying neurological mechanisms that contribute to the therapy's effectiveness. Gottfried Schlaug's team conducted an enlightening study with six patients suffering from chronic motor (Broca's) aphasia following a stroke in the left hemisphere. Despite ongoing speech therapy, they continued to struggle with speech even a year after the stroke.[5] These individuals participated in daily MIT sessions for fifteen weeks. MRI scans were used to map the brain's nerve fibres both before and after the therapy. Impressively, the study unveiled the formation of new nerve fibres, also known as 'axons', in all six patients' *right* hemispheres. Specifically, these axons transmitted information between the areas of Broca and Wernicke within the right hemisphere (as depicted in Figure 3.1). Furthermore, there was a marked improvement in the patients' speech fluency following the intervention. For instance, they demonstrated an increased vocabulary, using more diverse and complex words when tasked with describing pictures.

It is important to remember that language and music are processed in overlapping brain networks, with language predominantly processed in

---

[4] Van der Meulen, I., van de Sandt-Koenderman, W. M. E., Heijenbrok-Kal, M. H., Visch-Brink, E. G., and Ribbers, G. M. (2014). The efficacy and timing of melodic intonation therapy in subacute aphasia. *Neurorehabilitation and Neural Repair*, 28(6), 536–544; Merrett, D. L., Peretz, I., and Wilson, S. J. (2014). Neurobiological, cognitive, and emotional mechanisms in melodic intonation therapy. *Frontiers in Human Neuroscience*, 8, 401.

[5] Schlaug, G., Marchina, S., and Norton, A. (2009). Evidence for plasticity in white-matter tracts of patients with chronic Broca's aphasia undergoing intense intonation-based speech therapy. *Annals of the New York Academy of Sciences*, 1169(1), 385–394.

the left hemisphere and music in the right. In patients with Broca's or Wernicke's aphasia, the fibre tract connecting Broca's and Wernicke's areas in the left hemisphere is typically largely disrupted, and it is often significantly weaker in the right hemisphere than in the left. Therefore, the application of MIT can stimulate the growth of new nerve fibres, thereby strengthening the language functions of the right hemisphere.

I distinctly remember when Gottfried revealed these groundbreaking findings to me at a conference, before they were officially published. On his laptop, he displayed images of a centimetres-long neural pathway in the right hemisphere. This right-hemispheric pathway connected regions analogous to Broca's area in the frontal lobe and Wernicke's area in the temporal lobe of the left hemisphere. In the MRI images of a patient, I could discern each newly formed nerve fibre with incredible clarity. The significant increase in nerve fibres following the MIT intervention was immediately apparent. The brain's inherent ability to guide the growth of these new nerve fibres further underscored the incredible marvel that is the brain. While my anatomy students find it challenging to identify this specific neural pathway, the brain effortlessly navigates its growth, utilizing its innate ability. These compelling results were later reinforced by the same research team through an additional study involving five more patients.[6] The combined evidence indicates that individuals who have lost their speech due to a left-hemisphere stroke retain their ability to sing, utilizing their undamaged right hemisphere. This intriguing ability can stimulate the reorganization of language areas in the right hemisphere, aiding in speech recovery – even in stubborn cases where other therapies have proven ineffective in restoring fluency after a year.

Interestingly, this fibre tract is considerably more developed in musicians, in both the left and right hemispheres.[7] This suggests that musicians have a more facilitated path to recovery from aphasia following a stroke. It is also worth noting that the left-hemispheric dominance of

---

[6] Wan, C. Y., Zheng, X., Marchina, S., Norton, A., and Schlaug, G. (2014). Intensive therapy induces contralateral white matter changes in chronic stroke patients with Broca's aphasia. *Brain and Language*, 136, 1–7.

[7] Halwani, G. F., Loui, P., Rueber, T., and Schlaug, G. (2011). Effects of practice and experience on the arcuate fasciculus: Comparing singers, instrumentalists, and non-musicians. *Frontiers in Psychology*, 2, 156.

language processing is, on average, less pronounced in women than in men. While men commonly rely primarily on the left hemisphere for linguistic processing, women frequently utilize both hemispheres. As women already have more developed speech functions in their right hemisphere, they often recover more quickly from aphasia than men.

In conclusion, music therapy can play a pivotal role in restoring speech capabilities, particularly in cases of motor aphasia. When other therapeutic interventions fail and chronic aphasia develops, neurocognitive music therapy becomes a highly recommended approach. The likelihood of successful speech recovery increases when music therapy is individualized to the patient, incorporating MIT along with a variety of techniques tailored to their specific condition. Depending on the patient's ailment, this could involve different levels of singing, chant speech, breathing exercises, instrumental playing, or rhythmic exercises. Music therapists are also trained to look beyond the patient's functional needs; they value, as Claudia Dill-Schmölders succinctly put it to me, a holistic approach unifying music, body, and individual, considering their unique personality and emotions.

Recommendations for Speech Therapists and Family Members for Conducting MIT with Patients

If you are a speech therapist interested in incorporating MIT or elements of it into your routine, you can use these guidelines as a starting point. Family members can also use this method, particularly during lengthy waiting periods for speech or music therapy. Do not worry if you are not musically inclined; you can still follow these steps effectively. As long as the patient enjoys the process, and you follow these guidelines, you won't do any harm, and it is likely to be beneficial.

Patients with motor aphasia (also known as Broca's aphasia) are well suited for these exercises if they can understand spoken words, can sing songs with some understandable words, and possess the concentration and motivation to try this approach. Typically, these patients have suffered a stroke in the left hemisphere, not the right.

The exercises can begin a few weeks after a stroke, and you should perform them on a daily basis. Sit across from the patient at a table, allowing them to observe your mouth during the exercises. For the initial session, opt for a selection of common words and phrases with two to three syllables. Examples include 'water', 'hungry', 'How are you?', 'Thank you', and 'Excuse me'. Then perform the following steps, explaining each one to the patient before performing it.

1. In the first step, only you will perform the actions. Choose a word to practise, such as 'hel-lo' or 'cof-fee', point to your mouth and hum the word first, then sing it twice. Use two pitches: accentuated syllables on the higher pitch, and the unstressed syllables on the lower pitch. Choose a *starting pitch* within the patient's vocal range. Typically, this is a comfortable pitch at which the patient can hum or sing. For instance, find out in which vocal range the patient can comfortably sing or hum 'Hey Jude' and start with that pitch. The *second pitch* should be about a minor third below the starting pitch. For those unfamiliar with these terms, the song 'Hey Jude' begins with a minor third, thus your second pitch can be the second tone of that song. Hum or sing slowly, at about one syllable per second. Start with simple rhythms, using the same length for each tone. (As you progress to short sentences, use longer and shorter notes as appropriate.) While humming or singing, tap gently on the patient's left hand with each syllable to coordinate the sensorimotor speech processes in their right hemisphere.
2. In the second step, sing and tap the word or phrase together with the patient in unison.
3. The third step is a variation of the second step: once the patient is comfortable singing and tapping the word or phrase together with you, allow them to continue to sing and tap solo, while you stop.
4. In the fourth step, you sing and tap the word or phrase first, and then have the patient repeat it while they tap with their left hand on each syllable.
5. The fifth step is a variation of the fourth step. You sing and tap the word or phrase first, the patient repeats it, but then you sing the question 'What did you say?', and the patient repeats the word or phrase again, singing and tapping.

6. Intersperse the sessions with well-known songs that you and the patient sing together. Over several weeks, as the patient improves, you can gradually introduce longer and more complex speech formulas and idioms, such as 'Every cloud has a silver lining', or 'When one door closes, another opens.' You can also transition to less common phrases.

Remember, it is crucial to perform these exercises only if the patient is willing and comfortable. Avoid inducing stress as it could be detrimental to the patient's recovery. Keep a close eye on their facial expressions and demeanour to catch any signs of distress or fatigue. Always aim to provide a calm, supportive, and cooperative environment to make the process enjoyable and foster a sense of progress and hope.

HEMIPARESIS: MUSIC'S THERAPEUTIC EFFECTS ON PARALYSIS

A stroke frequently affects only one hemisphere of the brain, thereby often causing weakened motor functions on the body's opposite side. Consequently, a stroke in the left hemisphere typically results in motor impairment on the body's right side, and vice versa. The severity of this impairment can vary: when patients retain some ability to move the affected arm or leg, this condition is termed *hemiparesis* (partial weakness), while a complete loss of movement is referred to as *hemiplegia*. Manifesting in approximately two-thirds of all patients, hemiparesis is a prevalent consequence of strokes. This condition significantly diminishes quality of life as it severely restricts one's independence and mobility. Therefore, it becomes paramount to offer aid to those struggling with motor difficulties, particularly in their arms, hands, or gait.

HEMIPARESIS OF THE LEGS: A RHYTHMIC THERAPEUTIC APPROACH

Among various interventions, *rhythmic auditory stimulation* (RAS) has emerged as a music therapy approach that is both remarkably effective and ingeniously straightforward. The structure of a typical RAS session unfolds as follows: initially, the therapist determines the patient's natural walking pace. Music, either performed live or played from a recording, is then set to this tempo, and the patient walks in time with the music for a few minutes. Gradually, the tempo of the music is increased from one piece to the next, as long as the patient can maintain a stable gait. Subsequently, the patient practises manoeuvring across ramps and steps. The session culminates in periods where the music is purposefully faded out, providing the patient with practice in walking without rhythmic guidance.

Patients afflicted with hemiparesis commonly exhibit steps that are short, slow, and asymmetrical. Their gait often demonstrates rigidity, with little variation or flexibility between steps. Michael Thaut, a co-developer of RAS, documented marked improvements in the ambulatory abilities of hemiparesis patients following several weeks of RAS, surpassing the gains achieved through standard physiotherapy.[8] Thaut divided patients into two groups: one group received RAS, while the other was treated with physiotherapy following the 'Bobath concept'. (The average age of the patients was just below seventy years.) In both groups, therapy sessions, lasting half an hour each, were conducted daily over a span of three weeks. All patients had to have the capacity to take a minimum of five steps independently at the start of the therapy, which commenced four weeks post-stroke. After three weeks, RAS-treated patients showed significant progress, as they were able to perform more steps per minute and achieve larger and more symmetrical steps than those in the control group; they were able to perform an extra nineteen steps per minute and traversed an additional thirteen metres.

Thus, even a brief three-week course of RAS can yield dramatic improvements in a patient's gait. However, the pace of most patients remained approximately half as quick and less symmetrical than prior to the stroke, indicating potential for further improvement. Consequently, Michael Thaut's team doubled the intervention duration from three to

---

[8] Thaut, M. H., Leins, A. K., Rice, R. R., Argstatter, H., Kenyon, G. P., McIntosh, G. C., Bolay, H. V., and Fetter, M. (2007). Rhythmic auditory stimulation improves gait more than NDT/Bobath training in near-ambulatory patients early poststroke: A single-blind, randomized trial. *Neurorehabilitation and Neural Repair*, 21, 455–459.

six weeks, and applied RAS alongside conventional physiotherapy.[9] This integrated approach resulted in a markedly improved gait in patients compared to those subjected only to three weeks of RAS. Hence, an ideal treatment plan seems to be a combination of physiotherapy and RAS, extending over a period of at least six weeks, if not longer. Subsequent studies have consistently demonstrated RAS' effectiveness, not only during the subacute phase but also in patients experiencing chronic hemiparesis following a stroke.[10]

The biomechanics governing our upright gait are a marvel of intricate precision and synchronized dynamics. With every stride, a multitude of movements must seamlessly synchronize and coordinate. These individual actions need to be not only meticulously timed but also modulated in their acceleration and deceleration to integrate seamlessly into the overall kinetic sequence. Optimal performance arises when each movement segment is executed with just the right amount of force – neither excessive nor insufficient. When the brain, which serves as the command centre for this intricate walking mechanism, incurs damage, music emerges as a key tool. It assists in coordinating both isolated movements and complete kinetic sequences by providing a temporal framework. Consequently, music therapy interventions such as RAS can appreciably enhance the flexibility and fluidity of individual movements. Furthermore, music holds the power to motivate and bring joy, thus facilitating muscle relaxation and the smooth flow of movements – a universally applicable benefit for any muscular or movement issue.

Thanks to the simplicity and straightforwardness of the RAS principle, physiotherapists can proactively integrate music into their therapy regimen, rather than merely using it as an ambient background. For

---

[9] Thaut, M. H., McIntosh, G. C., and Rice, R. R. (1997). Rhythmic facilitation of gait training in hemiparetic stroke rehabilitation. *Journal of the Neurological Sciences*, 151, 207–212.

[10] Moumdjian, L., Sarkamo, T., Leone, C., Leman, M., and Feys, P. (2017). Effectiveness of music-based interventions on motricity or cognitive functioning in neurological populations: A systematic review. *European Journal of Physical and Rehabilitation Medicine*, 53(3), 466–482; Cha, Y., Kim, Y., Hwang, S., and Chung, Y. (2014). Intensive gait training with rhythmic auditory stimulation in individuals with chronic hemiparetic stroke: A pilot randomized controlled study. *NeuroRehabilitation*, 35, 681–688.

instance, they can choose music with an appropriate tempo and then explicitly instruct the patient to move in synchrony with it. This strategy aids significantly in the restoration of motor functions.[11]

Notably, patients themselves can directly apply RAS techniques (refer to the recommendations below). These music-assisted activities can also be organized within group settings such as day clinics, self-help groups, or residential homes. This approach not only makes therapy more cost-effective but also ensures its continued application long after hospital discharge or rehabilitation.[12] Furthermore, group therapy has the added advantage of fostering social interactions and facilitating mutual support. Regrettably, such group-based interventions are often in short supply across most institutions. As a result, I recommend that individuals unite with others undertaking a similar therapeutic journey, possibly sharing the financial responsibilities involved in hiring a qualified music therapist.

> **RECOMMENDATIONS FOR PATIENTS WITH GAIT DISORDERS**
>
> 1. *Finding your walking pace with music.* First, calculate your steps per minute. Use online platforms such as YouTube or getsongbpm.com to find music that matches this tempo. For instance, if you take twenty steps per minute, multiply this by four to search for songs at eighty BPMs (beats per minute). Walk in time with the music, taking a step every four beats. If you take sixty steps per minute, search for songs at 120 BPMs and step every two beats. Have variations of music at slightly different tempos to adjust your pace as needed. Regularly walking to this music can significantly benefit you. (Also see 'Recommendations for Walking with Music for Parkinson's Patients and Therapists' in Chapter 13).

---

[11] Whitall, J., Waller, S. M., Sorkin, J. D., Forrester, L. W., Macko, R. F., Hanley, D. F., Goldberg, A. P., and Luft, A. (2011). Bilateral and unilateral arm training improve motor function through differing neuroplastic mechanisms: A single-blinded randomized controlled trial. *Neurorehabilitation and Neural Repair*, 25, 118–129.

[12] Jeong, S., and Kim, M. T. (2007). Effects of a theory-driven music and movement program for stroke survivors in a community setting. *Applied Nursing Research*, 20, 125–131.

2. *Consistency is key.* Make it a habit to walk to your chosen music consistently. This will help your brain form associations between the music and your walking pattern. If you find yourself in a situation where music is not available, you can mentally replay the tune to help maintain your walking rhythm.
3. *Explore partner dancing.* When it is safe to do so, consider gentle partner dancing to music. Start with simple steps. Face your partner with hands joined. The leader starts by taking a half-step forwards with the right foot, followed by the left foot. Then the leader takes a half-step backwards with the right foot, followed by the left, returning to the original position. The follower's steps mirror the leader's but start with the left foot moving backwards. Dancing with a partner can provide additional balance and reduce the risk of falls.
4. *Safety first in dancing.* Keep dance steps simple and avoid stepping more than a half-step backwards. The primary goal is to maintain balance and minimize the risk of falls. Dancing with a partner is not just fun but also therapeutic.

HEMIPARESIS OF THE ARMS: MUSIC-SUPPORTED TRAINING

Neurocognitive music therapists have also devised specialized methods for treating patients with arm hemiparesis. Sabine Schneider, Eckart Altenmüller, and Thomas Münte have pioneered an intervention, known as *music-supported training* (MST), that engages patients – even those who are not musically inclined – in creating music with their arms.[13] This groundbreaking approach utilizes two musical instruments to refine gross and fine motor skills respectively.

The first instrument, aimed at enhancing gross motor skills, resembles an electronic drum set. It comprises eight drum pads, arranged in a semicircular pattern around the patient, thereby making some pads

---

[13] Schneider, S., Schönle, P. W., Altenmüller, E., and Münte, T. F. (2007). Using musical instruments to improve motor skill recovery following a stroke. *Journal of Neurology*, 254 (10), 1339–1346.

easier to reach than others. A simple tap of the hand activates each pad, which produces a piano tone instead of a drum sound. This setup enables the production of a full major scale with the eight pads. The second instrument – a digital piano – is utilized to refine fine motor skills, focusing on only eight keys.

The level of patient engagement with each of the instruments during a session, in terms of difficulty and duration, is adjusted based on the extent of their hemiparesis. Some patients may interact solely with the pads or the piano, while others may alternate between both. Throughout this experience, the patient remains seated, either on a stool or in a wheelchair. The therapist models a note or a sequence of notes, which the patient then replicates. The music playing evolves from single tones to repetitions, eventually advancing to incorporate all eight tones in children's and folk songs. Initially, only the paralysed hand is used, before progressing to use both.

Much like the RAS concept, the brilliance of MST lies in its simplicity. The research team demonstrated its efficacy in a study involving patients at a rehabilitation clinic. These patients, who suffered hemiparesis in one arm, retained the ability to independently move the arm and index finger on the affected side. The participants were randomly assigned to either a conventional physiotherapy group or a group receiving both conventional therapy and MST. The conventional physiotherapy regimen consisted of nearly thirty half-hour sessions over three weeks, conducted individually or in groups. In contrast, the MST group partook in an additional fifteen music sessions, each lasting thirty minutes.

For those undergoing music therapy, the results indicated a substantial reduction in the severity of paralysis, along with marked improvements in the range and speed of movement. Additionally, these patients exhibited improved practical daily skills, such as moving more cubes from one box to another or inserting more wooden pegs into a pegboard. It is important to note that while the group receiving only conventional physiotherapy did not exhibit similar significant improvements, the study did not explore the full range of physiotherapy techniques, and a longer duration of physiotherapy might have resulted in comparable effects.

Interestingly, the study authors reported that some patients found the musical intervention particularly enjoyable – so much so that it became their favourite part of the therapy process. The enjoyment derived from such therapies is critical, as it fuels additional motivation – a crucial element for instigating plastic brain changes. These transformations are most pronounced when an individual finds the activity enjoyable or feels motivated to engage in it.

The marked improvements in hand and arm motor skills were not solely the result of the extra therapy sessions that the patients received in addition to their standard physiotherapy; rather, they stemmed specifically from the unique effects of the MST intervention. In a subsequent study, the research team discovered that the combination of conventional physiotherapy and MST significantly outperformed a fusion of conventional physiotherapy and another well-known therapy approach, *constrained-induced movement therapy*.[14]

While both conventional physiotherapy and constrained-induced movement therapy have established effectiveness, my aim is not to rank their efficacy but to emphasize that music serves as an additional, empirically validated tool in rehabilitation. Depending on the specific needs of patients, the integration of physiotherapy and MST often proves to be the optimal strategy. Given the simplicity of MST, therapists, whether they are physiotherapists or occupational therapists, can effortlessly incorporate it into their treatment methodologies, particularly if they personally enjoy music. MST is especially recommended for patients whose progress with traditional therapy is not satisfactory.

For patients with an affinity for music, this technique can significantly enhance enjoyment and motivation. However, it should be noted that it may not be suitable for patients with severe paralysis. Administering the method in a group setting can create an even more enjoyable atmosphere. Consider, for instance, forming a 'hemiparesis band' where the members play percussion instruments in sync with a stereo system's rock music.

---

[14] Schneider, S., Münte, T., Rodriguez-Fornells, A., Sailer, M., and Altenmüller, E. (2010). Music-supported training is more efficient than functional motor training for recovery of fine motor skills in stroke patients. *Music Perception: An Interdisciplinary Journal*, 27(4), 271–280.

In therapeutic contexts, the *emotional* aspects of therapy – such as enjoyment, relief, and relaxation – along with muscle relaxation and their associated neurochemical reactions in the brain are of vital significance.

Neither MST nor RAS constitute a miracle cure. Even with rigorous and sustained training, the hand may not fully regain its pre-stroke mobility. However, these methods can assist in restoring movement abilities to the greatest extent possible. Patients who enjoyed the musical activities during therapy and wish to sustain the associated benefits can continue these practices at home after their treatment has concluded. Further guidance for this continuation is provided in the recommendations below.

GUIDANCE FOR PATIENTS WITH MILD ARM PARALYSIS

- *Explore easy-to-use musical instruments.* This could be an excellent time to begin learning a lightweight musical instrument. Many affordable keyboards, for instance, come with built-in learning programmes featuring a broad range of music pieces. When selecting your instrument, make sure it accommodates simple songs and aligns with your musical tastes. A music therapist can offer advice on the most suitable instruments for you, and provide support throughout your musical journey.
- *Form a 'hemiparesis band'.* Gather a variety of percussion instruments such as bongo drums, djembes, egg shakers, tambourines, or claves. Your bandmates need not share your condition; this approach is adaptable to most neurological or psychological challenges. Healthy participants are, of course, also welcome. Assemble a playlist of dance music that all band members enjoy, play it on a stereo system, and then let everyone join the rhythm – the heat is on! This activity helps train both fine and gross motor skills and is guaranteed to be a fun and rewarding experience.
- *Engage with interactive music games.* Games such as *Guitar Hero* or *Rock Band* offer an accessible way to engage with music and improve motor skills. These games are played on consoles with toy instruments such as guitars and drums that resemble their real counterparts while being remarkably easy to handle. The games offer a wide

variety of styles, songs, as well as difficulty levels, and it is possible to play them solo or in a group. Before purchasing, ensure you can handle the instruments comfortably – for instance, you are able to bend your hand to grip the guitar neck, or hold drumsticks and strike a drum pad.

CHAPTER 12

Alzheimer's Dementia

Pioneering Neural Therapy

A RE YOU OFTEN ON A QUEST TO find your misplaced keys? Do names or appointments sometimes escape your memory? If so, the question 'Could I be developing Alzheimer's?' might have crossed your mind. Unfortunately, a neurologist can diagnose Alzheimer's disease only when it has significantly advanced, usually in the senior years. However, the disease's insidious onset typically begins much earlier, often around the age of forty. What are the initial signs of Alzheimer's dementia? Current research suggests that the first warning signs present themselves when *both* you and a close relative notice a decline in your cognitive abilities over the past two years in areas such as memory, concentration, multitasking (carrying out two or more tasks concurrently or alternating swiftly between them), conversational skills, and the use of electronic devices. This could be a harbinger of a probable future onset of *mild cognitive impairment*, a condition that often progresses to Alzheimer's disease.

In the event of such early warning signs, addressing unhealthy lifestyle habits becomes urgently important, given that these are significant risk factors. It is now of utmost importance to embrace a healthy diet, ensure regular physical activity or exercise, rigorously manage negative emotional stress, and engage in music making, singing, or dancing. The window of opportunity for preventing Alzheimer's dementia is still open at this stage, thus making it highly advisable to adopt protective measures against dementia sooner rather than later. This urgency is heightened by the fact that, at present, there are no known medications that can halt or cure dementia. Furthermore, making lifestyle changes is generally easier at this stage. For instance, if you are in the early stages of dementia, you can still head without help to music lessons, choir practice, music therapy, or dance classes.

Of course, adopting such changes remains advisable even if you have started noticing more pronounced symptoms of Alzheimer's dementia such as the following:

- You suddenly draw a blank on a route you frequently take, such as your commute to work.
- Occasionally, you cannot remember how you got to your current location.
- You forget names, keys, or appointments without them subsequently coming back to you. You ask the same question repeatedly and still forget the answer. You constantly find yourself ordering new bank cards and discover family jewellery in unexpected places, such as the oven.
- Keeping track of time occasionally poses challenges, or you forget the current season or even the year.
- Routine tasks that used to be straightforward now present challenges. You skip critical steps or execute them out of order – for instance, forgetting to add flour when baking a cake or putting coffee into the machine without first inserting a filter.
- Common words increasingly evade you. You create your own terms, such as 'hand clock' instead of wristwatch, and communicate in brief sentences.
- You find yourself repeatedly being tricked by junk mail, such as that promising a sizeable inheritance for a small fee.
- You wear a blouse and shorts in snowy weather or boots with a coat and scarf in the height of summer.
- At this stage, it is common to experience diminished enjoyment in life. You might struggle to look forward to things. You might find yourself withdrawing from social activities, and those close to you may observe that your mood swings have become more frequent.

THE RESILIENCE OF MUSICAL MEMORY IN ALZHEIMER'S PATIENTS

Music proves to be a potent tool with profound benefits for Alzheimer's patients. The starting point of our exploration is the striking phenomenon where these patients often sustain an impeccable *musical memory* – even at advanced stages marked by severe memory deficits in other areas. Lola Cuddy and Jacalyn Duffin reported on an eighty-four-year-old former teacher (patient EN), a non-professional yet ardent music lover. Mrs EN was deeply affected by advanced Alzheimer's disease, characterized by severe atrophy of the inner (medial) temporal lobe, which also encompasses the hippocampal formation. (Recall that the hippocampus is important for memory, among other functions.) She was no longer able to conduct a coherent conversation and could not recognize her family members anymore. Yet, even in her advanced state, her love and memory for music remained undimmed. She liked singing songs, remembering the melodies as well as the lyrics. Lola presented Mrs EN with a series of familiar melodies, and Mrs EN delightedly sang or hummed along to the tunes she recognized. Every so often, Lola introduced an incorrect (out-of-key) tone into a melody. In such instances, Mrs EN's facial expression noticeably changed – she would express surprise, laughter, a frown, or exclaim, 'Oh dear!' Despite her severe dementia, she recognized twenty-five out of twenty-six melodies.[1]

Lola Cuddy's team corroborated these observations in full-blown studies. One study involved fifty Alzheimer's patients, spanning the spectrum from mild to severe dementia. Patients with mild to moderate dementia displayed an intact memory for familiar melodies. Even some of the patients with severe dementia could still recall melodies and continue to sing songs when prompted. Likewise, the ability to detect incorrect notes in these melodies remained unimpaired in patients with mild dementia and was still present in some patients with moderate dementia. All patients could even recall parts of the sung texts, irrespective of the severity of their dementia. By contrast, most patients were unable to complete familiar proverbs, thus underscoring that lyrics, when embedded in music, are more memorable.[2]

---

[1] Cuddy, L. L., and Duffin, J. (2005). Music, memory, and Alzheimer's disease: Is music recognition spared in dementia, and how can it be assessed? *Medical Hypotheses*, 64(2), 229–235.

[2] Cuddy, L. L., Duffin, J. M., Gill, S. S., Brown, C. L., Sikka, R., and Vanstone, A. D. (2012). Memory for melodies and lyrics in Alzheimer's disease. *Music Perception: An Interdisciplinary Journal*, 29(5), 479–491.

These observations underline that even patients in the advanced stages of Alzheimer's disease, when both long-term and short-term memory are severely compromised, can still have a well-preserved memory for music. This captivating phenomenon hints at the existence of a unique type of memory, one yet to be addressed in cognitive science textbooks – a *musical memory*. In Alzheimer's patients, this form of memory remains remarkably resilient, outlasting many other types of memories. Importantly, musical memory is not simply a form of 'muscle memory', or what is scientifically known as *procedural memory*. The patients involved in these studies were not musicians, and therefore had not learned the songs through extensive repetition. Even though they had likely sung some of these melodies before, their memory – particularly of rock or pop songs – was primarily rooted in listening experiences.

Intriguingly, in professional or amateur musicians with Alzheimer's dementia, the procedural memory for music is often remarkably well preserved. I have witnessed patients who, despite their cognitive decline, could still play their instruments with notable finesse. Although their performances might lack their youthful fluidity, these individuals can often reproduce previously learned pieces with surprising precision, and usually from memory – although they can no longer remember the title or composer of the piece. The ability to read sheet music also often remains startlingly intact. Even amid other motor difficulties, many of these patients maintain their musical skills. One patient, for instance, struggled with donning his jacket or tying a tie, while another could no longer simply wave, yet both were still able to play the piano with relative fluency. Thus, the procedural memory for musical movements proves particularly resilient against neurodegeneration.

More remarkably, Alzheimer's patients can not only replay known pieces but are also capable of learning new ones. This ability is notably impressive, particularly when considering that these patients have lost their capacity to learn new texts, images, or faces. Once again, the exceptional capacity to learn music extends beyond the realm of 'muscle memory'. This was highlighted in a study involving individuals with early Alzheimer's dementia. Participants were exposed to texts, some spoken repeatedly and others sung (set to both familiar and unfamiliar melodies). Astonishingly, ten minutes and even four weeks after the initial exposure, the patients recalled more words from the sung texts.[3] This finding underscores that music has a considerable impact on enhancing the retention of non-musical information, such as text, in Alzheimer's patients.

We have established that Alzheimer's patients often retain memory for melodies, for procedural memory of music, and even exhibit facilitated learning of texts with music. An additional facet of musical memory that remains preserved in some individuals with Alzheimer's – even those with severe dementia – is the *implicit memory* of musical regularities. (As we recall from Part I, this unconscious learning of musical regularities is not exclusive to musicians.) Lola Cuddy's team offered further evidence for this in a study where they presented Alzheimer's patients with *unfamiliar* melodies, some of which contained irregular, out-of-key tones. Remarkably, half of the patients were able to detect these irregularities, regardless of their advanced stage of the disease and the unfamiliarity of the melodies.[4]

MUSIC AS A CATALYST FOR EPISODIC MEMORY RETRIEVAL

In the previous section, we looked at the intricacies of musical memory. Now we transition to an even more riveting discovery: the power of music to stimulate autobiographical memory, which encapsulates our recollection of personal life events. This phenomenon is particularly striking in Alzheimer's patients who, notwithstanding their substantial loss of episodic memory, can recollect life events with greater vividness when music is played either prior to or during reminiscence. This intriguing phenomenon occurs even when the music played bears no apparent relation to the memory in question.

In an experiment, neuropsychologist Mohamad El Haj asked individuals in the early stages of Alzheimer's to recollect and narrate a random event

---

[3] Moussard, A., Bigand, E., Belleville, S., and Peretz, I. (2014). Learning sung lyrics aids retention in normal ageing and Alzheimer's disease. *Neuropsychological Rehabilitation*, 24 (6), 894–917.

[4] Vanstone, A. D., and Cuddy, L. L. (2009). Musical memory in Alzheimer's disease. *Aging, Neuropsychology, and Cognition*, 17(1), 108–128.

from their past.[5] The experiment was conducted in three different settings – without music, with the accompaniment of the participant's favourite tunes, or with music selected by the experimenters, with 'La Bohème' by Charles Aznavour proving to be popular among the French subjects. In the absence of music, the patients found it challenging to vividly recall their life events, a typical symptom of Alzheimer's disease. However, a significant transformation occurred when they listened to their favourite music: they reported a larger number of experiences and provided more specific and personal details – to such a degree that they remembered life events just as well as healthy control participants. Remarkably, this held true even though the music bore no relation to the memory they were recounting.

When the experimenters chose the background music, which was not necessarily the patients' favourite, their memory retrieval was not as robust. However, it still notably surpassed that achieved in the absence of music. This fascinating observation has been corroborated by a similar study involving Alzheimer's patients in the early to moderate stages.[6] Astoundingly, music can facilitate episodic memory retrieval, granting access to memories once thought to be irretrievably lost. To achieve this effect, the music does not even have to be related to the autobiographical event.

Autobiographical memory is intertwined with self-identity. Many of the events we remember most vividly hold significant importance in our personal development. They signify milestones, transformative shifts in our thoughts, feelings, or behaviours, marking the commencement of new chapters in our lives. These can be pivotal events such as graduations, significant career advancements, the first kiss with the person we will later build a family with, the birth of a child, a family breaking up, experiencing violence, losing someone close, or enduring an accident. These key moments in our personal history, interwoven with self-discovery, self-development, and self-understanding, make a significant contribution to our sense of identity and self-definition. Consequently,

---

[5] El Haj, M., Antoine, P., Nandrino, J. L., Gély-Nargeot, M. C., and Raffard, S. (2015). Self-defining memories during exposure to music in Alzheimer's disease. *International Psychogeriatrics*, 27(10), 1719–1730.

[6] El Haj, M., Fasotti, L., and Allain, P. (2012). The involuntary nature of music-evoked autobiographical memories in Alzheimer's disease. *Consciousness and Cognition*, 21(1), 238–246.

Alzheimer's patients, with the loss of their autobiographical memory, also experience a fragmentary loss of their identity. Their ability to recount personal experiences gradually diminishes, often reducing their remembrance to mere factual information such as the names and number of their children, tragically devoid of the rich memories associated with those facts.

Mohamad El Haj's study thus also revealed that Alzheimer's patients recalled more self-defining experiences when they listened to music. It is easy to imagine the profound solace, perhaps even a momentary reprieve from their condition, an Alzheimer's patient might feel when, through the gentle nudge of music, they can reconnect with fragments of their own identity.

THE ENIGMATIC EMOTION-MEMORY TUNNEL

What is the driving force that allows Alzheimer's patients, with their severe memory impairments, to remember and even learn music with such remarkable proficiency? We can find a plausible answer in a specific region of the brain, which I refer to as the *emotion-memory tunnel*. Predominantly situated in the cingulate cortex (refer to Figure 8.3), this region is one of the last havens resisting the devastation of Alzheimer's disease. It remains relatively unscathed from tissue attrition in most patients. The emotion-memory tunnel facilitates the interaction of four fundamental musical functions: musical memory, emotion, prediction, and synchronization.

As highlighted in Part III, this region becomes active when music evokes *emotions*. Moreover, my colleagues from the Max Planck Institute in Leipzig discovered that this region plays a pivotal role in *musical memory*. In a brain-scanning experiment with healthy participants, they played various tunes, and based solely on the brain signals emanating from the emotion-memory tunnel, they could determine whether a tune was familiar or unfamiliar to the participant.[7]

---

[7] Jacobsen, J. H., Stelzer, J., Fritz, T. H., Chételat, G., La Joie, R., and Turner, R. (2015). Why musical memory can be preserved in advanced Alzheimer's disease. *Brain*, 138(8), 2438–2450.

Our personal experiences attest to the intimate relationship between musical memory and emotion. The music we truly cherish is typically music that we have known for a while, and to which we have frequently listened. At times, a song may evoke strong emotions because it is associated with a significant life event (as detailed in Chapter 5).

The emotion-memory tunnel also plays a key role in our *predictions*. When a piece's progression of sounds deviates from our prediction, this region generates an error signal.[8] This error signal feeds back into our predictive system, refining it for future predictions. Predictions share a close association with memory and emotion: when we are familiar with a musical genre, we have implicit knowledge about its musical regularities, which aids us in anticipating what comes next. Even if a tune is unknown, as long as we are familiar with its musical style, it can still give us pleasure because we can predict its continuation. Composers often play with our expectations to elicit emotional effects, a topic we explored in Part II.

Finally, the emotion-memory tunnel plays a vital role in our ability to coordinate movements with music, that is, to *synchronize* movements with music.[9] Our ability to synchronize is tightly linked to memory, predictions, and emotions: familiarity with a piece of music, coupled with the ability to make accurate predictions, facilitates our synchronization with the music. We find it more natural to swing along to music we know well than to music that is unpredictable for us.

From these observations, the emotion-memory tunnel emerges as a nexus for musical memory, emotions, predictions, and synchronization. Although these functions are orchestrated by comprehensive networks across the brain, the emotion-memory tunnel is the unique region intersecting all these networks. Consequently, I posit that music, by activating this tunnel through emotion, synchronization, and prediction, opens the pathway for memory recall.

Might even simple acts of rhythm synchronization, such as clapping to the beat of a metronome or pacing oneself to a tune, activate this tunnel

---

[8] Tsogli, V., Skouras, S., and Koelsch, S. (2022). Brain-correlates of processing local dependencies within a statistical learning paradigm. *Scientific Reports*, 12(1), 15296.

[9] Grahn, J. A., and Brett, M. (2007). Rhythm and beat perception in motor areas of the brain. *Journal of Cognitive Neuroscience*, 19(5), 893–906.

and thereby enhance memory recall in dementia patients? This tantalizing question reveals a compelling avenue for future research.

HOW CAN MUSIC HELP?

Music can have a profound influence on the *emotional* well-being of patients with Alzheimer's disease. Particularly, those residing in care homes often exhibit a wide range of negative affective symptoms, chiefly including anxiety, depression, agitation, and apathy. Recent reviews cautiously suggest that musical interventions might alleviate these symptoms.[10] However, despite the prevalence of these debilitating symptoms, there is a surprising dearth of studies examining the impact of music therapy.

The potential therapeutic effects of musical interventions arise from social interactions that elicit feelings of belonging and togetherness, distractions from pervasive negative moods, the calming effects on agitated patients, and the empowering realization that they can still remember certain pieces of music or even learn new ones. These experiences can instil renewed hope and emotional uplift in Alzheimer's patients as they perceive that they retain the capacity to remember and learn in the domain of music.

> **RECOMMENDATIONS FOR CAREGIVERS OF PATIENTS WITH ALZHEIMER'S IN MODERATE TO ADVANCED STAGES**
>
> 1. *Music selection and initial assessment.* Evaluate whether a patient enjoys music or not. If the reaction is positive, integrate music into their care routine. Start with songs from their youth – preferably their personal favourites. Family members can often provide valuable insight into the patient's musical tastes. The music should be

---

[10] Goris, E. D., Ansel, K. N., and Schutte, D. L. (2016). Quantitative systematic review of the effects of non-pharmacological interventions on reducing apathy in persons with dementia. *Journal of Advanced Nursing,* 72(11), 2612–2628; Cammisuli, D. M., Danti, S., Bosinelli, F., and Cipriani, G. (2016). Non-pharmacological interventions for people with Alzheimer's disease: A critical review of the scientific literature from the last ten years. *European Geriatric Medicine,* 7(1), 57–64.

played at a comfortable volume, creating a calming environment, but loud enough for clarity. It is crucial to ensure that the music does not induce stress, particularly when using headphones for patients in advanced stages of the disease. Start with music that has a moderate tempo, steering clear of pieces that sound overly agitated or excessively calm.

2. *Observing reactions and tailoring the playlist.* Be acutely attentive to your patient's facial expressions and overall demeanour, looking for signs of distress, particularly in those who can no longer verbalize their discomfort. If they react negatively, cease the music immediately. Music that elicits a positive response can be revisited, and new pieces can be introduced gradually that resemble familiar pieces in terms of artists, genre, and style.

3. *Enhancing environment and caregiver familiarity.* Many patients will respond to music with a serene demeanour, reduced anxiety, and more cooperative behaviour. This is particularly important if they struggle to remember their environment or their caregivers. In such cases, music can help the patients feel more at home in their environment and establish a sense of familiarity with their caregiver. Simply singing or whistling the same song consistently when entering the room can already be helpful.

4. *Group singing and professional guidance.* If practicable, participate in singing activities with the patient or a group of patients. In nursing homes, regular singing groups should be a staple, ideally guided by a trained music therapist.

HARNESSING MUSIC FOR COGNITIVE RESILIENCE

Can music also serve as a strategic instrument in combating the *cognitive decline* associated with Alzheimer's disease? Just as with its impact on behaviour and emotional state, scientific studies suggest cautious optimism about the potential of music in mitigating cognitive decline, albeit with certain reservations. The primary reason for this hesitancy lies in the absence of a sufficient number of high-quality studies to substantiate more robust claims.[11] In a review article, Rong Fang advocates for the implementation of music interventions as soon as possible after a diagnosis has been made.[12] I wholeheartedly endorse this advice, largely due to music's potential to mitigate neurodegeneration and possibly even stimulate neurogenesis. In addition to music, it is also essential to engage in physical activity and other non-musical pastimes that promote cognition, such as board games and card games.[13] Physical activity not only promotes general health but also helps maintain bodily balance, thus mitigating the risk of falls. Dancing serves as an excellent medium to synergize music with physical exercise. It is crucial that the activity not only brings joy but also fosters social interaction.

Besides the emotion-memory tunnel, another brain area is also associated with both memory and emotions: the 'happiness system', specifically the anterior hippocampus (refer to Figure 8.3). I have already pointed out three significant aspects of this region: first, it functions in learning, memory, and spatial orientation. Moreover, music has the power to trigger emotions, which markedly activate this area. And lastly, surrounding the hippocampus is the 'dentate gyrus', which can generate new nerve cells, even in old age – a stem cell producer that rejuvenates the brain (refer to Chapter 8).

Intrigued by music's unique ability to stimulate activity in this brain region, I felt compelled to explore whether music might stimulate neurogenesis in the hippocampal formation of Alzheimer's patients, potentially slowing down both neurodegeneration and brain ageing. Several years ago, I submitted a proposal to the Norwegian Research Council for a research project that embodied this idea, which subsequently received approval. The following box illustrates the practical aspects and aims of this ongoing research endeavour.

---

[11] Fang, R., Ye, S., Huangfu, J., and Calimag, D. P. (2017). Music therapy is a potential intervention for cognition of Alzheimer's disease: A mini-review. *Translational Neurodegeneration*, 6(1), 2; Peck, K. J., Girard, T. A., Russo, F. A., and Fiocco, A. J. (2016). Music and memory in Alzheimer's disease and the potential underlying mechanisms. *Journal of Alzheimer's Disease*, 51(4), 949–959.

[12] Fang et al., Music therapy is a potential intervention for cognition of Alzheimer's disease.

[13] Brett, L., Traynor, V., and Stapley, P. (2016). Effects of physical exercise on health and well-being of individuals living with a dementia in nursing homes: A systematic review. *Journal of the American Medical Directors Association*, 17(2), 104–116.

A GLIMPSE INTO THE LABORATORY: CAN SINGING MITIGATE BRAIN DEGENERATION IN ALZHEIMER'S PATIENTS?

My research team in Bergen has embarked on an exploration journey to study the impact of singing on individuals either diagnosed with, or at risk of, Alzheimer's disease.[14] Our participants engage weekly in either a music therapy or a physical activity regimen. For comparison, a third group of individuals does not partake in either of these interventions. All the participants in our study continue to live at home, providing a unique opportunity for us to explore how our interventions might aid in prolonging their independence. This is of considerable importance, as home living generally provides a significantly better quality of life compared to that experienced in care facilities or hospitals. Plus, care home placements are costly. Therefore, it is crucial to discover strategies that allow individuals with early Alzheimer's to live independently for as long as possible, lest we risk overburdening our social systems due to the continuous rise in dementia cases. Every additional month that these individuals can maintain independent living has significant socioeconomic implications, potentially saving billions of pounds annually.

Participants in our music intervention engage in weekly singing lessons, led by experienced music therapists, and practise the songs daily using recordings we prepared for them. Twice a month, we meet and sing together in our 'memory choir'. Aligned with the philosophy that values participation over performance, many pieces are quite easy, often sung in unison, and performed in a circle, like a tribe around a campfire. This creates a shared experience, encouraging participants to connect and bond. It is not about rehearsing for a perfect stage performance but experiencing a sense of community and belonging through singing. Everyone can participate, by singing, clapping, or stamping their feet, fostering an environment of mutual trust, care, and compassion. Some pieces present a higher level of complexity, resembling the harmonic

---

[14] Flo, B. K., Matziorinis, A. M., Skouras, S., Sudmann, T. T., Gold, C., and Koelsch, S. (2022). Study protocol for the Alzheimer and music therapy study: An RCT to compare the efficacy of music therapy and physical activity on brain plasticity, depressive symptoms, and cognitive decline, in a population with and at risk for Alzheimer's disease. *PLos ONE*, 17(6), e0270682.

structures found in traditional choir compositions with multiple vocal lines. The selection of pieces spans various genres and epochs, ensuring something for every musical palate. Some pieces are familiar, evoking memories among the participants, while others are new, enabling individuals to experience their capacity to learn and remember songs – even with lyrics. These experiences, coupled with the sense of community they inspire, bring happiness to the individuals, uplift their spirits, and instil hope. Participating in these choir sessions moves me so profoundly that I sometimes cannot help but shed a tear.

The music and physical activity interventions last one year. We conduct comprehensive assessments of cognitive functions (such as memory and attention), mood, quality of life, and independence before and after that year. This enables us to determine whether the musical engagement impacts cognitive decline, mitigates depressive symptoms, and leads to a better quality of life. In addition, we obtain anatomical and functional measurements of the brain using MRI. We are particularly interested in assessing the 'brain age' of our participants, which can be inferred from the MRI data. (We explored this method in Chapter 7.) The MRI-estimated brain age of an individual with Alzheimer's is typically much greater than their chronological age.

Our preliminary data show promising results: the music therapy intervention appears to prevent hippocampal volume loss in the left hemisphere, while the physical activity intervention prevents hippocampal volume loss in the right hemisphere. This suggests that dancing, which combines musical engagement and physical activity, might be particularly effective in preserving brain health. Additionally, depression decreased in both intervention groups but increased in the passive control group – a typical finding in this condition. Notably, short-term memory scores improved in the music therapy group, further underscoring the benefits of musical engagement.

It is my fervent hope that our study will ultimately demonstrate a slower rate of brain ageing in the intervention groups compared to the control group, or perhaps even a rejuvenation of their brains. We keenly anticipate sharing our initial findings next year.

CHAPTER 13

Parkinson's Disease

Shall We Dance?

A DECADE AGO, A PSYCHIATRIST FRIEND ACQUAINTED me with an innovative treatment for Parkinson's patients known as *deep brain stimulation* (DBS). This surgical procedure involves implanting electrodes into the brain to electrically stimulate specific regions. Without this electric pulse, the patient reverts to the characteristic symptoms of the disease – with tremors, stiffness, a slow pace, and intervals of movement freezing. However, once the stimulator is activated, the patient's movements become relatively normal and fluid. 'We can turn Parkinson's symptoms on and off with deep brain stimulation!' my colleague declared proudly. I responded, 'We can do that too – with a *stereo system!*'

As remarkable as it may seem, even individuals with advanced Parkinson's disease can, despite their debilitating symptoms, move fluidly to music and even dance – with such elegance that one might assume they were never afflicted. Mrs D is in her early fifties and was diagnosed with Parkinson's disease seven years ago. She shares her experiences of this miraculous capacity of music with me, recounting an episode that occurred a year post-diagnosis. Like many other times during that period, she felt unusually stiff; even her medication was not enough to facilitate normal movement. She enjoyed sketching, but it had become increasingly challenging to draw smaller details. Hoping to relax with some music, she once decided to listen to a Bob Marley tune. As she started humming the song in her mind while searching for the CD, she noticed her movements becoming significantly smoother. Markedly inspired, she began singing out loud, dancing, and finally playing the song on her stereo. She found herself standing and dancing as if

PARKINSON'S DISEASE: SHALL WE DANCE?

Parkinson's had never cast its shadow on her life. As Mrs D opens up to me about this experience, she speaks fluently, her voice is not reduced to the typical Parkinson's monotone, and her expressions are lively and not as rigid as those of many patients with the disease. She does not exhibit the reserve or aloofness that is seen in many with Parkinson's. In the early to moderate stage of the disease, her hands and feet, especially on the right side, had significantly slowed down. However, when making or listening to music, astonishingly, she faced no such issues.

She can invariably dance to music – even when the rhythm exists only in her mind. Yet, the positive effects on her movements are more pronounced and immediate when the music is actually playing, enabling her to return to her normal movement speed. For this reason, she has saved her personal music collections on her smartphone, ensuring easy access to music at all times. Sometimes, a louder volume works better. She often leans on music as a comforting ally in her daily battle with the condition. For example, when morning stiffness makes preparing breakfast challenging, simply playing music not only improves her mobility but also helps prevent potential injuries, such as when slicing bread.

Interestingly, Mrs D's symptoms also show improvement when she draws or paints, or in general, when she adopts a more creative mindset – for instance, when her goal while slicing bread is to 'make the bread look more beautiful'. She confides that in situations where her movements are stiff and slow, her mind seems to mirror this rigidity and sluggishness. She becomes more vulnerable to distractions and struggles to focus on one thing – she needs to concentrate intensely on walking, and additional distractions such as phone calls make walking even more challenging. Consequently, loud noises such as traffic require her to muster her full concentration. Additionally, her perception of time has altered significantly: she often loses track of how much time has elapsed while performing an activity – another typical symptom of Parkinson's disease. Music serves as a reliable anchor, helping her grasp the elusive flow of time and estimate durations with greater precision. Stimulating music works best in this regard. However, Mrs D shares with me that, along with these changes, she has become more sensitive to sensory information. An action-packed movie, once a source of enjoyment for her, has now become an overwhelming ordeal, leaving her mentally and emotionally drained.

Mrs D manifests a spectrum of hallmark symptoms characteristic of Parkinson's disease, spanning from motor challenges to cognitive and emotional disturbances. The characteristic motor symptoms include stiffness, tremor, and noticeable sluggishness, sometimes even complete cessation of movement. Stiffness, or *rigor*, refers to a perpetual tension in the muscles, predominantly apparent in the limbs. The muscles often feel constricted, leading to cramping and the bent posture commonly associated with Parkinson's. *Tremor* describes the persistent, involuntary shaking seen in a hand, or sometimes both hands and even the legs, oscillating at a frequency of approximately 4–7 Hz. Interestingly, these tremors often subside when the individual engages in deliberate actions. The clinical terms *akinesia* and *bradykinesia* refer to halted and slowed movement, respectively, underscoring the escalating challenges patients encounter in executing fluid actions, such as walking. As this ailment advances, patients might experience abrupt halts in movement, rendering them temporarily solidified. Another concerning feature is their progressively unsteady posture, which heightens the unpleasant risk of sudden falls.

These motor challenges significantly reduce the autonomy of those with Parkinson's disease. Over time, their gait undergoes noticeable changes and deteriorations. Their steps become slower, adopting a shuffling rhythm, and at times their stride might come to a complete halt. Activities once taken for granted, such as simply sitting down or standing up, become increasingly challenging, and the ever-present threat of falls erodes individuals' confidence in their daily routines. While current medical treatments may offer relief from some *symptoms* and afford patients a semblance of normality for a few years, it is important to note that they are not a *cure* for the disease. In addition, most medications have little effect on gait irregularities, and their overall efficacy tends to diminish with prolonged use. As the disease advances, patients find it distressing when medication effects lessen between doses, causing extended intervals of both physical and emotional discomfort until the next dose. Fortunately, Parkinson's is among the diseases where music can have miraculous effects.

HOW CAN MUSIC ASSIST?

Music provides therapeutic benefits that offer a beacon of hope for Parkinson's patients. We will begin with gait improvement. Imagine a patient grappling with a laboured gait – each step they take is slow, rigid, and occasionally halted. Yet, the moment they hear music, the transformation is immediately visible. Using the steady beat of a metronome or a tune as a guide, Parkinson's patients find enhanced fluidity and ease in their movements. Even when the tempo of the music increases beyond their habitual slow pace, they are able to match it effortlessly. Remarkably, patients not taking pharmaceutical drugs often show stronger gait improvements than those taking medication but without the benefit of music. Even individuals who regularly encounter walking blockages find relief by synchronizing their steps with music.[1]

A study examined patients experiencing such gait blockages prior to their next medication dose. Activating a metronome led to a substantial reduction in these blockages – by as much as 20 per cent. The duration of the blockages also decreased by a third.[2] This astounding effect can be harnessed therapeutically. Similar to the application of *rhythmic auditory stimulation* (RAS) for stroke patients, this method has also proven beneficial for Parkinson's patients. After training with RAS for several weeks, patients can walk more efficiently even without accompanying music. This phenomenon was first identified by Michael Thaut in a seminal study involving Parkinson's patients aged around seventy and in the moderate stage.[3] Over a span of three weeks, these patients engaged in daily half-hour walks while listening to music and pacing each step to the pulse of the songs. The tempo of the music was set slightly above the patients' usual walking speed and was incrementally increased over time. Patients were also encouraged to climb stairs, navigate more difficult

---

[1] McIntosh, G. C., Brown, S. H., Rice, R. R., and Thaut, M. H. (1997). Rhythmic auditory-motor facilitation of gait patterns in patients with Parkinson's disease. *Journal of Neurology, Neurosurgery & Psychiatry*, 62(1), 22–26.

[2] Arias, P., and Cudeiro, J. (2010). Effect of rhythmic auditory stimulation on gait in Parkinsonian patients with and without freezing of gait. *PLoS ONE*, 5(3), e9675.

[3] Thaut, M. H., McIntosh, G. C., Rice, R. R., Miller, R. A., Rathbun, J., and Brault, J. M. (1996). Rhythmic auditory stimulation in gait training for Parkinson's disease patients. *Movement Disorders: Official Journal of the Movement Disorder Society*, 11(2), 193–200.

terrains such as small hills, and practise stopping and resuming their walk. Remarkably, after three weeks of RAS training, they walked with a significantly improved gait, almost a newfound lightness and freedom, even without music playing. Post-training, their strides had lengthened by 10 per cent, enabling them to cover an additional ten metres per minute. No such improvements were observed in patients who took part in a walking programme without music. Intriguingly, some patients in the study reported that they had begun humming or singing internally to help their movements and bypass blockages when no music was playing.

Subsequent research conducted by various scientists has validated these findings. Today, it is a well-established fact in neurocognitive music therapy that patients who can still walk without assistance show enhanced walking abilities with music. Furthermore, after training with music, these patients can maintain a faster pace and take larger strides even without musical accompaniment.[4] Improved gait not only boosts mobility but also fosters independence and overall quality of life. Moreover, an enhanced walking pattern with elongated strides is crucial to minimize the risk of falling and potential injuries. Although the benefits of RAS interventions may last from several days to weeks, continuous practice appears essential for maintaining these advantages (see the recommendations below). It is also worth noting that combining RAS with physical activity, such as treadmill training, brings added benefits in regaining a normal walking pace.[5]

MUSIC SUPPORTS TEMPORAL PERCEPTION

Parkinson's patients, hindered by their movement difficulties, not only face challenges in producing a steady beat but also in *recognizing* one. This challenge originates from their altered perception of time and duration. Their perception of time is distorted; for example, when instructed to press a button for precisely five seconds, they frequently

---

[4] Spaulding, S. J., Barber, B., Colby, M., Cormack, B., Mick, T., and Jenkins, M. E. (2013). Cueing and gait improvement among people with Parkinson's disease: A meta-analysis. *Archives of Physical Medicine and Rehabilitation*, 94(3), 562–570.

[5] Ghai, S., Ghai, I., Schmitz, G., and Effenberg, A. O. (2018). Effect of rhythmic auditory cueing on Parkinsonian gait: A systematic review and meta-analysis. *Scientific Reports*, 8(1), 506.

hold it down for longer, even while counting the seconds. To them, a real second elapses more quickly than what they conceptualize as a second. The more advanced the disease, the more pronounced this effect becomes.[6] Timing movements is essential for accurate and steady movements. This links impaired timing perception with movement disorders.

Music can support temporal perception by amplifying the activity in the brain's impaired temporal perception system. Additionally, a rhythm naturally prompts the brain to predict when the next tone will occur. This also facilitates movement coordination and execution because the brain's predictive and sensorimotor processes are closely intertwined. A pulse inherently sets up a temporal framework, aiding the synchronization and stabilization of movements. These processes can be orchestrated or compensated by brain structures that are less or not at all affected by the disease.

In the typical, 'idiopathic' Parkinson's disease, more and more dopamine-producing nerve cells in the midbrain – the upper part of the brainstem – degenerate. These then no longer supply the basal ganglia with sufficient amounts of dopamine. The basal ganglia are depicted in Figure 8.3 (centre). This brain unit essentially acts as a conduit, enabling non-motor regions of the cerebral cortex to interface with its motor areas. Imagine you want to pick up an instrument. In this situation, the basal ganglia, in collaboration with the cerebellum, create a programme for this action plan, including the selection of muscle groups, the inhibition of other muscle groups, and the determination of each movement's direction, speed, and force. Subsequently, this programme can be executed by neurons in the motor regions of the neocortex.

Neuroscientists have discovered that when individuals attempt to discern the beat of music, this system – comprising motor areas, basal ganglia, and the cerebellum – springs into action.[7] This finding shows us that the pulse of music can rhythmize and energize this very system. For

---

[6] Allman, M. J., and Meck, W. H. (2011). Pathophysiological distortions in time perception and timed performance. *Brain*, 135(3), 656–677.

[7] Tsogli, V., Skouras, S., and Koelsch, S. (2022). Brain-correlates of processing local dependencies within a statistical learning paradigm. *Scientific Reports*, 12(1), 15296.

Parkinson's patients, activation of this system by perceiving a beat can assist in organizing the temporal sequence of movements.

Biologist Charles-Étienne Benoit studied patients with mild to moderate Parkinson's who underwent RAS training three times a week for thirty minutes over a month.[8] One month post-training, patients were better able to estimate the length of tones. They were also more adept at determining whether sounds played alongside music matched the rhythm. Furthermore, they demonstrated increased accuracy in tapping to a beat and showed adaptability when the tempo changed. This indicates that RAS training not only aids in the recognition but also the production of time intervals. Through the medium of music, patients effectively train neural networks to mitigate their compromised sense of rhythm and time perception.

MOOD ENHANCEMENT AND DOPAMINE RELEASE

Beyond benefits to gait and time perception, music has profound therapeutic effects on emotions and moods. Music, by evoking positive emotions such as pleasure and joy, triggers the release of dopamine into the basal ganglia, particularly in the area I refer to as the brain's 'fun motor' (refer to Chapter 8). The limited dopamine in the pleasure system might account for the diminished joy in individuals with Parkinson's, underscoring the therapeutic significance of fun and pleasure for them.

Many individuals with Parkinson's frequently grapple with feelings of depression and anxiety. Their demeanour often mirrors that of children who live under the constant threat of physical punishment for mistakes, engendering a perpetual state of fear and tension. This resulting rigidity can be seen as a precursor to the characteristic tremor of Parkinson's disease. This subdued demeanour is evident in their infrequent laughter and the rarity of their expressions of immense joy or excitement. They might display restrained facial expressions and possess a notably monotone emotional voice. Their ability to discern emotional nuances in voice and facial expressions is significantly reduced. Such emotional

---

[8] Benoit, C. E., Dalla Bella, S., Farrugia, N., Obrig, H., Mainka, S., and Kotz, S. A. (2014). Musically cued gait-training improves both perceptual and motor timing in Parkinson's disease. *Frontiers in Human Neuroscience*, 8, 494.

challenges are compounded by issues within the autonomic nervous system, causing symptoms such as incontinence, circulatory problems, and occasionally even excessive sweating or heart complications.

Music emerges as a potent remedy for these emotional burdens, particularly the pervasive anxieties and worries. Thus, music therapy is highly recommended for those with Parkinson's disease, especially if they do not play an instrument or sing in a choir.[9] It activates the vitalization system, introduces rhythm to the sensorimotor system, and can induce feelings of pleasure and even happiness when the experience is shared with others.

Individuals with Parkinson's disease can engage in music making to alleviate their fears of mistakes, especially in group settings that value participation over performance. Conversely, listening to music can promote introspection. How does the body feel? How does it react to the music? How does the breathing feel? What do the muscles and limbs feel like? What are the face and voice expressing in this moment? Immersing oneself in these sensations, devoid of judgment or self-evaluation, fosters a feeling of self-acceptance in the present moment. To encapsulate the therapeutic power of joy and the importance of living fully in the current moment, a fitting mantra for individuals with Parkinson's could be, 'Don't worry, be happy.'

> **RECOMMENDATIONS FOR WALKING WITH MUSIC FOR PARKINSON'S PATIENTS AND THERAPISTS**
>
> 1. *The basics of RAS*
>   - For those diagnosed with mild to moderate Parkinson's disease, incorporating RAS exercises into their daily routines can yield significant benefits. Walking in sync with music serves as an excellent entry point, with early stages being the optimal time to start.

---

[9] Ueda, T., Suzukamo, Y., Sato, M., and Izumi, S. I. (2013). Effects of music therapy on behavioural and psychological symptoms of dementia: A systematic review and meta-analysis. *Ageing Research Reviews*, 12(2), 628–641.

- This method is primarily intended for those with moderate walking challenges, meaning individuals who maintain good balance and are not dependent on walking aids. If in doubt, consult a medical professional.
2. *Safety first*
    - For those with pronounced walking difficulties, exercises at home on even ground (avoiding stairs) are recommended. For added safety, having a companion or caregiver nearby can be helpful.
    - Stay alert to potential distractions during walks, such as phone calls or walking with dogs, as these can elevate the risk of mishaps.
3. *Tuning into the right musical tempo*
    - The goal is to synchronize the steps with music that matches the tempo of one's natural walking pace. A straightforward way to find your tempo is to count the steps you take during one minute of regular walking. For instance, eighty steps would equate to searching for 'music 80 BPM' on platforms such as YouTube.
    - To add a layer of challenge and variation, include tunes that are around ten beats faster or slower. However, it is advisable to stay within a tempo of 120 BPM for safety and comfort.
    - To find the tempo of your favourite tracks, consider using a metronome or a metronome app on your smartphone.
4. *Musical selection and variability*
    - Choose songs with a distinct rhythm, preferably in 2/4 or 4/4 time, and with pronounced drum beats; these tend to be most effective.
    - While rotating music over days or weeks keeps the exercise refreshing, having steadfast favourites allows the brain to establish a robust connection between certain melodies and walking. Mentally recalling these tunes can be beneficial in challenging situations, even without music playing. Another option is to simply count, ideally in a rhythmic sequence such as 'one, two, three ...'
5. *Engaging with music during walks*
    - Aim for rhythmic walks lasting at least thirty minutes, ideally three to five times a week.
    - Occasionally, pause the music and halt your steps. After a brief moment, restart the music and continue your walk in sync.

- From time to time, keep walking even when the music stops. Then pause, resume the music, and continue walking.
- As your gait improves, attempt to walk for one or two minutes without the music.

6. *Practical tips and tools*
   - Keeping music (alongside headphones) easily accessible, perhaps on a smartphone, ensures one is always ready for a rhythmic walk.
   - Consistency is key. Regular practice of these exercises is vital to support and enhance motor functions.
   - In our digital age, various smartphone apps are tailored specifically for those with Parkinson's. However, their effectiveness can differ from person to person, so it is advisable to try before you buy.
   - For physiotherapists and patients keen to integrate physiotherapy with RAS, synchronizing music with treadmill workouts or comparable activities can enhance the benefits.

7. *Embracing a holistic approach*
   - Alongside the physical exercises, nurturing a positive mindset is of utmost importance. Emphasize experiences and personal growth over perfection. Ultimately, it is the journey and ongoing self-development that truly matter.

DANCING PATIENTS

While the therapeutic influence of music on walking is considerable, its potential to inspire dance in those with Parkinson's disease is nothing short of remarkable. Even those patients who rely on canes, walkers, or crutches begin to waltz briskly after a few steps. Beyond auditory cues, dancing incorporates other sensory signals – visual, tactile, and, especially when dancing with a partner, communicative cues – enriching the experience. In this respect, dancing offers a richer multisensory experience than walking. Furthermore, a large number of individuals find the act of dancing more pleasurable than simply walking. Engaging in dance programmes tailored for individuals with Parkinson's not only bolsters balance and walking patterns but also amplifies mobility and elevates overall quality of life. Maintaining balance is of particular importance, given the significantly heightened risk of falls and ensuing fractures. Dancing naturally encompasses a variety of movements, executed at varying tempos. Notably, the Argentine tango is characterized by its pausing and resuming movements. Practising these types of movements is essential for managing episodes of freezing. Additionally, dancing facilitates social interaction, fulfilling an important human need. Considering that dancing enhances balance, coordination, muscle strength, flexibility, and fosters human connections, it is recommended not just for Parkinson's patients but for everyone, especially older people, if they can still move safely.

In an insightful study, Madeleine Hackney and Gammon Earhart assigned individuals with mild to moderate Parkinson's disease to either tango, waltz, foxtrot, or a passive control group.[10] The dancing groups participated in an hour of dance lessons twice a week for several months. Upon completing the programme, individuals involved in the dance-based interventions exhibited improved balance, demonstrated increased stability while standing on one leg, and found it easier to rise from a seated position. Even when walking without music, they were taking larger steps. Moreover, patients from the dance groups reported fewer daily movement blockages and improvements in mood and endurance. They also rated their quality of life higher in terms of social support and mobility.

While it is not possible to entirely rule out placebo effects in these studies, existing literature reviews cautiously suggest that the observed benefits surpass those of mere placebo influence, and that the therapeutic impact of dancing even exceeds that of simple RAS.[11] The efficacy of dance also emerges from music therapy studies including movements to music, such as breathing and stretching exercises to music, rhythmic gymnastic movements, or clapping and stomping to music, singing, and

---

[10] Hackney, M. E., and Earhart, G. M. (2009). Effects of dance on movement control in Parkinson's disease: A comparison of Argentine tango and American ballroom. *Journal of Rehabilitation Medicine*, 41(6), 475–481.

[11] Sihvonen, A. J., Särkämö, T., Leo, V., Tervaniemi, M., Altenmüller, E., and Soinila, S. (2017). Music-based interventions in neurological rehabilitation. *The Lancet Neurology*, 16 (8), 648–660.

group improvisation. All of these approaches appear to reduce Parkinson's motor symptoms and enhance mobility and quality of life.[12]

While music or dancing can assist with walking and improve balance, mobility, and quality of life, there is currently no evidence suggesting that music can cure Parkinson's disease. The degeneration of nerve cells in the brain apparently cannot be reversed with music. Whether music can slow or even halt the progressive degeneration has not yet been researched. However, Kathrin Rehfeld and colleagues from the University of Magdeburg did investigate whether the brains of healthy seniors change when they participate in a dance or sports course. Each course, conducted over eighteen months, had sessions once or twice a week.[13] The dance group received dance lessons, while the sports group performed strength, endurance, and stretching exercises to music in a sports studio, as well as nordic walking. After the course, the volume of the (left) hippocampus was larger in both groups. Furthermore, in the dance group, the volume of additional regions around the hippocampus increased in both hemispheres. A likely explanation for the increase in hippocampal volume in both groups is that individuals performed movements together in synchrony with music, fulfilling social needs and eliciting emotions associated with social bonding.

These findings highlight the positive impact of group sports, especially those synchronized with music, on the hippocampus region. This effect is further enhanced when dance is part of the exercise regimen. Therefore, I strongly encourage individuals with Parkinson's disease to explore combining music with physical activity, particularly through dance, as a transformative way to enhance their well-being.

---

[12] Pohl, P., Dizdar, N., and Hallert, E. (2013). The Ronnie Gardiner rhythm and music method: A feasibility study in Parkinson's disease. *Disability and Rehabilitation*, 35(26), 2197–2204; Pacchetti, C., Mancini, F., Aglieri, R., Fundarò, C., Martignoni, E., and Nappi, G. (2000). Active music therapy in Parkinson's disease: An integrative method for motor and emotional rehabilitation. *Psychosomatic Medicine*, 62(3), 386–393.

[13] Rehfeld, K., Müller, P., Aye, N., Schmicker, M., Dordevic, M., Kaufmann, J., Hökelmann, A., and Müller, N. G. (2017). Dancing or fitness sport? The effects of two training programs on hippocampal plasticity and balance abilities in healthy seniors. *Frontiers in Human Neuroscience*, 11, 305.

RECOMMENDATIONS FOR DANCING

1. *Seeking the right class*
   - Look for dance classes tailored to individuals with Parkinson's. If unavailable, senior dance programmes can be a great alternative.
2. *Safety first*
   - If dancing outside a therapeutic setting, partner with someone steady-footed for extra stability.
   - Ensure you are equipped to handle a fall without severe injuries. If uncertain about your physical ability, consult a doctor or physiotherapist.
   - Adequate vision is essential for a safe dance experience.
3. *Mastering the basic dance position*
   - Start with a face-to-face stance with your partner, holding both hands, elbows bent, and forearms parallel to the floor. As you gain confidence, you can venture into other dance positions.
   - For specific dance steps tailored to mobility challenges, refer to the 'Hemiparesis of the Legs: A Rhythmic Therapeutic Approach' section in Chapter 11.
4. *Balancing roles in dance*
   - Embrace the art of alternating roles in dance. Regardless of gender, alternating between leading and following roles enriches the dance experience and enhances its therapeutic benefits.

CHAPTER 14

Autism

DEREK PARAVICINI HAS ESTABLISHED HIMSELF AS A celebrated pianist in the musical world. With the Derek Paravicini Quartet, he has taken to stages for concerts and released a CD. In collaboration with piano teacher Adam Ockelford, he offers lecture concerts. I recently had the privilege of witnessing one of these captivating events. Derek's interpretation of Claude Debussy's 'Clair de Lune' was profoundly moving, capturing an essence that few renditions ever reach. That evening, his repertoire spanned various genres, from Art Tatum's jazz to Michael Jackson's tunes and more. Born prematurely, Derek lost his vision soon after birth. He has never glimpsed a musical score; every piece he performs he learns by ear. He was diagnosed with autism during his childhood. Yet, through music, he overcomes the limitations associated with his diagnosis. While he grapples with a significant learning disability, he knows how to play thousands of compositions by heart. His everyday vocabulary is limited, but he can name hundreds of pieces and their composers. Even though he struggles with conventional social cues, Derek demonstrates an uncanny ability to understand and convey emotions through music. Far from mere reproductions, his performances are animated with life and emotion, adjusting tempo and dynamics to capture the very essence of each piece. He plays not just to perform but to connect, to evoke emotions, and to share the joy of music.

When Derek was four, a piano became his world. This was years after his autism diagnosis. Without formal training, he intuitively taught himself pieces, echoing melodies he had heard. A few months later, he met Adam Ockelford. For Derek, this encounter was an epiphany, a realization that he was not alone in his fervour for music. Music, with its inherent structure and predictability, became his haven. Spoken words and ambient noises often felt unpredictable and overwhelming for him, exacerbated by his blindness and linguistic challenges. Yet, with Adam, a harmonious musical bond blossomed. By the age of ten, Derek had already showcased his prodigious talent with a professional orchestra, mastering Nikolai Rimsky-Korsakov's intricate 'Flight of the Bumblebee'. An unexpected hiccup arose when the orchestra's sheet music was discovered to be in a different key mere hours before a live radio broadcast performance. For Derek, this was not a problem – he easily adapted and played the piece in another key.

The term 'autism' encompasses a spectrum of conditions, affecting 1–2 per cent of the population, often referred to as autism spectrum disorder (ASD). Its manifestations are diverse. Some autistic individuals perform average or even above on intelligence tests, a trait often associated with what was previously diagnosed as Asperger's syndrome. However, approximately one-third of individuals with autism are classified as having pronounced intellectual disabilities. Many with ASD face communication challenges. Some remain non-verbal throughout life, while others master only rudimentary speech. Many have a greater capacity for understanding language than for expressing themselves. These challenges are particularly acute in autism diagnosed in early childhood, typically identified within the first two years of life, where language development is often significantly delayed. Even among autistic individuals with strong cognitive abilities, articulating emotions often proves challenging, despite seemingly typical emotional experiences.

Common to all forms of autism is their emergence in childhood as developmental disorders, predominantly characterized by distinct patterns of social interactions and communication. These patterns encompass challenges in adapting behaviour across social scenarios, engaging in reciprocal social-emotional interactions, and establishing social relationships. This often results in a reduced frequency of shared emotional experiences, such as laughter. The challenges often manifest in both verbal and non-verbal realms, although the symptoms can vary greatly from person to person. Expressing and interpreting through facial cues, gestures, and even eye contact become challenging. Even when speech capabilities emerge, they sometimes remain confined to basic functions such as counting or requesting a desired item. Many autistic individuals experience challenges in understanding the intricate weave of human emotions, desires, and thoughts. Coupled with this is a tendency for deeply rooted interests and repetitive behaviors, often stemming from a profound need for predictability and structure to help manage the sensory experiences that can be challenging for them. Predictability makes the world less frightening.

MUSICAL STRENGTHS OF INDIVIDUALS ON THE AUTISM SPECTRUM

In the realm of music, the challenges associated with autism often recede into the background. Many children with autism discover their voice through melodies and instruments. Even children with autism who cannot articulate a single word might hum melodies or play instruments.[1] When someone sings, children with autism are more likely to focus on the singer's face than during regular conversation. Music often becomes a bridge, enabling these children to communicate. During joint musical activities, they often establish eye contact, synchronize their attention with peers, and forge social connections – achievements that demonstrate their capacity for social interaction.

Music emerges as a genuine strength for many on the autism spectrum. A significant portion of individuals with autism who do not have intellectual disabilities exhibit normal or even superior musical talents. These skills include perceiving rhythm and melody, distinguishing between major and minor scales, discerning various timbral qualities, recognizing emotions in music, and understanding the regularities of chord progressions.[2]

---

[1] Ockelford, A. (2017). Towards a developmental model of musical empathy using insights from children who are on the autism spectrum or who have learning difficulties. In King, E., and Weddington, C. (eds). *Music and Empathy* (pp. 39–88). London and New York, Routledge.

[2] Heaton, P. (2009). Assessing musical skills in autistic children who are not savants. *Philosophical Transactions of the Royal Society of London B: Biological Sciences*, 364(1522), 1443–1447; DePape, A. M. R., Hall, G. B., Tillmann, B., and Trainor, L. J. (2012). Auditory

The profound connection many individuals with autism establish with music is truly captivating. Adam Ockelford shared a touching anecdote with me that illustrates this. He once met a five-year-old boy who seemed glued to the piano, producing what appeared to be nonsensical tunes and failing to replicate even basic melodies. As a result, he was dismissed as having no potential for the piano, and the idea of music lessons was abandoned. However, in a serendipitous encounter, Adam discovered the truth: the boy was playing everything with utter precision – just in reverse. Such a feat is so extraordinary that even experienced musicians struggle to identify or replicate melodies played backwards. It took a brilliant mind like Adam's to recognize that what sounded peculiar was, in fact, a remarkable manifestation of genius.

The focus on the challenges faced by autistic children often overshadows their strengths. For example, while they show abnormal activity of Broca's area during *language* perception, mirroring their language disorder, many show normal activity of this very brain structure during *music* perception. (Broca's area is illustrated in Figure 3.1.) Neurosurgeon Grace Lai and her team conducted a study using functional MRI (fMRI), comparing a group of children with autism against another group without developmental disorders.[3] The autistic children exhibited pronounced speech developmental disorders or outright speech disabilities. While many were virtually non-verbal, resorting to rudimentary sentences at best, they all harboured an affinity for music and could identify familiar melodies akin to the control group. The study incorporated two brain-scanning experiments: one centred on language and the other on music.

Data from the language experiment revealed the expected pattern: children with normal development exhibited activation in Broca's area when exposed to spoken language, while their autistic counterparts displayed no such activation. An astounding result, however, emerged in the music experiment. Here, the autistic children displayed significant

---

processing in high-functioning adolescents with autism spectrum disorder. *PLoS ONE*, 7 (9), e44084.

[3] Lai, G., Pantazatos, S. P., Schneider, H., and Hirsch, J. (2012). Neural systems for speech and song in autism. *Brain*, 135(3), 961–975.

activation in Broca's area in response to melodies, a pattern not evident in the control group. Similarly, my own research group has observed that adult individuals with autism show abnormalities in the processing of speech melody, while they process a musical melody normally.[4] These findings imply that those with autism do not inherently have a compromised language network – they prefer to use this network for music, rather than language.

Beyond the atypical development of language and communication, many individuals with autism frequently struggle with emotional recognition. However, given the tendency of individuals with autism to avoid eye contact, it is not very surprising that they do not recognize facial cues of emotions as well as others. By contrast, when expressed through music, most of them can accurately discern emotions. This stems from their ability to experience music-evoked emotions just like non-autistic individuals.[5]

Reinforcing this notion, Italian neuroscientist Andrea Caria discovered that brain activity during music-evoked emotions aligns remarkably well between individuals with and without autism. This study involved a cohort of eight individuals diagnosed with Asperger's syndrome, complemented by fourteen control participants.[6] Throughout the experimental phase, they were exposed to musical compositions, some effusing joyfulness, others resonating with melancholic undertones. Both groups responded similarly to the music, feeling pleasure, activation, or calmness. The brain activation patterns were virtually indistinguishable across groups. Intriguingly, those affiliated with Asperger's syndrome manifested unique activations within the so-called 'happiness system', a nuance absent among the control group.

---

[4] DePriest, J., Glushko, A., Steinhauer, K., and Koelsch, S. (2017). Language and music phrase boundary processing in autism spectrum disorder: An ERP study. *Scientific Reports*, 7(1), 14465.

[5] Quintin, E. M., Bhatara, A., Poissant, H., Fombonne, E., and Levitin, D. J. (2011). Emotion perception in music in high-functioning adolescents with autism spectrum disorders. *Journal of Autism and Developmental Disorders*, 41(9), 1240–1255; Allen, R., Davis, R., and Hill, E. (2013). The effects of autism and alexithymia on physiological and verbal responsiveness to music. *Journal of Autism and Developmental Disorders*, 43(2), 432–444.

[6] Caria, A., Venuti, P., and de Falco, S. (2011). Functional and dysfunctional brain circuits underlying emotional processing of music in autism spectrum disorders. *Cerebral Cortex*, 21 (12), 2838–2849.

Thus, even though persons on the autism spectrum are generally considered to be emotionally 'atypical', their neurological responses to music remain astoundingly normal. Whatever emotional blockages they might have in other contexts, music can pervade them.

To research how those with autism integrate music into their daily routines, Rory Allen interviewed twelve high-functioning adults with ASD, nine of which were diagnosed with Asperger's syndrome.[7] Ten actively engaged with music in their daily routines; one exhibited an exclusive interest in Wagner operas, while another only enjoyed music as a background to movies. A significant number utilized music to modulate their emotions and positively steer their thoughts. Some also resorted to music to foster social ties and engender a sense of belonging. A few even recounted deploying music as a therapeutic tool to mitigate negative emotional states such as depression, despair, anger, or fear. This further substantiates the notion that individuals with autism engage with the emotional resonance of music in a manner akin to any passionate music enthusiast.

HARNESSING MUSICAL ABILITIES FOR THERAPY

Given the innate musical abilities of most autistic children, even those with severe speech challenges, Gottfried Schlaug and his research team devised a variation of melodic intonation therapy (MIT) tailored for autistic children, naming it *auditory-motor mapping training* (AMMT). (For a description of MIT see Chapter 11.) In the therapy sessions, individuals learn speech through melody: words and short phrases are intoned over two distinct pitches, with the emphasis falling on the syllable sung at the higher pitch. Initially, the therapist sings alone; this is followed by a duet, and eventually the child sings solo. Contrary to MIT, which involves rhythmic tapping on a table using the left hand, AMMT entails tapping two drum pads using both hands. These drums produce tones that correspond to two specific pitches, matching the sung melody. To reinforce comprehension, an appropriate image corresponding to the word is shown beforehand.

---

[7] Allen, R., Hill, E., and Heaton, P. (2009). Hath charms to soothe ...': An exploratory study of how high-functioning adults with ASD experience music. *Autism*, 13(1), 21–41.

An initial study involved school-aged children diagnosed with autism. Despite having received speech therapy for over a year, they remained non-verbal. These children participated in forty therapy sessions spread over eight weeks. The teaching materials included basic, everyday words and phrases broken down syllable by syllable for easier singing, such as 'I-want-more', 'I-am-an-gry', 'It's-too-noi-sy'. Following the eight weeks of AMMT, and an additional observation period of the same length, significant improvements emerged: when shown relevant images, the children started to describe them, often extending beyond the vocabulary initially introduced during the therapy. They assimilated the skills acquired during the sessions into their daily lives, independently picking up new words. Although the children did not achieve complete fluency, and results varied among them, their initiation into speaking marked a noteworthy milestone.[8]

In a successive study by the same team, AMMT was investigated with 'minimally verbal' children – those with a sparse vocabulary, seldom formed into sentences. This investigation also incorporated a placebo control group, which underwent a regimen resembling AMMT, but here words were neither sung nor accompanied by drums; they were merely repeated. Each child underwent only twenty-five sessions since AMMT's pronounced effects typically manifest after this period. Once again, AMMT yielded outstanding results: the children articulated a significantly greater number of words and accurate syllables, even employing vocabulary not specifically trained during therapy. The placebo group demonstrated no significant improvements. Although this was not formally assessed, children in the AMMT ensemble were more inclined to synchronize their attention with the therapist, collectively focusing on images, faces, or drums. Through the act of singing, these children also honed their social skills.[9]

Due to the inherent musical interest and abilities in autistic children, music therapy has shown to be beneficial even for preschoolers. Music therapists Jinah Kim, Tony Wigram, and Christian Gold conducted an

---

[8] Wan, C. Y., Bazen, L., Baars, R., Libenson, A., Zipse, L., Zuk, J., Norton, A., and Schlaug, G. (2011). Auditory-motor mapping training as an intervention to facilitate speech output in non-verbal children with autism: A proof of concept study. *PLoS ONE*, 6(9), e25505.

[9] Chenausky, K., Norton, A., Tager-Flusberg, H., and Schlaug, G. (2016). Auditory-motor mapping training: Comparing the effects of a novel speech treatment to a control treatment for minimally verbal children with autism. *PLoS ONE*, 11(11), e0164930.

insightful study focusing on *music therapy improvisation* with children aged between three and six years.[10] Within this group, some were non-verbal but others had almost typical linguistic development. The therapeutic approach encouraged children to embark on a musical journey, introducing them to diverse instruments, from the rhythmic beats of percussion to the rich notes of pianos and xylophones. In this therapeutic milieu, the therapist became a musical ally, echoing the child's melodic expressions, refining them, and sculpting these sounds into harmonious sequences. Beyond the tangible instruments, the therapist's toolkit included modulated vocal tones, engaging eye contact, and a palette of facial expressions and gestures. The exchange of sounds established genuine communication and social interaction – thus fulfilling the deep need for connection in both the child and the therapist.

Each child participated in twelve music therapy sessions. Although one child remained ensconced in a cocoon of non-responsiveness, the remaining eleven blossomed. As sessions unfolded, these children unveiled a tapestry of emotions – spontaneous laughter, faces illuminated with joy, deeper eye engagements, and heightened mutual attentiveness. Their burgeoning self-assurance became evident as they initiated non-verbal musical dialogues, weaving narratives that drew the therapist into their musical realms. The children, over time, became more attuned to the therapist's prompts, epitomizing the growing cooperation between them. These moments bore testament not only to a burgeoning bond of trust but also highlighted the instrumental role of music in this therapeutic setting. In control sessions devoid of the musical element, no such effects emerged, thus emphasizing the pivotal role of music in the therapeutic outcomes.

Numerous other investigations corroborated the findings of this study. In an exhaustive meta-analysis of placebo-controlled studies, Monika Geretsegger and her team found that music and music therapy can assist children with autism in refining their social interaction skills.[11]

---

[10] Kim, J., Wigram, T., and Gold, C. (2009). Emotional, motivational and interpersonal responsiveness of children with autism in improvisational music therapy. *Autism*, 13(4), 389–409.

[11] Geretsegger, M., Elefant, C., Mössler, K. A., and Gold, C. (2014). Music therapy for people with autism spectrum disorder. *Cochrane Database of Systematic Reviews*, 6(6), CD004381.

According to their research, children enhanced their verbal communication and socio-emotional exchange during music therapy sessions. Furthermore, the experiences from music therapy positively influenced parent–child relationships. The authors noted that the study's results did not definitively indicate that the social skills nurtured in music therapy translated to everyday life. However, such a transition demands more patience and time than research studies can typically afford. Considering that the brain changes with practice and experience, the socio-emotional breakthroughs experienced during music therapy sessions likely translate into daily life over time. This principle applies not only to children but also to adolescents and adults. However, a conclusive answer would require further, high-quality research. Taken together, these findings underscore the transformative potential of music therapy across diverse age groups and developmental stages.

THE POWER OF MUSIC IN AUTISM

What is it about music that can lead to such pronounced effects in individuals with autism? Music offers a clear structure, evident in its metre, scales, and the inherent regularities of melodic and harmonic progressions. Such predictability renders the world less intimidating. At the same time, the structural scaffold beckons participation, compelling continuation until its conclusion. Within these boundaries, music provides ample room for personal freedom – finding one's own continuation, altering the tempo, or modulating the volume.

This predictable scaffold facilitates engagement in social functions: participants pursue a common goal and share their attention. They communicate, and their movements and emotions harmonize in rhythm, which in turn fosters cooperation and cultivates a deep sense of community and social bonding.

Given the divergent social behaviour of individuals with autism, the people surrounding them often forget that autistic people need social contact, community, and bonds just like any other human being. Music, owing to its intrinsic social attributes, can facilitate a bond with a therapist, thereby advancing social development. As surprising as it might sound, in music therapy, children with autism engage more strongly in social communication when they take the lead, compared to segments directed by the therapist. Those on the autism spectrum prefer clear structures yet often resist directed instruction – they are always ready to learn, although they do not always like being taught.

While my passion for this topic runs deep, and I feel a profound sense of solidarity with those on the autism spectrum, parents of children with autism would do well to manage their expectations. Music does not hold the power to instantly alleviate all symptoms. Patience is paramount for symptoms to lessen with music therapy or music lessons. For many children with autism, music's allure lies in its inherent structure blended with flexibility, its simplicity paired with complexity, and its predictability. It stands as a playful realm, untouched by coercion, pain, or punishment. Therefore, for many, immersing themselves in music becomes a profound source of relief. Language, with its intricacies, often poses challenges or feels threatening. Music, on the other hand, provides an avenue for human connection and social bonding – structured and safe. Those on the autism spectrum desire such experiences just like anyone else. Consequently, they place great value on the fulfilment gained from this musical journey, as it aids them in understanding their emotions, developing their talents, and achieving personal growth. Dispelling a common myth, individuals with autism do not inherently shun human contact. They merely prefer scenarios where they are not irritated and misunderstood.

> **RECOMMENDATIONS FOR CAREGIVERS AND GUARDIANS OF INDIVIDUALS WITH ASD**
>
> 1. *Initial assessment*
>   - Determine whether the individual – be it a child, teenager, or adult – has an affinity for music and responds positively to it. Future steps hinge on this assessment.
> 2. *Supporting musical exploration through instruments*
>   - If the child independently chooses music and exhibits interest in it, introduce them to the opportunity of learning an instrument. Through music, the child can establish social connections, improve communication, and engage more in social environments.

3. *Therapeutic interventions*
   - Music therapy can serve as a potent tool to cultivate socio-emotional skills in children on the spectrum.
   - For children with minimal to no verbal skills, it might be beneficial to consult a speech or music therapist who is open to learning and implementing AMMT. Preschoolers can already participate in this intervention.
4. *Musical communication*
   - If the child connects with music, think about using songs as a medium of communication instead of just spoken words. This infuses a playful element into interactions. Keep in mind that spoken language can be ambiguous and potentially overwhelming for the child, while music offers clarity and playfulness. Even simple clapping of a rhythm and a short melody can have a profound impact. As you progress, incorporate sung words, elementary phrases, or nursery rhymes.
5. *Providing structure*
   - Providing a child with a predictable structure, whether through rhythmic patterns, musical scales, or a consistent daily routine, is paramount. However, it is also essential to empower the child with choices, allowing them to lead occasionally. Their actions and preferences, although sometimes elusive to others, often have a personal rationale for them.
6. *Encouraging caregiver involvement*
   - If the individual shows a musical interest, nurture it through activities such as listening to music, singing, playing instruments, attending concerts, or participating in music therapy.
7. *Dance as a therapeutic outlet*
   - For adolescents and adults, a dance class might be a venture worth considering. If you're not sure which dance style to try, Argentine tango is a popular choice among autistic individuals. The structured framework of dance not only facilitates human interaction but also hones sensorimotor skills – all while being delightfully enjoyable!

CHAPTER 15

Chronic Pain

INDIVIDUALS ENDURING CHRONIC PAIN FREQUENTLY FACE a protracted and unpredictable cycle, characterized by episodes of intense discomfort that can last for days, weeks, months, or even years. Chronic pain manifests in diverse forms, from the debilitating grip of migraines to tension headaches, musculoskeletal aches like back pain and arthritis, the discomfort associated with fibromyalgia, the enigmatic sensations of phantom limbs, and the distressing pain associated with cancer, including tumor-related pain and the side effects of chemotherapy.

Some forms of chronic pain arise from the activation of pain receptors, a process known as *nociception*. Nociception can be triggered by factors such as inflammation-induced tissue damage or muscle tension. However, some chronic pain forms, such as fibromyalgia, may present themselves even when nociception is absent. It is vital to note that the absence of nociception does not diminish the validity or intensity of the pain experienced. Rather, it might suggest that while the pain is real and deeply felt, there is not always an underlying physical ailment to address. This highlights the nuanced difference between nociception and pain, emphasizing that pain can sometimes be a complex interplay of the mind's perceptions, even without direct physical stimuli.

The unremitting ache, coupled with the looming anxiety of its recurrence, often drives sufferers into patterns of withdrawal and avoidance. Regrettably, such reactions can magnify the very issues they aim to mitigate. If the distress persists, it can plunge individuals into a deep chasm of despair, accompanied by a profound sense of powerlessness.

Considering the well-documented effects of music on acute pain (as discussed in Chapter 8), it is surprising that only a single placebo-controlled study exists that explores the impact of music therapy on chronic pain. Such studies are imperative given the significant placebo effects observed with pain medications: a placebo pill could present a more cost-effective alternative to multiple music therapy sessions. In that study, music therapists Julian Koenig and Thomas Hillecke included individuals with migraines and tension headaches.[1] These patients received either music therapy or music education training, both spanning eight weeks, with six distinct sessions. In the music therapy group, participants engaged in relaxation exercises, harmonized with music, honed their body awareness, and practiced emotion regulation.

Participants from both groups reported a reduction in pain, both immediately post-intervention and persisting for up to six months. But there was a catch: this effect was not stronger in the music therapy group, so placebo effects could not be ruled out. Still, this does not necessarily negate the therapeutic potential of music. It is worth considering whether the use of music education as a control group inadvertently set an excessively high benchmark. It is plausible that music exerted pain-reducing effects in both groups, extending beyond mere placebo effects.

After presenting his high-quality study at an international music therapy conference, Julian faced a wave of disappointment from colleagues over the negative results, leaving him notably solitary at the breakfast table the next morning. It was an emblematic moment, reflecting the challenges of pioneering research. Yet, undeterred by such setbacks, Julian and I remain steadfast in our shared conviction: music and music therapy can provide profound solace to individuals grappling with chronic pain across a wide spectrum of challenges.

In the *physical realm*, music therapy can guide individuals towards relaxation, specifically targeting pain rooted in muscle tension.

---

[1] Koenig, J., Oelkers-Ax, R., Kaess, M., Parzer, P., Lenzen, C., Hillecke, T. K., and Resch, F. (2013). Specific music therapy techniques in the treatment of primary headache disorders in adolescents: A randomized attention-placebo-controlled trial. *The Journal of Pain*, 14(10), 1196–1207.

In addition, the inherent training of body awareness with music facilitates a clearer localization and articulation of pain. Moreover, engaging in singing, dancing, or drumming during music therapy sessions frequently prompts patients to adopt movements that counteract their typical pain-relieving postures.

Within the *emotional realm*, music is an effective catalyst through which suppressed emotions find a voice, paving the way for verbal articulation. Often, chronic pain is rooted in an emotional conflict or an unresolved trauma. In these contexts, music therapy serves as a bridge, facilitating trauma management and prompting individuals to look at the underlying causes of their pain. Frequently, music making unfolds a transformative power by opening emotional doorways, serving as a sanctuary for genuine emotional expression or as a conduit for 'letting it all out'. Specifically, the act of creating music provides an expressive avenue for the intricate tapestry of experiences related to pain, experiences that words often struggle to capture. It fosters a channel for patients to convey their pain narratives to others. Furthermore, music therapy leverages the power of improvisation to hone the art of emotional regulation. It assists in soothing emotional distress, such as anger and frustration, and dispelling negative thoughts, by redirecting attention to music's *Good Vibrations*.

Within the *social realm*, group music therapy rekindles social support and fosters optimism. While some self-help groups might unintentionally amplify feelings of desolation, music therapy consistently brings about renewed hope and joy. This resurgence of positive emotions often stems from experiencing human connections, both with the therapist and fellow group members. Throughout this therapeutic journey, music therapists craft environments of understanding, establishing bonds free from judgment and anchored in genuine compassion.

Loaded with these insights, I wholeheartedly advocate for music therapy as a guiding light for individuals navigating the arduous terrain of chronic pain, especially as they seek solace across various domains of their lives.[2] Beyond active music therapy, patients can use music as a

---

[2] Bradt, J., Norris, M., Shim, M., Gracely, E. J., and Gerrity, P. (2016). Vocal music therapy for chronic pain management in inner-city African Americans: A mixed methods feasibility study. *Journal of Music Therapy*, 53(2), 178–206.

balm during pain episodes. Immersion in music can redirect focus, reducing awareness of pain and diminishing its intensity. As previously discussed, the pain and pleasure systems overlap, and music's ability to activate the pleasure system offers potential relief for chronic pain. The following recommendations aim to alleviate the distress associated with this condition.

> **RECOMMENDATIONS FOR PATIENTS WITH CHRONIC PAIN**
>
> Music can provide solace to many coping with chronic pain, offering dual benefits: uplifting mood and diverting attention from discomfort. Additionally, music can help develop an awareness of pain control, helping individuals realize they are not entirely at the mercy of their pain.
>
> Not every tip may suit every type of pain or individual, but exploring what resonates with you personally is worthwhile. Generally, select music with a very positive emotional tone – encouraging, uplifting, or relaxing. Note that your music selection is strongly dependent on your taste and preferences. What works for others might not work for you.
>
> 1. *Deep breathing with calming music*
>   - Breathe gently, syncing your breaths to the soothing rhythms of calm music. Try music without a strong beat or accents, such as meditation music by Yuval Ron. With every breath, exhale pain and inhale relaxation. (For proper breathing techniques, refer to Chapter 20. Exhale until there is no more air in your abdomen; when inhaling naturally, the abdomen inflates like a balloon, while the chest barely rises.)
>   - Try humming a tone on the exhale. Then, on the next exhale, hum a second tone. Opt for pitches that are most comfortable for you. Alternate between the tones (one tone per breath). You can also add a third tone. Try humming a lullaby if the associated feelings are pleasant and peaceful for you.
>   - Focus only on your breathing and humming; avoid negative thoughts, worries, or irritations. Counting the beats of each

inhale and exhale helps distract attention away from the pain. For example, exhale for six and inhale for four beats. Vary the number of beats for each inhale and exhale to align with your own comfortable breathing pattern.
- Using music as a relaxation tool can aid in achieving restful sleep. (For more details, refer to Chapter 17.)

2. *Gentle stroking*
   - Gently stroke your arm, leg, or torso, slowly up and down. This activates nerve fibres that reduce pain. While doing so, reassure yourself, 'Everything will be fine!'

3. *For migraine or tension headaches*
   - Individuals with these conditions often become hypersensitive to music, which can occasionally exacerbate the pain. In such cases, breathe and hum slowly and quietly without music. Earplugs can aid in enjoying the silence, allowing you to focus on your body.

4. *Empowering music*
   - While many patients find faster, more rhythmic music uncomfortable during pain, some benefit from its distracting qualities.
   - Others take comfort in powerful tracks, particularly during moments of intense pain (excluding migraines or tension headaches). The epic, heroic, or empowering nature of such music can foster a sense of strength and resilience, making pain feel less overwhelming.

5. *Focusing on music*
   - Engage deeply with the music by tracing its melody and harmonic progressions, or following its emotional arcs, noticing how the tension continually rises and falls.
   - Tap the beat with your hand or foot, or sing along. If others are around, you can sing silently in your mind. Sync your breathing to the rhythm of the music.

6. *Counteract medication-induced fatigue*
   - If certain medications leave you feeling fatigued or exhausted, consider invigorating music as a way to energize and revitalize yourself.

7. *Overcome restrictive postures*
   - Certain pain conditions may result in restrictive postures. Engaging in dance or rhythmic movement in harmony with the

music can counterbalance these postures, potentially offering pain relief. Consult with your doctor before trying this.
8. *Consider regular music therapy*
    - Regular music therapy sessions can provide significant relief for those grappling with chronic pain.

CHAPTER 16

Addiction

Music over Chocolate

HAVE YOU EVER FOUND YOURSELF REACHING FOR that extra piece of chocolate, even when you are not hungry? If so, rest assured, you are not alone. Addiction, be it to substances such as alcohol or to behaviours such as online gaming, carries profound implications. Often, it deeply disrupts relationships, shatters families, and challenges the foundational essence of personal identity. The societal toll is likewise substantial.

The World Health Organization presents a grim picture: approximately forty-two *million* healthy life years vanished in the shadow of drug abuse in 2017, a significant portion of them due to opioids. In the US alone, an estimated 16.5 per cent of the population aged twelve or older is ensnared by the chains of alcohol or drug addiction.[1] However, these startling figures likely only touch upon the actual extent of the issue. Reflect upon this: if an individual grapples with forgoing alcohol for just three days, even without a clinical label of an alcoholic, does this not hint at a concealed dependency?

Yet, let us focus on an addiction that is both astonishingly widespread and frequently overlooked: sugar. Ponder this intriguing comparison: which substance holds a greater addictive pull, sugar or cocaine? The answer may surprise you: it is sugar. In experiments, rats were observed to work several times harder, and even endure more stringent

---

[1] Substance Abuse and Mental Health Services Administration (SAMHSA). National Survey on Drug Use and Health (NSDUH). (2021). www.hhs.gov/about/news/2023/01/04/samhsa-announces-national-survey-drug-use-health-results-detailing-mental-illness-substance-use-levels-2021.html

punishments, to obtain sugar over cocaine.[2] The allure of sugar, especially when combined with fats, is powerful and can be a rapid route to obesity. From sugary drinks and processed foods to seemingly healthy snacks and condiments, sugar is often hidden in plain sight. Given the omnipresence of sugar, this chapter casts a spotlight on sugar dependence, showcasing music's potential to provide solace and serve as a therapeutic tool.

Do you find yourself reaching for that chocolate bar when stressed? What if music could be your new go-to comfort? Becoming overweight often goes hand in hand with succumbing to sugar addiction. For many, this addiction is an insidious shadow, often undetected, yet its consequences for health are irrefutable. Beyond the visible weight gain, sugar addition lays the groundwork for a slew of life-threatening health conditions, including coronary heart disease, heart attack, stroke, and Type 2 diabetes. Moreover, sugar both instigates and exacerbates inflammation, thereby heightening susceptibility to a diverse array of diseases, from common colds to more severe conditions such as arthritis or cancer.[3]

In the brain, habitual consumption triggers subtle micro-anatomical alterations akin to inflammation.[4] The inflammation caused by sugar in the brain can lead to cognitive impairments and even dementia.[5] Excess weight, as an independent factor, can even diminish attention spans, impair learning, and lead to memory lapses.[6] As with all substance abuse that muddies cognitive clarity, excessive sugar consumption casts an

---

[2] Ahmed, S. H., Guillem, K., and Vandaele, Y. (2013). Sugar addiction: Pushing the drug–sugar analogy to the limit. *Current Opinion in Clinical Nutrition & Metabolic Care*, 16(4), 434–439.

[3] Flegal, K. M., Kit, B. K., Orpana, H., and Graubard, B. I. (2013). Association of all-cause mortality with overweight and obesity using standard body mass index categories: A systematic review and meta-analysis. *JAMA*, 309(1), 71–82; Peeters, K., Van Leemputte, F., Fischer, B., Bonini, B. M., Quezada, H., Tsytlonok, M., Haesen, D., Vanthienen, W., Bernardes, N., Gonzalez-Blas, C. B., and Janssens, V. (2017). Fructose-1, 6-bisphosphate couples glycolytic flux to activation of Ras. *Nature Communications*, 8(1), 922.

[4] Kälin, S., Heppner, F. L., Bechmann, I., Prinz, M., Tschöp, M. H., and Yi, C. X. (2015). Hypothalamic innate immune response in obesity. *Nature Reviews Endocrinology*, 11(6), 339.

[5] Profenno, L. A., Porsteinsson, A. P., and Faraone, S. V. (2010). Meta-analysis of Alzheimer's disease risk with obesity, diabetes, and related disorders. *Biological Psychiatry*, 67(6), 505–512.

[6] Miller, A. A., and Spencer, S. J. (2014). Obesity and neuroinflammation: A pathway to cognitive impairment. *Brain, Behaviour, and Immunity*, 42, 10–21.

analogous fog. The formidable addictive power of sugar has catapulted childhood obesity to a pressing public health concern in Western societies. It is almost surreal to think of a time when Coca-Cola contained traces of cocaine – an ingredient that lent its name to the beverage. Fast forward to the future, and these generations will reel in disbelief at the thought of the beverage being laden with sugar, consumed in vast quantities by children. The imperative is clear: we must champion legislative actions that hold sugar-infused products to the same standards of warnings and taxation as tobacco.

Current estimates suggest that nearly half the population in countries such as Germany, the wider European Union, and most notably the US grapple with sugar addiction. My own journey with sugar abuse began during my teenage years. Amid the emotional turmoil of my parents' divorce, I sought solace in the sweet comfort of sugar. It was only in subsequent years that I came to recognize the full extent of my dependence, prompting me to identify myself today as a 'recovering sugar addict'.

If you are contemplating your relationship with sugar, set yourself a challenge: abstain from sugary products for just three days. If this proves difficult, sugar addiction might be the culprit. Overcoming this dependency mirrors the process of overcoming other addictions, with the initial thirty days being the most challenging. After this stage, a healthier lifestyle begins to feel more natural. However, even small indulgences can reignite old cravings. While I now stand resilient against sugar's grip, the temptation of a single spoonful of cheesecake still sparks powerful cravings the very next day.

THE HARMONIC ANTIDOTE TO ADDICTION

My friend Dominic wrestled with alcohol dependence before encountering the transformative power of music on his journey to recovery. Inspired by its impact, he pursued a career as a music therapist and now works closely with individuals confronting their own addictions. Recounting his experiences, Dominic shared the following with me:

> At its core, musical engagement serves as an invaluable *diversion*. It becomes more than just a distraction; it's a sanctuary – a place for the mind to find

respite from the ever-present temptations. Moreover, music has the innate power to modulate our *mood*, offering encouragement and lifting our spirits. Through music, we can also amplify our *self-efficacy*, reinforcing our belief in our own capacity to bring about positive change. There were moments when just playing a heroic song and telling myself, 'I can do it!' felt transformational. Furthermore, music can act as an *alternative source of satisfaction*, significantly reducing the allure of cravings. Engaging in group music therapy introduces a communal dimension, fostering emotional bonds and nurturing *human connections*. Many resort to drugs to fill a void left by a scarcity of social connections. Tragically, those fortunate enough to have such bonds often witness them erode or vanish entirely due to their addiction.

Regrettably, high-quality clinical studies in this field are not yet available. An exhaustive review by my team suggests that the efficacy of music in treating addiction is promising but requires scientific substantiation.[7] Yet, prevailing neuroscientific insights underscore music's undeniable impact. For example, as described in Chapter 8, the neural circuits governing pleasure, pain, and craving intersect significantly. Owing to this intersection, moments of pleasure elicited by music alleviate the pain emerging from cravings. While no studies investigating the effects of music therapy on these brain mechanisms are currently available, the compelling need for such research is evident. Not only is group music therapy cost-effective but it also often garners overwhelming acceptance and commitment from those with addictions.

While the healing properties of music are undeniable, it is also pivotal to recognize its double-edged nature. Certain tunes or genres can inadvertently reignite latent cravings through associations with past addictive experiences. I recall a patient who mentioned that songs from a particular band triggered her heroin cravings. Another noted that a whole genre kindled his alcohol cravings. On a more personal and light-hearted note, the melodies of the Christmas season evoke within me a profound craving for traditional German Christmas treats. Conveniently, this gives me just the reason I need to avoid the busy shopping areas during that period!

---

[7] Hohmann, L., Bradt, J., Stegemann, T., and Koelsch, S. (2017). Effects of music therapy and music-based interventions in the treatment of substance use disorders: A systematic review. *PLoS ONE*, 12(11), e0187363.

Recommendations: Music in Addiction Management

1. *Crafting the right playlist*
   - Selection criteria: prioritize tracks suitable to command your full attention. While brisk tempos with intricate harmonies and melodies are often effective, it is essential to tailor your selection to what resonates with you. Some may find solace in slower yet complex tunes. Steer clear of songs that evoke memories of past addictive behaviours.
   - Mood management: depending on your current emotional state, choose uplifting melodies to counter low spirits and calming tunes to mitigate overexcitement.
   - Accessibility: always have your therapeutic playlist readily available, especially during vulnerable moments.
2. *Tackling acute cravings*
   - Immediate distraction: When a craving strikes, it is crucial to disrupt the associated thoughts as quickly as possible. Use music to redirect your focus away from the addictive substance or behaviour, breaking the craving cycle before it intensifies. Cravings grow stronger when we dwell on them, so engaging with music acts as a mental 'reset,' much like breaking negative thought loops.
   - Active engagement: do not just listen – *participate*. Whether it is tapping your feet, synchronizing your breathing with the music, dancing, or singing along, active engagement can intensify the therapeutic effects. Another option is to visualize yourself as the artist, tapping into their energy.
   - Step by step: to ease into the process, take only one, small step: commit to immersing yourself in just one song. After that initial song, consider adding another, then another, continuing in this manner until the craving subsides. Remember, every journey starts with a single step, and each song is a stride towards overcoming the craving.
   - Evoke emotion: opt for songs that stir emotions, serving as a wholesome substitute for the pleasurable feelings often associated with addictive behaviours.
   - Healthy substitutes: when a craving hits, consider other enticing but healthy alternatives alongside music, such as fresh fruits or savoury foods without sugar.

3. *Mood modulation with music*
   - Emotional upheavals, such as sadness or anxiety, can trigger cravings. In these situations, try to utilize music as a therapeutic balm for elevating your mood.
4. *Building positive associations*
   - Regularly engage with tracks that have proven beneficial in managing your cravings. Over time, your brain will associate these melodies with successful craving resistance. Periodically review your playlist and weed out less beneficial tracks.
5. *Engaging in personal musical expression*
   - If you are musically inclined, do not limit yourself to passive listening. Play an instrument, sing, or compose. Actively engaging with music offers a potent diversion from cravings and allows you to channel emotions constructively.
6. *The power of group music activities*
   - Social connections: consider joining a band or dance group. Shared musical experiences can forge social bonds, potentially filling the emotional voids that might contribute to addictive tendencies.
   - Music therapy: beyond casual groups, structured music therapy can foster mutual understanding and solidarity, help rebuild emotional connections, and activate the brain's pleasure pathways.
7. *Navigating with awareness*
   - Recognize that while music offers vast therapeutic benefits, it is essential to tread with caution. Some tracks, artists, or genres might inadvertently trigger cravings, especially if they are linked to past addictive episodes. Approach your musical environment with keen awareness of these potential triggers.

PLEASURE, PAIN, AND ADDICTION IN THE BRAIN

To fully grasp the therapeutic efficacy of music in alleviating addiction, we now look at the neural circuits associated with pleasure, pain, and craving. As highlighted in Part III, these circuits are not isolated players; they intersect, forming a delicate ballet within the realm of addictive disorders. At the heart of this intricate ballet lies the pleasure system, with the hypothalamus taking centre stage. It plays a multifaceted role – from adapting nerve cell functions to monitoring chemical levels.

As a result of frequent drug intake, the pleasure system's activity undergoes significant changes. For instance, nerve cell function in the hypothalamus adapts to the presence of the drug. This adaptation can lead to addictions tethered to substances such as opioids, alcohol, or sugar. The hypothalamus even adjusts to the presence of specific neurotransmitters such as serotonin, a known brain pain dampener capable of eliciting euphoria. Consequently, activities associated with the release of serotonin, such as jogging, can possess addictive qualities.

Constantly vigilant, the hypothalamus does more than merely monitor the activity of neurotransmitters within the brain. It also keeps a keen eye on the levels of various chemical substances in our bloodstream, with glucose being a prime example.[8] If any of these levels fall below a predetermined threshold, the hypothalamus sounds an alarm, signalling a 'craving'. The further these levels deviate from this set point, the more intense our desires become, often compelling us to undertake risks to satiate such longings. In its most intense form, this craving manifests as palpable pain. When we satisfy these desires and cravings, our brain's pleasure system lights up, rewarding us with sensations of profound delight or exhilaration.

However, there is a caveat. The pleasure system, as it gets accustomed to frequent drug intake and the ensuing shifts in chemical messengers, recalibrates its set points for these substances. Take alcohol as an example: when consumed, it prompts a mix of neurotransmitters and hormones to release. Some of these are tied to the pleasure system's role in regulating stress. Regular alcohol consumption alters the brain's baseline levels of blood alcohol and stress hormones within the hypothalamus.[9] When the level of a substance deviates from this newly adjusted standard, the hypothalamus generates a longing for alcohol. This principle does not just

---

[8] Burdakov, D., Luckman, S. M., and Verkhratsky, A. (2005). Glucose-sensing neurons of the hypothalamus. *Philosophical Transactions of the Royal Society of London B: Biological Sciences*, 360(1464), 2227–2235.

[9] Koob, G. F. (2008). A role for brain stress systems in addiction. *Neuron*, 59(1), 11–34.

apply to alcohol. Sugar, opiates, and even certain neurotransmitters related to stress or pain follow a similar pattern.

Additionally, alongside the recalibration of these set points, frequent drug use leads to a reduced release of reward-linked neurotransmitters. For instance, the consistent release of dopamine into the 'fun motor' gradually loses its efficacy in sparking pleasure. (We introduced the fun motor in Chapter 8.) An infrequent indulgence in sweet chocolate can evoke sheer delight. However, with daily consumption, the brain's pleasure system recalibrates, causing the euphoria from chocolate to diminish. Critically, if one skips their habitual sugar fix, the hypothalamus interprets this absence as a shortfall, triggering intense cravings. Such cravings command our attention, perception, and thoughts, directing them singularly towards obtaining something sweet. Now, redirecting one's focus away from the captivating allure of chocolate becomes an increasingly Herculean task.

This principle applies across a range of substances that modulate brain chemistry, from alcohol and amphetamines to cannabis and opioids. Merely the mental image of consuming these substances can coax a slight release of dopamine, offering a tantalizing foretaste of the pleasure that awaits.[10] This is why, during moments of intense cravings, it is imperative to immediately shift one's focus away from the desired substance. Although it may appear to be a daunting challenge, music emerges as a formidable ally in this endeavour.

From this exploration, it becomes evident that the essence of addiction lies in a misalignment of the brain's pleasure system. The neurotransmitters activated by addictive substances induce a wide range of sensations, from relaxation to euphoria, thereby teaching our brain to regard a particular substance as a beacon of pleasure. In the absence of this beacon, the brain experiences a perceived deficit, leading to an uncontrollable craving. Thus, the roots of addiction lie deeply entrenched in our brain's biochemistry, constituting a disorder rather than a lapse in moral fortitude. Opiates are celebrated for their potent pain-relieving properties, and frequently prescribed to manage pain.

---

[10] Volkow, N. D., Wang, G. J., Fowler, J. S., and Tomasi, D. (2012). Addiction circuitry in the human brain. *Annual Review of Pharmacology and Toxicology*, 52, 321–336.

However, their use presents a cruel irony as they are highly addictive and their withdrawal can thrust one into agonizing pain. This paradox accentuates the importance of considering music as a healthier alternative to prolonged opiate consumption.[11]

As we have journeyed through the complexities of addiction and the brain's intricate dance of pleasure and pain, the therapeutic potential of music in aiding recovery becomes unequivocally clear. Its melodies and rhythms can captivate the mind, redirecting it from cravings and providing a wholesome distraction from harmful substances. By attuning ourselves to music's *Good Vibrations*, we can orchestrate a sanctuary from the clutches of addiction. Furthermore, engaging in communal musical experiences nurtures a sense of belonging and human connection, thus filling those emotional voids that cause addictive tendencies. Next time the allure of chocolate tempts you, remember: striking a chord or humming a tune might just be the sweeter, harmonious remedy you have been searching for. Let us share this melody with others and amplify this symphony of healthier choices, thereby making the world more attuned to the healing effects of music over mere temptations.

---

[11] Chai, P. R., Carreiro, S., Ranney, M. L., Karanam, K., Ahtisaari, M., Edwards, R., Schreiber, K. L., Ben-Ghaly, L., Erickson, T. B., and Boyer, E. W. (2017). Music as an adjunct to opioid-based analgesia. *Journal of Medical Toxicology*, 13(3), 249–254.

CHAPTER 17

Non-organic Sleep Disorders

WHILE ENGROSSED IN CRAFTING THE ORIGINAL GERMAN EDITION OF THIS BOOK, I was interrupted by a thought-provoking enquiry from my agent. She mentioned a close friend struggling with sleep difficulties and wondered if music might hold the key to a reprieve. At that juncture, the complexities of sleep had not been charted in my work. But as I set out to articulate my insights, the vast expanse of music's potential in alleviating sleep disturbances unfurled before me. Blending scholarly findings, insights from respected peers, and my own musical experiences, what began as a simple email evolved into a comprehensive exploration. Recognizing the magnitude of this subject, I felt compelled to devote an entire chapter to it, especially considering the multitude silently craving the gentle embrace of restful slumber.

A staggering proportion of the global populace – nearly one-third of adults – grapples with sleep disorders. Vulnerable groups include shift workers, the elderly, and those subjected to pronounced stress. Psychological burdens, be they workplace challenges, interpersonal tensions, familial conflicts, or monetary concerns, can precipitate both transient and chronic sleep disturbances. A meta-analysis underscores music's healing prowess, illuminating its capability to significantly enhance sleep quality in those afflicted with sleep disorders.[1] Unlike some pharmacological interventions, which may come with the risk of

---

[1] Wang, C. F., Sun, Y. L., and Zang, H. X. (2014). Music therapy improves sleep quality in acute and chronic sleep disorders: A meta-analysis of 10 randomized studies. *International Journal of Nursing Studies*, 51(1), 51–62.

HOW MUSIC HELPS WITH ILLNESS

addiction and leave one feeling groggy upon awakening, music remains free from such drawbacks.

The musical selections you embrace are paramount. They should harmonize with your individual tastes and the specific nature of your sleep ailment. If you struggle with initiating sleep, maintaining it, or reaching its restorative depths, the following recommendations could serve as your guiding light.

RECOMMENDATIONS FOR SOUND SLEEP

1. *Sleep-inducing playlists*
   - Choose music that emanates tranquillity, positivity, and relaxation. Meditation melodies or gentle guitar tunes are typically fitting choices. For lovers of classical music, harpsichord compositions by Bach may offer particular solace. However, it is advisable to avoid their piano renditions, as abrupt forte passages could jolt you awake.
   - Continue listening to tracks that work, and sideline those that do not.
   - When we know familiar tunes so well that they lose their initial allure, they often transform into gentle lullabies, effortlessly guiding us into slumber.
   - Use the tracks of your sleep playlist exclusively for your nightly routine. This consistent pairing helps the brain forge a connection between these melodies and sleep. Once this association takes root, the melodies act as 'sleepy cues', ushering you into slumber.
   - Try to recall those audio tales and lullabies from your younger years. Can you source them? While it might sound unconventional, giving them a listen could be surprisingly effective. The brain often holds deep-seated associations between these familiar audios and a restful state of sleep. Reacquainting yourself with them could be the unexpected key to unlocking peaceful slumber.
   - Engage in conversations with others about their sleep-enhancing playlists and explore various genres and tracks to discover what

genuinely works for you. Remember, the journey to find your ideal sleep soundtrack is as individual as you are.

2. *Nightly resonance*
    - Although it is advisable not to have music playing continuously, playing gentle ambient sounds softly throughout the night can be beneficial. Soundscapes, such as the gentle ebb and flow of ocean waves or the sound of birds chirping, offer a comforting background. These sounds not only create a cocoon of tranquillity but also help mask any sudden, potentially disruptive noises from the environment. For those interested, tailored eight-hour tracks are available on platforms such as YouTube and various smartphone apps, designed to align with a full night's rest.
3. *Defensive sleep tactics*
    - For those disturbed by external noises, foam earplugs may offer a solution. Over time, most users become accustomed to them. Music can still be enjoyed with headphones placed over these earplugs.
4. *A musician's trick*
    - For those with musical inclinations, visualize playing a memorized piece note by note, finger by finger. Personally, when I mentally perform Bach's E major Partita for solo violin, I often fall asleep before reaching the third page. And if sleep still eludes you, at least you've rehearsed the piece.
5. *Relaxing body, mind, and soul*
    - Music's healing effects are strongest when we pair it with both physical and mental relaxation. As your sleep melodies play softly in the background, immerse yourself in progressive muscle relaxation. Deliberately relax each muscle, starting from your toes and working your way up to your scalp. As you breathe, let each exhale drive away tension and each inhale usher in serenity, allowing any residual stress to evaporate. Embrace this mantra: 'breathe, relax, let it flow'.
    - Achieving mental tranquillity is vital. If urgent tasks burden your mind, postpone thinking about them until tomorrow. Exciting ideas that captivate your thoughts? Jot them down for later

reflection. For pressing issues, designate a dedicated time slot tomorrow to tackle them. Should distressing topics preoccupy your mind, deliberately redirect your focus. Let your evening routine become like a meditation in which you only focus on the music or the relaxation of your muscles. (Also see Chapter 20.)
- When you consciously redirect negative thoughts, your mood begins to harmonize with the *Good Vibrations* of the music, dispelling the negative moods that poison restful sleep.

6. *Beyond the melody.* The following techniques can enhance your sleep journey. While they are not inherently musical, pairing them with gentle tunes can amplify their effectiveness, fostering a harmonious sleep environment.
    - Patterns in darkness: as you lie with closed eyes, tune into the subtle patterns emerging from the darkness, resembling distant light phenomena or faint grey clouds. These patterns might take a moment to appear, but when they do, engage with them. Let them guide your mind into the embrace of peaceful sleep. Remember, even if you feel you are not drifting off, spotting something in these patterns often means you *are* already in a light sleep.
    - Evening rituals: cultivate a serene pre-sleep routine, signalling to your body it's time to wind down. Engage in calming activities such as reading, listening to gentle music or an audiobook. Ensure your environment is conducive to relaxation, opting for warm-toned lighting that contrasts with the invigorating blue spectrum of screens. To further aid in this transition, avoid engaging with brightly lit screens before bedtime; if you must use a computer or device, activate its night mode to minimize blue light exposure.
    - Consistency is key: adopt a regular routine for sleeping, waking, eating, and other daily activities. Strive to go to bed and wake up at the same times each day. This consistency aligns your body's natural circadian rhythms, making it easier to fall asleep as bedtime approaches and to wake naturally before your alarm sounds.

- Night's natural ebb and flow: sleep has its deeper and lighter phases, with waking during lighter stages being common. If you struggle to drift back into sleep, apply the techniques outlined in this guide during those wakeful moments.
- Limit stimulants and fluids before bedtime: While a soothing cup of herbal tea can be comforting, avoid stimulants such as coffee, cigarettes, and chocolate at least three hours before sleeping. If you choose alcohol, consume it in moderation to prevent a decrease in sleep quality. For those who experience frequent nighttime trips to the lavatory, maintain hydration during the day but reduce fluid intake in the two hours before bed.
- Dream control: recurring nightmares can be daunting, but the technique of *lucid dreaming* offers a potential remedy. This skill lets you consciously direct your dreams. There are numerous resources to assist you in mastering this.
- Morning energizers: upon hearing your alarm, rise promptly and dive into a structured morning routine. Allow music to set the tone for your day, invigorating you with energy and positivity. For inspiration, consider tracks from Chapter 10.
- Anticipating important events: before significant events such as exams or concerts, excitement or anxiety may hinder sleep. This nervous energy can create a self-reinforcing cycle: the more you worry about not sleeping, the harder it becomes to fall asleep. To counteract this, remember that even two hours of sleep the night before can be sufficient, as long as you've rested well in the preceding nights. Instead of focusing on the potential effects of one restless night, prioritize consistent, quality sleep in the days leading up to pivotal moments.

7. *Setting realistic expectations.* The strategies outlined in this chapter are not quick fixes, but consistent application over a month is likely to result in noticeable improvements in sleep quality. However, if the underlying causes of your sleep challenges are rooted in neurological or psychiatric conditions, these recommendations may not be sufficient. In such scenarios, it's essential to seek specialized medical advice.

Drawing the curtain on this chapter, we stand poised to investigate the intricate interplay between sleep disturbances and depression. In this relationship, one can often be the harbinger of the other: insomnia may intensify feelings of sadness, while depression can give rise to sleep problems. These intertwined threads emphasize the delicate balance of our well-being.

Reflecting on the origins of this book, there is a delightful irony: while my agent's friend now basks peacefully in the realm of dreams, the task of translating this chapter into English has continued well into the night. Having meticulously documented my own sleep-enhancing strategies, the only thing remaining for me is to muster the discipline to follow them. Yet, I find solace in knowing that music's embrace is ever ready to lull me into slumber. Onwards to the next chapter, where the depths of mood and mind beckon.

CHAPTER 18

Depression

CLASSIFIED AS AN AFFECTIVE DISORDER, depression intricately weaves together a tapestry of subdued moods, diminished interest and enthusiasm, heightened fatigue, and a noticeable decline in motivation. Within this emotional tapestry lie pervasive feelings of guilt, a profound sense of worthlessness, eroded self-confidence, and a marked reduction in focus. While brief spells of sadness are natural, clinical depression, also known as *major depressive disorder*, presents a significantly more debilitating challenge, distinguished by the unyielding gravity of its symptoms. This intense suffering often engulfs individuals, encapsulating them in a cocoon of desolation and inertia. Life's triumphs and joys struggle to penetrate this melancholic shield. More often than not, the individuals feel trapped, and require external help to navigate their way out. Over time, the brain, in its remarkable adaptability, reshapes itself to these depressive states, adjusting its neural pathways, brain chemistry, and overall function. This neural transformation further complicates the restoration of positive thought patterns, making the emotional landscape of those with depression elusive to the external world.

Depression's manifestations are multifarious. It can manifest at any life stage, with varying intensities, across diverse durations, and may progress in numerous ways. Many individuals with depression experience physical symptoms – such as chronic pain, sleep disturbances, fatigue, and changes in appetite or weight – despite the absence of an identifiable underlying medical condition. Some may also experience cardiovascular issues or diminished libido. At times, depression alternates with episodes of mania, marked by heightened euphoria and vigour, leading to the diagnosis of *bipolar disorder*. Between these oscillations, periods of mood stabilization may occur.

Factors that elevate the risk of developing depression include exposure to trauma during formative years and a family history of the disorder, particularly when a parent has been affected. Negative thought patterns acquired in childhood, coupled with low self-esteem or pervasive feelings of helplessness, often lay the groundwork for depression. Life's tumultuous events or circumstances – such as job loss, relationship turmoil, the death of a loved one, or prolonged stress – can also act as catalysts. In some cases, individuals may internalize their distress, suppressing emotions rather than addressing them. Other triggers include seasonal transitions, the postpartum period, stages of dementia, or the onset of severe physical illnesses. Additionally, depression may be linked to nutritional deficiencies, such as a lack of vitamin D, or underlying chronic inflammation.

The complex nature of depression can hinder accurate diagnosis for both individuals and medical professionals, particularly in its early stages. Initial symptoms are often mistaken for fleeting mood fluctuations or misattributed to physical ailments. Societal stigmas, intensified by personal reservations, frequently deter people from seeking professional help. Without treatment, depressive episodes can last for extended periods, shadowed by a significant risk of recurrence. In some individuals, depression may evolve into a chronic condition, persisting relentlessly for years.

Globally, the World Health Organization estimates that nearly 300 million people live with depression. The combined costs of treatment and lost productivity make depression one of the most economically taxing illnesses. Tragically, depression is a leading contributor to suicide, with an estimated 800,000 people taking their own lives each year. Experiencing suicidal thoughts warrants immediate action, whether through emergency services, a psychiatric clinic, or a specialized helpline. (For example, in the UK call 116 123; in the US, call 1-800-273-8255.)

Conventional treatments for depression include medication, which can have side effects, and psychotherapy. While patient and empathic support from loved ones can be highly valuable, unsolicited advice or criticism can be detrimental. Therapy aims to help individuals understand and change entrenched negative thoughts and behaviors, replacing them with healthier coping mechanisms. This often involves exploring past traumas, establishing new routines of thinking and acting, and learning new strategies to manage emotions. In addition to therapy, lifestyle factors play a crucial role. Other powerful tools in overcoming depression include physical activity, a balanced diet – and engagement with music.

MUSIC'S THERAPEUTIC ROLE IN MANAGING DEPRESSION

Within the sphere of mental health, music serves as a potent instrument, providing comfort, insight, and healing. However, it is important to be aware of the potential pitfalls of music use for those experiencing depression.

Many of these individuals, often without conscious awareness, employ music in ways that may be counterproductive, particularly during the depths of depressive episodes. They may find themselves drawn to melancholic tunes, even though this type of music often evokes negative thoughts and emotions rather than eliciting enjoyment. While sombre tunes can provide a sense of understanding by giving voice to shared struggles, they can also reinforce destructive thoughts and emotions. In fact, those with depression frequently report heightened despondency after listening to such melodies.[1]

Notably, individuals at risk for depression, marked by difficulties in controlling and regulating their negative emotions, are impacted in similar ways. They frequently experience feelings of nervousness, insecurity, and anxiety without manifesting the clinically relevant symptoms of depression. (This particular tendency is often termed 'neuroticism' within the realm of personality psychology.) Immersing themselves in sorrowful music exacerbates their depressive symptoms and heightens the risk of full-blown depression. One reason is that such tunes can

---

[1] Garrido, S., and Schubert, E. (2013). Adaptive and maladaptive attraction to negative emotions in music. *Musicae Scientiae*, 17(2), 147–166.

instigate a downward spiral of negative moods and prolonged rumination. At times, individuals intentionally select music to nurture and intensify these adverse moods and memories – a potentially risky practice that can make the onset of depressive symptoms more likely.

However, as they listen to music mirroring their current negative mood, they remain caught in the emotional undertow of despondency. Despite feeling burdened by such music, they still 'like' it and frequently choose it over uplifting tunes. Most are unaware that the music they listen to perpetuates their depression. One constructive approach involves not merely listening to music that mirrors one's *existing* mood but also to melodies that align with the *desired* emotional state. One potentially effective solution is to create a playlist that begins with a song resonating with the current mood and gradually transitions to tracks with a more positive tone.

Social interactions significantly influence our relationship with music and mood. Individuals with depression, or those at elevated risk, often gravitate towards listening to sombre music in group settings. This shared experience can lead to co-rumination, where conversations are laden with negativity, painful memories, and persistent pessimism.[2] Such group rumination is even more harmful than solitary brooding, as shared negative emotions amplify each other. This is particularly detrimental for those with depressive tendencies, as ruminating on negativity against the backdrop of melancholic music can deepen destructive thought patterns and emotions. If conversations within your social circle frequently focus on negativity without seeking constructive solutions, it might signal underlying depression or unhealthy dynamics. Encouraging positive interactions or seeking professional guidance may help break these cycles.

Conversely, when individuals with depression intentionally choose music that *avoids* provoking negative rumination, they frequently discover it to be a proficient means of managing symptoms (see the subsequent recommendations below). Dancing also appears to offer benefits for some with depression. In a study, researchers divided participants

---

[2] Garrido, S., Eerola, T., and McFerran, K. (2017). Group rumination: Social interactions around music in people with depression. *Frontiers in Psychology*, 8, 490.

into three groups: a dance group, an ergometer exercise group, and a group that listened to music.[3] Each group engaged in their respective activities for twenty minutes. Surprisingly, all groups reported a reduction in depressive symptoms afterwards. However, it was the dance group that experienced the most significant decrease in symptoms. Strikingly, the effects emerged after a mere single session, illuminating the remarkable benefits of even a fleeting dance experience.

> **RECOMMENDATIONS FOR INDIVIDUALS WITH DEPRESSION**
>
> For those navigating depression, music offers both therapeutic benefits and potential pitfalls. The incorrect use of music can intensify negative moods or ruminative thoughts. This guide aims to assist individuals, whether diagnosed with depression or at risk, in harnessing music's therapeutic effects for their well-being. Note that these guidelines are meant to complement, not replace, essential medical advice.
>
> 1. *Crafting mood-lifting playlists*
>   - To positively affect your mood, include music that aligns with the emotional state you aim to *achieve*. Do not focus solely on tracks that echo the typical negative moods you experience at times.
>   - Mood-transition playlist: ideally, during a time of well-being, take the time to curate a playlist. It is perfectly fine to begin with a track that resonates with the mood you often find yourself in during melancholic or even depressive episodes. Such tracks can provide emotional resonance and convey understanding. However, it is crucial to thoughtfully transition, track by track, towards music that mirrors the emotional state you aim to inhabit – whether that state is motivating, uplifting, or calming.
>   - Classical music lovers might appreciate such mood transitions in all Bach cantatas in minor, and most of Beethoven's compositions in minor. Meanwhile, jazz enthusiasts might start with a

---

[3] Koch, S. C., Morlinghaus, K., and Fuchs, T. (2007). The joy dance: Specific effects of a single dance intervention on psychiatric patients with depression. *The Arts in Psychotherapy*, 34(4), 340–349.

soulful blues piece, progressing towards the lively rhythms of bebop or swing. You might also think about incorporating pieces from Chapter 10 into your playlist.
- Exclusively positive playlists: consider creating playlists that consist exclusively of tracks with a positive tone. You can use these in times of good health to practise cultivating positive thoughts.

2. *Immersion in the musical experience*
   - Do not simply let the music play in the background – immerse yourself fully in the experience. Engage by tapping to its rhythm, silently humming the melody, or even synchronizing your breathing with its tempo. Such active involvement not only deepens your connection to the music but also serves as a diversion from negative ruminations by occupying your mental resources.
   - If your mind strays into less positive terrains, gently remind yourself that now is not the time for such thoughts. Redirect your focus back to the music or pivot to positive thoughts, as outlined in the next recommendation. For additional strategies, see Chapters 5 and 20.

3. *Channelling positive thoughts*
   - As you listen to music, intentionally direct your thoughts towards positivity. Music that radiates positivity often acts as a potent catalyst for this shift. However, during challenging phases, such a task might seem daunting. To assist in these moments, during a period of wellness, prepare a note listing a few of your personal strengths, cherished memories, and affirmations. Read this note during your listening sessions to bolster positive thinking, and let the music's *Good Vibrations* unleash their healing effects within you.
   - Mantras such as 'breathe, relax, let it flow' or 'it is right that I exist', accompanied by a gentle, slow stroke of your arm or torso, can be grounding.
   - To help prevent new episodes, incorporate this practice into your daily routine. Doing so will bolster your resilience and enhance your ability to counteract rumination and negative emotional spirals. You might consider using those of your playlists consisting exclusively of positive-sounding tracks for this practice.

4. *Setting small, achievable goals*
    - Dedicate yourself to manageable, music-related tasks. For instance, aim to listen to at least one track from your therapeutic playlist each day. Alternatively, dance or take a walk, syncing your movements to the rhythm of a single song. Even if the joy you feel is not as intense as in the past, these small actions are vital stepping stones in your journey through depression.
    - Let music be a motivating force for physical or mental activities. Upbeat or invigorating tunes can energize you to engage in physical movement or tackle tasks you've been postponing. Try aligning your pace and actions with the rhythm – this can make tasks feel easier and more enjoyable.
5. *Shared music experiences*
    - Consider joining group musical activities such as choirs, dance groups, or ensemble performances. Participating in these activities offers multiple benefits: it facilitates social interaction, fosters a sense of belonging, and mitigates the feelings of isolation that often accompany depression.
    - Strive for positive experiences in these group musical activities. Aim for sessions that evoke feelings of joy, fulfillment, and connection.
6. *Beyond music*
    - Helpful resources: Consider utilizing workbooks tailored for individuals with depression, such as *Depression for Dummies*. These resources provide structured guidance and are invaluable not only for individuals navigating depression but also for their loved ones seeking to better understand and support them.
7. *Music therapy*
    - Consider formal music therapy. A typical course involves twelve to twenty sessions and can yield significant therapeutic benefits. During these sessions, a trained music therapist employs a range of music-based activities designed to help individuals express emotions, build self-esteem, and manage stress.

MUSIC THERAPY IN MANAGING DEPRESSION

Beyond listening to music and engaging in music making or dance, music can also unfold its healing effects through music therapy. The Finnish music therapist Jaakko Erkkilä spearheaded a clinical study to examine the therapeutic benefits of music therapy in patients with clinical depression.[4] Adult participants were divided into two groups: one received standard treatment, which included medication and psychotherapy, while the other received music therapy in addition to standard care. The research team utilized *improvisation-based music therapy* as their method. In this therapeutic framework, the therapist's role is multifaceted: they may accompany the patient's musical activities, offer creative cues, or mirror the patient's musical expressions. (For a more detailed account, see Chapter 14). Each therapy session was structured to alternate between phases of collaborative music making and open discussions. These discussions focused on the patient's moods, thoughts, or current feelings. The study employed a variety of instruments that are easy for non-musicians to play, including a marimba, an African djembe, and an electronic drum. Each patient participated in a total of twenty sessions, scheduled twice a week. Notably, compared to the standard treatment group, those engaged in music therapy experienced a significantly greater reduction in depression and anxiety.

While these findings offer cause for optimism, an important limitation must be acknowledged: thus far, no study has included a placebo-controlled group. This absence significantly limits the findings, particularly given the well-documented impact of placebo effects in treating depression. For instance, the mere act of leaving one's home twice-weekly to participate in a structured activity can itself yield tangible psychological improvements. As it stands, the absence of placebo-controlled studies leaves a gap in our definitive understanding of music therapy's efficacy in treating depression. Nevertheless, several studies such as the one by Jaakko Erkkilä indicate that music therapy reduces

---

[4] Erkkilä, J., Punkanen, M., Fachner, J., Ala-Ruona, E., Pöntiö, I., Tervaniemi, M., Vanhala, M., and Gold, C. (2011). Individual music therapy for depression: Randomised controlled trial. *British Journal of Psychiatry*, 199(2), 132–139.

depressive symptoms when added to standard treatment.[5] Moreover, I firmly believe that the therapeutic effects of music therapy extend far beyond mere placebo effects; here are several compelling reasons to support this assertion:

- *Emotional awakening.* Music therapists frequently report instances where patients reveal that music therapy has helped them feel, understand, and articulate emotions they had long been unable to confront. For example, Jaako Erkkilä shared a moving account of a patient who remarked, 'Today, for the first time in years, I was able to permit, articulate, and comprehend my emotions.' Another patient, initially hesitant to participate, experienced a profound breakthrough during an intense drumming session, later exclaiming, 'For the first time in my life, I could let it all out.' Remarkably, this patient displayed no symptoms of depression after completing the music therapy sessions.
- *Non-verbal emotional expression.* For individuals who find it difficult to verbalize their emotions, particularly when dealing with traumatic experiences, conventional psychotherapy might fall short. Music therapy can provide an alternative by offering a non-verbal medium for emotional expression, thereby creating a safe space for emotional exploration and healing.
- *Strong patient engagement.* Many patients demonstrate remarkable motivation to participate in music therapy. Jaako's study revealed not only exceedingly low dropout rates but also indicated that the majority of patients were keen to continue music therapy post-study.
- *Physical activation.* The physical act of engaging in music making offers therapeutic benefits, analogous to the positive effects attributed to physical activity in treating depression.
- *Experience of meaning.* For music to emerge, movements need to be synchronized to an underlying pulse. Therefore, music as the result of synchronized movements makes sense. This experience of meaning is crucial for individuals with depression, who often grapple with

---

[5] Aalbers et al., Music therapy for depression.

thoughts of meaninglessness, such as the belief that their existence lacks purpose or value.
- *Emotional activation.* Engaging in synchronized movements during musical activities triggers pleasure and stimulates dopamine release in the reward system. This is an important brain mechanism mitigating anhedonia – a restricted ability to feel pleasure or joy, and a common symptom in depression.
- *Human connection and social reintegration.* The formation of a personal bond with the therapist not only satisfies the human need for connection but also offers a foundation for patients to establish and maintain social bonds in their everyday lives.
- *Neurological activation of the hippocampus.* In many psychological disorders, including depression, the activity of the hippocampus – the brain's *happiness centre* – is compromised. Music has an extraordinary ability to mobilize this brain region, offering hope for those with mood disorders. Furthermore, given that depression is associated with reduced hippocampal volume, one might hypothesize that music therapy could contribute to increasing hippocampal volume through emotional stimulation of neurogenesis in the hippocampal formation (also see Chapter 12). This hypothesis warrants further investigation in future research.

MUSIC THERAPY ACROSS DEPRESSION TYPES

The diverse therapeutic advantages of music therapy underscore its role as a comprehensive and deeply impactful therapeutic approach. Those grappling with depression, as well as relatives concerned about a loved one's mood disorder, may be curious about the specific forms of depression most frequently addressed by music therapy. The following list provides answers on this matter.

- *Major depressive disorder.* Also known as clinical depression, this disorder's hallmarks include sustained feelings of sadness, worthlessness or excessive guilt, loss of energy, and diminished interest in previously enjoyed activities. As outlined in the previous section, many music therapists treat major depressive disorder.

- *Postpartum depression.* Postpartum depression is a prevalent psychological condition, affecting millions of parents after childbirth worldwide each year. It primarily impacts mothers but can also affect fathers. Postpartum depression has severe psychological repercussions on the infant. Infants of depressed parents display behavioural abnormalities just days or weeks after birth, such as avoiding faces and voices, which can persist over the long term and affect other developmental aspects, such as language development.[6] Music therapy interventions often begin with the therapist taking the lead, singing or humming lullabies to the newborn. Parents are gently encouraged to join in, either following the therapist's lead or singing on their own, all while rocking their baby to the rhythm. The musical interaction not only fosters positive bonding with the baby but also enhances the parent's sense of competence, self-worth, and overall well-being.[7]
- *Depression in older adults.* In the elderly population, depression is one of the most common ailments, often spurred by factors such as loneliness, limited interaction with younger generations, diminishing abilities due to age, or severe medical conditions. Group singing, music making, and improvisation-based music therapy have shown promise for seniors, including individuals with mild to moderate dementia.[8]
- *Stroke patients.* A significant number of individuals recovering from a stroke also suffer from depression. Therefore, hospitals and rehabilitation clinics should consider integrating music therapy techniques that aim to alleviate depressive symptoms, in tandem with the neurological treatments detailed in Chapter 11.

---

[6] Schaadt, G., Zsido, R. G., Villringer, A., Obrig, H., Männel, C., and Sacher, J. (2022). Association of postpartum maternal mood with infant speech perception at 2 and 6.5 months of age. *JAMA Network Open*, 5(9), e2232672–e2232672.

[7] Yang, W. J., Bai, Y. M., Qin, L., Xu, X. L., Bao, K. F., Xiao, J. L., and Ding, G. W. (2019). The effectiveness of music therapy for postpartum depression: A systematic review and meta-analysis. *Complementary Therapies in Clinical Practice*, 37, 93–101.

[8] Dhippayom, T., Saensook, T., Promkhatja, N., Teaktong, T., Chaiyakunapruk, N., and Devine, B. (2022). Comparative effects of music interventions on depression in older adults: A systematic review and network meta-analysis. *EClinicalMedicine*, 50, 1–17.

- *Cancer patients.* The gravity of a cancer diagnosis often leads to significant emotional distress. In addition, the disease itself and its treatments are often accompanied by severe physical pain. Music-based interventions can alleviate symptoms of anxiety, depression, pain, and fatigue in both adult and paediatric cancer patients.[9] Patients can utilize music listening to reduce anxiety and worries, as well as to manage pain; if possible, active participation in music therapy is likely to offer even greater benefits.
- *Sleep disorders and substance abuse.* Both of these conditions often coexist with depression and can benefit from music therapy. (Refer to Chapters 16 and 17.)

EMPOWERING YOUR RESILIENCE AGAINST DEPRESSION

We have seen the diverse benefits that make music therapy a comprehensive and impactful approach to treating depression. In addition to its therapeutic role, music can also help *mitigate the risk of depression.* The most effective safeguard against depression is building resilience – our ability to cope with traumatic events without enduring lasting negative impacts. Much of the guidance in this book is designed to strengthen resilience (see Chapter 7 for a focused approach). For those who have experienced a depressive episode before, regularly practising meditation exercises with music can be particularly helpful (refer to Chapter 20). Recognizing the early signs of a depressive episode is crucial, including early awakenings, persistent low moods, negative thought loops, or diminished pleasure in activities. When these signs appear, creating and following a personalized action plan can be invaluable. The earlier you identify a depressive downward spiral, the easier it is to interrupt it.

---

[9] Bradt, J., Dileo, C., Magill, L., and Teague, A. (2016). Music interventions for improving psychological and physical outcomes in cancer patients. *Cochrane Database of Systematic Reviews* (8), 1–154; Köhler, F., Martin, Z. S., Hertrampf, R. S., Gäbel, C., Kessler, J., Ditzen, B., and Warth, M. (2020). Music therapy in the psychosocial treatment of adult cancer patients: A systematic review and meta-analysis. *Frontiers in Psychology,* 11, 651.

DEPRESSION

Resilience training for those managing depression begins with maintaining a balanced diet and a consistent exercise routine – even if it is as simple as taking regular walks. Avoiding refined sugar is crucial, as it can exacerbate depressive symptoms. Instead, opt for whole fruits (but avoid fruit juices and smoothies) and incorporate a variety of fresh vegetables such as tomatoes, bell peppers, and avocados. Legumes, seeds, and nuts are also excellent additions to your diet. For vitamin D, consider fish like salmon, herring, sardines, oysters, or shrimp. Foods rich in antioxidants – such as strawberries, raspberries, and walnuts – help the immune system combat inflammation. For your next mood-boosting experience, why not pair uplifting music with a nourishing mix of strawberries, raspberries, and walnuts? Remember, resilience is a potent capacity for protecting against depression. Embracing a healthy lifestyle with music as your companion can significantly empower your journey toward mental well-being.

CHAPTER 19

How This Book Led Me to a Music Recipe for Patients with Schizophrenia Spectrum Disorder

Individuals with schizophrenia spectrum disorder (SSD) frequently encounter auditory hallucinations, perceiving voices that are, to them, virtually indistinguishable from genuine external voices. These hallucinations can coexist with delusions and are frequently accompanied by enduring challenges such as depression, social isolation, and memory issues.

During episodes of voice hallucinations, the brain's auditory and speech systems are activated in a manner similar to hearing genuine external voices. Compounding this challenge, these hallucinated voices often convey negative messages, eliciting feelings of threat, powerlessness, despair, depression, worthlessness, or irritation in those affected.

While crafting this book, a novel idea emerged: could music serve as both an emotional and a cognitive distraction to assist SSD patients during episodes of auditory hallucinations? I distinctly recall the moment when this idea crystallized; I was seated in my university's cafeteria, and it suddenly became clear: from a neurophysiological perspective, music should have the potential to assist patients with SSD.

Their potent negative moods and thoughts can only originate from what I refer to as the *subconscious*, a realm we can effectively divert through the medium of music. Furthermore, music and speech are processed in overlapping networks in the brain. Hence, focusing on music – especially music with lyrics – engages brain mechanisms that interfere with those underlying auditory hallucinations, effectively muting the voices.

For music to function as an *emotional* distraction, it should ideally be counteractive to the negative emotional states elicited by the hallucinations. The patients themselves are most qualified to choose this music, as they uniquely understand the emotional nuances induced by their hallucinations. Clinicians would act in an advisory capacity, offering guidance in the selection of suitable music, while also imparting their own emotional reactions to the pieces chosen by the patient.

As a *cognitive* distraction, the music's effectiveness could be maximized if the patients fully focused on it. The exercises outlined earlier in this book to disrupt negative thought loops would serve to enhance this focus. Furthermore, tapping the rhythm with the *right* hand or foot engages the language-dominant *left* hemisphere, thereby disrupting the speech-processing mechanisms effectively through rhythmic movements.

I discussed these considerations with a friend, who serves as the director of a psychiatric clinic. She found the methodology intriguing, and we resolved to test the approach on a select group of patients, aiming to assess its efficacy and refine the method. The ensuing recipe stems from these collective endeavours.

RECOMMENDATIONS: A MUSIC RECIPE FOR INDIVIDUALS EXPERIENCING AUDITORY HALLUCINATIONS

This music recipe is specifically designed for individuals with SSD who appreciate music, hold no adverse associations with it, and experience emotionally negative states triggered by auditory hallucinations, particularly hearing voices.

- *Assess the specific emotional impact.* Evaluate the specific emotional impact that your auditory hallucinations, particularly the voices, have on you. Then, create a playlist of pieces that express the opposite emotions. For instance, if the voices are typically threatening, choose heroic-sounding music, or if the voices are typically disheartening, choose uplifting music. Ensure that the selected music does not evoke any distressing memories and is not associated with any negative experiences or previous drug use.
- *Participate in the music.* When you experience auditory hallucinations, or anticipate their onset, utilize your curated playlist. Subtly tap the beat with your right hand and foot. For added

distraction from the voices, either sing along in your mind or breathe in rhythm with the music, counting the beats as you inhale and exhale. For variety, you can also follow how the musical tension increases and releases, or focus on how phrases begin, reach their central point, and then conclude. If musically inclined, consider also visualizing playing the song yourself. For example, you might envision your fingers strumming the chords on a guitar or striking the keys on a piano.
- *Maintain focus.* Keep your thoughts securely focused on the music and abstain from dwelling on any negative thoughts. If you find your mind wandering, immediately redirect your focus back to the music.
- *Be prepared.* Make certain that your chosen music and, if applicable, headphones are always within easy reach.
- *Iterate.* Persistently refine your playlist, keeping the tracks that work well for you and removing those that do not.

I have tested these recommendations with numerous patients afflicted by SSD. My role primarily involved advising them on the curation and optimization of their playlists, customizing each recommendation to suit the individual's unique profile and needs. For example, a patient with a passion for singing found the technique of internal singing to be particularly beneficial. Another patient, an amateur guitarist, found value in visualizing himself playing the chords of his chosen heavy metal songs.

The feedback received so far has been overwhelmingly positive. 'The voices disappear when I listen to music,' expressed one patient. A young man experiencing auditory hallucinations as buzzing and whistling sounds, rather than as voices, reported remarkable control over these symptoms through music. All the patients expressed profound relief at finally having a way to silence the intrusive voices, freeing them from the continual dread of their next appearance. Moreover, the discreet nature of these techniques – such as tapping a foot or finger, or internally singing along – facilitates their use in everyday settings without drawing undue attention, be it on public transport or during shopping.

This methodology does not constitute 'music therapy' in the traditional sense, which generally aims for broader therapeutic outcomes, such as coping with trauma, facilitating emotional release, or enabling other psychological breakthroughs. While unquestionably advantageous for tackling the emotional and social complexities frequently accompanying SSD, my 'music recipe' has a more targeted, immediate aim: providing swift relief via music. This is akin to my recommendations for managing chronic pain, disrupting depressive thought cycles, or controlling addiction cravings.

In the years to come, I aim to delve further into these therapeutic properties of music through rigorous scientific investigation. Considering the significant distress auditory hallucinations inflict on those with SSD, it is remarkable how straightforward yet effective music can be as a therapeutic tool – another testament to the still untapped healing power of music's *Good Vibrations*.

PART FIVE

IN CONCLUSION

At a Glance

CHAPTER 20

Music Meditation

PLAY MUSIC THAT SOUNDS PLEASANT, UPLIFTING, encouraging, or calming to *you*. You can find suitable tracks in a variety of genres and styles (my current favourites are Bach cantatas BWV 140, 115, and 66, Standard Time Vol. 6 by Wynton Marsalis, and meditation music by Yuval Ron). Lie down and close your eyes. The more relaxed and inviting your surroundings, the more effective the exercise will be. Wear comfortable clothing or loosen your belt. Turn off your phone and internet for the duration of this exercise.

Aim for a calm and rhythmic breathing pattern. Exhale through either your nose or mouth; if through the mouth, pursing your lips like you are whistling can help (or actually whistle while exhaling). Inhale solely through your nose. Imagine your abdomen as a balloon that expands and contracts with each breath, while keeping your chest relatively still. Exhale longer than you inhale (for example, six seconds out and four seconds in). Try to match your breathing to the music's rhythm, timing your inhalations and exhalations to the beat. Again, make sure that you exhale longer than you inhale. For example, exhale to the count of nine musical beats and inhale to the count of six.

If you start to feel light-headed or experience tingling due to excess oxygen, you can pause briefly after exhaling before inhaling again. However, always follow an inhalation immediately with an exhalation; do not pause after inhaling. Slow and prolonged exhalation will naturally slow your heartbeat, contributing immediately to relaxation. With each breath, exhale tension, tightness, negative emotions, pain, and illness. Inhale relaxation, peace, renewal, and health. Focus solely on your breathing, avoiding negative thoughts.

Progressively relax different parts of your body, from your extremities to your torso and head. If your mind starts to wander, simply steer your focus back to either relaxation, breathing, or the music. For a deeper state of relaxation, think of calming places or experiences.

Key point. Focus exclusively on relaxation, your breathing, or the music. Do not let your thoughts wander off into negative territories; should they stray, gently guide them back. If you wish to continue the exercise and feel deeply relaxed, feel free to think about positive, relaxing places or experiences.

A variant. In addition to focusing on your breath, pay attention to the musical structure of the piece. Follow the musical phrases and emotional arcs, experiencing how expected or unexpected the musical events sound. If your mind drifts away from the music, simply guide it back. This focus can free your mind from negative thought loops, and sometimes even alleviate pain. Enjoy the relaxation and inner peace that such concentration on music brings; it is pleasant and regenerative.

Another variant. Reiterate positive affirmations to yourself in full sentences. These can relate to your personality, your life, your current situation, or your current physical state. Make relaxation a daily habit, whether through this practice or other techniques such as different forms of meditation, mindfulness, or yoga. By doing so, you train your brain to detect stress more quickly and to relax more readily. You also become adept at recognizing negative thoughts and converting them into positive ones. Healthcare professionals refer to this ability as resilience, aiding us in coping with traumatizing events or life crises without enduring health impairments.

CHAPTER 21

Engaging in Physical Activity with Music

EVERY SMALL STEP IS EASY, EXCEPT FOR THE FIRST ONE. Taking that first step in physical activity might seem daunting, but it is crucial for our health and well-being. According to the World Health Organization, a minimum of two and a half hours, but ideally five hours, of physical activity per week is recommended. Therefore, incorporate physical activity into your weekly schedule, preferably at regular times to establish a consistent rhythm that your body can adapt to. Alter the intensity, rather than the duration, to suit your fitness level.

Prepare for your next physical activity a day ahead. Have your sports gear readily accessible and select the appropriate, motivating music – perhaps one of your courage-boosting songs. Visualize yourself the following day turning on the music, embarking on your workout, commencing the exercise, breaking a sweat, and persevering throughout.

Follow through with your plans the next day. Turn on your music at the planned time, without hesitation or second thoughts, and set off. If you find that specific music works well, make it a regular part of your routine. Dismiss any music that does not yield results.

Music can also help you sustain your activity. If possible and helpful, listen to music while you exercise. To maintain your stamina, perform your movements in time with the music and consider singing along. If you are not listening to music, sing in rhythm with your movements. If necessary, sing internally so that no one can hear. Anything that distracts from negative thoughts and emotions is welcome! Imagine that your movements produce or influence the background music. You can also simply breathe in and out in time with your movements (for more on breathing, see Chapter 20). When your body breaks down fat, it's

IN CONCLUSION: AT A GLANCE

primarily converted into carbon dioxide, which you exhale. When exertion becomes uncomfortable, take solace in knowing that each breath expels fat.

Commit to this routine for at least thirty days. It will become more manageable over time. Consider your initial twenty-minute sessions a success, even if you had planned for a longer duration – your next session might be a minute or two longer. Set achievable goals to make success more attainable; even the smallest success counts.

During or after exercise, opt for water, herbal tea, or non-alcoholic wheat beer instead of sugary beverages, fruit juices, or smoothies. Make your first post-exercise meal healthy and free of added sugars.

Remember, music will always be your ally in perseverance.

CHAPTER 22

Negative Side Effects of Music

MUSIC'S IMPACT IS NOT ALWAYS POSITIVE. Here are some of the most significant side effects of music. Keep in mind that 'music' may refer not only to specific pieces but also to the works of a composer, a band, or even entire styles of music.

- *Music and addiction.* Music can trigger relapse or incite addictive behaviour in individuals with a history of substance abuse. The risk is particularly high if certain music is associated with memories of previous drug use and the brain has stored an association between this music and substance abuse.
- *Music and depression.* For those with depression or a predisposition towards it, certain types of music can worsen existing depressive symptoms. Often, these individuals unknowingly use music in a way that exacerbates their depression, especially when they are already feeling low. Music that evokes gloominess can trigger negative thought loops and attract thoughts, memories, and perceptions that resonate with the melancholy conveyed by the music. Such thought loops and emotional attractor effects elevate the risk of depression and exacerbate depressive symptoms.
- *Music and trauma.* For trauma survivors, specific music can bring back traumatic memories, potentially leading to a crisis.
- *Music and epilepsy.* For individuals with epilepsy, specific genres or rhythms in music may trigger an epileptic seizure. Consulting a neurologist can help clarify which music should be avoided.
- *Music and emotional health.* Even for mentally healthy individuals, certain negative-sounding music can adversely impact thoughts, emotional cycles, and moods.

IN CONCLUSION: AT A GLANCE

- *Music and earworms.* Music can give rise to bothersome 'earworms', which are snippets of a song that seem to play on a loop in one's mind. These can occur with any genre or complexity of music, from classical to modern, simple to intricate. Neurologically, the experience is akin to auditory hallucinations, activating regions in the brain such as the auditory cortex and areas associated with repetitive thought loops or rumination. To dislodge an earworm, one can employ a strategy akin to breaking free from negative thought loops: focus intently on a different piece of music. One does not necessarily have to hear that different tune but can also mentally 'sing' it. If more suitable, listening to an audiobook can also be effective, especially when played at a faster speed, such as one and a half times the normal rate, to fully engage the auditory processing resources.
- *Music and manipulation.* While music has the power to foster peace and community, it can also be weaponized to incite hostility, isolation, and aggression. Examples include music used by extremist groups to spread hate, nationalist anthems that fuel division and prepare nations for war, or military marches that instill discipline and aggression among troops. Many subcultures use music for dancing and celebration, yet 'outsiders' are not welcome. As a result, music can reinforce subconscious impulses toward violence, discrimination, and destruction. Ultimately, music's potential to foster peace depends crucially on the humanistic values with which individuals engage its community-building capabilities.

CHAPTER 23

Emergency Help for Negative Emotions and Moods

DESIGNED AS A TRUSTED RESOURCE FOR MY children, friends, and myself, this emergency guide has been meticulously refined based on first-hand experiences with overcoming challenges. If these strategies can even spark positive change in my life – a life brimming with challenges and my own stubborn resistance – they're bound to work for you too. While some recommendations may appear unconventional or daunting, I encourage you to embrace them. Regular practice will rewire your brain, creating and fortifying new neural pathways, thereby making this approach progressively easier and more effective over time.

STEP 1: START WITH MUSIC

Have you realized that you are feeling angry, worried, sad, or experiencing another negative emotion? Congratulations! Recognizing this is an important first step. It is normal and human to experience negative emotions. Regrettably, life inevitably involves problems, suffering, and change. The key is not to let these negative emotions linger and evolve into a lasting mood – that would be a waste of our lives. Now, play some music that you find both uplifting and encouraging. Let its *Good Vibrations* resonate within you. If you can't think of any music, try a song by Elvis Presley or a Bach cantata (such as BWV 147), or Mojo Club Dancefloor Jazz (Vol. 10, 4, or 7). Remember, such moments happen to everyone. Proceed to the second step to transform your negative emotions into positive ones.

STEP 2: BREATHE, RELAX, LET IT FLOW

Engage in slow, deep breathing; for instance, exhale gently to the count of six musical beats and inhale to the count of four. Repeat this several times to establish a rhythmic breathing pattern, which will naturally calm your body. Relax your muscles one by one. Slowly stroke your left arm with your right hand up and down, telling yourself, 'Everything will be alright.' A warm cup of tea can also help to calm down and relax.

STEP 3: FIND SOMETHING POSITIVE

Identify a positive aspect of your current situation, even if it's simply that things could have been worse, or that the experience will help you grow – some of life's most important lessons come from our mistakes and crises. So never, never, *never* give up! Remember the Kölsch Constitution's Article 3: 'In the end, it has always worked out.' We can always surrender to despair and think or act self-destructively in the face of challenges. Alternatively, we can accept the challenge to discover and develop our inner strengths, resilience, perseverance, and tenacity, thereby growing through the challenge. To do this, we do not need negative emotions.

STEP 4: THINK CLEARLY

If you are currently engulfed in strong negative emotions, your perception of the world, yourself, your problem, and anyone involved is likely irrational and distorted. This suggests that you are likely harbouring several misconceptions right now. For example, you may be overestimating the threat, fearing unrealistically negative outcomes ('worst-case scenarios'), filling information gaps with the worst assumptions, and treating these unproven assumptions as irrefutable facts. These irrational thoughts, frequently characterized by unwarranted pessimism and negativity, are known as *cognitive biases*. Perhaps you are also giving in to all-or-nothing thoughts such as, 'Either everything is perfect, or my life and I are failures,' or 'If X happens, my whole life will fall apart.' You might even fear that you will lose everything and that you and your family will never be happy again, or that something like this will keep happening.

Irrational negative thoughts typically arise in situations that your brain classifies as threatening, upsetting, or disheartening. They are part of what we have labelled in Part II as *emotional attractor effects* – negative emotions attract only those thoughts, memories, and perceptions that fit with the current mood. However, instead of playing fortune teller, filling information gaps, and making negative assumptions without actual facts, consider that it is precisely these cognitive distortions that contribute to your fears, worries, anger, and stress.

Furthermore, remember that experiencing negative emotions does not necessarily signify an inherently negative situation. It is usually our own perspective that makes something annoying, sad, and so on. Instead, focusing your attention on positive-sounding music will help dissolve the emotional attractor effects of negative emotions.

STEP 5: SEE YOUR STRENGTHS

Refrain from blaming yourself, tearing yourself apart, or feeling overwhelmed by shame due to your mistakes. Everyone makes mistakes, and we grow from them. Try to get it right next time. Now, focus on your strengths. (If you have previously written down your strengths, take a moment to read that list now.) Avoid trying to find someone to blame, – whether yourself or others. Remember, your worth is not defined by your actions or mistakes. It is inherent and equal to that of any other human being. Your dignity and intrinsic value remain intact, irrespective of any mistakes you have made.

STEP 6: FOCUS

Channel your focus into an activity or thought that holds both benefit and meaning for you, be it music, your work, or problem solving. Further suggestions for this include playing music yourself, entertaining yourself by playing a game, tidying up, reading a book you've wanted to read for a long time, going outside, doing some light physical exercise, or taking a shower. Or do a mindfulness exercise or meditation and tell yourself a dozen positive things about your life in full sentences (that start with 'I am glad that ...', 'How fortunate that ...', 'I am happy that ...', 'How wonderful that ...'). Then, repeat these positive affirmations. What is crucial in all of this is that you direct your full attention to yourself, allowing your negative thoughts and emotions to subside so you can be present in the moment again.

Remember: the less time you spend on destructive thoughts, the more time you have for constructive ones. If you notice that your thoughts wander or negative thoughts emerge, comment on this with an 'aha' and then tell yourself that it is normal for this to happen. Redirect your attention back to your initial focus or activity. Do not devote any negative thoughts to the thing or person triggering the negative mind wandering. If you keep thinking of such a person, say, 'Sorry, I don't have time for you right now' and direct your focus on thoughts that are good for you. You will notice that negative *thought loops* begin to fade and occur less frequently, much like dense clouds that gradually dissipate.

STEP 7: TALK TO OTHERS

Speak constructively with another person about your problem. Do not keep worries and problems to yourself. Simply verbalizing things often has very positive effects, and support from others often works wonders. Others often have ideas for solving a problem. Preferably speak with people who, if necessary, criticize your behaviour, not you as a person. Be prepared for this person to also share some unpleasant truths – real friends have the courage to tell you things you may not wish to hear. To generate a variety of ideas and develop diverse perspectives, consult with up to three people, as this is usually sufficient to capture the critical aspects of a situation.

If conversing with someone else is not feasible at the moment, speak aloud to yourself. I know it sounds embarrassing, but when we speak aloud to ourselves, we form our thoughts into full sentences and give them more logic, instead of thinking irrational thoughts.

If you believe you have a moral obligation to experience negative emotions and remorse, consider postponing these feelings to specific, pre-allocated time slots. Additionally, allocate specific times to work on problem solving. If worries and problems come to your mind during the day, quickly write them down on a piece of paper and postpone them to your 'problem-solving time'. Take solace in the knowledge that you need not worry at this moment as you have specifically allocated time for it later.

Generally, it is especially important in times of crisis that you also do things that are good for you and your health, that give you pleasure or joy. If the music you are currently listening to is pleasant and enjoyable, this is an ideal start. Some people find it helpful to do sports or cook something particularly delicious *and* healthy. Avoid seeking comfort in sweets, alcohol, or other substances, and exercise caution with salt intake due to the risk of high blood pressure. Instead, eat fish, fruits, and vegetables right now. Consider supplementing these with additional vitamins C and D to bolster your immune system and mitigate potential mood symptoms associated with vitamin D deficiency.

Be careful comforting yourself with sad music or music that fits your mood. Sometimes it helps to have a good cry to sad music, but then start again from Step 1 and make sure to end with positive-sounding music.

Finally, the following additional tips can also help with specific emotions or situations:

- *Someone has ended a relationship with you.* Identify a positive aspect that allows you to feel relieved or glad that the relationship has ended. Wish that person happiness and well-being. Then stop thinking about them.
- *Worrying.* When consumed by worry, your subconscious mind tends to focus exclusively on the negatives. Counter this by playing music that lifts your spirits, and then make a list of seven or more positive scenarios that could unfold in your life. Note: frame these scenarios not as possibilities but as future certainties. For instance, if you are anxious about an upcoming exam and passing is realistically achievable, write, 'The exam will be a success.' Other examples include, 'The project will be a success' and 'I will feel relieved and happy this evening.' Read this list out loud to yourself. Take into account which elements you have control over – such as studying for an exam – and differentiate between problems you can solve and those you cannot. If a solution to your concern exists, do not delay – take steps to resolve it. (For detailed guidance, I recommend the book *Managing Your Mind*

by Gillian Butler, Nick Grey, and Tony Hope.) Steer clear of obsessing over uncontrollable issues. Life is full of uncertainties; therefore, redirect your energy towards steps you can take on your way to achieving your personal goals.

- *You have messed up.* We have all been there: making a major mistake can plunge you into a cycle of guilt or shame. In moments such as these, it is crucial to remember that your past is not solely defined by this blunder; you have also made positive impacts on your life and on the lives of those around you. The next step is to formulate a plan for making amends. This also includes informing those affected that you acknowledge your mistake, express your regret, and assure them it will not recur; for instance, 'I realize I have made a mistake; I am sorry – it won't happen again.' Remember, every blunder is also a learning opportunity, inviting us to acknowledge our limitations and take responsibility for our actions.

CHAPTER 24

Concluding Remarks

As we close the final pages, we return to the questions posed in the Preface: how can we use music to stay healthy or regain health? How does music evoke healing and regenerative effects? What happens in our brain and the rest of our body when music plays this role?

The journey through this book has illuminated music's unique power to promote health and happiness. I have underscored the idea that health and happiness derive not solely from music itself but from the mindset with which we approach our musical experiences. That is, when we engage in music in a peaceful, compassionate, and prosocial way, I believe that it supports our inner healing powers more than anything else. Similarly, I assert that music surpasses all in its ability to foster social cohesion and community on a grand scale – and bonding with other individuals and belonging to a group is a fundamental human need and source of happiness.

Therefore, music not only has a fundamental place in human evolution, but attaining health and well-being with music also defines our humanity, extending beyond mere artistic and emotional expression. The scientific evidence presented in this book corroborates music's enduring capacity to heal, unite, and inspire.

From the evolutionary necessities discussed in Part I to the profound emotional connections explored in Part II, and the intricate neurobiological processes unveiled in Part III, music emerges as a vital component of human life. Part IV's examination of music's therapeutic applications in addressing a wide range of illnesses and disorders further solidifies its importance, not just as a cultural or artistic endeavour but as a necessary element of human health and happiness.

IN CONCLUSION: AT A GLANCE

Moreover, this book has explored the vast expanse of human musicality, from the inherent musical abilities present even in infants to the sophisticated cognitive processes that underlie musical perception and enjoyment. We have seen how music can evoke profound emotional responses, facilitate language recovery, aid in movement for those with Parkinson's, and even provide comfort and memory recall for patients with Alzheimer's disease.

As we reflect on the myriad ways music influences our lives and well-being, it is my hope that you, the reader, will find new appreciation for the sounds that surround us and the melodies that move us. Let the knowledge and stories shared here inspire you to integrate music's *Good Vibrations* more consciously into your daily life, whether for health, healing, or simply the joy of shared musical experience.

In essence, this book is an invitation to recognize and harness the transformative power of music. As we step forward from this reading journey, may we all carry with us the understanding that music is much more than a background soundtrack – it is a fundamental pillar of our health, happiness, and humanity.

Index

Page numbers: **bold** = box; *italics* = figure.

accents, 28, 30
AC/DC, 99
Adams, D., vii
addiction, 272–280
  harmonic antidote, 274–275
  management (music recommendations), 276–277
  pleasure and pain in brain, 277–280
adolescents, 80, 133
adrenal cortex, 118, **122**
adrenaline, 119, 120
adrenocorticotropin, **121**
affect systems, *146*, 146, 195
aggression, 110, 177, 181, 188, 194, 208, 312
'aha' experiences, 102–103, **105**
akinesia, 244
alcohol, 274, 275, 278, 279, **285**
Allen, R., 260
Altenmüller, E., 224
Alzheimer's dementia, viii, 133, 175, 320
  enigmatic emotion-memory tunnel, 235–237
  future research, 237, 239
  harnessing music for cognitive resilience, 238–239
  music as catalyst for episodic memory retrieval, 233–235
  pioneering neural therapy, 229–241
  'profound influence' of music on emotional well-being, 237
  recommendations for caregivers, **237**
  resilience of musical memory, 230–233
  singing (mitigation of brain degeneration), 240–241
  symptoms, 230

amateur musicians, 41, 92, 93, 232
  rejuvenating effects of music, 130
amusia, 211
amygdala, 94, 95, *149*, 164, 168
  'conductor of brain's emotional orchestra', 164
anaesthetics, 165
analgesia, *161*
anger, 13, 14, 46, 60, 63, 78, 177, 268
anger management: four steps, 61–64
anterior hippocampus, *161*, 170, 172, 175, 239
  in footnote, 173
anterior insula, 50
anterograde amnesia, 170
anxiety, 126, 175, 177, 248
aphasia: patients who sing when they cannot speak, 213–215
appraisal theories (emotion psychology), 60
arm paralysis: recommendations, **227**
Armstrong, L., **117**
arrogance, 71, 139
art music, 10, 87
ascending system (in brain), 148
Asperger's syndrome, 256, 259
atmospheres, 78–79
  definition, 78
attachment-related emotions, 170–172
attention: therapeutic effect of music, 132–133
attention-deficit hyperactivity disorder (ADHD), 133, 175
audiobooks, 209, 210, 284, 312
auditory cortex, 22, *32*, 34, 39, 40, 41, 44, 198, 199, 312

INDEX

auditory motor-mapping training (AMMT), 260–261, **265**
auditory-limbic pathway, *149*
Austria, 105
autism, 176, 200, 255–264
  harnessing musical abilities for therapy, 260–263
  individuals' musical strengths, 257–260
  power of music, 263–264
  recommendations for caregivers, **264**
autism spectrum disorder (ASD), 256
autobiographical memories, 81, 82, 233
  evocation by music, 82–84
autonomic nervous system, 113, 114–117, 118, 148, 154, 167, 249
  illustration, *115*
autopilot network (Koelsch), 189, **190**
Aznavour, C.: 'La Bohème', 234

babies, 16, 20, 29, 109, 154, 180, 201
  emotional contagion, 74
  talking, singing, dancing with, **17–19**
Bach, J. S., vii, 24, 26, 78, **117**, **282**
  cantatas, 150, **291**, 307, 313
  'Chaconne', 58, 133
  cheerful exclamations, 154
  'Musical Offering', 87
  'Partita in E major for violin', 283
  suites, 65
Backstreet Boys, 20
bad vibrations, 182, 186
balance, 132, 148, *149*
basal ganglia, *161*, 247, 248
Baumeister, R., 178
beat, 10, 19, 36
  ability to harmonize, 11
  language versus music, 12
Beatles, The
  'Hey Jude', **219**
  'Yesterday', 75
beauty, 136, 138
Beethoven Duo, 83
Beethoven, L. van, 24, 26, 83, 99
  compositions in minor, **291**
  defiant accents, 154
  'Moonlight Sonata', 200
  'Symphony (No. 9)', 58
  'Violin Concerto', 56
'Bele Mama' (song), 105
beliefs, 126
Bell, J., 57, 58
Bengtsson, S., 43–44

Berg, A., 107
Berlin: Charité Hospital, 139
Bhattacharya, J., 64
bilingualism, 28
bipolar disorder, 175, 288
birds, 20, 172, 283
Bizet, G.: 'Carmen', 104
blame, 60, 129, 184, 192, 315
blindness, 255, 256
blood pressure, 117, 119, 317
Blood, A., 159
Blues Brothers, 203
  'Everybody Needs Somebody', 203
Blutner, Dr, 69
Bobath Concept, 221
borderline personality disorder, 174
Bradt, J., 156
bradykinesia, 244
Brahms, J., 104, 154
brain, 9, 134, 287
  electrical responses to chords, **24**, 25–26
  emotional structures activated by music, *160*
  evocation of emotions by music, 142
  feeling cortex, 195–199
  'intrinsic ability for recuperation', 209
  listening to music, 23
  music and language, 28–38
  music-language network, 31–35
  neuronal activity, 22
  pleasure, pain, addiction, 277–280
  'pre-factual' affect system within, 192
  processes of music and language in overlapping networks, 25
  processing of chord progressions, 23
  shaped by our engagement, 39–52
brain age, 130, 239, **241**
brain anatomy, 39, 51
  impact of musical engagement, 41–44
brain correlates of musical tension, 95–96
brain function, 51
  effects of music training, 39–41
brain health, **105**
brain networks, 22, 33, 43, 108, 216
brainstem, 22, 118, 148, 150, 151, 153, 154, 164, 247
Brazil, 21, 194
breach of expectation, 97
'breathe, relax, let it flow' (mantra), **283**, **292**, 314
breathing, 23, **68**, 113, 147, **153**, **269**, 307
breathing rate, **117**, 117, 165

INDEX

Bremen Philharmonic Orchestra, 56
Bremen Youth Symphony Orchestra, 73
Broca's aphasia, 32, 216, 217, **218**
Broca's area, 31, *32*, 33, 34, 214, 216, 217, 258
Brubeck, D.: 'Take Five', **117**
Buddhist tradition, 50
burnout, 50, 76, 139
buying pleasure, 181–182

Cambridge, University of, 36
Cameroon, 15
cancer, 46, 67, 84, 102, 189
  comorbidity with depression, 298
Cannon, W., 126
carbon dioxide, 79, **121**, 309
cardiac nervous system, 116
cardiovascular disease, 46, 67, 136
care activities, **18**
Caria, A., 259
caudate nucleus, *161*
Cave, N.: 'Song for Bob', 77
cellists, 82–84
cerebellum, 247
Chaplin, C., 203
cheering, 108, 154
chemosignals, 78, 79
child carriers: musical movement, **38**
childhood, 82, 182, 255, 256, 274, 288
childhood trauma, 81, 174
children, 135, 173
  musical training, 35
  'particular benefits of music', 166
  perception of language as music, 30–31
children's songs, 14, **36**, 83, 225. *See also* lullabies
chocolate, 161, 181, 272, 279, 280
choirs, 108, **293**
choir singers: versus listening to choir performances, 121
chord progressions, **24**, 90, 91, 257
chord sequences, 23, **24**, 27, 34, 91
  resolution with final tonic, 97
Christmas songs, 82
chronic pain, 84, 124, 156, 164
  forms, 266
  music therapy, 266–269
  recommendations for patients, **269–271**
cinemas, 79, 178
cingulate cortex, 164, 235
clapping, 36, 106, 198, 236, **265**
Clapton, E.: healing through music, 75

classical concerts, 96, 185
classical music, 5, 14, 20, 34, 83, 99, 282, **291**
  focus on compositional ideas, **59**
clinical depression: same as 'major depressive disorder', 296
clinical psychology, 48, 61
Coca-Cola, 274
cocaine, 161, 272, 274
cochlea, 72, 148, *149*
coffee, 203, 230, 284, **285**
cognitive biases, 314
cognitive resonance, 78, 139, 140
collective expression: advantage of music, 12
collective music making, 10, 169, 193
Cologne: Carnival Law, 142
commonalities, 191, 192
  collective music making, 192
communication: music as 'versatile medium', 109
community, 72, 106, 128, 137, 169, 185, 194, 263, 312, 319
compassion, 72, 111, 138, 178, 197, 268
  versus 'empathy', 75–77
compassion training, 49, 50
concert guides, 104, **105**
concert musician, 45, 47
concerts, viii, 22, 56, 57, 58, **73**, **79**, 84, 107, **112**, 178, 255, **285**
conflict, 11, 97, 129, 192, 268, 281
  role of music in, 193–194
conflict mitigation, 12
conscious will, 184, 187
consciousness, 116, 201–202, 207
consonants, 30, 40
constrained-induced movement therapy, 226
cooking, 9
cooperation, 11, 110
  impact on social relationships, 11
co-pathy (Koelsch), 77, 108
  definition, 108
corpus callosum, 44
  definition, 43
  'thicker in professional musicians', 44
correlation is not causation (mantra), 125
cortex, 22, 300
cortisol, 118, 119, **122**, 177
  impact of music (meta-analysis), 119
couple dancing, 98, **224**
courage centre (of brain), 148, *149*, 152
  engagement through music, **150**

323

courage songs, **150**, **152**
Cramon, Y. von, 32
craving, 167–168, 202, 275, **276**, 279
Crohn's disease, 175
C's (Seven C's: facilitation by music of engagement in social functions), 106–111
  cognition (social), 107
  cohesion (social), 110
  communication, 109
  contact, 106
  cooperation, 110
  coordination, 109
  co-pathy, 108
C-tactile nerve fibres, 107
Cuddy, L. L., 231, 233

dance, 2, 36, 65
  autism, **265**
dance groups, 252, 253, **277**, 291, **293**
dance music, **18**, 65, 89, 203
dancing, 36, 37, 71, 89, 100, 107, 108, 109, 111, 120, 156, 203–204, 243, **276**, 312
  benefits for some individuals with depression, 290
  'especially beneficial for health', 130
  recommendations (Parkinson's disease patients), **254**
dancing patients, 251–253
Danner, D. D., 55
Davies, J., 81
Dead Poets Society (film), 173
death, 32, 33, 126, 157, 207
Debussy, C.: 'Clair de Lune', 255
deceptive cadence, 91, 92, 97, 103
deep brain stimulation (DBS), 242
default mode network, 189, **190**
dendritic spines: definition, 42
dentate gyrus, 176, 239
depression, **66**, 124, 136, 140, 174, 176, 189, 248, 286, 287–299
  annual cost (Germany), 128
  diagnosis, 288
  further research, 294, 296
  improvisation-based music therapy, 294
  management (music therapy), 294–296
    emotional activation, 296
    emotional awakening, 295
    experience of meaning, 295
    human connection and social reintegration, 296
    neurological activation of hippocampus, 296
    non-verbal emotional outlet, 295
    physical activation, 295
    strong patient engagement, 295
  manifestations, 287
  music's therapeutic role, 289–291
  negative side effects of music therapy, 311
  older adults (music therapy), 297
  physical symptoms, 287
  placebos versus pharmaceuticals, 125
  resilience, 298–299
  risk factors, 288
  treatments (conventional), 289
  types (music therapy), 296–298
depression (recommendations), **291–293**
  channelling positive thoughts, **292**
  formal music therapy, **293**
  immersion in musical experience, **292**
  mood-lifting playlists, **291**
  beyond music, **293**
  setting small, achievable goals, **293**
  shared music experiences, **293**
Der Narr tut . . . (German saying), 141
Derek Paravicini Quartet, 255
development section (sonata form), 104
diabetes (Type 2), 273
diencephalon, 157, 168
  'central hub for pleasure, pain, and craving system', 157
  'multifaceted roles', 157
diet, 127, 131, 229, 289, 299
Dill-Schmölders, C., 213–215
djembes, 227, 294
dopamine, 80, 104, 161, **162**, 165, 180, 211, 247, 279
  'essential for various brain functions', 131
  'keeps brain young', 162
dopamine release, 162, 296
Drexel University (Philadelphia), 156
drumming, 4, 106, 109, 268, 295
drum music, 10
drum pads, 224, **228**, 260
drums, 156, 261
drum sequences, 19, 20
dubstep songs (2010), 80
Duffin, J., 231
Dukas, P.: 'Sorcerer's Apprentice', 98
Dunbar, R. I., 109
dyslexia, 36, 38, 41

INDEX

Earhart, G. M., 252
earworms, 312
Eerola, T., 20
El Haj, M., 233
'El Sistema' initiative, 44
electroencephalography (EEG), **24**, **33**
  experiments with toddlers, 27
electronic drum, 224, 294
Ellis, A., 187
embedded constructions: 'Goodbye Yellow Brick Road', 134
emergency help, 313–318
  Step 1 (start with music), 313
  Step 2 (breathe, relax, let it flow), 314
  Step 3 (find something positive), 314
  Step 4 (think clearly), 314
  Step 5 (step your strengths), 315
  Step 6 (focus), 315
  Step 7 (talk to others), 316
emotion, 319
  components contributing to feelings, 196–198
  and consciousness, 201–202
  feeling cortex, 195–199
  impact of voice, 13–17
  therapeutic effect of music, 136
  when music is 'worth a thousand words', 199–200
emotion percept, 198
emotion psychology
  dominant theories, 60
  in footnote, 63
emotional activation: depression management (music therapy), 296
emotional attractor effects, 61, 187, 315
emotional contagion, 73–74, 76, 78
emotional health: negative side effects of music, 311
emotional outlets: non-verbal, 295
emotional resonance, 72–73, **74**, 77, 79
emotional speech: imitated by music, 15
emotional spirals: negative (interruption in four steps), 61–64
emotion-memory tunnel (Koelsch), 164, 235–237, 239
emotions, viii, 126, 235, 236, **276**
  evocation by music, 55–111
  evocation by music (impact on brain), 142
  'impact immune system', 113

music and, 55
  regulating (resilence strategy using music), 138
emotions in brain (how music affects us), 145–194
  attachment-related emotions and social bonding, 170–172
  buying pleasure and earning happiness, 181–182
  craving, 167–168
  effect of music on subconscious, 187–189
  goosebumps and 'fun motor', 158–162
  happiness, 177–178
  happiness system, 169–170
  hedonic happiness, 179–181
  hippocampus (neurobiological substrate soul), 172–175
  invigorating power of music on soul, 175–177
  medical procedures, **166**
  music (impact on subconscious), **189**
  music (peacemaking potential), 191–193
  music (role in conflict), 193–194
  physical exercise, 150–152
  pleasure network, 163–164
  pleasure network (overlaps with pain network), 164–166
  pleasure, pain, and craving system, 156–158
  relaxation, 153–154
  social norms and irrational beliefs, 184–186
  subsconscious (blame and shame), 182–184
  thought loops (counteracted with music), **190**
  unlocking pleasure (simple steps), **162**
  vitalization system, 147–150
empathy, 50, 73, 78, 199
  versus 'compassion', 75–77
endocrine system, 113, 119
endogenous opioids, 109, 157, 165, 171
endorphins, 109, 157, 171
energy levels, **100**
enteric nervous system, 116
Epic Instrumental Background Music: 'Addicted to Success', 99
Epic Soul Factory: 'Legendary', 99
epigenetic changes, 45–47
epileptic seizures, 1, 2, 311

INDEX

episodic memory, 82, 84
  retrieval (music as catalyst for Alzheimer's disease patients), 233–235
Erben, F.-M., 69
Erkkilä, J., 294, 295
ethical emotions, 192
ethics, 4, 71, 181
eudaimonia, 179, 180, 181, 182
European Humanist Federation, 129
evaluations
  conscious and unconscious, 57–59
  'give rise to emotions', 57
event-related potential, **25**
everyday life, viii, 27, 60, 61, **156**, 263
evoked potential, **25**
evolution, 9–21, 28, 158, 172, 182, 319
  fundamental principles, 110
  music and language, 12–13
examinations, ix, 86, **285**, 317
exercise, **101**, 127, 138, **150**, 239, 299
  using music, 150–152
  using music (self-motivation), **152**
expectations, 70, 86, 87, 89, 95, 97, 98, 125, 126, 198, 264
exposition (sonata form), 104
eye contact, 1, **190**, 256, 257, 259, 262

fairness, 108, 129, 192
fake news, 71, 192
family members: MIT recommendations, **218**
Fang, R., 239
fantasy and imagination, 98–100
fear, 126, 177
feeling cortex (Koelsch), *161*, 164, 195–199, 200
feelings, 195
  'percepts of emotions', 199
feelings (biological components), 196–198
  affective component, 196
  cognitive component, 198
  motor component, 197
  somatic component, 196
film music, 77, 99
films, 87, 98
Finland, 21
first theme (sonata form), 104
fish, 172, 299, 317
foetus, 31, 47
folk music, 14, 147, 211, 225

foreign languages, 30, 31
Formenlehre (theory of form), 103
Franklin, A., 203
Free University of Berlin, viii, 146
Friederici, A., 23
Fritz, T., 15, 151
fruits, **276**, 299, 317
fun, 180, 181
'fun motor', 158–162, 168, 180, 248, 279
  same as 'nucleus accumbens', 163
functional MRI (fMRI), 32, 33, 95, 120, 145, 189
Furrer, B.: in footnote, 15

gait, **223**, 248, **251**
  Parkinson's disease, 245
  upright (biomechanics), 222
Gaser, C., 41–43
genius, 47, 258
Geretsegger, M., 262
German Democratic Republic, ix
Germany, 3, 105, 128, 274
'give-up-itis', 126
Glennie, E., 72
glucose, 118, 167, 278
Gold, C., 261
Good Vibrations, 46, 47, **74**, 111, 129, 154, 186, 203
  book hope, 5, 320
  book structure, 319
  conclusion, 319–320
  essence, 320
  'exploration of vast expanse of human musicality', 320
  findings underpinned by empirical research, 4
  music's capacity to heal (presentation of scientific evidence), 319
  music's 'unique power to promote health and happiness', 319
  original German edition, 281
  source material (systematic reviews and meta-analyses), 4
goosebumps, 23, 88, 97, 98, 145, 156, 158–162, **163**, 163, **179**
Goswami, U., 36
grey matter, 41, 42, 210
group therapy, 223, 268, 275
growth and development, 49, 142
Guarneri violins, 69
guided imagery and music, 101

INDEX

Guitar Hero (game), 227
Gunter, T., 23

Hackney, M. E., 252
halo effect (Kahneman), 186
happiness, 76
  promotion by music, 177–178, **178**
happiness system, 168, 172, 173, 176, 179, 180, 181, 239, 259
  soul within brain, 169–170
'Happy Birthday to You' (song), 35
harmonic sequences, 23, 35, 98
  transitional phase, 97
harmonies, 88, 90, 92
Harrison, P. M., 88
Harvard Medical School, viii, 28, 33, 35, 41
Harvard University, 126, 177
hate music, 194, 312
Haydn, J.
  string quartets, 77
  'Surprise Symphony', 89
Head, H., 196
headphones, 59, **166**, **212**, **238**, **251**, **283**
healing powers (natural), 123–142
healing processes (natural): use of music, 126–128
health, 11, 46
  effects of music, 1–5
hearing, 131, 132
heart attacks, **68**, 147, 200, 273
heart rate, 16, 114, 117, 145, 158
  effects of music, **117**
heart: 'possesses own nervous system', 116
heartbeat, 23, 74, 113, 114, 115, 148, 149, **155**, 195, 307
hedonic happiness, 179–181, 182
Heine, A., 147
hemiparesis
  arms (music-supported training), 224–227
  legs (rhythmic therapeutic approach), 220–223
  'prevalent consequence of strokes', 220
hemiparesis band, 226, **227**
hemiplegia, 213, 225
Herbert, G., 164
heroic music, **100**
heroin, 172, 275
Herrmann, B., 15
hi-hat, 29, 30
Hillecke, T. K., 267
hippocampal formation, 231, 239, 296
  in footnote, 173

hippocampus, 168, 169, 171, 176, 253
  neurobiological substrate of soul, 172–175
  neurological activation, 296
  'pivotal role in emotional processing', 170
Hippocrates, 127
Hitchcock, A.: *Psycho* (film), 15
Hocheck Hospital (Austria), 147
holistic perspective, 2, 5, 218
holistic well-being, 129, 138
Holmes, G., 196
home living, **240**
homeostasis, 157, 179
  definition, 167
Homo sapiens, 9, 10, 12, 20, 21
hope, 84, 125, 137, 139, 237, **241**, 245, 296
hormonal responses: effects of music, **121**
hormonal system, 113, 167
hormone release, 74, 127
hormones, 118–120, 171
  dance to beat of music, 113–121
horror films, 15, 120
human connections, 252, 268, 275
human rights, 129, 192
human survival: role of music, 9–21
humanistic orientation, 194, 312
humanity, 70–72, 319
humans
  ability to synchronize rhythmically in group, vii
  distinguished from 'animals', vii
  world without (would be world without music), 7
hunger, 57, 157, 167
hunter-gatherers, 12
  singing duels, 193
hypothalamic-pituitary-adrenal (HPA) axis, 118
hypothalamus, 157, 167, 172, 278
  'brain's hormonal control centre', 120
  'craving centre' (Koelsch), 167
  role, 158

identity, 101, 234, 235, 272
illness, 106, 111
  turning to music, 85
illness (how music helps), 303
  addiction, 272–280
  Alzheimer's dementia, 229–241
  autism, 255–264
  chronic pain, 266–269
  depression, 287–299

327

illness (how music helps) (cont.)
  Parkinson's disease, 242–253
  schizophrenia spectrum disorder, 300–303
  sleep disorders, 281–286
  stroke, 207–227
imagination, 98, 99, 101, **102**
  harnessing (music therapy), 101–102
immune system, 120–121, 127
  effects of music, **121**
immunoglobulin A, 120
implicit knowledge, 26, 90, 92, 236
improvisations, 14, 100, 156
infants, 154, 320
  already recognize unusual chords, 27
  communication to (during care activities), **18**
  engaging in music, **37**
inflammation, 82, 113, 189, 266, 273, 288, 299
initiative: resilence strategy using music, 140–141
inner ear, 73, 148, *149*, 177
inner peace, 48, 49, 76, **96**, 128, 133, 154, **179**, 308
insula, *161*, 164, 197, 198, 199
intelligence: therapeutic effect of music, **122**, 134–135
interleukin-6, **122**
International Humanist and Ethical Union, 129
interoception, 197, 199
  definition, 197
interoceptive cortex, 197, 198
intestinal nervous system, 116
Ireland, 194
irrational beliefs, 184–186
  commonly held, 186–187

Jackson, M., 255
Jäncke, L., 116
jazz, 5, 14, 65, 105, 211, **291**
Jennings, W., 75
John, E., 89
  'Goodbye Yellow Brick Road', 134
Joplin, J., 99
Juslin, P. N., 13–14

Kahneman, D., 183, 186
keyboards, 156, 227
Kim, J., 261
kindergarten, 27, 35, 142
kindness, 50, 126, 139, 142, 181, 192

Kirschner, S., 21
Klimecki, O. M., 49
Kodály, Z., 36
Koelsch, S., 69, 267
  brain correlates of musical tension (experiment), 95–96
  doctoral student (MPI, Leipzig), 145
  experiments exploring effects of music on autonomic activity, **117**
  hormonal and immune responses to music (collaborative study), **121**
  investigation of social cognition, 107
  meta-analysis (with Jäncke) regarding impact of music on ANS, 116
  meta-analysis (with Stegemann) regarding impact of music on cortisol levels, 119, 121
  meta-analysis on music, emotion, and brain, 163, 168
  'most frequently cited study in field', 145
  music student, 73
  musical background, 5
  music's impact on subconscious (experiment), **190**
  own life 'not without obstacles', 313
  playing piano pieces, 93
  preference for NewStrad violin (reason), 70
  quartet theory of human emotions, 146
  sociologist, 128
  use of music by Bach to stay focused, 78
Koenig, J., 267
Kölsch Constitution, 142, 314
Kraft, J. A., 1–2
  patient 'AC' (cellist), 83–84
Krems University, 147
Kreutz, G., 121
Kubrick, S.: *'2001: A Space Odyssey'* (film), 10

Lai, G., 258
language, viii, 12–13, 216
  'decisive difference' from music, 13
  'music distorted by semantics' (Reich), 12
language development disorders, 131
language skills: enhancement (use of music), 35–37
lateral orbitofrontal cortex, 95
laughter, 64, 74, 106, 114, 256, 262
Laukka, P., 13–14
learning disability, 132, 255
left hemisphere, 31, *32*, 33, 34, 301
Lehne, M., 93

INDEX

Leipzig Gewandhaus Orchestra, 69, 83
leucocytes, 121
'Libertango', 98
life balance: resilence strategy using music, 141
Ligeti, G.: 'Atmosphères', 10
Lindsen, J. P., 64
Liszt, F.: first 'Mephisto' waltz, 98
loneliness, 106, 137, 297
long-term memory, 23, 133
Los Angeles Philharmonic Orchestra, 44
loud noises, 148, 243
Lourdes, 125
love of neighbour, 138–139
lucid dreaming, **285**
lullabies, 16, **18**, 269, **282**, 297
   tone of voice (importance), **18**

Mafa people, 15–16
Mahler, G., 200
major depressive disorder, 287
   music therapy, 296
mammals, 21, 172, 182
Mandarin language, 28, 40–41
Mansell, C.: 'Death Is Road to Awe', **189**
marching songs, 151
Marley, B., 242
Marsalis, W., 307
Matsumoto, M., 169
Max Planck Institute (Leipzig), viii, 23, 33, 35, 83, 145, 164, 235
McFerrin, B., 29, 156
   'Don't Worry, Be Happy', 249
medial forebrain bundle, 163
medical procedures: use of music (by patient), **166**
mediodorsal thalamus, 164
meditation, 78, **102**, 202, 298, 315. *See also* musitation
meditation music, 10, 65, 211, **282**
melodic intonation therapy (MIT), 215–218, 260
   recommendations for speech therapists and family members, **218**
melody, 12, 23, 30
memory systems, 172
memory training, 49
memory: therapeutic effect of music, 133–134
Mendelssohn, F.
   'Venetian Gondellied' (Op. 30, No. 6), 93
   'Violin Concerto', 173

mental disorders, 136, 179
mental health, 129, 138
messing up, 318
meta-analyses, 4, **67**, 174, 176
Mettā meditation technique, 50
midbrain, 163, 247
migraine, 124
mild cognitive impairment, 229
Milstein, N., 173
mindfulness, 189, 308, 315
mindset, 46, 71, 76, 186, 243, **251**, 319
mind wandering, 188, **189**, 189, **191**, 316
minimum wage, 128
mixed emotions, 201
modulation (music theory), 91
Mojo Club, 65, 313
mood management, **276**
mood uplift, 84
moods, 63, 64, 121, **122**, 126, 275
   in footnote, 63
   transformation with music, 64–65
moral emotions, 192
Moreno, S., 41
morning dance, **67**, 203–204
mother's voice, 31
motor aphasia, 136, 214, 215, 216, **218**, 218
motor cortex, 41, 44
moving together: 'social function' stimulated by music, 21
Mozart, W. A., 24, 89, 91
   'Eine kleine Nachtmusik', 14
   'Magic Flute', 104
   'Piano Sonata' (KV 280), 93
   Requiem, 98
   'Requiem', 14
   'Symphony (No. 31)', 90, *90*, 92
MRI, 32, 43, 95, 120, 145, 216, 241
Müller, S.: *Das Publikum macht die Musik* (2014), 58
multidisciplinary approach, ix, 4
multilingual music benefits, **38**
Münte, T. F., 224
muscle memory, 232
music
   'activates array of brain functions', 210
   'alternative source of satisfaction', 275
   beneficial effects on health, 48
   'can function as barrier', 194
   effective use 'depends on our values', 110
   effects on endocrine system, 119
   effects on health, 1–5

INDEX

music (cont.)
  effects on heart rate, respiratory rate, and perspiration, **117**
  effects on hormonal and immune responses, **121**
  epistemic offering, 86–88
  essential for human survival, 9–21
  evocation of autobiographical memories, 82–84
  evocation of emotions, 55–111
  evocation of emotions (impact on brain), 142
  evolutionarily adaptive functions, 21
  facilitating natural healing processes, 126–128
  facilitation of engagement in social functions (Seven C's), 106–111
  healing effects, 130–131
  impact on subconscious, **189**
  innate sense, 22–27
  life with 'longer life', 55
  origins, 9
  overcoming negative emotions and moods, **65**
  peacemaking potential, 191–193
  positive-sounding, **66**
  profound healing effects (case of patient 'AC', cellist), 82–84
  promotion of happiness, 177–178
  promotion of more equitable society, 70–72
  role in conflict, 193–194
  social functions, 105–106
  'super melodic speech', 35
  taking it easy, **68**
  therapeutic benefits, 46, 117, 319
  therapeutic effects (remarkable increase in research), 3
  therapeutic versatility, 5
  transforming negative thoughts into positive ones, **51**
  'unique category within the realm of sound', 10
  when 'worth a thousand words', 199–200
music (helping with illness), 303
  addiction, 272–280
  Alzheimer's dementia, 229–241
  autism, 255–264
  chronic pain, 266–269
  depression, 287–299
  Parkinson's disease, 242–253
  schizophrenia, 300–303
  sleep disorders, 281–286
  stroke, 207–227
music (negative side effects), 311–312
  and addiction, 311
  and depression, 311
  and earworms, 312
  and emotional health, 311
  and epilepsy, 311
  and social influence, 312
  and trauma, 311
musical activities: participation, **111**
musical analysis, 103
musical anhedonia, 159, 296
musical appreciation
  advanced analysis, **105**
  biographical data (about composers), **105**
  enhancement, **105**
musical engagement (active), **66**
musical grammar, 23, **25**, 27
  rules, 10
musical imagery: supporting recovery, **102**
musical instruments, **38**, 49, **101**
musicality: 'natural ability of every human being', 46
musically untrained: not the same as being 'unmusical', 26
musical memory, 79–81, 235, 236
  emotional potency, 81–82
  resilience (Alzheimer's dementia), 230–233
musical performance: looking on bright side, **59**
musical predictions, 85–86, 89–91, 93
  paradoxical (when familiar pieces remain surprising), 92
musical structure, **96**
  rewards of understanding, 103–104
  stability, 93
musical surprises
  pleasant, 88–89
  reaction of body, 91–92
musical tastes: men versus women, 80
musical tension, 93
  brain correlates, 95–96
musical training, 29, 35, 40, 51
musical vault (personal), **84**
music box, 17
music breaks, **66**
music lessons, 76
  preschool age, 35

INDEX

music listening, 145, 209, 210, **212**, 298
  active versus passive, 165
  emotional benefits, 210
music meditation, 189, 307–308
  key point, 308
  variants, 308
music reflex (Koelsch), 147
music therapists, **19**, 79, 156, 213, **240**, 294
  case of 'Mrs A', 147
music therapy, 176
  efficacy, 4
  emotional realm (chronic pain), 268
  enhanced walking abilities, 246
  harnessing imagination, 101–102
  holistic impact, 2
  improvisation, 14, 100, 156
  irreplaceable form of treatment, 3
  physical realm (chronic pain), 267
  research, 205
  research complexities, 3
  scientific base, 3
  social realm (chronic pain), 268
  traditional sense, 303
music-supported training (MST)
  hemiparesis of arms, 224–227
musitation (music meditation), **155**
Mussorgsky, M.: 'Pictures at Exhibition', 98
mutism, 1, 2

negative emotions, 46, 125, 154, 289
  controlling, 59–61
  'detrimental to health', 67–68
  emergency help, 313–318
  'impede regeneration and healing', 56
  transformation with music, 64–65
  triggers, **66**
negative evaluations: fewer 'lead to more positive life', 56–57
negative moods, 50, 61, **66**, 113, 147, 237, **284**, 290, **291**, 300
  'detrimental to health', 67–68
  emergency help, 313–318
negative stress, 119, 120, 121, 127, 128, 131, **179**
negative thoughts, 4, 61, 77, 127, 135, 187, 188, **284**, 316
  reduction (following tension arcs), **96**
  transformation into positive ones (through music), 51
negativity, 187, 290, 314
Nena: '99 Luftballons', 80
neocortex, 73, 75, 158, 182, 247

nerve fibres: definition, 43
Neue Deutsche Welle (1980s), 80
neurobiology, 146, 172, 179, 192, 199, 319
neurodegeneration, 162, 232, 239
neurogenesis, 176, 239, 296
neuronal Big Bang, 22
neurons, 22, 44, 148, 151, 163, 247
neuroscience, 5, 159, 169, 170, 216
neuroticism, 289
neurotransmitters, 64, 114, 127, **191**, 211, 278, 279
newborns, 34, 197, 297
  recognition of voices and languages, 31
  speech recognition, 31
NewStrad, 69, 70
Nietzsche, F., 203
nocebo effects, 125–126
nociception, 266
non-musicians, 91, 93, 95, 130
  musicality, 22–27
  sensorimotor cortex, 43
noradrenaline, 119, 120, **121**
norepinephrine, 119, 165
Norway, 29, 77, 128
Norwegian Research Council, 239
nucleus accumbens, 110, 159, *161*
nursery rhymes, 35, 36, **37–38**, **265**
nursing homes, 238
nutrition, 138, 288
Nyman, M.: 'À La Folie', **189**

obesity, 273, 274
obsessive-compulsive disorder, 175
Ockelford, A., 255, 258
Odetta, 99
oestrogen, 171
off-beats, 89
'Old MacDonald Had a Farm', 10
opera, 77, 104
opiates, 172, 279
  'cruel irony', 279
opioids, 171, 272, 278, 279. *See also* endogenous opioids
optimism, 64, 68, 147, 268
  longer lifespan, 55
orbitofrontal cortex, 50, 70, 95, 164, 182, 185, **190**
Orff, C., 36
osteoarthritis, 124, 136, 266
  'striking example' of placebo effect, 124
osteoporosis, 67
our tune, 79–81

out of key, 24, 231, 233
oxytocin, 120, 171, 178

pain, 102, 133. *See also* chronic pain
  reduction (following tension arcs), **96**
pain network, *160*, 167, 196
  overlaps with pleasure network, 164–166
pain threshold, 151, 165
painting, 36, 41
Panksepp, J., 158
Pantev, C., 39–40
parasympathetic nervous system, 114
Paravicini, D., 255–256
Parkinson's disease, viii–ix, 124, 136, 152, 175, 203, 242–253, 320
  dancing (recommendations), **254**
  dancing patients, 251–253
  music (therapeutic benefits), 245–246
  temporal perception (supported by music), 246–248
  walking with music, **249–251**
patience, 60, 62, 142, 263, 264, 289
Pearce, M. T., 88
Peking opera, 87
pelog and slendro, 10
pentatonic scale, 10
Perani, D., 34
perception: therapeutic effect of music, 131–132
percepts (of emotions), 195
percussion instruments, 30, 72, 148, 156, 226, 227, 262
perfection, 44, 48, 59, 85, **251**
peripeteia, 97
perseverance: 'can be transformative factor', 126
perspiration, 114, **117**, 196
  effects of music, **117**
pharmacy, 123
phonemes, 34
physical activity, 130, 309–310
physiological changes, 195, 201
pianists, 39, 43
piano genius, 258
piano lessons, 44
piano tones, 40
pianto motif, 14
Piazzolla, A., 98
pill colour, 124
pitch, 41, **219**
  ability to synchronize, 11
pituitary gland, 118, **122**, 157, 167

placebo effects, 123–125, 126
  conditions, 124
  factors, 124
Planet Earth II (film), 99
playlists, 290, 302
pleasure centre, 168
  same as 'hypothalamus', 163
pleasure network, 163–164, 168, 169
  overlaps with pain network, 164–166
pleasure system, 158, 172, 179, 180, 195, 248, 278
  capacity of music to activate, 158
pleasure, pain, and craving system, 156–158, 164, 172, 179, 267, 277
pleasure: unlocking with music, **162**
Ploner, C. J., 82, 83
plucked guitar tone, 30
positive emotions, 46, 47, 55, 125
positive experiences, 55
positivity, **51**, **84**, **191**, **292**, **314**
  affirmation (daily), **51**
  cultivation of resilience, **51**
  expressing aloud, **51**
  sharing, **51**
  writing down, **51**
positron emission tomography (PET), 159, 162
postpartum depression, **19**
  music therapy, 297
post-traumatic stress disorder, 174
potential, **25**
poverty, 128
practice, 46, 49, **101**
  daily 'essential in developing unique skills', 45
practice makes perfect (adage), 51
predictions, 103, 236
predictive evaluation: impact on emotions, 69–70
premature birth: professional help from music therapist, **19**
preschool children, 10, 27, 36, 40, 131, 142
Presley, E., 16, 65, 99, 313
problem solving, 140, 316, 317
  tips, 141
procedural memory, 232, 233
professional musicians, 41, 44, 46, 69, 130
programme music, 98, **105**
progressive muscle relaxation, **155**
Prokofiev, S.: 'Peter and the Wolf', **105**
prolactin, 120, 171
propofol, 166

INDEX

proprioception: definition, 197
prosocial behaviour, 21, 108, 110, 138, 194
psychological distress, 81
psychology, viii, 4, 5, 23, 137, 289. *See also*
   clinical psychology
psychoneuroimmunology, 46, 67
Puccini, G.: 'La Bohème', 104
pulse, 9, 10, 20, 21, 36, 194
   isochronous, 19
puppet neurons (Koelsch), 151, 152

quality of life, **67**, 128, 132, 180, 226,
   240–241, 252, 253
quartet theory of human emotions (Koelsch
   et al.), 146

ragas, 10, 14
Ravignani, A., 19
reading difficulties, 36, 37, 132
reading skills, 36, 41
recapitulation (sonata form), 104
recovery: use of musical imagery, **102**
Rehfeld, K., 253
Reich, U., 12
relationship endings, 317
relaxation, 11, 62, 93, 97, 106, 307, 308
   use of music, 153–154
resilience, **51**, 63, **84**, 308, 314
   musical memory (Alzheimer's
      dementia), 230–233
   tips, 138, 139, 140, 141
resilience (seven nurturing strategies using
   music), 137–142
   clear values and goals, 140
   life balance, 141
   love of neighbour, 138
   nutrition, sleep, exercise, 138
   regulating emotions, 138
   self-confidence, 139
   self-efficacy and initiative, 140
respiratory rate: effects of music, **117**
restless legs syndrome, 124
restrictive postures, **270**
reward network, 158, 160, *163*
rhythm, 12, 30
   human preference, 19–21
rhythm training, 37
rhythmic auditory stimulation (RAS),
   220–223, 227, 246, 248, **249**, **251**, 252
   Parkinson's disease patients, 245
right hemisphere, *32*, 33, 34
right that I exist (mantra), **292**

Rimsky-Korsakov, N.: 'Flight of the
   Bumblebee', 256
rock, 5, 14, 108, 226
Rock Band (game), 227
Rohrmeier, M., 93
Ron, Y., 65, **269**, 307
Rossini, G., 102
   'Barber of Seville', 104

Sack, U., **121**
sadness, 14, **100**
safety, **250**, 254
Saint-Saëns, C.: 'Carnival of Animals', 20,
   98, **105**
saliva, 121
salt, 317
Särkämö, T., 208–211
savants, 257
saxophone, 26
scale, 10, 11, 21
   language versus music, 12
Scandinavian countries, 128
Schellenberg, G., 37
schizophrenia, 136, 174, 176, 300–303
schizophrenia spectrum disorder (SSD)
   further research, 303
   music as cognitive distraction,
      301
   music as emotional distraction,
      300
schizophrenia spectrum disorder music
   recipe, **301–302**
   assess emotional impact, **301**
   be prepared, **302**
   iterate, **302**
   maintain focus, **302**
   participate in music, **301**
   'targeted, immediate aim', 303
Schlaug, G., 33, 41–43, 44, 216, 217, 260
Schneider, S., 224
Schönberg, A., 107
   'String Trio' (Op. 45), 200
school curriculum: incorporation of music
   'only natural', 103
School Sisters of Notre Dame, 55
Schubert, F., 26
second theme (sonata form), 104
secondary somatosensory cortex: same as
   'feeling cortex', 198
sedation, 124, 166
self-acceptance: unconditional (positive
   impact), 47–49

INDEX

self-confidence, 137, 140, 287
  building (resilence strategy using music), 139–140
self-efficacy, 140–141, 275
self-fulfilling prophecy, 70, 125, 126
self-healing, 123–125
self-recognition, 197
semantic memory, 82
  definition, 78
sensorimotor cortex, 43
sensorimotor functions, 22, 23, 37
  therapeutic effect of music, 135–136
sensory integration, **37**
sensory memory, 22
sensory percepts, 200
serotonin, 211, 278
Seven C's: facilitation by music of engagement in social functions, 106–111
'Sex, Drugs & Rock 'n' Roll' (Ian Dury song), 161
sexual abuse, 174
sexual activity, 161
Shackleton, E., vii–viii, 11
Shakespeare, W., 97
  Much Ado about Nothing, 173
  Romeo and Juliet, 96
shame, 63, 182, 186, 315, 318
shanties, 151
short-term memory, 23, 133, 134
shrink choir, 139
singing, 17, 111, 120
  mitigation of brain degeneration (research project), 240–241
singing duels, 193, 194
singing groups, 238
singing hospitals, 105–106
singing tones together: music-specific skill, 9
skeletal muscles, 150
skills: interplay between genetics and environment, 45–47
skin orgasm (Panksepp), 158
sleep, 106, 118, 138, **270**
sleep (recommendations for sound)
  beyond melody, **284**
    anticipating important events, **285**
    consistency 'key', **284**
    dream control, **285**
    evening rituals, **284**
    morning energizers, **285**
    night's natural course, **285**
    night's natural ebb and flow, **285**
    patterns in darkness, **284**
  defensive tactics, **283**
  musician's trick, **283**
  nightly resonance, **283**
  relaxing body, mind, and soul, **283**
  setting realistic expectations, **285**
  sleep-inducing playlists, **282**
sleep disorders, 281–286
  comorbidity with depression, 298
sleep–wake cycle, 148
Sloboda, J., 81, 97
smartphone, 140, **150**, 243, 250, **251**, **283**
Smetana, B.: 'Vltava', 98
social bonding, 9, 17, 120, 170–172, 180, 181, 264
social bonds, 169, 177, **277**, **296**
social cognition, 107
social cohesion, 11, 77, 110, 138, 319
  music 'unique tool', 106
social connections, **277**
social contact, 107, 127, 171, 263
social functions, 105–106
  facilitation by music of engagement in (Seven C's), 106–111
social influence: negative side effects of music, 312
social interaction, 138, 192, 239, 262
social isolation, 127, 137, 178, 300
social network, 137, 141
social norms, 59, 184–186, 192
social participation: therapeutic effect of music, 137
sociology, viii, 71, 128
somatosensory cortex, *161*, 164
sonata form, 103, 104, 134
song duels, 12
songs, 2, **212**, 250
songwriting, 101
soul, 172–175
  definition (in footnote), 173
  invigorating power of music, 175–177
soul in brain, **179**
sound, 12–13
  perception of, 72
  recognized as music, 10
  vibrations, **73**
soundbed, 1, 2, 214
speech formulas, 215
speech therapists: MIT, **218**
speech therapy: integration of music, **38**
speech: 'super-fast music', 35
spelling difficulties, 36, 37

INDEX

Spirit of America Ensemble: 'Heroic March', 99
spiritual: as 'sense of harmony', 111
Spotify, 80
St Thomas Choir (Leipzig), 35
Star Trek: The Next Generation, 97
Stegemann, T., 119, 121
Steinbeis, N., 107
stem cells, 176
Stephens-Davidowitz, S., 79
Stradivari violin, 57
  reputation put to test, 69
  superiority 'subjective', 70
stress, 78, 114, 116, 135, 154
  healthy versus unhealthy, 119
stress alleviation, **101**
stress hormones, 119, 177, 278
stroke, viii, 136, 207–227, 273
  acute phase, 208–211
  aphasia, 213–215
  arm paralysis, **227**
  comorbidity with depression, 297
  gait disorders, **223**
  hemiparesis (music's therapeutic effects), 220–223
  hemiparesis of arms, 224–227
  immediate and subsequent phase (recommendations), **212**
  left-hemispheric, 209, 213, 216
  medical attention (urgency), 207
  melodic intonation therapy (MIT), 215–218
  MIT recommendations, **218**
  right-hemispheric, 211
  survival (but usually with disabilities), 208
  warning signs, 207
stroking, **270**
structured routines, **18**
subconscious, 168, 300
  blame and shame in brain, 182–184
  effect of music, 187–189
subconscious autopilot mode, 188
substance abuse, 81, 127, 138, 167, 272
  comorbidity with depression, 298
  negative side effects of music therapy, 311
sugar, 272–274, **276**, 278, 279, 299
surgeries: placebo effects, 124
Survivor: 'Eye of the Tiger' (song), 99, **152**
Switzerland, 21, 105
sympathetic nervous system, 114
symphony, 134
synapses, 22, 42, 45, 208, 210

synchronization, 236
System 1 and System 2 (Kahneman), 183

tactus, 11, 86
taking it easy with music, **68**
  practice makes perfect, **68**
  professional help, **68**
  reflection, reassessment, and proceeding positively, **68**
  selecting mood music, **68**
  use of proven pieces, **68**
tango, 98, 252, **265**
tapping along, 162, 165, 188, 191, **219**, 248, 260, **270**, **276**, **292**, 301, 302
Tatum, A., 255
taxes, 128, 274
'Tears in Heaven' (Eric Clapton and Will Jennings, 1992), 75
tempo, vii, **117**, 221, **223**, 245, **250**, 255, 263, **292**
tension arcs, 92–95, 103
  aesthetic devices across art forms, 96–97
  reduction of negative thoughts and pain, **96**
tension curves, 93, 95
tension headaches, 267, **270**
Tetzlaff, C., 56, 57
thalamus, 22, 157, 196
  'centre of brain's pain network', 157
  'registers signals of danger or reward', 158
Thaut, M. H., 221, 245
theory of mind, 107
therapeutic effects of music (seven underlying factors), 131–137
  attention, 132
  emotion, 136
  intelligence, 134
  memory, 133
  perception, 131
  sensorimotor function, 135
  social participation, 137
thought loops, 64, 96, 188, 312, 316
  counteracted with music, **190**
thoughts: influence of music, 77–78
thrillers
  films, 16
  television series, 15
'Thula Baba' (lullaby), 17
Thum, T., 29
timbre, 12, 22, 31
time intervals, 10, 74, 248

INDEX

time perception, 248
tinnitus, 133, 177
toddlers, 27, 30, **37**, 78
Tomasello, M., 21
tonal centre, 34, 93
tonal expectancy violation
   resolution, 93
   transitional phase, 93
tone languages, 30, 40
touch, **18**, 132
Toy Story 2, 173
train delay, 60, 62
trauma: negative side effects of music therapy, 311
trumpet tones, 40
trust, 2, 110, 137, 262
'Twinkle Twinkle Little Star', 17

umlauts, 28, 29
UN Charter of Human Rights, 71
uncertainty, 86, 87, 88, 93, 103, 318
unipolar depression: definition, 288
United States, 272, 274
University of Bergen, viii
University of Magdeburg, 253
unresponsive wakefulness syndrome, viii, 147, 152, 154

values, 101, 110, 129, 140, 182, 192, 194
Van Gelder, R., 65
vanity, 71, 139
vasopressin, 171, 178
Vater-Pacini corpuscles, 72
vegetables, 299, 317
vegetative nervous system: same as 'autonomic nervous system' (*qv*), 114
vegetative state. *See* unresponsive wakefulness syndrome
Verdi, G., 89
   'La Traviata', 104
vestibular apparatus, 72, 148, *149*, **150**, 154
Vienna Academy, 58
violin, 2, 5, 14, 41, 69, 132, 133, 169, 173, 200
violin soloist, 56, 57
violin tone, 29, 30, 40, 57
Viotti, G. B.: 'Violin Concerto in A Minor' (emotional contagion), 73

visual imagery, 98, **105**
vitalization system, 147–150, 249
vitamin C, 317
vitamin D, 288, 299, 317
Vivaldi, A., **117**
voice, 248
   acoustic features, 14
   emotional impact, 13–17
'Volver', 173
vowels, 29
   melodic pitch variations, 40

Wagner, R., 260
   'Lohengrin', 102
waltz, 19, 98, 251, **252**
Wang, Z.-J., 69
Weber, C. M. von: 'Oberon', 77
Webern, A., 108
well-being, 146
   individual 'requires healthy society', 128–130
   'profound influence' of music (Alzheimer's dementia), 237
Wernicke's aphasia, 33, 217
Wernicke's area, *32*, 33, 216, 217
West-Eastern Divan Orchestra, 169
whales, 20
Wigram, T., 261
wine, 70, 161
Wong, P. C., 40–41
working memory, 23, 135, **191**
World Health Organization, 127, **152**, 272, 288, 309
world view, 60, 129, 192
worry, 56, 60, 63, 106, 114, 127, 177, 317
Wünnenberg, E., 106

xylophones, 262

Yanomami, 14
YouTube, **223**, **250**, **283**
   video of cockatoo 'Snowball', 20
'Yurikago No Uta' (lullaby), 17

Zatorre, R., 159, 161
Zentner, M., 20
Zimbabwe, 185
Zimmer, H., 99